The Boston Globe

Historic Walks in Old Boston

Fourth Edition

BY JOHN HARRIS

EDITED BY ERICA BOLLERUD

The Globe Pequot Press

Guilford, Connecticut

Cover photo: © Kindra Clineff; www.kindraclineff
Cover design by Saralyn D'Amato
Text design and maps by Libby Kingsbury

Photographs by Ulrike Welsch except page 42 courtesy Erica Bollerud; pages 216, 282, 290 courtesy Greater Boston Convention & Visitors Bureau; pages 310 and 313 courtesy Cambridge Tourism.

Library of Congress Cataloging-In-Publication Data

Harris, John, 1908–
The Boston globe historic walks in old Boston / by John Harris ; edited by Erica Bollerud.—4th ed.
p. cm.
Includes index.
ISBN 0-7627-0519-1
1. Boston (mass.)—Tours. 2. Walking—Massachusetts—Boston—Guidebooks. 3. Historic sites—Massachusetts—Boston—Guidebooks. I. Title: Historic walks in old Boston. II. Bollerud, Erica. III. Title.

F73.18 .H37 2000
917.44'610443—dc21 00-035339

Manufactured in the United States of America
Fourth Edition/First Printing

KEY MAP

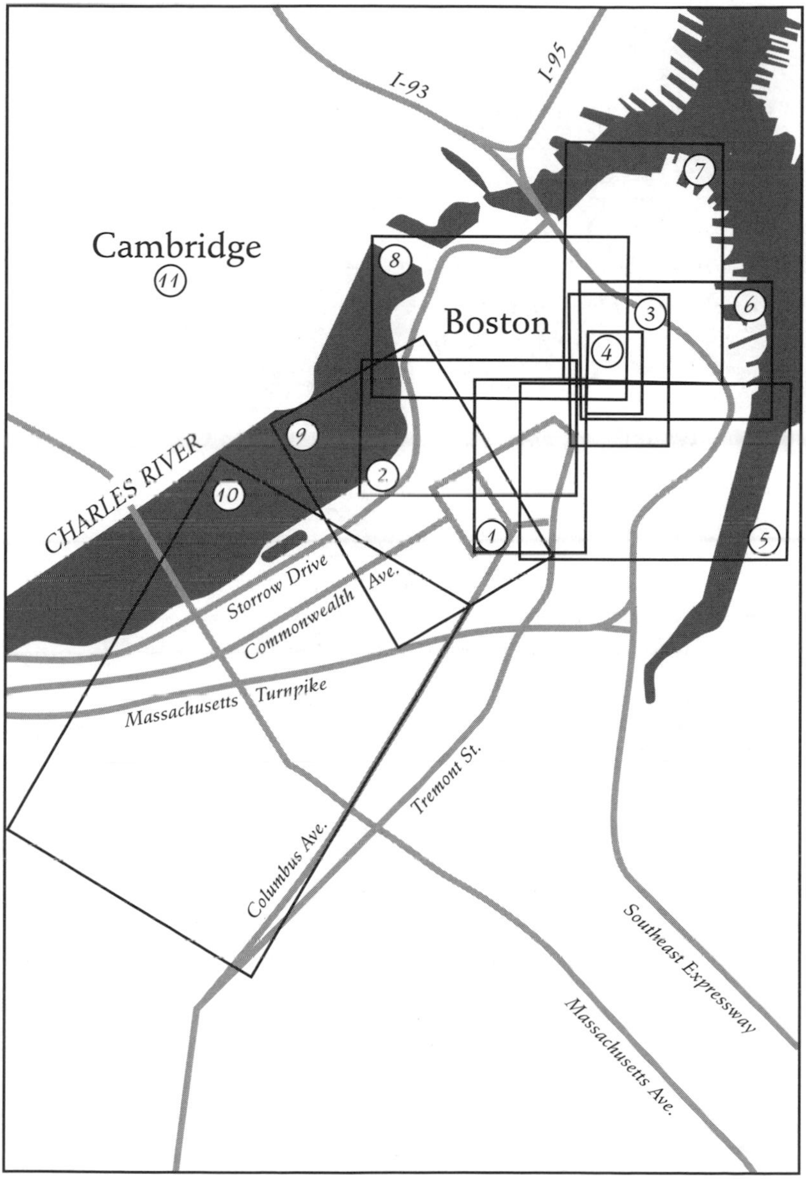

1. THE COMMON
2. BEACON HILL
3. CENTRAL BOSTON
4. BOSTON'S MOST HISTORIC BLOCK
5. DOWNTOWN BOSTON
6. CENTRAL BOSTON AND THE WATERFRONT
7. NORTH END
8. WEST END
9. BACK BAY I
10. BACK BAY II
11. CAMBRIDGE

CONTENTS

BOSTON THE BEAUTIFUL	vii
THE COMMON	1
To Brimstone Corner and the Long Path	1
Frog Pond to Flagstaff Hill	8
Railroad Mall and Abe Lincoln to "Round Marsh"	12
BEACON HILL	17
Beacon Street and up Beacon Hill	17
Spruce Street to Walnut Street	22
Walnut Street to the State House	28
Mount Vernon Street	35
Chestnut Street, a Beacon Hill Delight	43
Roaming Blackstone's Acres and Louisburg Square	50
Pinckney Street	55
Smith Court to Bowdoin Street	61
Upper Beacon Street—Brahmin Land	68
CENTRAL BOSTON	75
To Old Scollay Square via Pemberton Hill	75
Old Scollay Square and Government Center	82
BOSTON'S MOST HISTORIC BLOCK	91
Court Street	91
Old Newspaper Row	99
Old Corner Bookstore and School Street	105
Tremont Street to King's Chapel	113

DOWNTOWN BOSTON 119
Tremont Street to Old Granary 119
Brimstone Corner and Park Street 127
Tremont to Boston's Theater District and Old Park Square 134
Old South Meeting House to Tea Party 143
Province House to Canyonland 151
Federal Street to Where the Great Fire Began 159
Summer Street Mall to West Street 165
Old Movieland to Liberty Tree 174

CENTRAL BOSTON AND THE WATERFRONT 183
The Old State House and State Street 183
Lower State Street and around the Custom House 192
Walkway to Old Dock Square and the Sea 205
Faneuil Hall and Quincy Market 211

NORTH END 219
Washington's Route through the North End 219
North Square to St. Stephen's Church 229
Old North Church and Copp's Hill 236

WEST END 249
Bowdoin Square to St. Joseph's 249
First Otis Mansion to the County Jail 256
Between Charles Street and the Charles River 261

BACK BAY 271
What the Old Mill Dam Hath Wrought 271
Public Garden to the Hoffbauer Murals 280
Mid-Boylston to Mrs. Jack Gardner's 287
Copley Square and Westside Back Bay 296

CAMBRIDGE 307
Cambridge Constitutional 307

PUBLIC TRANSPORTATION TO NEARBY HISTORIC SIGHTS 317

INDEX 319

BOSTON THE BEAUTIFUL

The beloved American hero, the Marquis de Lafayette, a guest of the nation, went up Flagstaff Hill on the Common during his 1824 visit to Boston to watch the New England Guards at artillery practice. Their cannon pointed toward a floating target not far from present Copley Square in the Back Bay.

"With his own hand," a witness joyfully recorded, Lafayette, on invitation, touched off a cannon. The ball flew over what is now the Public Garden and out over the water of the bay to a bull's-eye hit. The cheering was deafening, said those present, for Lafayette, who had been wounded at Brandywine and had led victorious American assaults at Yorktown.

For us today, the incident spotlights the way old Boston has grown since the summertime of 1630 when Governor John Winthrop and his Puritans came ashore.

The 700 to 800 acres of the Back Bay over which Lafayette sped the cannonball just about equal the area of the Boston peninsula when Winthrop got here, a piece of land about 2 miles long and a mile wide, eaten by coves like a pear with bites in it. When the coves and the Back Bay were filled in with gravel, old Boston tripled its original size.

But Boston's size is not what has made it a city with magnetism like London, Paris, or Rome, a place with endless fascination. People and deeds, they did it. And as we walk around Boston today, we can see it all firsthand:

> Where Governor Winthrop lived, governed, and put in place some of the foundation blocks of our nation.
>
> Where Anne Hutchinson suffered for religious freedom.
>
> Where heroes James Otis, Samuel Adams, and Joseph Warren rallied the Sons of Liberty to a war for independence.
>
> Where the taxed, detested tea was dumped and where the victims were struck down in the Boston Massacre.
>
> Where Paul Revere got his orders, arranged for the lanterns, and set off to the first battlefield of the American Revolution.

The deeds that added luster to the community did not end when the new nation began. Boston annals tell of

> Sailors on the *Columbia,* sailing from Boston wharf when former British empire ports were no longer open to them, who began the fur trading on the Northwest Pacific coast that gave America exciting access to the rich markets of China and the Indies.
>
> William Lloyd Garrison and a small band who formed the Anti-Slavery Society, which at long last successfully stirred the conscience of America.
>
> Elizabeth Peabody, "Boston's grandmother," who opened America's first English-speaking kindergarten.
>
> Julia Ward Howe, who fought for women's suffrage.
>
> The Reverend Martin Luther King, Jr., who did graduate study and shaped his struggle for civil rights to the nonviolent tenets of Thoreau and Gandhi.

Most striking to visitors—and particularly to Bostonians—is the way high-rise structures now dominate the city scene. The golden dome of the State House was unrivaled in height right into this century. Now forty-story towers have risen in Old Boston like asparagus shoots in springtime. And highest of all, the sixty-two–story Hancock and fifty-two-story Prudential towers, stand now uptown in the area toward which Lafayette was shooting.

The gusty winds that high-rises create have brought new experiences to Boston, and wind barriers have begun appearing. High-rises, though, in effect create land in old Boston, which has no more coves to fill. If we look carefully, we may find shortcuts through the high-rise lobbies to nearby streets. And at night, high-rise grids of light do give a modern aspect to the landscape.

Eccentricities nowadays are not so routinely associated with Bostonians. Boston's squares, however, are an exception. In Boston we most often find that something called a "square" designates merely an intersection or an irregular open space. Old Scollay Square had little resemblance to a square, and old Brattle Square was actually a street making a right angle. Washington Square, on vanished Fort Hill, was a circle.

Just one legend of what was called the heyday of proper Bostonians involved the august St. Botolph Club in the Back Bay, where the death of a club member went undiscovered for three days. The gentleman seemed to be sleeping in his club chair, and no one had the brashness, let alone effrontery, to speak to him unless he spoke first.

IN WHATEVER PART OF THE WORLD YOU MAY MEET HIM YOU CAN TELL A BOSTONIAN A MILE OFF. . . . THE BOSTONIAN KNOWS THAT HIS OWN IS PREEMINENTLY THE HISTORIC CITY OF AMERICA, AND HE FEELS THAT NO SMALL PART OF ITS WORLDWIDE RENOWN HAS DESCENDED TO HIM AS HIS PECULIAR INHERITANCE.

—Samuel Adams Drake

It is old Boston, to which Emerson came from Concord and Longfellow from Cambridge, that Bostonians love best, the one Charles Dickens fell in love with and called "the beautiful."

In 1796, when the patriot Samuel Adams was governor and living just off the Common, the town's second directory was published. It gave a rapturous account of the place as seen by visitors arriving on State Street, which was described as "very spacious, being on a line with Long Wharf where strangers usually land." The editor ran on: "The view of the town as it is approached from the sea is truly beautiful and picturesque. It lies in a circular and pleasingly irregular form around the harbor, and is ornamented with spires, above which the monument on Beacon Hill arises preeminent; on its top a gilt eagle." The monument was Charles Bulfinch's creation, and at that moment Bulfinch's State House, as the editor related, was being built.

We can still see these and many more of the buildings Bulfinch built that transformed colonial Boston into a Federal city. Bulfinch, America's first great professional architect, did so much that he told friends that he would not train his son to be an architect. He explained that there would not remain much in the way of architecture for the young man to do.

Yet there was, and new ideas in architecture have adorned and continued to transform Boston, from H. H. Richardson and Charles McKim in the nineteenth century to I. M. Pei in the twentieth.

To be seen, too, are a multitude of attractions, many of them the first or among the first in our nation: schools, museums, libraries, medical centers, and milestones in commerce, finance, and manufacture—from Francis Cabot Lowell using a waterfront building to develop his epochal power loom to sophisticated high technology.

Harvard, the first American college, was established across the river in Cambridge in 1636, when the Bay Colony was only six years old. It is said to have been inspired chiefly by an early immigrant to Boston, the Reverend John Cotton, formerly of Boston in Lincolnshire, England. The nation's first public school, created in Boston a year earlier, and the new college must have done their jobs well. A president of Yale, visiting Boston in 1796, asserted: "Knowledge is probably more universally diffused here than in any other considerable town in the world."

If Boston has had its difficulties along the way, and it has, we must realize that Boston was New England's first large community to experiment with becoming a city. Time put an end to expelling the Anne Hutchinsons, whipping Quakers, and hanging witches. Dickens, a keen social critic, said of Boston in 1842: "I sincerely believe that the public institutions and charities of this capital of Massachusetts are as nearly perfect as the most considerable wisdom, benevolence and humanity can make them."

Boston still has, as we will see, so many of the things that have contributed to its fame. Some treasures, like John Hancock's mansion, are gone. But others survive, like the Old State House and the Old South Meeting House, both of which had eleventh-hour escapes from the wreckers.

We begin our walks through a treasure linked with Boston's first white settler, the Reverend William Blackstone's Common, most of it still intact.

THE COMMON

To Brimstone Corner and the Long Path

Boston has a red line in mid-sidewalk—a line going uphill, downhill, across marketplace and waterfront—which is called the Freedom Trail. It connects sixteen or so of Boston's historic buildings, places, and sights. There are many, many other places of historic import in the oldest sections of this city — not far from the Common. To see them we shall be taking short walks both on and off the red line of the Freedom Trail.

The Common, as Bostonians have long called it, has been Boston's foremost landmark since the 1630s, when the founders of the community, John Winthrop and his Boston neighbors, each contributed pounds, shillings, or pence so that Bostonians would own and enjoy forever the Common's roughly fifty acres. Appropriately, the Freedom Trail starts on the Common, at the Boston Visitor Information Booth on the Tremont Street (east) side of the Common opposite West Street. Adjacent to the Information Booth is Parkman Plaza. The sculptures around the plaza were created by two well-known Boston artists, Arcangelo Cascieri, dean of the Boston Architectural Center, and Adio DiBiccari. In the fall of 1908 George F. Parkman, whose elegant dwelling we shall see standing high up on Beacon Hill overlooking the Common, wrote a codicil to his will bequeathing his residence and $5 million for Boston's public parks in the "hope and expectation"

THE COMMON

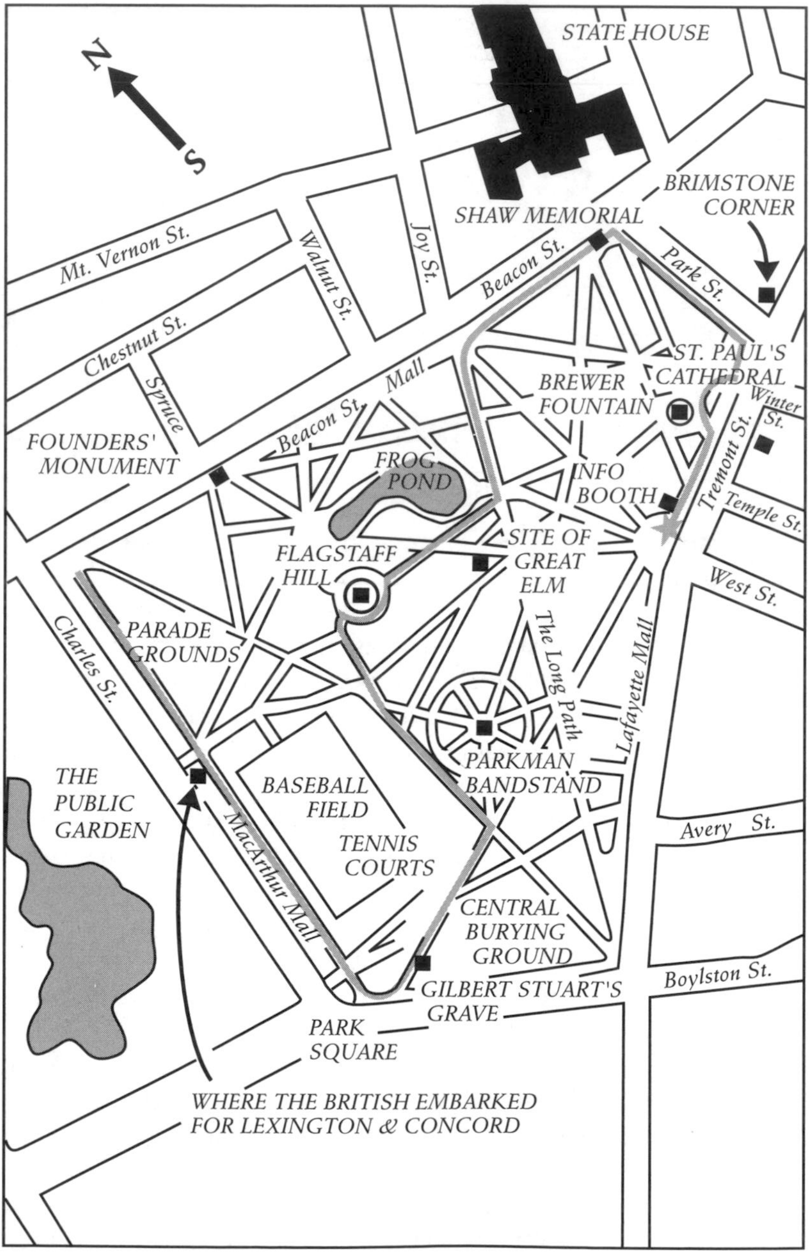

N
S
STATE HOUSE
BRIMSTONE CORNER
SHAW MEMORIAL
Mt. Vernon St.
Walnut St.
Joy St.
Beacon St.
Park St.
Chestnut St.
Spruce
Mall
ST. PAUL'S CATHEDRAL
Winter St.
BREWER FOUNTAIN
Beacon St.
FOUNDERS' MONUMENT
FROG POND
INFO BOOTH
Tremont St.
Temple St.
FLAGSTAFF HILL
SITE OF GREAT ELM
West St.
Charles St.
PARADE GROUNDS
The Long Path
Lafayette Mall
PARKMAN BANDSTAND
THE PUBLIC GARDEN
BASEBALL FIELD
MacArthur Mall
TENNIS COURTS
Avery St.
CENTRAL BURYING GROUND
Boylston St.
GILBERT STUART'S GRAVE
PARK SQUARE
WHERE THE BRITISH EMBARKED FOR LEXINGTON & CONCORD

that the Common "shall never be diverted from its present use as a public park. . . ."

To get a quick impression of the setting Boston delightfully and frequently can offer as Birthplace of the American Revolution, we can pause at this nearby plaza and glance up and down Tremont Street. Had we been standing here as the clock approached 9:00 A.M. on April 19, 1775—the day the Revolutionary War began—we would have seen a resplendently dressed British officer, young Lord Percy of Northumberland, dashing up and down the street on his white horse to organize a column of 1000 redcoats, infantry, and marines, mustered for the rescue of the British troops sent late the previous night to Lexington and Concord. It was at 9:00 A.M. that Lord Percy gave the command to march, curiously, it now seems, to the tune of "Yankee Doodle." With him were two six-pounders, one of which would fire the first cannon shot of the war. Through blunders, the men of Lord Percy's column had lost a fateful five hours in gathering on the Common parade ground before forming in their line of march. Those lost hours would be a blessing to the embattled farmers on the patriot firing line.

The red line from the information booth leads toward the State House with its golden dome, but we will go toward Park Street. Walk a few hundred yards northeastward along the Tremont Street Mall toward Brimstone Corner, at Park and Tremont Streets; across the intersection is the Park Street Church. On the way we pause to enjoy, on our left, one of the Common's beautiful ornaments, Brewer Fountain, the gift of Gardner Brewer in 1868. The fountain is a bronze replica of a Parisian fountain that was a sensation of the Paris Exposition of 1855.

Brewer shares another Boston distinction, for he had the pleasure of residing at 30 Beacon Street on the site of John Hancock's mansion atop Beacon Hill. Brewer was one of two Boston merchants who purchased and demolished the old landmark in 1863 and built brownstone mansions (later cleared away to enlarge the State House grounds).

Boston has used the Common to welcome many distinguished visitors with illuminations, fireworks, festivity, and parades since George

Washington, the newly elected president of the United States, came here in 1789 to the scene of his first military victory. The greatest celebration after that was the 1824 visit of Washington's revered aide, the then-aging but still debonair Marquis de Lafayette. It was in tribute to that visit that the mall we have been walking was rechristened Lafayette Mall.

The one-story granite subway entrances and exits we see close to Brimstone Corner are for the Park Street subway, central transfer point of Boston's rapid-transit system. This, too, is a piece of history. This first streetcar subway in America was dug along two of the five sides of the Common—one right here along Tremont Street. When the pioneer streetcar entered the subway September 1, 1897, the *Boston Globe* dramatically headlined the event "First Car Off the Earth!"

There is usually a touch of London's Hyde Park Corner in this section of the Common, with soapbox orators, performers, strolling musicians, a variety of religious devotees appealing for support from passersby, and peddlers with carts hawking their goods mixed in with loungers at what is one of Boston's busiest spots.

The slate memorial near the corner, seemingly a part of the iron fencing, tells how and for what purposes Governor Winthrop acquired the Common in 1634. When they had arrived in Boston in 1630, the Puritans held the charter from King Charles I that granted them the entire Bay Colony. The sole white occupant they found on the peninsula, the Reverend William Blackstone (he spelled it Blaxton), was in effect a squatter. So the Puritans were indeed generous in 1633 when, establishing bounds, they set aside fifty acres near his cottage for Blackstone "to enjoy forever." Even a year later they were still apparently in a charitable mood to pay him thirty English pounds ($150) and to leave him six acres and his dwelling—a site we will be seeing and where we will learn how he felt about these benefactors. To meet the levy that paid Blackstone, some Bostonians gave more and some less than the fixed six shillings.

The Common, as we read on the tablet, was to be used as "a trayning field . . . and for the feeding of cattell." So it has been used, over the centuries, for military purposes. During our nation's wars the Common has recurringly been the scene of recruiting, bivouacking, drill, and ceremony. But the history has been different with cattle. Free use for cattle even caused the death of a general who, returning home in the dark from military exercises, hit a cow, was thrown, and died. Cows and other cattle continued to munch on the Common even after Boston became a city. One of its greatest mayors, Josiah Quincy, son of the patriot, discovered in 1823 that one man was keeping thirteen cows and selling milk. The limit was one. Mayor Quincy ordered that cows henceforth carry an owner's name, and any strays were promptly put in a pound at the corner of Boylston and Charles Streets. But city growth and pasturage became so incompatible that Quincy's successor, Harrison Gray Otis, put that Common out-of-bounds to cattle in 1830, especially to prevent accidents and annoyance to women pedestrians.

Let us now head uphill along the red line, on the path inside the railing along Park Street. Park Street, on the other side of the railing, began life as a pathway across the then-larger Common to the beacon atop Beacon Hill. This was the pathway most convenient for Samuel Adams, "Father of the Revolution," between his house on Winter Street and the hilltop. It was Samuel Adams as governor who laid the cornerstone for the State House.

Park Street (where we will spend more time later) was laid out in 1804 by Boston's preeminent architect, Charles Bulfinch, and in that period he designed nine dwellings built on Park Street facing the Common. These included the much-altered but still-standing structure at the prestigious Boston location ahead at the corner of Park and Beacon Streets. These houses were long known as Bulfinch Row.

The supreme accomplishment of Bulfinch's genius, however, is directly ahead of us, the State House on the present crest of Beacon Hill, in what was once the pasture of John Hancock's mansion. We will visit the State House shortly.

Meantime, as we reach Beacon Street we are standing just about where the nearly thirty-year-old, newly famous Charles Dickens stood on his first visit to Boston in 1842 before he went to the House and Senate chambers of the State House. Describing the "green inclosure called the Common," he said, "The site is beautiful; and from the top there is a charming panoramic view of the whole town and neighborhood." Today's higher structures limit that prospect but make us value even more the beauty of restful green space in the center of a busy metropolis.

After ascending the steps to Beacon Street, we can see the entire Robert Gould Shaw Memorial, by Augustus Saint-Gaudens, which reminds us that Boston before and during the Civil War was the nation's foremost center for the abolition of slavery. It was in Boston that the first regiments of free blacks were enlisted. The very first was the 54th. There was a grand review on the Common before Colonel Shaw, scion of one of Boston's wealthiest families, led his regiment off to war. The distinguished black orator and abolitionist Frederick Douglass was among the spectators, for in the ranks of the soldiers were two of his sons. Shaw, then twenty-five years old, and many of his men were killed in the battle for Fort Wagner in the harbor of Charleston, South Carolina. Note on the street post here a marker for the Black Heritage Trail, which takes in historic sites that we will later visit on our walks. We will also visit memorials on the Women's Heritage Trail that honor two victims of Puritan intolerance: Anne Hutchinson, banished from Boston, and Mary Dyer, hanged on the Common. We will shortly see their statues in front of the State House.

Descend the steps on either side of this monument and to your right, running parallel to Beacon Street, is a tree-bordered mall along the north side of the Common, a promenade we now walk along. It is well known for its literary associations.

William Makepeace Thackeray, author of *Vanity Fair,* on his visits here in the 1850s regarded the elms along this mall to be in a class with "those in the long walk" at Windsor Castle. As for the residences on Park and Beacon Streets, he declared to a companion that they "could hardly be surpassed, for elegance and the appearance of comfort, even in London!"

Poet Walt Whitman relates how he and Emerson, "for two hours of a bright, sharp February mid-day" in 1860, walked up and down this mall in deep discussion as Emerson sought to have the younger Whitman delete some lines from Whitman's forthcoming third edition of

Leaves of Grass. When Whitman issued—and even set the type for—his first edition of poems in 1855, he sent copies to several prominent authors. Emerson prophetically wrote back, "I greet you at the beginning of a great career." Some of Whitman's poems were criticized as sensual and potentially offensive. Emerson had urged Whitman to remove these lines, some in "Children of Adam," so that his poems could reach a wider audience. Whitman listened respectfully, agreed that Emerson's criticism "was unanswerable. I could never hear the points better put." But, decided Whitman, "I felt down in my soul the clear and unmistakable conviction to disobey all, and pursue my own way." Friends they remained and went off to share "a bully dinner."

There was an aftermath. Twenty-one years later Whitman was back in Boston on the invitation of John Boyle O'Reilly, a distinguished Boston editor, to prepare a new edition of *Leaves of Grass.* Whitman was entertained by many prominent Bostonians and often refreshed himself with walks on the Common. But suddenly the edition was suppressed here by the state's attorney, whereupon Whitman returned to New York and published it anyway.

EVEN BOSTON PROVINCIALITY IS A PRECIOUS TESTIMONY TO THE AUTHORITATIVE PERSONALITY OF THE CITY. COSMOPOLITANISM IS A MODERN VICE, AND WE'RE ANTIQUE, WE'RE CLASSIC. . . YES, I'D RATHER BE A BOSTONIAN, AT ODDS WITH BOSTON, THAN ONE OF THE CURLED DARLINGS OF ANY OTHER COMMUNITY.

—William Dean Howells

Pause at the steps, on your right, leading up to Joy Street and look, to your left, down the diagonal path now called Oliver Wendell Holmes Walk. It leads past the Frog Pond to Tremont Street near the corner of Boylston Street, the southern side of the Common. In Holmes's era it was called the Long Path.

Right here was a famous love scene. The Autocrat of the Breakfast Table, as Holmes was called, had fallen in love with the beautiful schoolmistress. Fearing that his proposal of marriage might be rejected, he had taken tentative passage on a steamer to Liverpool leaving that noon. Twice the suddenly timid master of the breakfast table asked his question before the words became audible. Would she take the Long Path with him? He meant, he told her, that it would signify that they would part no more. "The schoolmistress stepped back with sudden movement, as if an arrow had struck her." There was a stone seat near the gingko tree. Would she like to sit down? Instead, as he joyfully recalled, she softly replied, "No, no . . . I will walk the Long Path with you."

We now take the Long Path.

Frog Pond to Flagstaff Hill

The Frog Pond (filled, if we are in luck, with water) lies just west of the Long Path and spreads along the foot of Flagstaff Hill. It is the sole survivor of several ponds that once furnished drink to cattle on the Common, just as (if you except Beacon Hill's slope) Flagstaff Hill is the last of several hills and hillocks once within the Common.

In the summer the pond long afforded youngsters a place to wade, swim, or sail toy boats. In the winter there was ice skating. The pond came into its real glory in the early 1800s when foresighted Mayor Josiah Quincy, whose house overlooked the Common, had a stone curbing, both decorative and protective, placed around the edge of the pond.

One of the pond's greatest moments came in October 1848, when Mayor Quincy's son and namesake was serving as Boston's mayor. There was a spectacular celebration, with soldiers parading, bands playing, and cheering crowds all over the malls, the slope, and around the pond. Schoolchildren sang poet James Russell Lowell's new ode. And when Mayor Quincy gave the signal, a 6-inch column of water shot up 80 feet above the pond. Boston, its growth as a city no longer menaced by a water shortage, was thus connected with a great new supply from a lake miles away in Framingham that Mayor Quincy rechristened Lake Cochituate, its Indian name. "After a moment of silence," said an enraptured onlooker, "shouts rent the air, the bells began to ring, cannon were fired, and rockets streamed across the sky. In the evening there was a grand display of fireworks, and all the public buildings and many of the private houses were brilliantly illuminated."

Edgar Allan Poe knew the Common well and thought it "no common thing." Just about all his other reactions to "Frogpondium," as he satirically styled Boston, were highly negative. For him the city lacked a soul. He even said that he was "heartily ashamed" that he had been born in Boston. The poet, unlike his mother, never found much joy in Boston, for he was either penniless or miserably ill when he was here.

Boston has offered little but pleasure for other famous visitors, having welcomed—often on the Common or along the traditional parade route along the Common's borders—most of our Presidents. The unprecedented crowds that welcomed George Washington were not matched until after the War of 1812, a particularly unpopular war in this seaport, when the welcome given on the Common to newly elected President James Monroe in 1817 confirmed that the Era of Good Feeling had genuinely arrived.

On the slope by the Joy Street steps, President Andrew Jackson, with his cabinet and presidential aides also on horseback, received a military salute in 1833 as crowds roared approval. Monroe, well versed in law, had been given an honorary degree at Harvard, so former Mayor Quincy, who had gone on to be president of Harvard, saw to it that Jackson got an honorary law degree, too. Both times big tents were raised and there was feasting on the Common.

We turn right at the path leading from the Long Path to Flagstaff Hill, with its towering Soldiers' Monument, but before proceeding along it, let us take note (on our Common map) of the site of the Great Elm, Boston's most remarkable tree. It was located a few steps farther down the Long Path. The tree took considerable space, rose above 72 feet, had a spread of more than 100 feet, was flourishing when the Puritans first arrived in Boston, and survived endless storms until leveled by a merciless one that struck in 1876. It so impressed Bostonians that its site was marked for many years with a big round iron fence, now vanished.

The tree provided early Boston with a device for imposing stern justice. The Puritans developed quite a ritual for these executions.

"Many and many a weary hour did I spend in prison," bemoaned Reverend Cotton Mather, "to serve the souls of these miserable creatures." Prisoners, often in chains, were brought to sit through church meetings. The condemned provided vivid Thursday lecture material and were then led to the gallows. Often there were soldiers "with drums and colors, guns, swords, picks and half-picks." The gallows consisted of a rope around a limb of the tree and a ladder that could, at the selected moment, be suddenly pushed away. Clergy attended the place of execution to pray with the prisoners to the final moment.

Some generations might be astonished to read, in Governor Winthrop's Journal, that two lovers were executed for adultery and that the woman, before dying, gave "good exhortation to all young maids to be obedient . . . to take heed of evil company." The date: 1643.

What gave the Great Elm special distinction was that it was the scene not just of executions but of martyrdoms. It became part of the tragic history of several hangings prompted by religious oppression and the hysteria over witchcraft.

The saddest tale was that of the Quaker Mary Dyer. We will see her sculpted resolute countenance in front of the east wing of the State House when we visit there. Brave Mary Dyer, in protest, quit the Puritan colony when it banished the famous dissenter Anne Hutchinson. But Mary came back, was led to the gallows, and, at the last moment, in response to desperate appeals from her son, was permitted to leave the colony. She returned to champion religious freedom. Boston's first minister, the Reverend John Wilson, urged her until the last moment to repent as Governor John Endecott rigidly enforced imposition of the death sentence. Normal burial was taboo, so her ashes and those of her fellow martyrs are mingled with the nearby soil we tread.

Flagstaff Hill is the one where Lafayette fired the cannon during his 1824 visit. This hill has had long military associations. From early times the town's powder was stored atop the hill. Soon there was at its foot a watch house. Its use for recruiting during the Civil War, as well as its eminence, fit beautifully into its selection for the Soldiers' Monument, a 70-foot-high creation by sculptor Martin Milmore, erected in 1877. The bronze bas-reliefs depict Civil War scenes—particularly Civil War Governor John A. Andrew, with poet Longfellow near him, bidding farewell to the first Bay State soldiers to respond to Abraham Lincoln's call to arms.

Near this hill two young men of socially prominent families, their swords drawn, faced each other in Boston's most famous fatal duel. This was on a July evening in 1728. The duelists had quarreled over cards in an elegant tavern near the Old State House and the younger man, nineteen-year-old Benjamin Woodbridge, was urged on to issue a challenge. Thrust through the chest, he died almost instantly, while the wounded victor, who would die in a year from remorse, was helped to flee to France by no less a person than Peter Faneuil, donor of Faneuil Hall and a close relative.

The Common has played host to a succession of noted military activities far beyond just "trayning." Sir William Pepperell assembled 2,000 volunteers in camp in 1745 and set out from here to capture France's key fortress in North America, Louisburg in Nova Scotia. And when one of our greatest colonial governors, William Shirley, who sent Pepperell, received news of victory, there were drums beating, bells ringing, banqueting, and marching all over town and bonfires and fireworks on the Common.

Lord Jeffrey Amherst, a "soldier of the king," brought forty-five hundred redcoats, in dozens of transports convoyed by men-of-war, to Boston in 1758 as part of the plan to conquer Canada. They set up tents on the Common and bivouacked for three days; then Amherst headed his troops toward Albany and Lake George, pathway to Canada.

General Thomas Gage, whose "secret expedition" to Lexington and Concord touched off the Revolutionary War, quartered redcoats on the Common for years. Here he held reviews and, as an object lesson, had his regiments drawn up under arms for the execution of a young deserter. General Gage raised fortifications on Beacon Hill, around the Common, and along the shore of the Back Bay to forestall General Washington's attempting, as Washington eventually did, to land troops from his siege positions in Roxbury, Brookline, and Cambridge.

We can still study all the details on a neat military map made by one of Gage's engineers, Lieutenant Thomas H. Page, who fought and lost a leg at Bunker Hill. The lieutenant even marked the residences of the officers who would be top British commanders during the war, General Clinton and General Burgoyne in Hancock's house and patriot James Bowdoin's house respectively, the two biggest mansions then on Beacon Hill.

When General Washington, after forcing the redcoats to flee, entered Boston, he inspected the British fortifications on and around the Common and ordered them all dismantled. For years youngsters played in the abandoned trenches.

Railroad Mall and Abe Lincoln to "Round Marsh"

Down Flagstaff Hill to our left, take a path that curves past the sets of benches around the Parkman Bandstand to Railroad Mall, a much-traveled walkway crossing the Common from West Street, where we first started, and going past the Central Burying Ground to Park Square, where one of Boston's first railroads had a terminal in 1835. Around the spot where we enter Railroad Mall, about midway along that busy footwalk, no end of interesting events have occurred.

There have been private doings, like Louisa May Alcott as a child merrily rolling her hoop and becoming a "lost little girl" to the deep distress of her family. Or Oliver Wendell Holmes as a youngster, paying ten cents for "a peep through a telescope on the Common," seeing the transit of Venus, and declaring, "I have never got over the shock, as it were, of my discovery."

There have been doings that produced big crowds. Crowds always morbidly congregated when some wretch or rascal was punished in a public spectacle. Crowds appeared near the arched West Street entrance when the whipping post, painted red, was moved to the

Common. The stocks and pillory were movable and had been variously located around town and the Common, attracting onlookers to see helpless victims pelted with mud and rotten eggs.

One of Boston's biggest crowd-producers was the arrival of word that King George III had signed a repeal of the abominated Stamp Act in the spring of 1766. Church bells rang, cannon boomed. Everywhere joy was boundless. By evening, related the *Boston Post* Post-Boy, "The whole town was beautifully illuminated;—on the Common the Sons of Liberty erected a magnificent pyramid illuminated with 280 lamps." Liberty Tree was only a short way off and Paul Revere, besides making a print of the merrymaking, drew upon his talent and wit to create political cartoons for the pyramid. "About 100 yards from the pyramid," continued the Post-Boy, "the Sons of Liberty erected a stage for the exhibition of fireworks, near the work-house [on present Park Street] in the lower rooms of which they entertained the gentlemen of the town." John Hancock's house on Beacon Hill "was magnificently illuminated," and popular Hancock had servants convey a pipe—a wine cask of 126 gallons—of his Madeira to the Common for all to drink. Still later that night rockets were fired amid wild cheers from the crowd. King George learned little from it. In the fashion of tax-reapers, he went on to impose a three-pence tax on each pound of tea. We all well recall what that led to.

Turn right at Railroad Mall and we come, on our left, to the cemetery on the Common, the Central Burying Ground. The town purchased two acres for it in 1756, thus increasing the Common on that side, on petition of the residents in the growing South End. Gravediggers had testified that the town's oldest cemeteries—two of them still on downtown Tremont Street—were then "so filled with dead bodies that they are obliged oft-times to bury them four deep."

Gilbert Stuart is the most famous person buried here. Passersby for decades have trod unknowingly on the tomb of the great portraitist. It is directly under this mall, and if we look inside the railing as we near Boylston Street, we see a memorial tablet from fellow artists to the man who made masterful likenesses from life of George Washington and our other early presidents. For years Stuart's date of death or place of burial was uncertain. He was suffering from old age, wavering talent, cancer, and penury when he died in a dwelling a couple of blocks from here. Old records at last showed that the date was July 9, 1828, and that he was buried the next day in the vault of friends, Tomb 61. This tomb does not even bear Stuart's name.

Names on other vaults and stones are of many well-known Boston families—Codman, Coolidge, Fowle, Harris, Sprague, and more. The oldest extant stone was set in 1755. Here also lie the remains of the largest family group to take part in the Boston Tea Party, the four Bradlee brothers, aged nineteen to thirty-one, and their sister. Their house, one of several in Boston where Tea Party participants foregathered, was near the shore of the Back Bay, 3 blocks south of here on Tremont Street. It was there that the Bradlee boys' sister, who helped them get ready, concealed them afterward from British officers.

Many other Tea Party patriots and soldiers of the Revolutionary Army are buried here. So are many British soldiers mortally wounded in the Battle of Bunker Hill. Most are in unmarked graves. British casualties ran 50 percent in that fight; afterward, all the buildings around the Common or nearby, among them Hancock's mansion, were filled with British wounded and dying. A British regimental hospital was right beside the cemetery.

Railroad Mall is the Common path most likely familiar to Abraham Lincoln. The prairie congressman spent more than a week in Boston in 1848 to campaign here and in suburban towns for "Old Zach" Taylor and the Whig ticket. Between trips by rail and carriage he lodged in a Tremont Street hotel a block north of the Common. Twelve years later Lincoln came east to deliver his Cooper Union address in New York, which helped clinch the presidential nomination. At that time he also came to see his son Robert, a student at Phillips Exeter academy in New Hampshire. Lincoln had a couple of hours between stations, and the customary route was along Railroad Mall from the Boston & Providence Station, then in present Park Square, to West Street and on to the Boston & Maine Station, which was downtown in Haymarket Square. Lincoln, who traveled light with a cylindrical leather bag and umbrella, would have had ample time to catch a meal and take a walk, which he enjoyed.

At the time Lincoln visited Boston in 1860, the papers were filled with columns of a speech William H. Seward had just made in the U.S. Senate. Not a line appeared specifically on Lincoln's being here, save that he was tendered (and did not accept) an invitation to speak at the Republican state convention. But Lincoln's remarks at Cooper Union were already working their magic, particularly his declaration: "I believe this government cannot endure permanently half slave and half free."

The Illinois log cabin that Lincoln had helped to build in 1830 and had lived in until he was an adult was exhibited on the baseball field on your right shortly after Lincoln's assassination. Lincoln's cousin, farmer John Hanks, brought it from a showing in Chicago. Top public officials visited it here and so did future President Ulysses S. Grant, a victorious general who had taken Richmond only four months before his visit to Boston.

When we reach the corner of Boylston and Charles Streets, we turn right onto what is known as MacArthur Mall along Charles Street. This part of the street along the foot of the Common was built early in the 1800s atop a seawall. The seawall had been constructed as protection against tides rolling across the Back Bay, a large cove of the Charles River estuary.

A bronze marker, on one of the two 7-foot-high stone pillars about halfway along MacArthur Mall to Beacon Street, commemorates the embarkation from here, at the foot of the Common, of some 700 redcoats under portly Lieutenant Colonel Francis Smith, at 10:00 P.M. on the eve of April 19, 1775, in boats of the British fleet that were to be rowed to the Cambridge side of the river. Ahead for them at Lexington and Concord were the opening clashes of our American Revolution. They had their "oars muffled to prevent a noise," but their secret mission was already known to the patriots. Offshore, about where Lafayette would have his floating target in 1824, the redcoats were guarded by the guns of His Majesty's warship *Nautilus,* and nearer on the shore (to our left) there was a British battery atop Fox Hill, an islet off the Common that was later leveled in the filling of the Back Bay. The embarking redcoats were the ones that Lord Percy next morning set out to save after their defeat and flight from Concord and Lexington.

The parade grounds on our right on the west slope of Flagstaff Hill have seen swarms of people attending public events. Spectators have come to watch elaborate annual drumhead elections of the Ancient and Honorable Artillery company founded in 1638, America's oldest military order. In the earlier years these were held with a grand marquee and festivity on the hill's east slope, opposite the site of present St. Paul's Cathedral on Tremont Street.

There have been great annual outpourings on the parade grounds for the Fourth of July fireworks and displays. Memorable record-breaking throngs, seemingly covering just about every inch of Common land, have appeared throughout the long history of the Common: in 1936 and 1940 to greet magnetic President Franklin D. Roosevelt at the height of the New Deal years; in 1969 to demand an end to the war in Vietnam; in October 1979 to welcome, to the Common of the Puritans, His Holiness Pope John Paul II; and, in recent decades, crowds protesting or celebrating headline events.

The Great Elm was not the only execution setting on the Common. The former shore we have been walking (MacArthur Mall) skirted what the earliest Boston records called "the Round Marsh." It was along the beach, just before it went northward across present Beacon Street, that murderers were hanged. With normal burial denied, bodies of culprits were hastily interred near the gallows, and there was a tradition that the tide sometimes exhumed corpses.

In those days, of course, far from being a fashionable section of the community, this part of the Common was one of the most remote, uninhabited places on the small Boston peninsula.

BEACON HILL

Beacon Street and up Beacon Hill

Beacon and Charles—a beloved intersection. Children all over America, even though they have yet to see it, have already enjoyed it. For it was here that kindhearted Officer Clancy had four of his fellow Boston policemen rush to hold up traffic so that author Robert McCloskey's brave Mrs. Mallard and her eight ducklings following her in line—Jack, Kack, Lack, to Quack—could march across to celebrate their reunion with Mr. Mallard waiting in the Public Garden.

So many appealing tales go with Beacon Street that it is a puzzle where to begin, at the foot or at the top. Nathaniel Hawthorne's future wife, Sophia, just sweet sixteen, walking Beacon Street for the first time, wrote in her diary that she "could but just keep my feet upon the sidewalk, so bubble-like, balloony were my sensations—the full rich foliage, the hills, the water, inflated me. Oh that Common—that Eden in miniature!" That was in 1829, when there was still water of the Back Bay along Charles Street and the Blue Hills could be seen rising beyond the distant shore.

Beacon Street houses are pretty much today as Charles Dickens, happily reminded of London streets, saw them before and after our Civil War. Dickens dined in several Beacon Hill dwellings, and his

BEACON HILL

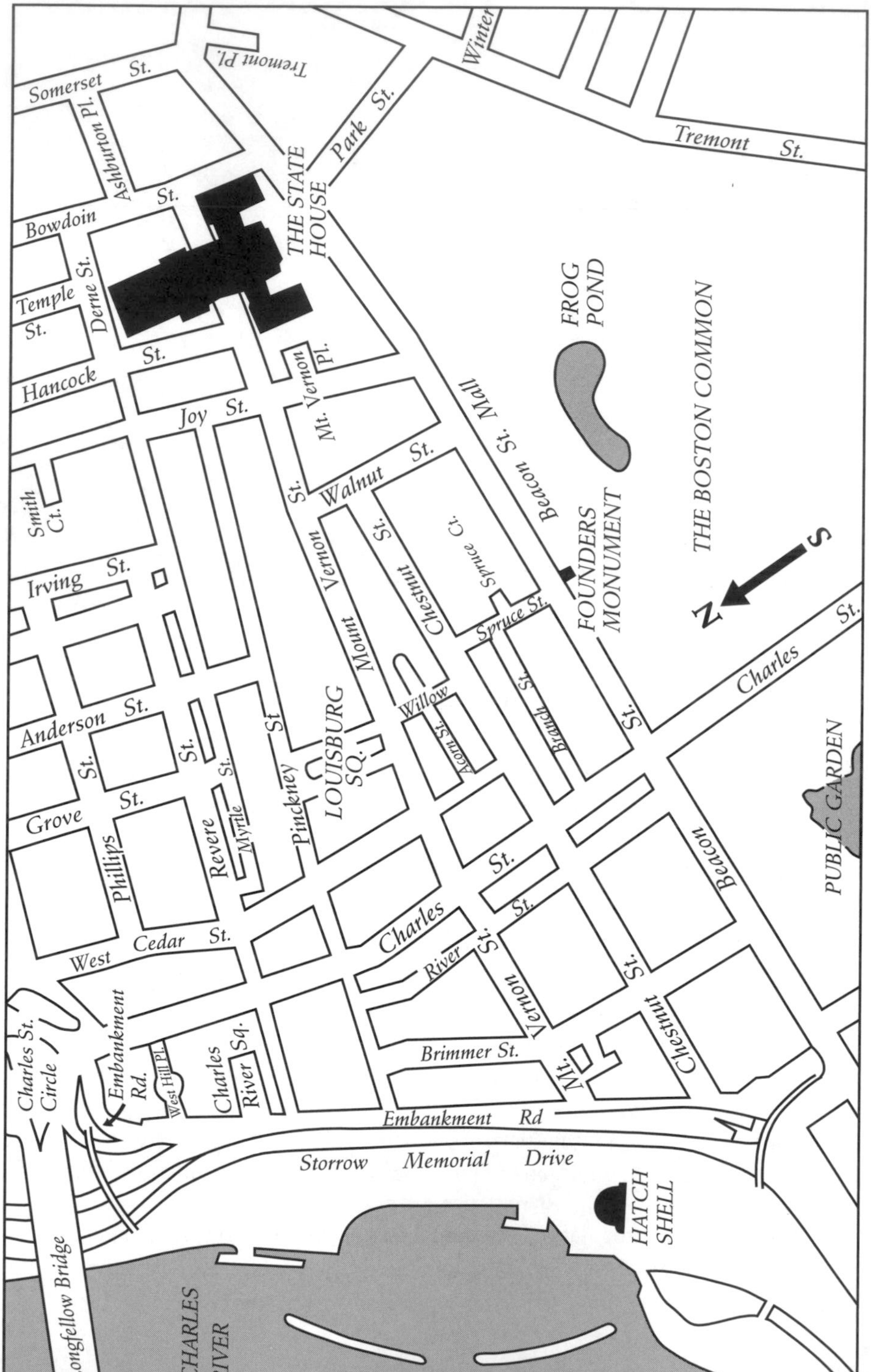
Somerset St.
Tremont Pl.
Ashburton Pl.
Park St.
Winter
Tremont St.
THE STATE HOUSE
Bowdoin St.
Temple St.
Derne St.
Hancock St.
Mt. Vernon Pl.
Joy St.
Mt. Vernon
Beacon St. Mall
FROG POND
THE BOSTON COMMON
Walnut St.
Smith Ct.
Vernon St.
Chestnut St.
Spruce Ct.
Beacon
FOUNDERS MONUMENT
S
N
Irving St.
Mount
Spruce St.
Anderson St.
Willow
Branch St.
St.
Charles St.
Pinckney St
LOUISBURG SQ.
Acorn St.
St.
Grove St.
St.
Revere
Myrtle St.
Phillips
PUBLIC GARDEN
Beacon
West Cedar St.
Charles
St.
River St.
Vernon St.
St.
Chestnut
Charles St. Circle
Embankment Rd.
West Hill Pl.
Charles River Sq.
Brimmer St.
Mt.
Embankment Rd
Storrow Memorial Drive
HATCH SHELL
Longfellow Bridge
CHARLES RIVER

many friendships, as he said in parting, had made "Boston a memorable and beloved spot to me." Daily, and usually setting the pace for his companions, Dickens walked 8 or 10 miles. Beacon Street was a favorite of his. When too ill to walk, he ordered a sleigh and pair of horses to ride over this road he loved.

We may, of course, go uphill by the Common's Beacon Street Mall or along the sidewalk. The latter seems better for our purpose, with the charm of the gas lamps and the full view of the Common all the way up.

Purple panes, a touch supposedly aristocratic, go traditionally with Beacon Hill. Actually, there are only a half-dozen dwellings that have the original purple panes—a result of sunlight bringing out an imperfection in glass shipped from Hamburg and installed in houses built a few years either side of 1820.

Twin houses with some original purple panes are directly on our left, 64 and 63 Beacon Street, respectively the parish house and rectory of a venerable Boston landmark, King's Chapel, over the hilltop near the head of Beacon Street. The parish house, with a Sunday school, a meeting room for church suppers, a library, and a small chapel with pulpit and organ, is modestly furnished. But the sunlight penetrating the front purple panes from across the Common brings, as a lady there recently remarked, "a lovely gentle tint into the room." Through the rear windows can be seen a large garden area, an unusual sight today on Beacon Hill.

An even more unusual sight from the parish house is an alleylike way between Beacon and Chestnut Streets, known as Branch Street. Just beyond our view, at 66 Branch Street, is a small converted coach house where the Aga Khan, one of the world's richest men, lived while he was a student at Harvard College. Branch Street used to be called Kitchen Street because it was a service access to great dwellings on Chestnut and Beacon Streets.

The delicately designed house at 61 Beacon, with its graceful ironwork, colonnade, and entrance, was the town house of Governor Christian A. Herter, later President Eisenhower's secretary of state. Herter's father, Albert, was a distinguished painter, and we may shortly enjoy his magnificent murals, *The Road to Freedom,* which adorn the great chamber of the House of Representatives in the State House, where Governor Herter once served as Speaker. The tallest windows we see here on the second floor are telltale of the location of the drawing room—as in so many of Beacon Hill's mansions.

Another beautiful pair of houses forming a double facade appear at 55 and 54 Beacon, built in 1808, quite an early date for construction on the lower part of Beacon Street. Both have had distinguished owners.

Historian William Hickling Prescott's house at Number 55 recalls the tale of British novelist Thackeray, a big, jolly, broad-chested man, on a snowy winter day during his 1852 visit "sturdily ploughing his way down Beacon Street with a copy of *Henry Esmond* [the English edition, then first issued] under his arm. He held aloft the volume," continued famous Boston publisher James T. Fields, "and began to shout in great glee. When I came up to him he cried out, 'Here's the very best I can do, and I am carrying it to Prescott as a reward of merit for having given me my first dinner in America.'"

Prescott's house also gave Thackeray an idea for his new novel Prescott had inherited the sword used by his grandfather, Colonel William Prescott, in commanding the fight for the key fort in the Battle of Bunker Hill. Prescott's bride had her grandfather's Tory sword, used when he commanded a British war vessel in the same battle. After their wedding they mounted the crossed swords on their library wall. Thackeray saw them there and used them for the opening scene in *The Virginians.*

Both authors were victims of schoolboy pranks. Thackeray's looks were marred by a broken nose. Prescott lost the sight of his left eye when, during a college mealtime rumpus, he was struck by a hard crust. Sight in his other eye was so impaired that his daily reading was painfully reduced, and to write at all he devised a ruled slate noctograph for the blind that he used in his fourth-floor study.

A glorious moment for Number 55—and for pre–Civil War Boston—came on the eve of the 1846 election. The old Whig Party, abandoned by the abolitionists, had begun to disappear. The nation had finally become outraged. The slave states, not content with trying to strangle freedom in "bleeding Kansas," tried "to crush it in the Senate by a slaveholder's bludgeon." Senator Charles Sumner, clubbed on the Senate floor, was coming home after months of agony. The welcoming parade went up Beacon Street. Prescott, like an increasing number of Beacon Hill bluebloods, was out cheering. Prescott even sent a note to Sumner: "I hope you saw me wave you a greeting from my piazza." He told Sumner he wished that he had known earlier about the reception as he would have hung "my house with flags and a canvas printed in enormous letters, 'Welcome Home!'"

Number 54, resplendent, too, with white Corinthian pilasters up to the roof and a pillared portico, was the early home of one of the greatest merchant princes of Boston, Nathan Appleton. He was only fifteen years of age, a New Hampshire country lad, when he came to Boston and worked for his older brother Samuel in a small store on lower Washington Street. At twenty-one he was running the business and, prospering, moved into this house in 1808 before he was thirty years of age. We will shortly meet with him again, in a bigger house farther up Beacon Street, after he and his colleagues introduced the first power loom on the Charles River in Waltham and created great mills on the Merrimac River in Lowell, named at Nathan's suggestion, for his colleague Francis Cabot Lowell. When Nathan left this house, he sold it to his cousin, wealthy merchant William Appleton, who also succeeded to Nathan's seat in Congress.

The slope of Beacon Street has seen so many houses called home by members of the Appleton family that it might be fairly styled Appletonland. Sam, like Nathan, would have a house farther up Beacon Street when, late in life, Sam took a bride. A year after brother Sam's death, his widow Mary, in 1854–1855, built for herself the house at 53 Beacon with the granite ground floor and brownstone bowfront. She had her husband's initials, S. A., lovingly worked into the metal grillwork (but that has vanished). Even though the heavy eave of her large, four-story mansion overhangs the five levels of Nathan Appleton's former dwelling at Number 54, Mary Appleton's residence was known to family members as a "bird cage." This was doubtlessly because its width on the ground floor allowed for but a single window beside the big front door.

The stone plaque on Number 50 at the corner of Spruce Street marks the northeast corner of the six acres remaining to Boston's first settler, the Reverend William Blackstone, after he sold the Common. The six acres, fronting on Beacon Street, stretched back along the shore (Charles Street) and in the direction of Spruce Street as far as Pinckney Street—and included the ever-famous social citadel of Louisburg Square. Exactly where Blackstone built his solitary cottage we do not know. Here, though, was his orchard—the colony's first apple orchard—commemorated on the plaque by the two incised branches bearing fruit. When Blackstone's new neighbors finally tried to get him to join their Puritan Church, he took off for Rhode Island a future colony for which he was the first white settler, too—and left this comment: "I came from England because I did not like the Lord Bishops but I will not join with you because I do not like the Lord Brethren." Hermit Blackstone turned out not to be a true loner. He did come back to Boston to get himself a bride, a widow; and grim old Governor John Endecott, strictest Puritan of them all, tied the knot. Just across Beacon Street, on the Common, is the Founders' Monument, where we can see Blackstone in convivial spirit inviting Winthrop and his followers to come ashore and share the peninsula and its springs.

Spruce Street to Walnut Street

Particularly in the next block as we move up Beacon Street from Spruce to Walnut, we should keep in mind that the Autocrat of the Breakfast Table described the place as "the sunny street that holds the sifted few."

On recrossing Beacon Street after a view of the Founders' Monument, notice the narrow, two-windows-wide building at Number 48 that rises a dozen levels. Today, in Boston, with high-rises sprouting, this may not seem upstart and out of character with its neighbors. At the beginning of the century, however, it led to this country's pioneer legislation to control the height of dwellings.

Its neighbor at Number 46 was the town house of Eben Jordan, merchant prince. Jordan, a Maine lad with few funds, came to Boston and began business life in a small dry goods store on old Hanover Street in downtown Boston in the 1840s and went on to reach the topmost rungs of the mercantile ladder. For this mansion Jordan joined two buildings and installed the single-pillared brownstone entrance.

Historically and architecturally, the next building, 45 Beacon—with its cobblestone carriageway and side entrance—is one of Beacon Hill's premier attractions. It is the third successive, and the last, mansion, all still standing around Beacon Hill, that the great architect Charles Bulfinch designed and built in 1805 for Harrison Gray Otis. The other two will be on later walks. Otis, with this new mansion a few steps from the Frog Pond, fitted exactly Holmes's phrase, "the sifted few." His mansion and then more extensive grounds were a center of civic and political influence, of regal hospitality and living.

THIS IS GOOD OLD BOSTON/THE HOME OF THE BEAN AND THE COD/ WHERE THE LOWELLS TALK TO THE CABOTS/AND THE CABOTS TALK ONLY TO GOD.

—DR. JOHN COLLINS BOSSIDY

Otis's rise was as meteoric as merchant Eben Jordan's. Otis did have a starting advantage of a not uncommon mixed heritage in Federal Boston. He was a nephew of the patriot James Otis and a grandson of the last Tory treasurer of the colony, for whom he was named. The Tory's vast estates were confiscated by the Commonwealth. So Otis began his legal—and later political and real estate—career with little money. Indeed, when he was married in 1790 he set a life goal of accumulating a $10,000 estate, a fortune in post-Revolutionary Boston. He was so personable, so tactful, and so amply endowed with sagacity that he came to have more than his goal as just an annual income. It was at age thirty, when he was already on the legal heights, that Otis entered political life, serving as a leader in both legislative branches and as Boston mayor, congressman, and U.S. senator.

Of all people associated with developing Beacon Hill into an enduring residential area, Otis was foremost. Otis, while on the town committee named in 1794 to select a site for Bulfinch's new State House, looked beyond the superb site of Hancock's pasture that the committee chose. To enterprising Otis the entire west slope of Beacon Hill, mostly covered then with huckleberries, bramble thickets, small cedars, and many cowpaths, could be converted into a grand residential district to go with the new State House. Otis and others, especially fellow lawyer and legislator Jonathan Mason, soon to be a U.S. senator, agreed to form the Mount Vernon Proprietors. Otis and Mason held more than a majority of the shares and proceeded to try to purchase the south slope land that belonged largely to artist John Singleton Copley.

Copley, in the six-year period before he departed for London in 1774, put together an even larger estate on Beacon Hill than John Hancock had. It comprised more than eighteen acres, including all of Blackstone's six acres at the foot of the hill. Copley did well financially on the deal with Otis and Mason. But he felt that his agent had been outsmarted and, to win redress in court, sent over his son, the Boston-born future Lord Chancellor of England; nevertheless, Copley's effort failed.

Otis eventually prospered spectacularly, but prosperity did not come to the Beacon Hill development in a rush because of Jefferson's embargo of 1807, war, and depression. The mansion at Number 45, with Bulfinch's classical touches, granite base, tall drawing room windows, and keystones, is a perfect example of how changing times made the Mount Vernon Proprietors change, too. Bulfinch, acting for them, drafted an original division plan for Beacon Hill of big estate lots with setbacks, formal gardens, greenhouses, barns, and coach houses with stalls for horses. Otis, at Number 45, after Mason on parallel Mount Vernon Street, built this sort of manorial setup to attract others to build in the former pastures. With rising costs, Bulfinch's expensive plans had to be set aside very early. Otis's dwelling at Number 45 once had formal gardens and an oval-ended drawing room on the uphill side that was later changed to provide space for the dwelling at Number 44 and expansion at Number 43, row house style.

Few dwellings we are looking at on the hill are open to the public. Like this one, they are private. But their charms have long been known.

When Otis moved into Number 45 with his wife, Sally, their seven youngsters, and a half-dozen servants, they had eleven bedrooms and a dozen fireplaces. The grandeur included a well but no plumbing. That did not become possible until Otis's last conscious day, just before he died, when he could look out and see on the Frog Pond the initial 80-foot geyser of Lake Cochituate water in 1848. The privies in an ell (reached through the woodshed) had to be pumped out every week into horse-drawn tank wagons nicknamed "the Brighton artillery," for the way their straining wheels struck the cobblestones.

Otis, the host supreme, was called "Harry" by all his intimates. He was a celebrated gourmet, drank choice Madeira, and kept ten gallons of punch in a remarkable blue-and-white Lowestoft bowl stationed in a niche on the stairs winding up to the drawing room so that guests could refresh themselves en route. He got gout at forty, not yet halfway through life. When he once asked his victualer if anyone purchased more delicacies than he did, the victualer replied, "only the Albion Hotel," then one of the city's two largest hostelries.

The mansion has seen some great moments. Among them would be the post–War of 1812 visit of President Monroe, last of the early Virginia presidential dynasty. When Otis, the Federalist nabob, opened the door to his palatial bow-end drawing room and presented Monroe to his 300 "sifted" guests, it was a reliable signal that even in Boston the Era of Good Feeling had replaced bitterness over the war's destruction of sea commerce.

One of the two structures that displaced Otis's formal gardens, Number 43, is the lower half of one of Boston's most exclusive clubs. The Somerset Club, which had its first quarters in 1852 farther up Beacon Street, at Somerset Street, acquired the Rockport granite mansion that Colonel David Sears had built in 1819 at Number 42. The design is by famous architect Alexander Parris, and the building very much resembled the grand mansion that Sears's father-in-law, Jonathan Mason, had built on Mount Vernon Street in 1801–1802 to encourage Beacon Hill development. The eminently historic Sears lot was also the sight of the last American dwelling of artist John Singleton Copley.

A 1772 visit to Copley's house by a young Harvard student helped to give America another great artist. Governor Jonathan Trumbull of Connecticut—ever-helpful "Brother Jonathan" to beleaguered George Washington—was determined to make his artistically inclined son, John, a clergyman. He sent the fifteen-year-old youth off to Harvard College in the charge of an older brother. En route the brother indulged John by taking him to see Mr. Copley and his paintings in "his house on the Common where Mr. Sears's elegant granite palazzo now stands." Trumbull's account in later life went on: "We found Mr. Copley dressed to receive a party of friends for dinner. I remember his dress and appearance—an elegant looking man, dressed in fine maroon cloth, with gilt buttons—this was dazzling to my unpracticed eye!—but his paintings . . . renewed all my desire to enter upon such a pursuit." And so he did, painting while at Harvard, bringing his work here to Copley, and winning Copley's praise and encouragement.

Sears's mansion originally had lavish surroundings, a coach yard, and stables, like the Otis mansion, which shared the garden area. On acquiring it in 1872 the Somerset Club built a second bow extension at Number 43 and an additional upper story. The Parris exterior was maintained, and the club even duplicated the decorative stone carvings made by Solomon Willard, distinguished architect of the Bunker Hill Monument.

The Somerset was Boston's first residential club and even provided a family dining room for ladies. A large, stately dining room took the place of the razed Sears stables. To this day, famous chefs are engaged. Members may still dine on Daniel Webster's beautiful silver service; to "The Divine Daniel" a great dinner was the apex of civilization. For Beacon Hill coziness and beauty there is a walled garden, called "The Bricks," a paradise for cocktails.

"Strictly private" the club most certainly is, but it has welcomed many distinguished guests: presidents, grand dukes, the Prince of Wales, military leaders, and noted authors and celebrities like Rudyard Kipling, Winston Churchill, and John P. Marquand. Throughout its life the club has been a citadel of conservatism. Bostonians may recollect how flamboyant, personable James Michael Curley, on winning election nights, would lead his rapturous, roaring victory parade up Beacon Street past the Somerset Club so that he could give the many dour faces at the windows what is politely called a waggish "raspberry."

Original purple panes can be seen in the next two twin buildings, with their pillars and walk-up granite steps, which textile tycoon Nathan Appleton and a partner had built for them in 1819 from designs of Charles Bulfinch. It was in the second-floor drawing room at Number 39 that Nathan Appleton's daughter Fanny, on July 13, 1843, became the bride of poet Henry Wadsworth Longfellow. Longfellow's sister Anne said of the famous wedding, "Oh, it was a beautiful scene!" Fanny wore a white muslin dress, bridal veil, and was adorned with flowers. "Darling brother never looked one half so handsome in all his life and Fanny was in all respects the perfection of brides." Presents covered two tables and "some 50 bridal-dressed" guests sat down to the wedding feast. That evening, by moonlight, the newlyweds drove to Cambridge to Longfellow's quarters in Craigie House on Brattle Street, headquarters of George Washington during the siege of Boston. Craigie House itself was among the wedding presents, a gift from Nathan Appleton and his wife.

An old Appleton clock long ticked in the Federal-style, four-story twin at 40 Beacon, the Women's City Club, founded in 1913. Dwindling membership forced the club to file for bankruptcy, and in Spring 1992 Suffolk University bid $2.6 million to take over the place for an alumni club and executive offices. But by June 1992 the university backed out and it was purchased by private owners. As for the purple panes, the Women's City Club manager enjoyed them but felt they were "hard to see through."

The building at the corner of Walnut Street, its original Federal style converted to Victorian fashion, was the first brick structure on Beacon Street when built in 1804 by John Phillips, who became president of the Senate after twenty-five years in the legislature and, in 1822, filled the role of Boston's first mayor. The structure is particularly noted as the birthplace of his son, Wendell Phillips, who braved the ostracism of many of his social peers and threats to his life as the inspiring trumpet, the "Orator of the Anti-Slavery Cause."

It is interesting to note how remote this part of town seemed to Bostonians even as late as the post-Revolutionary era. When the honorable John Phillips started his brick residence, after spending years around the Old State House as town counsel, there was considerable surprise. His uncle, Judge Oliver Wendell, was asked on State Street "what had induced his nephew to move out of town!"

The Phillips house, when it changed ownership in 1825 on Phillips's death, continued to have deep roots in Boston history. It became the dwelling of a direct descendant of the colony's first governor, Lieutenant Governor Thomas L. Winthrop, who was married to a granddaughter of the Revolutionary patriot Governor James Bowdoin.

Walnut Street to the State House

The short block just ahead of us from Walnut to Joy Street provided an unforeseen fortune for Dr. John Joy, for whom Joy Street, originally a pathway for transporting loads of hay from the pastureland, was named. Dr. Joy was actually an apothecary with a shop on present Washington Street at Spring Lane. He received medical advice that, for his wife's health, he should take her into the country, and so he purchased two-plus acres on Beacon Hill. It was, he said, "country enough for him," with only the two small Copley buildings downhill and the Hancock mansion near the hilltop. Mrs. Joy, a "townie," having been born on School Street, was not for such a far-off move until her husband promised to bring her back to town "at no distant day." In 1791, four years before the State House was erected, Dr. Joy put up his dwelling, a fairly elegant two-story structure with fluted Corinthian columns at the west corner of Joy and Beacon Streets. He soon recovered all his costs by selling off just a piece of his land on the north side of his acreage.

The tale of the west corner of his acreage at Walnut and Beacon Streets underscores the economic hazards of the period in which Beacon Hill was developed. Dr. Joy sold this land in 1806 to one of the most enterprising individuals ever to live in Boston, Uriah Cotting, the man who was developing a large portion of Boston's thriving waterfront, including Bulfinch-designed India and Central wharves, and who would presently be the creator of the Mill Dam extending Beacon Street across the Back Bay to Brookline. Cotting picked this Joy land for his own dream house. Feeling rich, he began putting in the foundation of Boston's "most magnificent mansion," a structure superior to any in Boston "for elegance or splendor." Then along came Jefferson's embargo and Madison's war. Real estate plummeted. Cotting took down what he had built and sold the land. On just one half of what Cotting sold, former 37 and 37½ Beacon, Nathan Appleton's brother Samuel raised a mansion for his new bride. This was 1819, the same year that Cotting, almost impoverished, died virtually on the eve of completing his greatest, most important development for Boston, the Mill Dam.

The Tudor apartment and office building at the corner of Joy Street is on the site of Dr. Joy's 1791 dwelling. The elder Robert Gould Shaw, wealthy merchant and grandfather of Colonel Robert Gould Shaw, who led the 54th Regiment of free blacks during the Civil War, lived and died in a mansion he built here after Dr. Joy's time. The Tudor for whom the present apartment/office building is named was Frederic Tudor, who also had a mansion here. He was an ingenious Yankee who, despite guffaws of skeptics, persisted in the idea that he could convert blocks of ice into gold. He proved it on a 1805–1806 voyage to Martinique, selling ice in the tropics. Soon he had repositories all the way to Calcutta for ice he had cut from local ponds.

As we cross Joy Street we enter upon what was John Hancock's land. Hancock, immortalized by the big signature he was the first to affix to the Declaration of Independence—big, so that George III and all the world could read it—was the nephew and heir of Thomas Hancock. The wealthy uncle acquired the summit of Beacon Hill in 1735 and built his stone mansion, great gardens, and coach house, all of which, and more, came to John Hancock in 1777 along with "chariots, chaises, carriages and horses." John Hancock added a large banqueting room in which he lavishly entertained countless distinguished guests—and some militarily unwelcome ones.

When the redcoats were encamped on the Common during the siege of Boston, General Gage had Lord Percy occupy the Hancock mansion to prevent pillage by the soldiers who enjoyed shouting that Hancock was a rebel and would be hanged. For most of the siege the mansion was headquarters for General Sir Henry Clinton, who would be the top British officer in America at the time George III lost all thirteen colonies at Yorktown.

General Washington visited the mansion more than once. The day after he drove the redcoats out of Boston, Washington inspected the mansion and wrote to Hancock, then president of the Continental Congress, "I have particular pleasure in being able to inform you, sir, that your house has received no damage worth mentioning. The furniture is in tolerable order, and the family pictures are all entire and untouched."

Cows roaming the Common enter one tale about the mansion. To show America's gratitude for the new 1778 treaty with France, Hancock invited forty French naval officers to a sumptuous meal when Admiral d'Estaing's fleet moored that year in Boston. Madame Hancock's dismay that she lacked sufficient milk was promptly resolved when she sent servants to the Common to milk any available cows.

The mansion stood until the middle of the Civil War. By then all efforts to keep it and its furnishings together had failed. Legislation to have the state purchase it at a bargain price was blocked by the rural districts, and the historic structure was demolished.

The summit area, from Joy Street east, has long attracted prominent residents. The Federal house at 34 Beacon on the east corner of Joy Street, built like its next neighbor in 1825, has been a dwelling of the Russells, Bradlees, and Cabots. The greatest devotee of the Common, George Francis Parkman, came in 1853 with his mother and sister to live at 33 Beacon in seclusion after the sensational murder of his father.

The plaque on the house tells how George Francis Parkman, on his death in 1908, left this house and a fortune to the city for "the Common and other public parks." The unmentioned amount of the fortune was $5 million. Boston has used the mansion for high-level conferences and entertainment of official guests, as the President uses Blair House opposite the White House in Washington.

Just prior to the Parkmans' occupying Number 33, it was the home of the Tuckerman family. A well-known ravine coming down from the highest point in New England, Mt. Washington, was named Tuckerman Ravine for a noted lichenologist member of this family.

John Singleton Copley's family made at least a partial return to Boston and his hill. The artist's daughter Elizabeth married Boston's wealthiest citizen, Gardiner Greene, during a visit that Greene made to London in 1800, and they returned to her birthplace. When widowed in 1832 she came to live in another 1825 house, one that used to stand next east of the Parkman house. She, too, loved the Common. On the Greene estate that had covered most of Pemberton Hill, the easternmost peak of Beacon Hill, was a Chinese gingko, or maidenhair, tree a much admired ornament of the elaborate Greene gardens. She had it moved and placed by the Beacon Street Mall on the Common opposite her new house at 32 Beacon. Its glossy dark foliage was a public delight until 1978, when the tree became hopelessly diseased and was severed to a stump.

The former Greene residence at Number 32 was demolished in 1924 and replaced the following year by a six-story building designed to harmonize with its neighbors. The erection of this structure by the Unitarian Universalist Association marked the association's centennial, and for this reason the new building, out of sequence, was given its old street address of Number 25.

To the east of this house once stood, until removed in 1916 for extension of the State House grounds, the home of two very eminent Bay Staters—President Charles W. Eliot of Harvard University, modernizer of college curricula, and the elder Henry Cabot Lodge, the statesman. Eliot's father was a mayor of Boston, 1837–1839, and his son was born here.

Lodge's father, Boston merchant John Ellerton Lodge, whose clipper ships plied the China trade, bought Number 31 from the Eliots in 1858. The future U.S. Senator attended Boston Latin and Harvard College and Law School while living here; edited the prestigious *North American Review;* and was twice elected to the legislature, although he ran from the Nahant district.

When we enter the first opening on our left to the State House grounds, there is a reminder that the Lodges once lived here: a memorial and likeness of Senator Lodge. This area was cleared for the west (white stone) wing of the State House. Among the buildings that were removed was the birthplace of Lodge's friend, author Henry Adams, and of Adams's noted brothers. It stood on now-vanished Hancock Avenue, just east of where John Hancock's mansion once stood.

Women's Heritage Trail

The men of Boston are hailed and hallowed by the dozen, sometimes to the seeming exclusion of the legions of formidable women educators, activists, advocates, and artists who once marched, upset meetings, organized neighborhoods, or wrote quietly persuasive letters of change with as much purpose, perspicacity, and panache as any "Jamie" Fields or Daniel Webster. The Boston Women's Heritage Trail seeks to rectify this situation by organizing a five-part walking tour that refocuses attention on the stories, accomplishments, and movements led by women, such as the struggle for the rights of women, African–Americans, Native Americans, and the mentally ill. The Trail starts here at the State House statues of Anne Hutchinson and Mary Dyer. To learn more, call (617) 522–2872.

The next opening on the left leads into the basement of the State House. The State Archives, formerly here, moved in 1986 to a new building next to the John F. Kennedy Library in Dorchester. In the Archives, eminently worth a visit, may be seen many of the original documents of our nation and later pieces of history such as muster rolls, Paul Revere's expense chits and the Bay State Charter, signed by King Charles I and brought to the new world by Governor John Winthrop.

On the lawn near the basement entry, in front of the west wing, is Cyrus E. Dallin's statue of Anne Hutchinson, fearless pioneer in religious freedom, who was banished by the Puritans. Later, fleeing to New York, she and all but one of her many children were killed by the Indians. Bible in hand, she looks touchingly to heaven. A memorial statue of President John F. Kennedy, an impressive 8-foot, 2-inch bronze by sculptor Isabel McIlvain, was erected at the main entry to the west wing of the

State House on May 29, 1990, the date of the martyred president's seventy-third birthday.

The next entry off Beacon Street is the main approach to the original 1795–1798 redbrick Bulfinch structure with its great dome. The cornerstone was laid July 4, 1795, by the patriot Governor Samuel

SACRED COD

"The rocky nook with hill-tops three/Looked eastwards from the farms,/And twice each day the flowing sea/Took Boston in its arms."—*Ralph Waldo Emerson*

Early settlers of Boston and environs discovered that tilling the land made for poor farming and quickly reoriented themselves and their livelihoods when they discovered that the surrounding waters were teeming with cod. Fishing became a cornerstone of Boston's economy, with Boston ships carrying dried cod to the West Indies to provision the British sugar plantations. The cod-based economy received another boost from an unlikely source: the Pope. Though he found no favor with Puritans, the Pope's edict forbidding the consumption of meat on Friday led to a large market for dried cod with the largely Roman Catholic population of the Mediterranean—and steady income for Puritan fishermen.

Bostonians were well aware of the debt they owed to the humble cod. In 1784 it was proposed "that leave might be given to hang up the representation of a Codfish in the room where the House sits, as a memorial of the importance of the Cod-fishery to the welfare of this Commonwealth." The proposal was duly approved, and the "Sacred Cod" adorns a wall in the representatives' chamber in the State House to this day.

Adams after it was borne to the scene by fifteen white horses representing the fifteen states. Paul Revere, as Grand Master of the Masons, participated and later sheathed the dome with his own rolled copper (as he did for the hull of Old Ironsides in 1803).

The main entrance stone steps lead up to Doric Hall, which is pretty much as Bulfinch designed it. President Monroe was given a banquet here, too, as well as at Otis's, and here Washington's beloved aide Lafayette held a reception during his 1824 visit. Free guides are available to show visitors treasures of the State House: original Bulfinch rooms for Governor, Senate, and House; the 1889–1894 extension over Mount Vernon Street to the north, in which may be seen the new House of Representatives; the Herter Murals; and the Sacred Cod.

The stone steps have traditionally been the pathway back to private life of a governor on his last day in office, a sentimental lone walk as his successor begins delivering an inaugural address in the Representatives' chamber, largest in the building. Governor James Michael Curley, master showman, made his departure most memorable when he quietly passed a surprise news tip—stealing all the inaugural day headlines—revealing that the beautiful lady he was about to meet at the foot of the stone steps had consented to become his bride.

Before entering the State House, note other statues on the State House grounds between tragic Mary Dyer's (in front of the east wing) and that of her companion in misfortune, Anne Hutchinson. The famous Daniel Chester French helped to create the popular equestrian figure of Civil War hero General Joseph Hooker we see in front of the entry to the east wing. On the elevated lawn forward of Charles Bulfinch's original colonnaded State House facade are likenesses of statesman-orator Daniel Webster and celebrated pioneer educator Horace Mann.

Mount Vernon Street

On leaving the back entrance of the State House under the arch, we arrive at Mount Vernon Street, which runs parallel to Beacon Street. Alongside the head of Mount Vernon Street we may see—in the legislators' former privileged parking area—the reconstituted Doric column that Charles Bulfinch designed and built in 1790 on the original site of the 1634 warning beacon that gave the hill its name. The hill was 60 feet higher in the eighteenth century than it is today. Legislators now enjoy a ninety-seven-car garage built beneath the Bulfinch beacon, with access from Derne Street.

Bulfinch's monument was to commemorate the triumphs of our American Revolution. When the 60-foot mound was carted away by horse-drawn tipcarts in 1811–1824, the workmen also removed Bulfinch's 60-foot-high monument and the gold eagle with outspread wings perched on its top. When placed here again in 1898, the monument carried, and still does, Bulfinch's wording that may be read on four slate tablets on the sides of the pedestal.

Meantime, a large reservoir, Beacon Hill Reservoir, was constructed and in 1849 was filled with Lake Cochituate water, a boon to Bostonians formerly relying mainly on well water. The large granite blocks that formed the sides of the reservoir were used in 1889 for some of the State House extension over Mount Vernon Street. That same year the reservoir, no longer needed, was filled with gravel and the Bulfinch monument was restored. Noted architect Henry H. Richardson used some of the reservoir's large granite blocks for bridges he designed to beautify the Fenway.

Interestingly, there were originally several lengthy ropewalks on the north slope of Beacon Hill. We can picture the nearest after we walk under the archway across Mount Vernon Street and reach Hancock Street. The ropewalk ran downhill along the right side of Hancock Street. The Commonwealth bought it, and it is now the site covered by the long State House extension to Derne Street.

Mount Vernon Street, from the State House archway to Joy Street, ran across John Hancock's former garden and was opened to connect with the Mount Vernon Proprietors' streetway. It was not until 1799 that the Proprietors started laying out streets, giving them, of course, to the town. These include Mount Vernon Street—all the way down to the river flats at present Charles Street—and Chestnut Street, which, as we will presently see, were the Proprietors' first Beacon Hill roadways.

A fascinating footnote: The Proprietors commenced their sale of lots for the largest development undertaken up to that time in Boston by inserting a 3-inch display ad in the leading Boston newspaper, Major Benjamin Russell's *Columbia Centinel,* the trumpet of the then-dominant Federalist Party.

Looking left as we arrive at Joy Street, we notice how the houses on the west side are set back 15 feet from the sidewalk as far as the Tudor Building, farthest down on the right. This setback was by gentleman's agreement almost two centuries ago between old Dr. John Joy, the developer, and Thomas Perkins so that the view toward the Common would not be blocked from the big brick Bulfinch mansion that Perkins built on the southwest corner lot at Mount Vernon.

Perkins was not the Boston multimillionaire Thomas Handasyd Perkins, social giant of that era; however, this Thomas Perkins was also exceedingly wealthy, built houses on adjoining lots for his children, was the grandson of a royal governor of Nova Scotia, and was connected by marriage with leading Boston families. His brother-in-law, Senator Jonathan Mason, the Mount Vernon Proprietor, was building his own elaborate mansion farther down Mount Vernon Street at the same time.

Thomas Perkins's mansion went up more slowly, 1803–1805, because the building had to await adornments he was buying in Europe, crystal chandeliers from London, and marble fireplaces from Italy. It was all demolished for row structures in 1853.

Before we walk down Mount Vernon Street, notice, on the left, a short way down Joy Street toward the Common, a short cul-de-sac opposite 1 Joy Street. It is called Mount Vernon Place, a byway so private that it accommodates just a few automobiles. On its lower corner, 8 Mount Vernon Place was the dwelling of one of Boston's distinguished mayors, "General" Theodore Lyman, who one afternoon rescued abolitionist William Lloyd Garrison from a howling mob. Lyman, also a longtime Beacon Hill legislator, founded and endowed America's first reformatory for youngsters.

Before walking back up Joy Street, observe again the block of redbrick houses with brownstone trim, 1 to 5 Joy Street, with their grass plots setting them back the agreed 15 feet. They are among Beacon Hill's venerable structures, having been built 1832–1834.

The top three are the property of America's oldest nonprofit organization devoted to exploring, preserving, and enjoying our outdoor resources, the Appalachian Mountain Club, founded in 1876. Headquarters is at Number 5. A similar nonprofit group, the Sierra Club, occupies Number 3.

Now back to the gaslights, brick sidewalks, and trees of Mount Vernon Street. On our right were built the first Bulfinch row houses on Beacon Hill, two blocks of four houses each in 1803–1804, with their showy stables and coach yard in back on Pinckney Street. Of the first four only one remains, 49 Mount Vernon, which was originally narrower and had its entrance on the west side of the house. The big brownstone entrance was installed by a Bay State chief justice when he had the building enlarged for his residence.

Only one member of the "Essex Junto" that exerted control over the Federalist Party in New England in its earlier years, Stephen Higginson, lived for any length of time high on Beacon Hill. These former Essex County merchants, lawmakers, and lawyers settled in the older areas of Boston. Higginson, who had an estate in Brookline, acquired Number 49 as a town house in 1811 to help his son and namesake, who had built the first block of four houses, survive financial reverses from Jefferson's embargo.

The elder Higginson, who died here in 1828, had a fabulous career as privateer and patriot in the Revolution and as a member of the Continental Congress for Massachusetts. He was as handy with pen as with pistol. In articles in Russell's *Columbia Centinel* he made John Hancock a political target. It was Hancock, in turn, a chief of the old Bay State squirearchy, who dubbed the ex-Salem area nabobs the "Essex Junto."

The block of four houses built by Jonathan Mason still stands, numbers 51 to 57, all but one nearly flush with the sidewalk. Mason built them for three of his daughters and willed the houses to them. The houses have had illustrious tenants. Daniel Webster, upon moving to Boston as he completed his term as a New Hampshire congressman, lived from 1817 to 1819 at Number 57, a base for the walks that he loved to take across the Common to his law office.

In later decades Number 57 was the residence of a founder of the Republican Party, Charles Francis Adams, son of President John Quincy Adams. Charles Francis's sons, his namesake and Henry, grew up here after moving from the top of the hill. At first Charles Francis Adams did not approve of his own father's forceful championship of abolition. Then, outraged by slaveholders' excesses, he formed and edited a publication of the "Conscience Whigs," ran on the Free Soil ticket, and became Abraham Lincoln's wartime minister to Great Britain, a post vital to the victory of the North in the Civil War.

It was on the sidewalk here outside Number 57 that ex-President John Quincy Adams, intent on a short walk before returning to his son's house for dinner, suffered a stroke of apoplexy in November 1846. The honored warrior against slavery, then almost eighty, was unable for some time to resume his crusade in Congress where, little more than a year later, he suffered another and fatal stroke on the floor of the national House of Representatives.

A chance for the public to see the interior of a Bulfinch-designed Beacon Hill mansion is before us at 55 Mount Vernon, the palatially furnished 1805 residence willed as a museum by Rose Standish Nichols, world traveler, author, and founder of the Women's International League. The Nichols House Museum here offers the only opportunity of this character on the Hill, with its ancestors' portraits and delicately fashioned spiral staircase.

The museum is entered from a delightful garden in which we may enjoy the garden statuary and rest on the stone settees.

As we leave the museum, let us pause and look downhill. The next five lots formed the site of Jonathan Mason's "elegant new house," which was going up in 1801—on the Proprietors' manorial theory—

about the time that Harrison Gray Otis's second residence was rising nine lots farther downhill. Both of these are Bulfinch-designed. By gentleman's agreement between Mason and Otis, their setback was 30 feet from the sidewalk, precisely as it still is for all the lots to and beyond Otis's mansion.

Before we look at this stretch of dwellings, with their historic associations, observe two adjacent dwellings on the even-numbered side at numbers 32 and 34.

The house at Number 32 was the town dwelling in 1870–1872 of Julia Ward Howe and her illustrious husband, Dr. Samuel Gridley Howe, for the few years before his death. After their marriage in 1843 they made additions to an "ancient cottage" on a few acres adjoining Dr. Howe's Institution for the Blind in South Boston, where he attracted world attention by the training of a deaf, mute, and blind person, Laura Bridgman. The Howes called their South Boston place, near the present Dorchester Heights battle monument, Green Peace. Still, to be nearer Boston's social, literary, and philanthropic life, of which they were an eminent part, they would take town houses at a number of different places but mainly on Beacon Hill. Their first places were on Mount Vernon Street at numbers 47 and 80, for two years each from 1848 to 1851.

Women's Heritage Trail

The Portia School of Law was established at 45–47 Mount Vernon Street in 1908 when two women asked Attorney Arthur MacLean to help them prepare for the Massachusetts bar exam. It was named Portia in reference to the character who disguises herself as a lawyer in Shakespeare's Merchant of Venice. *The school incorporated formally in 1919, becoming the only institution offering legal education exclusively to women. It later became the New England School of Law.*

Dr. Howe was a freedom fighter as well as intensely involved in the struggle for abolition. When he was twenty-one years of age, he heard that his idol, Lord Byron, was fighting for Greek independence and Howe hurried off to Greece. Byron had already lost his life when Howe got there, but Howe joined the fight and brought back the poet's helmet (so small, few could put it on) to grace his hat tree, not the least of the attractions at Number 32.

The house on the corner, originally 34 Mount Vernon but now with an entrance at 14 Walnut Street, was built in late 1802–1803 and is one of the oldest in the area. The entry was shifted when the town cut down the grade and exposed the foundation. It was for a time the rectory of old Trinity Church. The garden in back was once part of Dr. Joy's old garden.

The expansiveness of Jonathan Mason's now-vanished 59–67 Mount Vernon Street manor is easy to imagine. In the mansion's swelled front, Bulfinch had created a two-story-high, princely ballroom. Proprietor Mason and wife did need a big place; they had seven children. A brick wall surrounded most of his big lot but left open a coach yard on the Pinckney Street side, where Mason's unusual and large brick stable (with alterations) still stands at 24 Pinckney Street. In 1836 after the death of widow Mason, the 1802 mansion was demolished and replaced with five dwellings that have had noted tenants.

Thomas Bailey Aldrich, a few years after he succeeded to the editorship of the *Atlantic Monthly,* came to 59 Mount Vernon in 1885, and it was his town house until his death in 1907. By the time he moved to Mount Vernon Street the magazine was owned by Houghton Mifflin Company, with offices then at 4 Park Street opposite the Common. Aldrich's places were convivial gathering spots for Boston's men and women of letters.

From 1886 to 1892 Henry Cabot Lodge the elder, GOP grandee, lived at 65 Mount Vernon in the previous house on that site. By 1886 Lodge was elected to Congress and was then twice reelected. He was a champion of civil service reform and a close friend of future President Teddy Roosevelt. In 1892 he was elected U.S. senator, a post he held for the remainder of his life. After 1892, however, his Bay State residence was his North Shore family home on the Nahant peninsula.

Changes in ownership on Mount Vernon Street illustrate the financial difficulties that Bulfinch's architectural enthusiasm caused for both him and his family. The next four lots below Mason's would have belonged to Bulfinch, but he was forced to sell his share of the Mount Vernon proprietorship to Benjamin Joy, brother of old Dr. Joy. The new owner and another new proprietor, adventurous Hepzibah Swan, wife of the patriot James Swan, had "severally contemplated to build mansion houses" on these eight lots between the Mason and Otis mansions. But Joy and Mrs. Swan shifted their building attention to row houses on Chestnut Street.

Several distinguished residents have lived on what were Mrs. Swan's lots. The Reverend William Ellery Channing, pioneer of Unitarianism, welcomed Charles Dickens to breakfast at 83 Mount Vernon the morning after Boston's reception for "Boz" on his first American visit. Dickens, who corresponded with the clergyman, greatly admired Dr. Channing's staunchly opposing "that most hideous and foul disgrace—slavery."

We may see the influence of dynamic Mrs. Swan even before we get to Chestnut Street. On one of her sites, 77 Mount Vernon, is Boston's Club of Odd Volumes. It had its beginnings, however, across the street at Number 50, one of those one-story structures, numbers 50 to 60. Their seemingly stunted height of 13 feet was established by Mrs. Swan in their deeds. Originally these structures were coach houses for dwellings Mrs. Swan built on Chestnut Street. On their lower levels were stalls. One of the entries, between numbers 50 and 56, is actually by deed a "cattle" (horse) passage from Mount Vernon Street down to the stalls.

A Beacon Hill gem is the Otis mansion still standing at 85 Mount Vernon. Otis's stable and grounds, like Mason's, once extended back to Pinckney Street. The freestanding mansion has many Bulfinch embellishments, recessed windows, fluted Corinthian pilasters, cornice balustrade, and even an octagonal cupola. Many consider this the most attractive of Otis's three Bulfinch mansions still extant. He sold it in 1805 to go to his new one at 45 Beacon.

By 1805 Bulfinch had sufficient funds to try for his own dwelling. On the lot next to Otis's he built 87 Mount Vernon for himself and a companion building that once stood at Number 89. Again came financial woes and Bulfinch never got to live in his new house.

Acorn Street

"For the year I am a Bostonian," poet Robert Frost wrote just after his wife's death when, in the fall of 1938, he took quarters at 88 Mount Vernon. There, he observed, he and his tenement were "overlooking Louisburg Square and overseeing any little defects there may be in human nature in the rough."

While here Frost got both sad and happy news. The grievous message was that his troubled son Carol had taken his own life. The good news: Harvard President James B. Conant informed him that "Friends of Robert Frost" had created a Ralph Waldo Emerson fellowship in poetry, and Conant invited Frost to join Harvard's English Department to give a series of lectures and "meet groups of young men interested in poetry." Frost quickly accepted.

Notice the studio window atop 92 Mount Vernon, overlooking Louisburg Square. Here for two decades was the studio of sculptor Anne Whitney, who created many famous statues long admired and familiar to us all; among them are Samuel Adams, which we see outside Faneuil Hall, and Leif Ericson on Commonwealth Avenue.

By way of contrast, we go past Louisburg Square, which we will visit later, and turn left at West Cedar Street. As we near a picturesque, cobblestone byway named Acorn Street on the left, we come to a five-story redbrick house with brownstone lintels at 9 West Cedar. A distinguished architect, Asher Benjamin, who held Bulfinch to be the foremost architect of that day, built Number 9 as his residence. Unlike Bulfinch, Benjamin was fortunate enough to live at Number 9.

Chestnut Street, a Beacon Hill Delight

As we reach the south end of West Cedar Street, we seem to step back into the Federal era on one of the loveliest streets on Beacon Hill, Chestnut Street. The charm of this roadway, its gaslights along the curbing, the neat trees, the wrought-iron railings against red brick, shiny old brass door knockers, mudscrapers, even some genuine purple panes—all combine to provide a beautiful urban setting. The literary and professional achievements of its residents have brought renown to several of the houses.

Just to our right, on the corner at 57A Chestnut, is the clubhouse (its entry was originally on West Cedar Street) that especially appealed to Senator Ted Kennedy, who lived not far away. This is headquarters of the Harvard Musical Association, which was founded back in 1837 to vary Boston's puritanical repertoire of psalm singing and to provide Bostonians with Europe's rich heritage of chamber and symphonic music. Browsers are welcome to see its remarkable music library, oldest in the nation. Artists of note give recitals in its attractive chambers. It carries Harvard's name, not because of any direct link to the university but because, in the days when Harvard had no music department, it was a group of Harvard graduates, all of them musicians, who got together to bring great music to the public. This same group built Boston's old Music Hall to provide the city with a large auditorium and purchased for it one of the world's largest organs, fetched from Europe in mid–Civil War, 1863.

The composer Dvorak was on hand when their quarters were reconstructed in 1907. Six years later the Marsh Room was added. It is a beautiful music chamber with two grand pianos given by Julia Marsh, widow of Eben Jordan's partner in the Boston store, Jordan Marsh Company. In the chamber a guest may play a piano free of charge by appointment.

Two houses across the street and up the hill are notable. A three-story brick dwelling at Number 50, with a recessed doorway built in 1824, was for nearly three decades the residence of Francis Parkman, who, despite ill health, traveled wilderness and plain to tell of the Oregon Trail, early explorers, and the saga of the 150-French and English struggle for the American continent. Parkman, like his near neighbor and friend, historian William H. Prescott, had impaired eyesight and painstakingly pursued his research from transcribed documents in his third-floor study.

Architect Ralph Adams Cram, who lived in the adjoining house at Number 52, also dating from 1824, encouraged his Beacon Hill neighbors to expand their celebration of Christmas Eve. Back in 1893 young divinity student Arthur Shurtleff had initiated putting lighted candles in the Shurtleff family house windows at 9 West Cedar Street. Early this century Cram got the neighbors to start going about the hill singing Christmas carols.

This Boston area was associated with still another writer with eye trouble, Richard Henry Dana, Jr., author of *Two Years Before the Mast.* The dramatic experiences at sea were Dana's own. His sight had been so impaired by measles that he suspended study at Harvard when he was nineteen and put to sea from Boston's town wharf. He recovered his eyesight, and four years after his return to Boston published his windjammer classic.

Young Dana lived at 43 Chestnut, the dwelling of his father, the poet. Here Henry, Jr., met his future bride. They wed in Hartford and by 1851 had a house in Cambridge directly back of the poet Longfellow's mansion. Save for a few years the elder Dana spent at 37 Chestnut, he lived most of his life and died on the sunny side of the street at Number 43.

Chestnut Street has the distinction of still having the first house erected by the Mount Vernon Proprietors, Number 29A, a Bulfinch house facing Spruce Street with the Founders' Monument and the Common in view.

New proprietors Benjamin Joy and Mrs. Hepzibah Swan put up two houses here when the Mount Vernon Proprietors laid out the first streets in 1799. A fire followed at this site and Number 29A appears to have been built on the surviving cellar in the following year, 1800. This lot, in the expansive initial manner of the development, ran back all the way to Mount Vernon Street.

Proprietors Joy and Swan got construction going so early on Chestnut Street that Thomas Perkins rented Number 31 from 1803 to 1804 until his great mansion at the corner of Joy and Mount Vernon was finished in 1805. The swell front of Number 29A, with brick laid differently, was added by a later owner around 1820, accounting for the authenticity of its purple panes. The 25-foot-wide garden, a beauty, goes back to the era of more lavish lots.

The most noted occupant of Number 29A was the tragedian Edwin Booth. He was a Boston favorite, playing here when his brother John Wilkes Booth assassinated Lincoln. The next night's show was to complete, at the Boston Theater, Edwin's highly successful engagement in *The Iron Chest,* a drama of a murderer haunted by his crime. But the assassination was a prostrating blow to the tragedian. He was staying during this 1865 engagement at the home of the theater's manager and was told of it next morning by the valet, who awakened him after reading the morning newspaper. The nation was horrified. The theater was immediately closed. Booth left secretly in a private railway compartment for New York. It was nearly a year before Edwin felt able to appear again before an audience.

Next uphill is what was once the Theological School and Methodist Chapel of Boston University. The building has also been the New England School of Pharmacy. These institutions were quartered here after the remodeling of a once-resplendent, double granite residential structure that had been built in 1847 extending from Chestnut to Mount Vernon Street. On the latter street it has two entrances, at numbers 70 and 72.

It was back in the early period that plutocratic Captain Richard Crowninshield Derby, a Salem merchant prince, acquired these same lots and put up a sumptuous residence in 1804 with the Petit Trianon at Versailles as his model. Reversing Otis and Mason, Derby put his stables so that they had Mount Vernon Street itself directly at their rear. This all gave way to the 1847 double granite structure. In recent years, after changes made by various institutions, the former chapel was converted into almost a dozen condominiums. An old resident reminisced about the widespread remodeling into condominiums and apartments: "It used to be all families and everyone knew everyone else. The policeman on the beat knew everybody—who did and who did not live here. . . . There's no more caroling or open house. Oh, there's plenty of parties, but they're private." He then added something vaguely foreboding: "With a half-dozen owners—or more—occupying what was once just one family dwelling, where are they going to park all the automobiles?"

The history of these lots pretty much epitomizes what has been happening to old residences on Beacon Hill since the Mount Vernon Proprietors got their street plan and started building.

The most glamorous houses on Chestnut Street are the sister houses

Looking up Chestnut Street to the Golden Dome

at numbers 13, 15, and 17 designed by Charles Bulfinch and built in 1806 by Mrs. Swan, who gave them to her daughters on their marriages: Number 13 to Christiana in 1806, 15 to Sarah in 1807, and 17 to Hepzibah in 1808. For years they remained in the family. It was in back of these small houses that Mrs. Swan built the 13-foot-high (and no higher ever!) stables on Mount Vernon Street. All three dwellings were graced with furnishings sent from France by Mrs. Swan's husband, Colonel James Swan. He was abroad throughout the French Revolution and sent them on, treasures now to be seen at the Museum of Fine Arts. Most belonged formerly in palaces, castles, and chateaux of French nobles who fled or were guillotined. Mrs. Swan had many lots and at 16 Chestnut, across the street, built herself a town house to use when she was not summering in her Dorchester mansion with its array of French furnishings.

A Swan granddaughter born at Number 15 in 1807, when there were no other Chestnut Street houses blocking her view to the Common, recalled looking out upon artist John Singleton Copley's former Beacon Street dwelling. "It was," she said, "a low wooden house surrounded by a garden." Copley's twice-widowed mother, who remained in Boston after he left, described the Copley house much more eloquently back in 1785 when she placed this ad in Boston's *Independent Chronicle:* "To be let—the elegant mansion house, stables and grounds of J. S. Copley, Esq., near the Common, now in occupation of General Knox." The occupant was Bostonian Henry Knox, George Washington's chief of artillery during the Revolutionary War and his secretary of war.

During the Civil War, 1863–1865, 13 Chestnut Street became the town house of Julia Ward Howe and her husband. Julia had by this time became famous for her "Battle Hymn of the Republic." During November 1861 she and her husband, both busy with war work, had gone with the noted pastor, the Reverend James Freeman Clarke, to visit the national capital, then literally an armed camp. Their friend, Bay State Governor John A. Andrew, took them to the White House to see President Lincoln. Julia, meeting him for the first time, recalled the strain on his face and the "sad expression of Mr. Lincoln's deep blue eyes." Riding back in a carriage along soldier-clogged roads, she heard them singing the popular war song, "John Brown's Body." "Why do you not write some good words for that stirring tune," suggested Mr. Clarke. That sleepless night in her Hotel Willard room, Julia composed her "Battle Hymn" and with "an old stump of a pen" committed the words to paper at dawn before she forgot them.

Governor Andrew had long been a fellow abolitionist along with Dr. Howe. Andrew had even, by telegraph, hired and paid for a Washington, D.C., lawyer to handle the defense of John Brown after his Harper's Ferry raid failed. Julia recalled how the state's busy wartime governor would come from the State House to Number 13 "to take refuge when the need for rest was imperative. He would sometimes lie down on a sofa in my drawing room and snatch a brief nap."

These Swan houses were also celebrated for their hospitality. The "Boston Radical Club"—not a bomb-throwing crowd, just intellectuals—held a monthly meeting at Number 13 or 17 to hear and discuss some member's essay. Longfellow, Lowell, the elder Henry James, Julia Ward Howe, Lucretia Mott, Whittier, Holmes, Phillips, Emerson, Mr. Clarke—all came to the big parlor with its great fireplace and French furniture. Visiting celebrities to Boston came. The Swan ladies long remembered Emperor Dom Pedro of Brazil being the only one at Number 13 to rise and thank them when they passed the ice cream. Number 15 has been the residence of the British consul general since 1972, when it was purchased by the British government.

From earliest to modern times houses at the head of Chestnut Street have had well-known residents. The son of a signer of the Declaration of Independence, Robert Treat Paine, in 1803 built the twin Bulfinch buildings at numbers 6 and 8, now the Beacon Hill Friends House. Their driveways to their yard and stables on either side became, two decades later, sites for numbers 4 and 10. On the opposite side, Secretary of State Henry Kissinger resided at 1 Chestnut when he was teaching at Harvard.

Roaming Blackstone's Acres and Louisburg Square

Back when Boston's first settler, the Reverend William Blackstone, could choose from the whole of the Boston peninsula for his abode, he picked this area of Louisburg Square. A visit today confirms that Mr. Blackstone as a site-selector was a talented man. The area of his farmstead, Walnut Street west down to Charles Street and from Beacon Street north to Pinckney Street, offers many delightful sights for a stroller besides glimpses of the river one way and of the golden dome another. This is Beacon Hill's best section for wandering.

The handrail on the Walnut Street buildings as they reach to Mount Vernon Street confirms that Beacon Hill is still a genuine height—intown Boston's highest—and that the grade can be steep. While we are on Walnut Street, notice the five-story redbrick building nearly opposite the head of Chestnut Street, 8 Walnut, an attractive building with recessed entry and Doric pillars. Boston's greatest murder sensation began here when wealthy banker George Parkman, intent on collecting a long overdue debt, left this dwelling on the morning of November 23, 1849—and disappeared before lunchtime. On a later walk we shall see how quickly Charles Dickens put on his hat and coat when Dr. Oliver Wendell Holmes offered to show the eager British novelist where George Parkman met his fate.

Stroll back down Chestnut Street to Spruce Street, on the left. About midway down short Spruce Street, on the left, is a freestanding structure (this alone a rarity on Beacon Hill), and going around it is Spruce Court with cobblestones, a narrow paved sidewalk, and even trees. In fact, in this contemporary "city upon a hill," Spruce Court has parking (private, of course), and in the court's innermost part we may even see two-car garages—commonplace in the suburbs but, located here on the hill, something that can easily compete nowadays with any other Beacon Hill status symbol.

Before leaving Chestnut Street via Willow Street we should note still another Chestnut Street residence, Number 51. Parkman and Dana were not the only prominent literary figures to live on Chestnut. The poet James Russell Lowell spent part of his youth here. His father, the Reverend Charles Lowell, son of "Essex Junto" Judge John Lowell, was minister of Boston's Old West Church and lived at Number 51 for eight years before purchasing Elmwood estate in Cambridge, now the residence of presidents of Harvard University.

On our way up Willow Street to Louisburg Square we come about midway to a showpiece of Beacon Hill, steep Acorn Street. This was once the habitat of Beacon Hill servants, coachmen, and tradesmen. Cobblestones are photogenic but make rough walking. The north-side sidewalk may be as much as 2 feet in width including the granite curb. In view of the street's one-car width, the sign once on 20 Acorn suggested rueful built-in humor: PLEASE DON'T BLOCK THIS DOORWAY WHEN PARKING. THANK YOU. The handrails at the top of Willow Street offer an appreciated lift getting up to Louisburg Square—now directly before us.

If Charles Bulfinch's plan had been adopted by the Mount Vernon Proprietors, this celebrated square, a Beacon Hill treasure, would have been exactly three times larger. We can be certain because Bulfinch's plan still exists, and it included the peak of Mount Vernon itself just above the upper side of present Louisburg Square. Like Beacon Hill, this one was roughly (exact statistics are lacking) 50 or 60 feet higher than the existing square.

This peak was cut away by the Mount Vernon Proprietors by means of what was exalted as the nation's first railroad. "In 1803," asserted Harrison Gray Otis, "we began our great operation . . . carting down gravel from the mountain." Actually the arrangement was a gravity slide with the dirt carts on a rope so that as one cart went up, the other went down with gravel to create present Charles Street, where, as Otis added, "the tide rose 12–14 feet." The carts crossed and recrossed Louisburg Square.

It was more than three decades before any construction got going on Louisburg Square. The first was the building at the upper corner of Pinckney Street, 19 Louisburg, built in 1834. This became the home of Mayor Frederick Walker Lincoln, Boston's Civil War mayor and a descendant of the same Bay State stock as President Lincoln. The mayor played host here at a grand reception for the nineteen-year-old Prince of Wales (later King Edward VII) when he was royally welcomed to Boston in 1860.

The square, despite its hillside tilt, appears taken directly out of some London scene of the Regency period. It has a changeless, patrician air about it. Still it has had its share of change. Mayor Lincoln's dwelling and three of its neighbor structures were converted in 1881 into the St. Margaret's Convent with an Anglican chapel built in the rear. In 1991 the Episcopal nuns auctioned their buildings, 19, 17, and 13 Louisburg Square, and moved their charitable order to St. Monica's Home on Roxbury's Fort Hill.

We now know how Yuletide customs have changed, too. It was here, beyond all other Beacon Hill spots, that Boston long enjoyed a perfect setting for a Christmas Eve welcome to Santa and the Birth of Christ—with lights, wandering minstrels, bell-ringing, caroling, and "Silent Night" and "O Little Town of Bethlehem" echoing through the neighborhood and into all the hospitably open houses.

Lincoln's corner domicile at Number 19 was where the private character of Louisburg Square was established. The abutting landowners, twenty-two of them, in a pioneer neighborhood endeavor, signed an agreement that they would forever maintain their square. They would put up the iron railing, tend their park, allot parking space. The statues at either end, Aristides the Just and Columbus, were the gifts of a wealthy resident at Number 3 in 1850. He was the Turkish consul and the statues had crossed from Greece as ballast in one of his ships.

Beyond the charming aspect of the buildings on Louisburg Square's west side, four dwellings are of special interest. William Dean Howells, noted editor, author, and first president of the American Academy of Arts and Letters, lived briefly in two of them. Late in 1881, the year Howells resigned his editorship of the *Atlantic Monthly,* he suffered a debilitating illness and decided to leave the cozy Queen Anne cottage he had built in Belmont so that he could be nearer the center of Boston's literary world. He rented quarters the following January at 16 Louisburg Square and shortly was writing from there to a friend:

"We are quite a literary precinct." Henry James that winter was "only a few doors from us. I see him constantly," said Howells, "and we talk literature perpetually, as we used to do in our walks 10 years ago." Poet Whittier was a winter visitor on Mount Vernon Street. Thomas Bailey Aldrich was "in his old house on Charles Street," and Howells and his intimate friend Mark Twain, besides other writing, were working jointly on a stage play.

But for health reasons and to write a travel book, Howells took off in July for a year in Europe. When he got back he found himself "in a frenzy of house-hunting" that, as he wrote Twain, led to a year's lease, 1883–1884, at 4 Louisburg Square. "You can't come to see us in it any too soon," he wrote Twain. "We wish that Mrs. Clemens would come with you. Mrs. Howells joins me in love to all of you." Twain and Howells continued work on their play. "I would give anything if we lived within tongue-shot of each other," Howells told Twain. Howells also worked on the libretto for an opera to be performed at the Bijou Theater. Meantime, as he was preparing to leave Louisburg Square for a house "on the waterside of Beacon St.," the gentlemen organizing Boston's fashionable Tavern Club were preparing to ask the celebrated editor-author to be their first president.

The brick, bowfront building at Number 10 in midblock, with its stone steps and black railing, is associated with the Alcott family. The tale of their occupancy, like much of their economically distressed life, is poignant. Father Bronson Alcott, an unrealistic mystic, could blithely ascend the greatest heights of philosophy but—save for gifts from admiring friends, in particular Ralph Waldo Emerson—Bronson found it next to impossible to scrape together funds to sustain his family of devoted wife and four daughters. The Alcotts lived in innumerable places in Boston, Concord, and many other communities in the harrowing quest to keep a roof over their heads.

Louisa May Alcott was long the family breadwinner though it was not until she wrote the classic *Little Women,* published in 1868 when she was thirty-five, that she could count on a comfortable income. But life for Louisa had become even harsher. She had served as a nurse during the Civil War and, as part of treatment for a fever that hit her and wounded soldiers, she sustained creeping mercury poisoning.

In the fall of 1885 she leased 10 Louisburg Square for two years. It had become her custom to summer in Concord and rent in Boston in the winter. Year by year the effects of the poisoning grew more severe, incapacitating her. This dwelling was to be her last rental. Bronson had already suffered a stroke and Louisa, on the death of one of her sisters, had been left the care of baby "Lulu," her niece, a care that proved about Louisa's only joy. Months before her lease was up, Louisa had to enter a nursing home in Roxbury. Death was slow, terribly painful, her system wrecked, her legs crippled. She still went to visit Bronson in Concord, where he died just two days before Louisa passed away in the Roxbury nursing home in the spring of 1888. The five-story residence at 8 Louisburg Square was redone in magnificent Georgian style in 1923 when William K. Vanderbilt purchased it for his bride.

Tales that go with the bowfront at Number 20 are joyful. A wedding that delighted concert lovers was performed here in early 1852 when soprano Jenny Lind, "The Swedish Nightingale," became a bride. Host and owner of Number 20 was one of the nation's most distinguished bankers and intellectuals, Samuel Gray Ward, American representative (as his father was before him) of the preeminent British banking house of Barings of London.

Jenny Lind, who had been starring in top operatic roles since she was sixteen, was lured by showman P. T. Barnum to undertake one hundred concerts on an American tour. From the moment of her arrival in the fall of 1850 she became a sensation. Her first Boston appearance was a month later in Tremont Temple, the remodeled Tremont Theater of 1827. At the auction of seats for this concert, the first one brought a bid of $625. In a later Boston appearance she sang for the overflow crowd at the old Fitchburg Railroad depot on Causeway Street near the North Station. A year and a half later she married her pianist-conductor.

Ward (not to be confused with Julia Ward Howe's brother Samuel, also a banker) had many distinctions. He carried out the banking for America's purchase of Alaska from Russia for $7.5 million. Ward made the suggestion that was a key to the success of Boston's celebrated Saturday Club, of which he was a founder, that members be noted for sociableness as well as talent. He was also a founder of Boston's renowned Union Club.

About the only visitors who have not fallen in love with Louisburg Square were Mrs. Mallard and the little Mallards. They, though, were ducks, and Mrs. Mallard explained that they looked in Louisburg Square "but then there was no water to swim in." So, to the relief of worried fans, the Mallards took up their abode in the Public Garden.

Pinckney Street

Pinckney is the Cinderella street of Beacon Hill. The Mount Vernon Proprietors intended, when they laid it out in 1802, that it should be the farthest northward reach of their domain, and by furnishing only limited access to the north side of the hill, via Anderson Street, they put off-limits the less desirable part of the North Slope.

They considered it wise to locate stables protectively along Pinckney at the very back of the Mount Vernon Street mansion lots. After all, ropewalks still stood along the south side of Myrtle Street down to Grove Street. What they most wanted to exclude was a rough-and-tumble area then on the riverside extreme of the North Slope. The area was typical of seaports the world round, which gave that section, and even Beacon Hill, a stenchy name, Mount Whoredom.

The walk through Louisburg Square to Pinckney Street was a favorite of hearty, companionable publisher "Jamie" Fields as he went on foot between his downtown bookstore and the famed salon that his beautiful young wife, Annie, and he ran at their dwelling on Charles Street. A young editor of his, Thomas Bailey Aldrich, lived at 84 Pinckney, on the left just below Louisburg Square, having moved in with the bride he married in 1865.

Fields dropped by the Aldrich house on Thanksgiving Day morning, 1867, the only Thanksgiving Day that Charles Dickens would be spending in America. The public had been informed that Dickens's health required quiet, and it respected the request. Fields knew that

Dickens would be having breakfast alone in his Parker House rooms and set out to join him. Lilian Aldrich had her table set for Thanksgiving with flowers and all their wedding presents. "Dickens must see this," exclaimed Fields and hurried on through Louisburg Square. The day was snowy and cold. Presently he came walking back the same way with Dickens. Dickens was so delighted by what he saw that he wrote home to London. He was bewitched by a child making a curtsy and offering him wine and biscuits on a silver tray. He then went on to Fields's and then to Longfellow's in Cambridge for Thanksgiving dinner. When Dickens saw some of his own latest novels in the house, he winked at Longfellow's children and remarked to Longfellow: "Ah! I see you read the best authors."

It was in the house at 84 Pinckney that Aldrich, before moving downhill in 1870 to Charles Street to be closer to Fields, began writing his most successful novel, *The Story of a Bad Boy,* a tale of joyful adolescence in an oh-so-long-ago setting.

The house at 86 Pinckney, just below the one Dickens visited, was the dwelling of John J. Smith, a leader of Boston's black community in the mid-1800s when it was located on the slope to the north of Joy Street, before shifting to the new South End for better livelihoods and housing. In 1840 the Honorable Mr. Smith, then twenty years of age, came from his Virginia birthplace to Boston. A barber by training, he soon owned a shop near Bowdoin Square at now-vanished Howard and Bulfinch streets, and eventually owned several other shops. He served with the all-black Fifth Cavalry during the Civil War. After the war Smith, for three terms beginning in 1868, represented this district in the state legislature. Later, in 1878, he became the first black to serve in the Boston Common Council. Smith, as we shall see when shortly we visit Smith Court off Joy Street, was a crusader in the pre–Civil War struggle to integrate the Boston schools.

Louisa May Alcott included Pinckney Street in her shifting winter rentals after *Little Women* royalty checks started arriving in the household that Louisa, "duty's faithful child," long helped to maintain for the Alcott family. First she took quarters at 43 Pinckney and then came in 1880 to 81 Pinckney, the four-story brick house facing Louisburg Square. Louisa had sent a nurse to France to fetch back her sister

May's blond, blue-eyed baby, Louisa, whose birth had cost May (the Amy of *Little Women*) her own life. It was here at Number 81 that little "Lulu" first brought joy to her pain-wracked Aunt Louisa for whom she was named.

The attic of 57 Pinckney Street, after his climb of at least five flights, provided quarters for young author John P. Marquand in 1914 when, just out of Harvard College, he got his first newspaper job on the *Boston Transcript.* Marquand liked to climb through the skylight and sit precariously on the slate roof for a view of the city. By 1927 he was living down Pinckney Street in his own house at 43 West Cedar Street, and it was from there that he went on to New York City where he wrote his satire on the Boston elite, she *Late George Apley.*

On our right on Pinckney Street, uphill from Louisburg Square, is a line of five houses, numbers 58 to 66, which replaced the grand stables of Harrison Gray Otis's Mount Vernon Street mansion. But first we come to an address, curiously numbered 74½, that appears beside an iron gateway athwart a passage built on the left side of Number 74. Several of these right-of-way passages exist on Beacon Hill—at least three more of them when we get farther up Pinckney Street. The 74½ private passageway leads to what is known as Beacon Hill's "Hidden House," a four-story dwelling with seven rooms and baths and a delightful garden. Understandably, this modern Shangri-la, nestled between Mount Vernon and Pinckney Streets, is strictly private. Bostonians in general, and particularly tourists, should respect that privacy, for they are deeply in the debt of the gentleman who lived here with his wife and family, John Codman, Sr.

Mr. Codman, who died early in 1989 at age 90, was in the fourth generation of Bostonians directly responsible for preserving many historic Boston buildings. Indeed, it was Mr. Codman who helped get enactment of the law protecting Beacon Hill and its structures as an historic district. The famous Old Corner Bookstore, which we will visit on another walk, is an example of Mr. Codman's civic contribution to Boston. Back in 1960, when he learned that the Old Corner Bookstore and neighboring buildings were to go on the market, he and friends, working through the Bostonian Society and the Boston Athenaeum, raised funds to preserve them. Their campaign flier starkly pictured the alternatives: the Old Corner Bookstore at the height of its glory in 1850 or a mere marker; treasured building restored or its tombstone? Like other benevolent individuals, Mr. Codman, a veteran Boston realtor, explained his civic role in his modest way: "You can't be in real estate on the Hill or in Boston and not get interested in history. Also you just can't do things like this alone. There's always credit to others." He was particularly grateful to *The Boston Globe* for providing advance rent for the premises so that his rescue group could succeed. Again a bookstore, it is now called The Boston Globe Store.

The house at 62 Pinckney was the residence, in his later years, for a law partner of U.S. Senator Charles Sumner, George Hillard, legislator, U.S. district attorney, and warm friend of Boston nineteenth-century literary figures, who often gathered here as his guests.

The brick structure at 54 Pinckney, Hillard's earlier dwelling, was the setting for one of the happiest moments in the life of his friend Nathaniel Hawthorne. The impecunious author of *Twice-Told Tales* (his more famous novels were yet to be written) had been in love for more than three years with Sophia Peabody, his "sweet dove," and he had at last arrived at the eve of their 1842 wedding.

In 1839 Sophia's sister Elizabeth had gotten Hawthorne a job on the Boston waterfront from her friend, the historian George Bancroft, then collector of the port. Hawthorne came from Salem and Hillard invited him to use a bedroom and parlor at Number 54. Hawthorne found that the waterfront work left him no time to write. In the hope of getting a livelihood and dwelling for Sophia and himself, Hawthorne quit the job and put his meager funds into the new transcendental utopia of communal living, Brook Farm, in West Roxbury. That proved equally unproductive and he came back to Hillard's.

By July 1842 Hawthorne and Sophia found that they could lease the Old Manse in Concord for $100 a year. He sat down at Number 54 on July 8 and dashed off a note asking a family friend, the Reverend James Freeman Clarke, to perform the wedding, saying: "Unless it should be a decidedly rainy day, a carriage will call for you at half past 11 o'clock in the forenoon." In his ecstasy Hawthorne failed to give Mr. Clarke the date or place. But all went well. Mr. Clarke married the lovers the next day at Elizabeth's bookshop on the other side of the Common.

Although Harrison Gray Otis's brick stables no longer stand, we can still get an idea of the lavishness of early Mount Vernon Street manor life, because Jonathan Mason's stables, though of course altered, may be seen at 24 Pinckney—the two-story, gray-painted brickwork with the variety of elaborate window styles.

The row of houses, numbers 12 to 22, is also on land once at the back of Mason's extensive lot that he sold before his death. The only handy well was in the rear of Number 18, owned by a kind tailor who permitted his adjoining neighbor to draw water, provided that the neighbor build his own passageway from the Pinckney Street lot line. In some instances these arched, 2-by-4-foot passageways were retained as rights-of-way to the rear lots of later Mount Vernon Street owners. Barred, as many of them are, the passageways are unquestionably private.

"We are real Micawbers," was Louisa May Alcott's touching description of life among the Alcotts when they lived for three years, 1852–1855, at 20 Pinckney Street, the narrow brick structure still there. From age fifteen Louisa tried to help, baby-sitting for folks on Beacon Street, teaching school with her sister in the second-floor parlor, and writing in her third-floor room. Her patient mother, Marmee of *Little Women,* took in boarders and sewing to augment the pitiful earnings of their impractical father, Bronson Alcott.

When she was twenty, Louisa took her first major story down to the Old Corner Bookstore and handed it to "Jamie" Fields. Astoundingly for an editor of invariably acute perception, Fields, after reading it, plunged Louisa into a "slough of despond" by advising her to remain a teacher. Two years later she sold her first story for $10. *Little Women* and success were then fourteen more years in her future.

Father Bronson, with his admiring friend Emerson helping on expenses, took a trip westward to deliver lectures. He did send back a little money now and then and, in cold February 1854, came back to Number 20. At the sound of the bell, mother Alcott flew down the stairs crying, "My husband!" Louisa recalled the odd look he gave when the shivering, sleepy man finally opened his billfold and in it was a lone dollar bill. "My overcoat was stolen and I had to buy a shawl," he said; "Another year I shall try to do better." Louisa and her sister "choked down our tears and took a lesson in real love" when mother Alcott kissed him and said, "I call that doing very well. Since you are safely home, dear, we don't ask anything more." By July 1855, despite help from friends, even sufficient funds for rent ran out and the Alcotts left Beacon Hill and moved to live with cousins in Walpole, New Hampshire.

This part of Pinckney Street is also associated with Elizabeth Peabody's successful effort to introduce English-speaking kindergartens in America. She had studied the new methods of German educator Friedrich Froebel and started her experiment, as we shall see, on the other side of the Common at 24½ Winter Street in the fall of 1861. By 1862 she had learned that the work was "life-absorbing," she had to increase her rates to $1.00 per pupil per week, and she needed "to have another room, nearly as large as my largest . . . whose law shall be quietness. I have not been willing to impose this law in my one room which has caused a greater appearance of disorder . . . than was the reality of the case."

So Miss Peabody started her second kindergarten year on September 29, 1862, at 15 Pinckney Street. The building Miss Peabody brought her pupils to, unlike its successor building on the sidewalk line, stood back on the land, thus affording some "accommodations for growing plants or keeping animals" she had desired from the start. Julia Ward Howe's seven-year-old daughter Maud was a pupil and recalled: "We sat on tiny chairs, around a fascinating low table where we modeled birds' nests in clay and filled the nests with tiny eggs. Another useful art was the weaving of patterns with narrow strips of colored paper. My first lessons in arithmetic were had at the kindergarten with the help of a frame strung with red, green and yellow beads."

The site next to Peabody's kindergarten, 13 Pinckney, is of considerable interest as well, for it was here in 1847 that the noted publisher and builder Maturin M. Ballou lived and brought his bride. Ballou is particularly remembered as editor of two great nineteenth-century illustrated magazines, *Gleason's Pictorial* and *Ballou's Pictorial,* and for founding *The Boston Globe* in 1872.

Two more extant buildings at the head of Pinckney Street deserve our attention. Number 14, with its built-in backyard passageway, was once the home of the man who made possible the great publishing career of "Jamie" Fields, the man who made Fields a partner, William D. Ticknor of the original Ticknor & Fields. Ticknor was basically a businessman, and a good one. He came to live here in 1835 after his marriage.

The other building, pressed now between two four-story brick dwellings, is the two-story-plus-dormer, two-door wooden structure at numbers 5 and 7. This is, if not the oldest, one of the oldest buildings on Beacon Hill. The lot goes back to an early attempted development on the North Slope in the eighteenth century. It changed hands several times and, in 1786, like other lots after the Revolution, was purchased by workmen and mechanics. This one went for 30 pounds to two friends, George Middleton, a black coachman who served in the Revolutionary War, and Louis Glapion, a mulatto barber from the French West Indies. The house was completed by 1791, "a small house by south side ropewalk," as the assessing records put it, about a decade before the Mount Vernon Proprietors even laid out Pinckney Street. The building was later divided into two houses when the barber was married. It has undergone many changes but still has authentic signs of age, an old-style chimney of much depth and quite venerable timbering.

Smith Court to Bowdoin Street

We bear left on leaving Pinckney Street, and a short way downhill on Joy Street is the setting for the beginning of the abolitionist movement, so much a part of Boston's fame. The access is through Smith Court, which runs left off Joy Street at 46 Joy. The two-story brick structure on the corner, with its brick pediment, was erected in 1834 from a legacy left to the city by a white businessman, Abiel Smith, for whom the court was renamed. He gave funds for the education of black children, who had long been

The Black Heritage Trail

From the late eighteenth to the late nineteenth century, Boston was home to one of America's largest communities of free blacks. Many settled on the north slope of Beach Hill and in the North End. The fourteen stops on the Black Heritage Trail range from the Robert Gould Shaw and 54th Regiment Memorial at Park and Beacon Streets, commemorating the service of blacks in the Civil War, to The Charles Street Meeting House, which served as a pulpit for the oratory of abolitionists Frederick Douglass and Soujourner Truth, to houses that served as stops along the Underground Railroad. Complete information about the tour is available at the Museum of African American History, at 46 Joy Street.

shut out from the public school system, despite appeals to the Legislature and city going back to the first appeal in 1787 by a black veteran of the Revolutionary War, Prince Hall.

Black parents, to help their youngsters, formed a pioneer community school on the North Slope in the home of Primus Hall at Revere and West Cedar Streets in 1798. This school was moved to the basement of the African Meeting House still standing at 8 Smith Court, built by free blacks of the African Baptist Church Society in 1806. By 1820 Boston did establish a school for Afro-American children, and in 1834 the Abiel Smith School, open to black children throughout the city, enrolled the Meeting House School children.

The Meeting House, among this nation's oldest extant black churches, has been recently under restoration as the Museum of Afro-American History. Over the years, as waves of ocean-borne immigrants brought changes to seaport Boston's neighborhoods, this building has seen different uses. For a time it was a Jewish synagogue.

But the peak of its renown was reached the night of January 6, 1832, in its basement schoolroom under the church, when William Lloyd Garrison and twelve dedicated men signed a preamble that brought into existence the New England Anti-Slavery Society, with its demand for immediate emancipation.

"A fierce northeast storm, combining snow, rain and hail in about equal proportion, was raging, and the streets were full of slush." Garrison's friend, biographer, and one of the apostolic dozen, Oliver Johnson, continued: "On that dismal night, and in the face of a public opinion fiercer far than the tempest of wind and hail that beat upon the windows . . . was laid the foundation of an organized movement against American slavery that at last became too mighty to be resisted. . . . As the little company . . . were stepping into the storm and darkness . . . Mr. Garrison impressively remarked: 'We have met tonight in this obscure school-house; our numbers are few and our influence limited; but mark my prediction, Faneuil Hall shall ere long echo with the principles we have set forth. We shall shake the nation by their mighty power.'"

And they did, though ahead were three decades, and incalculable, life-threatening perils, until they reached their goal. Garrison, who seemed a mighty small David facing a Goliath that stormy night, would be present in Baltimore when the Republican convention, urged by Abraham Lincoln (as Lincoln predicted to Garrison on a visit to the White House), proposed the Thirteenth Amendment to abolish slavery.

Along the way Garrison's band inspired and aided many other reforms. The group's willingness to have women join in the abolitionist movement, helping to develop antislavery societies in other states, brought about their open participation at the formation of the American Anti-Slavery Society. "When Lucretia Mott arose to speak," said Johnson, "not one of the clerical members cried shame, or remembered to throw at her a text of St. Paul." Thus the women's liberation movement was launched.

Across the court from the African Meeting House is a large clapboard house at Number 3, built in 1799. William C. Neill, a black historian, dwelt here in the 1850s. He was already a leader, along with John J. Smith of Pinckney Street, William Lloyd Garrison, and the orator Wendell Phillips, in an early crusade to integrate the public schools. They asked: Why should blacks pay taxes for schools that bar their children? The landmark Abiel Smith School on the corner was boycotted and, in 1855, the legislature at last voted to approve integration.

A few Afro-American houses of the period still exist in Smith Court: the parsonage of the Meeting House minister at Number 5 and former black artisans' houses at numbers 7, 7½, and 10. But the high tides of immigration swept almost all away on the North Slope, and they were replaced by large tenements to shelter the newcomers.

It may seem peculiar to visitors that Boston, the birthplace of the Revolution, would have a street bearing the name of Great Britain's first consul in Boston directly following the war, Sir John Temple. But then Boston, like much of New England, still has streets that cling to names of well-known, even politically detested Tories of pre-Revolutionary days. Temple Street is back of the State House. We come to it by going back uphill on Joy Street and turning left at Myrtle Street, which, English style, becomes Derne Street as we walk back of the State House to a narrow street on our left, which is Temple.

Sir John Temple was a very popular man, particularly renowned in England for a duel. Temple Street, however, was really named for his wife, Lady Temple. She was the former Elizabeth Bowdoin, daughter of the patriot governor of Massachusetts, James Bowdoin—all of which made Sir John a natural selection for consul in Boston when the shooting was over.

Until their destruction by fire a few years ago, there stood on Temple Street about the only rivals to the wooden buildings we saw at 5 and 7 Pinckney Street for being the oldest on Beacon Hill. This pair was at 44 and 46 Temple Street, at the rear of the stone structure of the old Bowdoin Street Meeting House. The houses were built in 1787 and eventually were used by clergy of the meeting house. By agreement with the church and Suffolk University, the site, maintained by the University, is now—with its trees, shrubs, and benches—an attractive courtyard in front of the main entrance to the most recent addition to the University, founded in 1906.

As we resume walking along Derne Street into Bowdoin Street, we get a closer view of the great granite blocks in the wall at the rear of the State House grounds. These, as we noted earlier, formed a huge container for the former Beacon Hill reservoir, and there are some critics who claim that this granite formation is still a prizeworthy architectural showpiece.

Downhill at 35 Bowdoin Street, on the left, there is the eye-catching, early Gothic, castellated tower of the Church of St. John the Evangelist, designed by Solomon Willard. St. John's was built in 1831 by the congregation of the Reverend Lyman Beecher, the father of Harriet Beecher Stowe, who wrote *Uncle Tom's Cabin.* Dr. Beecher was a Boston preacher from 1826 to 1832, during which time this church replaced an earlier one on Hanover Street, which burned down.

Though Dr. Beecher's pastorate here ended in 1832, when he went to head a seminary in Ohio, he had become New England's leading evangelical preacher and had as a parishioner abolitionist William Lloyd Garrison. This led to a dramatic confrontation, for it was in this period that Garrison shifted from favoring gradual emancipation to demanding immediate emancipation. Dr. Beecher, like most clergy then, except mainly Unitarian and Quaker abolitionists, preached gradual emancipation or African colonization and assailed the position of the others as radical and insurrectionist. In *The Liberator* Garrison declared that Dr. Beecher would hardly use his pulpit to advocate gradual giving up of sin by "drunkards, tyrants, thieves and debauchees . . . It would hardly be tolerated even from the lips of Lyman Beecher. Yet he is foolish, in the Doctor's estimation, who tells the slaveholders to leave off their sins at once . . . For one, I cannot listen to any proposal for a gradual abolition of wickedness."

The membership of the stone church, originally called the Bowdoin Street Meeting House, disbanded in 1861. Two years after it became the Church of the Advent and moved, in 1883, to its present Gothic edifice on Brimmer Street. That same year the Society of St. John the Evangelist started services here on Easter Eve, renaming the church, and now it is a parish in the Episcopal Diocese of Massachusetts.

On Bowdoin Street, as well as treading on land that was part of the extensive acreage of Governor James Bowdoin, we are in John F. Kennedy's territory. Kennedy had his town apartment on this street, and it was Bowdoin Street he used when he went downhill to vote in the polling place of the Old West Church. He also used Bowdoin Street often when he went around the Beacon Street corner to use the library of the Boston Athenaeum.

Let us now go uphill on Bowdoin Street to see some of these places.

On our left is the twenty-two-story John W. McCormack Building (1973–1975), which holds a variety of state government offices. The main entrance into the grand lobby faces Ashburton Place, once part of a neighborhood center for some of Beacon Hill's most distinguished residents. Among them, besides President Kennedy, were Daniel Webster, Henry James, Elizabeth Peabody, and Horace Mann.

Kennedy was elected to Congress in 1946, the year after he was discharged from the navy, in James Michael Curley's old district. The public saw a slender, handsome youth but not the ugly, severe war wound he carried on his back from PT-boat service in the Pacific, a wound that more than once gave the future martyred President a brush with death. His third-floor apartment at 122 Bowdoin Street was his personal office, as well as dwelling, in his district. It was not always the tidiest of places, with heaps of things to be read and a pile of ever-mounting numbers of the *Congressional Record* to be consulted. There were always plenty of books, for he was a regular and very rapid reader. In 1952 he became the state's junior U.S. senator.

The McCormack Building was named in honor of a longtime public servant of Massachusetts, John W. McCormack. He served several years on Beacon Hill, 1920–1926, and then in Washington, where he became Speaker of the House. McCormack was a staunch supporter of President Franklin D. Roosevelt's administration and gave crucial backing to Roosevelt's leadership during the World War II era.

There are several large conference rooms on the twenty-first floor. Visitors—and cameras—are welcome when the rooms are not in use. From their ample windows the streets, buildings, and people of Beacon Hill we have been seeing look like a toy world. The hill, from this vantage, has no hidden gardens but a completely panoramic view is blocked oceanward by the growth of high-rise monoliths, which interrupt like pages ripped from a picture book.

The McCormack Building at 1 Ashburton Place stretches over the whole site of a number of once-smaller noted buildings on this short street. The Ford Hall Forum, which never rejected a speaker, however controversial, and which often drew mounted police to handle unruly, dissident mobs, was on the northwest corner, opposite Kennedy's apartment house.

The curved flower beds and shrubbery near the northeast corner at Somerset Street were pretty much the site of the boarding house at 3 Ashburton, run by the mother of the Reverend James Freeman Clarke when the street was called Somerset Court. Here the Peabody sisters lived and ran a school. Their friends gathered, with Elizabeth usually presiding, at Mrs. Clarke's long boarding-house table. Elizabeth pioneered lecturing here and held "reading Parties" in the evening—forerunners of Margaret Fuller's "Conversations," an intellectual breakthrough for women. And here the widower Horace Mann, then a state senator and educator, first saw the smiling face of Elizabeth's sister Mary and fell in love. Other lodgers included the future president of Harvard, Jared Sparks, who was then working on his major edition of George Washington's life and letters; George Hillard, beginning his legal career; and the future founder of the Transcendentalist paradise Brook Farm, the Reverend George Ripley.

The middle of the McCormack Building's main entrance is about the site of 13 Ashburton Place, the residence of the philosopher Henry James during the Civil War. James was drawn by Boston's intellectual life to further his sons' education. One of them, the novelist Henry, appeared to have used Elizabeth Peabody for a prominent character in his Bostonians. James protested that he had "no shadow of such an intention." Still he did concede that he was aware that his Miss Birdseye, a lifelong reformer, "would perhaps be identified with Miss Peabody."

Resuming our walk on Bowdoin Street, we come to the former nine-story Bellevue Hotel at the corner of Beacon Street. The hotel rooms, now apartments, once housed leading participants in the strenuous political life associated with the State House. The 21st

Amendment, beside the old marquee, was joshingly called the State House Annex and was used by press and pols convivially as a news exchange. Upstairs the Democratic State Committee played its role.

President Kennedy's maternal grandparents, after giving up their big family dwelling in Dorchester, lived here a dozen years in an apartment suite. John F. "Honey Fitz" Fitzgerald, the President's grandfather and namesake, used to regale listeners in the lobby, including his smiling grandson, by singing his mayoral campaign tune, "Sweet Adeline." No grandfather ever wore a happier or prouder look than "Honey Fitz" when he was campaigning in 1946 for his World War II–hero grandson for congressman in the same district that had three times sent "Honey Fitz" to Congress. The night Jack was elected, "Honey Fitz" jumped on a table in the lobby, danced a jig, and led everyone in a chorus of "Sweet Adeline." Someone shouted that twenty-nine-year-old Jack might one day be governor. Shot back his grandfather: "That young man will be President of the United States."

The hotel sheltered other noted guests. In the 1870s, Louisa May Alcott moved in for parts of four different winters to rest and to write. When she first took rooms at the Bellevue in 1874, her beloved youngest sister, May, gave a weekly class in drawing. On Louisa's last brief stay in 1878 she got word that May had given birth to "Lulu." Fearing further word of danger, she fled back to Concord, only to be followed by word of May's death.

Upper Beacon Street—Brahmin Land

At the corner of Bowdoin and Beacon Streets we are definitely strolling in old Brahmin land. On our right, the corner where we see the east wing of the State House, was once the magnificent, large double house built in 1760 by one of Boston's leading Sons of Liberty, the rich Irish merchant William Molineux, close friend of his neighbors, John Hancock and James Bowdoin. Molineux hailed from Dublin, where his father was a knight and surgeon.

The Sons of Liberty often met here to confer on the crown's abuse of their British birthright. Molineux was an original member of Samuel Adams's powerful revolutionary weapon, the Committee of Correspondence. Molineux was a member of the Boston Tea Party, at age fifty-seven by far the oldest member. He died on the eve of the war; his last words for the land and people he loved were, "Oh, save my country." Oddly, Molineux's mansion after his death came into the hands of a leading Loyalist and was confiscated by the Commonwealth for debts when the Loyalist became a refugee.

The Bellevue site on the northeast corner was the estate of Governor James Bowdoin, with the mansion set back and facing Beacon Street. There was then a ridge in its rear and a long flight of stone steps up to the main entrance. The mansion's attractiveness drew British General "Gentleman Johnny" Burgoyne, future loser at Saratoga's battlefield, to live in it during the siege.

The most illustrious visitor to Bowdoin's mansion was George Washington. He went at least twice on his final visit to Boston in 1789 after his election as President. On that visit Bowdoin was almost constantly Washington's companion. Two days after Washington recorded that he merely "drank tea with Gov. Hancock," he wrote in his diary, "I dined in a large company at Mr. Bowdoin's."

Governor Bowdoin, suppressor of Shays' Rebellion, has, like many Brahmin families, sturdy ties to our cultural as well as mercantile annals. He was an intimate friend of Benjamin Franklin, a regular correspondent of his, and the first president of Boston's oldest scientific and cultural institution, the Academy of Arts and Sciences, founded in 1779. The first college in Maine, then part of Massachusetts, was named in his honor and to it he made munificent gifts.

This Beacon Street area had few peers in the Revolutionary and Federal periods. There were only three mansions in the block between Bowdoin and Somerset Streets: Bowdoin's; in the middle the home of Boston merchant Edward Bromfield, later the residence of his son-in-law William Phillips the elder; and, on the Somerset corner, the dwelling of merchant prince David Sears. The great mansions stood until the mid-1840s, when the ridge in back was finally cut down. Like the Bowdoins, the Phillips family gave extensively to education. William Phillips's brother and nephew were the founders of the Phillips academies in both Exeter, New Hampshire, and Andover, Massachusetts.

On the opposite side of Beacon Street, facing the head of Bowdoin Street, is an educational landmark, the Claflin Building at Number 18–20. Built in 1884 in the early years of Boston University for its College of Liberal Arts, it was named for the Claflin family, which contributed generously to found this new major coeducational institution and gave to the state a governor, William Claflin (1869–1871). From 1935 to 1981 the building housed the well-known Boston bookseller, Goodspeed's.

> THAT'S ALL I CLAIM FOR BOSTON—THAT IT IS THE THINKING CENTER OF THE CONTINENT, AND THEREFORE OF THE PLANET.
>
> —OLIVER WENDELL HOLMES

The graceful, four-story 1808 brick building at 16 Beacon, with a portico of slender, fluted columns, headquarters of the Boston Bar Association since 1963, was the studio residence of Chester Harding from 1827 to 1830. Harding was a self-taught American portrait painter who attracted patrons from frontiersman Daniel Boone to British royalty in England just before he came to Boston. "Harding fever" was the way Gilbert Stuart sourly explained Harding's crowded studio and his own ill-patronized one. Stuart, of course, was a genius, but increasing age and illness had made him a difficult man. Harding, by contrast, was distinguished for his charm. A "mighty man bright as an eagle" was the way twenty-one-year-old Sophia Peabody, who came here to sit for him, described Harding. Some of his paintings may be seen when we get to the lobby of the Boston Athenaeum.

The Congregational House at Number 14, with four facade carvings of scenes ranging from the Mayflower Compact to John Eliot preaching to Indians, has on its second floor one of New England's most unusual libraries. Here are early original town records when meeting house and town hall were synonymous. Its collection includes a carved church pew from Scrooby, where Elder Brewster and his Pilgrim followers worshiped before fleeing to Holland and the New World.

On the same side of Beacon Street, in the area of the Boston Athenaeum at Number 10½, was the mansion that the widow Emerson used for herself and children while Ralph Waldo was a student at the Boston Latin School, just downhill. Boston shipping merchant Daniel Parker lent her his dwelling to take in roomers while he was abroad and while the twin Beacon Street mansions at numbers 39 and 40 were being built for him and his business partner, Nathan Appleton. A family cow was presented to the needy widow by grandmother Emerson of Concord. Twelve-year-old Ralph Waldo's chores included takingthe cow to graze on the Common, leading it from near what is now the small front yard of the Athenaeum. For years the entire site of the Athenaeum had been pasture for the Bromfield-Phillips mansion across the street.

The 1847–1849 Renaissance structure at Number 10½, designed by Edward C. Cabot, was not the Athenaeum's first. The Athenaeum had its beginning in a small literary-minded group of Bostonians who called themselves the Anthology Society and in 1803 published America's first literary magazine, *The Monthly Anthology.* Its editor was the pastor of Boston's First Church, the Reverend William Emerson, father of Ralph Waldo Emerson. He was succeeded as editor by William Tudor, brother of the ice merchant Tudor.

In 1807 the group was incorporated as the Boston Athenaeum, and raised funds for a reading room and library. The members were few but they were enthusiasts about making Boston truly the Athens of America. At first they were housed in old Scollay Square (to which our walk will shortly take us). By 1810 they moved a few yards south to a "large and capacious" house that replaced the old King's Chapel parsonage and stood on the north side of the burying ground. By 1822, and until 1849, it was located in the much larger mansion formerly at 13 Pearl Street, on the slope of old Fort Hill, that was a gift from Boston merchant James Perkins, older brother of the more widely known merchant Thomas Handasyd Perkins. Both brothers made possible the addition in back of a three-story building for a lecture room and art gallery.

In 1827 the Athenaeum staged its first exhibition of paintings. It was a sensation. Growing wealth among Boston's Federal-era merchants financed private collections that were shown on loan. Gilbert Stuart came. He was so sickly (he would die the next year) that the man in charge rushed out to help the famous artist up the steps. For this kindness, the man received from crotchety Stuart naught but a withering look.

Boston had won identity as an art center, and, at the next exhibition in 1828, the needy heirs of Thomas Jefferson sent his paintings for sale. Athenaeum members, especially Thomas Handasyd Perkins and George Ticknor, in 1831 bought Stuart's unfinished portraits of George and Martha Washington to help the widow Stuart. The Athenaeum provided the nucleus of the collection of the Boston Museum of Fine Arts. That museum, for the first six years of its life, 1870–1876, was housed on the third, then the top, floor at 10½ Beacon.

Boston was always a magnet for the Concord group of writers and their friends. Emerson, despite a three-hour trip by coach, loved to come to the Athenaeum on Saturdays. In later years his daughter Ellen came along to carry his books and papers. He enjoyed sitting by a window. It was like in childhood days when merchant Parker lent his dwelling and, as Emerson's dear Aunt Mary recalled, there was from the back windows "a full view of the Burying Yard." Longfellow chatted by these Athenaeum windows with Emerson. Hawthorne told "Jamie" Fields that he had "passed delicious hours . . . in old advertisements in the newspaper files at the Boston Athenaeum." A great moment for amorous Hawthorne came on his marriage eve, when Emerson told Hawthorne in the earlier Athenaeum that he could have the Old Manse at a manageable rent.

Besides unique memories, the Athenaeum has rare attractions. Most of George Washington's library with his private bookplates can be seen, as well as one of America's first great libraries, given in 1698 by the British monarchy to King's Chapel; the books of Henry Knox; newspaper files augmented for a century or more since Hawthorne perused them; beautiful paintings and sculptures; a wonderful collection of books; and, most of all, what Emerson loved, countless, comfortable nooks in which to research and read.

Diagonally across the street from the Athenaeum is Somerset Street. Boston's Somerset Club, named after this street, had long association with this intersection. On the lower corner once stood two adjoining stone mansions built by Boston merchant David Hinckley, structures said in 1810 to be Boston's most lavish. The Somerset Club first came here in 1851. On the opposite, upper corner was, as we mentioned, the mansion of David Sears the elder. On his death, his son and namesake built an elaborate new mansion at 42 Beacon into which the Somerset Club was moved in 1872.

The lower Hinckley mansion that stood at 7 Beacon, just below the first Somerset Club at 9 Beacon, became the residence of the Gardners, and in it the legendary, wealthy Isabella "Belle" Stewart of New York City—the flamboyant, future art patron Mrs. "Jack" Gardner—in 1860 began married life as John Lowell Gardner's bride. She started shocking Boston society quite early, wearing big hoop skirts from Paris at the first party for her given by the Gardners.

The thirty-six-story tower of polished pink granite built at 1 Beacon Street in 1972 was most considerately positioned to assure a large downhill view of ancient King's Chapel. The skyscraper itself occupies Beacon Hill sites that once belonged to Brahmins, too.

The original site of the Somerset Club has an interesting connection with the present towering skyscraper. The Boston book firm of Houghton Mifflin was once the prime tenant. The Mifflin of the firm was wealthy George Harrison Mifflin. He spent his childhood in the old Hinckley mansion on the corner that, before becoming the Somerset Club, was the residence of Mifflin's grandfather, Benjamin W. Crowninshield, congressman and secretary of the navy, from 1832 until his death in 1851.

Houghton Mifflin eventually succeeded to the publishing world of James T. Fields, taking over the Old Corner Bookstore, the *Atlantic Monthly,* and "Jamie" Fields's great list of authors. It also greatly enriched that heritage with a dazzling list of authors, which includes Franklin D. Roosevelt, Rachel Carson, and Winston Churchill.

Houghton Mifflin, now well into its second century, is one of the oldest book publishers in the nation. It has closed all its traditional Boston quarters at 1 Beacon Street, 2 and 3 Park Street, and 1 Memorial Drive, Cambridge, and moved to 222 Berkeley Street, Back Bay, as the major tenant of the twenty-two-story skyscraper.

Almost directly across Beacon Street from the skyscraper's main entrance is a short private street, Tremont Place, presenting a building-framed view of the Park Street Church. One of Boston's foremost Brahmins had his last Boston residence in Tremont Place, Francis Cabot Lowell, the son of Judge Lowell of the "Essex Junto." Francis Cabot Lowell, in whose honor the Bay State industrial city of Lowell was posthumously named, inspired the American-made power loom that brought textile prosperity to New England.

CENTRAL BOSTON

To Old Scollay Square via Pemberton Hill

Old Scollay Square—on the west edge of spacious, resplendent, new Government Center—can be approached by many routes of historic interest. One of the most appealing is via Pemberton Hill or old Cotton Hill, its earlier name, which long dominated the central part of old Boston and for nearly two centuries blocked the town's spread westward over its own and other peaks of Beacon Hill. Actually old Pemberton Square is what remains of what was once a 65-foot-higher eminence.

From Beacon Street we head along Somerset Street as far as the old courthouse, the immense gray granite structure on our right with its east front facing on old Pemberton Square. Farther down Somerset Street, on the right, was a row of Federal brick buildings. Daniel Webster lived in one (now gone) from 1820 to 1824, a period when his law practice flourished and he won fame as an orator; he then resumed his career in Congress.

Still another great Bostonian who lived in one of these patrician residences on lower Somerset was Dr. James Jackson, a founder of the first general hospital in the Commonwealth, the Massachusetts General Hospital. The cornerstone of the hospital's creation was a circular

CENTRAL BOSTON

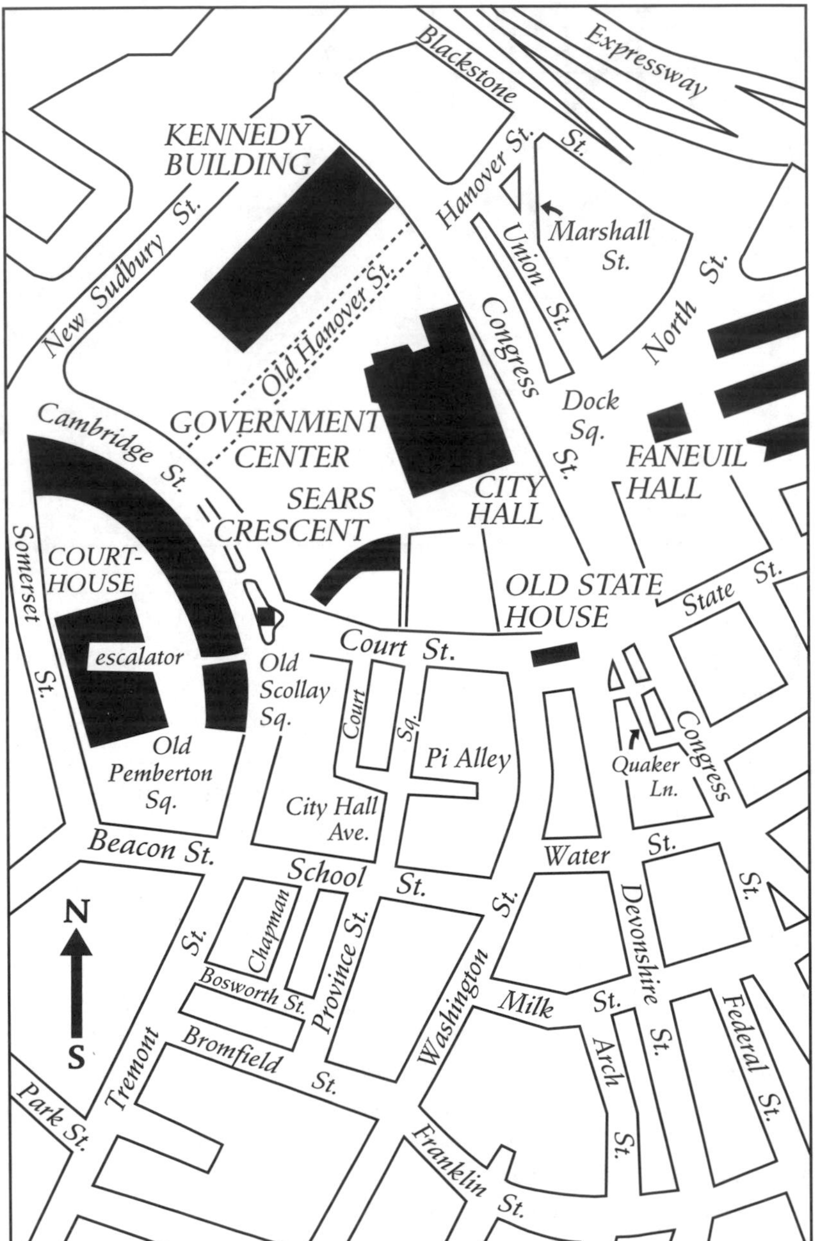

issued August 20, 1810, by Dr. Jackson and Dr. John Collins Warren declaring the public's need for its creation.

Turn right at the corner of the courthouse, and go down the ramp along its side into old Pemberton Square. The bollards with their inserted lights were ordered by a chief justice of the Supreme Judicial Court so that authorized vehicles could continue to use the once public highway to reach the ornate main entrance of the courthouse.

Pemberton Square in front of the courthouse is certainly ample enough, though the view seaward is blocked by the crescent of Center Plaza, a ten-story brick and concrete structure eight hundred and 75 feet in length, one of the city's largest office buildings, built 1965–1968. Penthouses on the two top floors are set back, which makes it difficult to see them from the street.

CRUSH UP A SHEET OF LETTER-PAPER IN YOUR HAND, THROW IT DOWN, STAMP IT FLAT, AND THAT IS A MAP OF OLD BOSTON.

—Walt Whitman

There is an across-the-centuries glimpse, though: Stand at the bottom of the ramp, the bronze plaque to your left designating probate court—insolvency court—registry, and the buildings frame a fascinating view of King's Chapel, the trees in its graveyard, the old City Hall mansard in mid–School Street with the appealing green tones time has brought to its copper roofing, and, for background, lofty towers in Boston's financial district.

We can only imagine how much more sweeping must have been the wide seaport prospect from the original peak before it was taken away by ox teams in 1835 to fill ten acres of river flats for the North Station and railroad yard area north of Causeway Street. Daniel Webster, always an outdoor man at heart, loved, while he lived on Somerset Street, to go to the top of the hill—he called it Sandy Hill—to enjoy the "magnificent panorama." Beyond the masts of ships thronging the waterfront wharves could be seen the islands of the wide harbor and in the distance the peninsula of Nahant. The hilltop and structures on it had been acquired by the fabulous developer Patrick Tracy Jackson, pioneer in both textile mills and railroading, for construction of the Boston & Lowell railroad station to those mills.

The hilltop portion of Jackson's purchase had been part of the showplace estate of artist John Singleton Copley's son-in-law Gardiner Greene. Greene, a forty-seven-year-old widower when he met and married beautiful twenty-nine-year-old Miss Copley in London in 1800, was considered Boston's richest citizen of his day. The Greene estate took in the lion's share of Pemberton Hill's east side and ran all the way uphill from old Scollay Square to his terraced gardens, greenhouse, and gazebo.

Greene's estate took in a lot of Boston history, as we may note on plaques around Pemberton Square, especially on the circular redbrick settees toward either end of the square. The south one marks the homestead of the Reverend John Cotton, once Puritan rector of St. Botolph's Church in old Boston in Lincolnshire, in whose honor Boston itself was named. Sir Harry Vane, a truly admirable man who was beheaded by King Charles II as a regicide in 1662, lived as Cotton's guest in an addition he had built on the south side of the Cotton dwelling; this was in the mid-1630s when young Vane was one of our early Bay State governors. Cotton recounted in his will how Vane deeded the addition "at his departure to my son Seaborne," then a four-year-old lad.

Still another interesting governor lived on this hillside immediately south of Mr. Cotton, Governor Richard Bellingham, who served four times as governor between 1635 and his death in 1672. When he was a widower at fifty years of age, he confronted the colony with what seemed an insolvable legal problem through his sudden marriage to a twenty-year-old beauty named Penelope. Penelope and her betrothed young man had published their banns and had come before Bellingham to be wed. Love-stricken, Bellingham seems to have fast-talked the young lady into switching and, thereupon, as chief magistrate, proceeded to unite himself and Penelope in marriage. He was charged with having failed, as the law required, to have published any banns. He announced that he would sit as judge and jury on any suit brought against him—and that put a prompt end to the legal issue.

There is another strange tale about Bellingham. Mrs. Ann Hibbins, one of the women executed as witches at the Common's Great Elm in 1656, when Bellingham was a magistrate, is said to have been his sister. No word of their relationship has come down from him. But many of that period did intimate that the widow Hibbins was unjustly condemned, as our last royal civil Governor Thomas Hutchinson observed, "for having more wit than her neighbors."

The old courthouse, still architecturally attractive, was built in 1886–1893. The new one, straight up twenty-four stories, eight of them mezzanines for jury deliberations, was completed during the period 1936–1939. Their height is quite disproportionate to the way mansions in Pemberton Square looked after Jackson in the 1830s had the lots auctioned off in a marquee temporarily raised in the square. The location was so convenient to the heart of Boston's commercial and financial life that the residences, their height harmoniously limited by deed, resembled in attractiveness Louisburg Square. The family names of its eventual dwellers included Winthrop, Forbes, Lowell, Coolidge, and Crowninshield, all Boston elite. But by the time the old courthouse rose, these families had departed and their dwellings were being torn down and replaced with offices in high buildings for lawyers. Construction of the new courthouse and the sweeping crescent of modern Center Plaza marked a renewal of one of the oldest parts of the town.

Besides its neoclassical, Louvre-like exterior, the old courthouse has interior charms not often to be found in our functional skyscrapers. It is worthwhile to work patiently through the necessary courthouse security to see the immense lobby of the old courthouse with its pillars and carvings. Elevators are handy for impressive views from the upper balconies.

The courthouse maintains one of the oldest, if not the oldest, collections of deeds, wills, and court records in the nation. Besides Mr. Cotton's will, there is a codicil that widow Hibbins wrote to her will the morning of her judicial murder, showing that she was a very sane, generous-hearted woman. Better-known treasures going back to 1629 are wills of the Winthrops, Paul Revere, John Hancock, Samuel Adams, and Daniel Webster, all with the customary opening, "In the name of God, Amen!" There also are John Adams's original notes on the Boston Massacre trial, tar-and-feathering suits, court records of the confiscation of Loyalist property, and even the papers of seventy-six lawsuits that spell out the agony of architect Charles Bulfinch's bankruptcy.

A plaque on the redbrick settee on the north side of Pemberton Square, in front of the entrance to the new courthouse, marks the dwelling that stern Governor John Endecott (he spelled it that way) rented, 1655–1665, when he came from Salem to run the colony once again.

Elihu Yale was born in 1649 in a dwelling in this same area of Governor Endecott's house. Yale's father, an original settler of New Haven who left there to come live in Boston, moved to England when Elihu was four years old. Elihu made a fortune trading in East India and sent such large gifts to the new college being built in New Haven that it was named Yale after him.

Steps and an escalator are available slightly to the left below the sign for Three Center Plaza. A few steps from the foot of the escalator we reach old Scollay Square. The escalator, by the way, replaces a public street that once linked Scollay and Pemberton Squares. By registered deed this escalator service must be provided literally "forever" in exchange for building over that short street.

To our right, as we arrive in what was Scollay Square, was the dwelling of Daniel Maude, in which for six years, 1636–1642, he conducted the first public school in America, Boston Public Latin School. It had started a year earlier a few blocks away in the dwelling of its first teacher, Philemon Pormont. The first actual school building, as we shall shortly see, was not built until 1645 in nearby School Street.

Government Center was developed in the early 1960s with the prize-winning Boston City Hall and the Federal Building named in honor of President Kennedy. The roughly ten-acre plaza was created in what was once a jumble of narrow London-like streets and decaying buildings, a delightful maze that sprawled in the heart of Boston from the redbrick Sears Crescent building, on our right, northward to our left, beyond the twenty-six-story split-tower Kennedy Building, to Sudbury Street on its north side.

All this acreage was part of the Puritans' original waterfront settlement around the town dock, once in Dock Square immediately in the rear of the new City Hall. Governor Winthrop and his followers

Faneuil Hall and the harbor from old Scollay Square

started their building hereabouts because of the many fine springs that abounded around the town cove, drainage no doubt of water from Beacon Hill. Building was already under way before they voted on September 7, 1630, to name the place Boston for a Puritan center they had left behind in the old world.

There are splendid sights from this vantage: Old Scollay Square itself, strictly speaking, was the space directly in front of us at the head of Court Street—down which you can catch a glimpse of the Old State House dating back to 1712, one of America's oldest extant public buildings. Immediately to the right of new City Hall, a bit in the distance and close to the original shoreline of the cove, is the beloved "birthplace of freedom," Faneuil Hall, started in 1740 to replace the old Market house. On the other side of new City Hall, between it and the Kennedy Building, a graceful spire rising above the rooftops of the North End identifies Christ Church (though it may be obscured by cranes from the ongoing "Big Dig"), the celebrated Old North Church in which Paul Revere's friend, the sexton, displayed in 1775 the two lanterns to signal that "the British are coming"—redcoats moving at that moment from the Common in boats and landing in Cambridge to head for Lexington and Concord.

Old Scollay Square and Government Center

Old Scollay Square, while at first just the area at the present junction of Tremont and Court Streets, grew over the years both in size and, ironically in view of its Puritan birthright, in notoriety. When the wooden buildings, named later for William Scollay, went up toward the close of the eighteenth century, they were considered a showpiece of improvement in the community. The block itself was a wedge shape between two streets running close together and converging, about 500 feet north, near the head of Hanover Street, the main street in Boston's North End. The two converging streets were Tremont Street (then called Tremont Row), where we are standing, and Court Street, which, on coming up from the Old State House to Tremont Street, made a right turn toward Hanover Street. Little wonder that a legend persists that Boston's original street layout developed from the paths made by wandering cattle.

Currently, as we see from the midstreet signs in front of us, the junction of the two converging streets has officially resumed its ancient name. The brick traffic island in the center of this renamed extension, from here toward old Hanover Street, is roughly where the wedge of Scollay Buildings was located. When we visit Boston's North End we will be walking along what remains of Hanover Street, so proudly named in colonial times for King George III's royal house of Hanover. The now missing portion of Hanover Street that once ran into Scollay Square directly crossed present Government Center. It ran through the trees and the sunken plaza in a line pretty much parallel to and about fifty yards from the south side of the Kennedy Building.

Once the Scollay Buildings were demolished Scollay Square was formed and was for generations a crossroads of the city, thronged and often plagued by traffic and tie-ups. Gradually through the nineteenth century as the seaport flourished, this square became known in every port on earth for its roaring nightlife as its bordering buildings were converted to shooting galleries, tattoo parlors, pawnshops, saloons, low-priced hotels, and all-night theaters.

Old Scollay Square, though strikingly transformed, has long been enjoyably recalled by Bostonians. Nostalgia reigned in 1987 as Mayor Raymond Flynn, responding to popular demand, revived the old name with a band playing, two aged burlesque queens frolicking, and a big throng cheering.

Crowds drawn to the square made it a political stumping ground for many decades prior to its transformation into a plaza area rivaling Europe's best. Charismatic James Michael Curley, whose oratorical talents fascinated even his political enemies, often stumped crowds in the square on foot, from the back of an open automobile, or in a storefront that was just to our left under the arcade. His Honor called that his "bull pen." Curley's energy was so inexhaustible, even after night-before campaigning into the wee hours, that he would be up and talking to a crowd in his bull pen before it was time for his listeners to start the day's work.

No less a national figure than former House Speaker Thomas P. "Tip" O'Neill, Jr., standing upstairs at an open window in the prow of the Sears block, could be seen during a campaign addressing throngs in the square below. O'Neill, a crowd-charmer, too, came to represent this former Curley district in Congress. O'Neill enjoys great appeal, for long before going to the national scene, he was the first Democrat ever to be chosen Speaker on Beacon Hill.

Notice an old landmark: the 227-gallon steaming kettle on the Sears block over the Starbucks coffee shop at the head of Court Street. The kettle was made in 1873 by a coppersmith as a trademark for what was then Boston's largest tea shop, the Oriental Tea Company, long a Scollay Square fixture a few doors from the kettle's present site. Steam is provided by a pipe to the nose of the kettle. The precise contents, as certified by 13,000 contestants who gathered here in 1875 to watch the measuring, is 2 quarts, 1 pint, and 3 gills beyond the 227 gallons.

Because the Scollay Square traffic island on which we started will be the starting point for our walks to Boston's downtown, waterfront, North End, and West End—all of them short walks—it may be well to present a few more insights on Boston's best-remembered square.

William Scollay, for whom the place was named, was an intimate friend and business associate of architect Charles Bulfinch. Their homes for years were close to either end of the square. Scollay's was on Tremont Street, on the left, about halfway to King's Chapel Burying Ground. Scollay's father was a Boston selectman during the Revolution.

Scollay ran an apothecary on Washington Street near the Old State House and was deeply interested in Boston's culture and development. It was in the Scollay Buildings that the Boston Athenaeum began. Scollay was a partner with Bulfinch in the pioneer but bankrupted building venture called the Tontine Crescent. Still, their benevolence provided early quarters in that crescent, on nearby Franklin Street, for another great Boston institution, the Massachusetts Historical Society.

The curve of the Sears Crescent, fortunately preserved, was one side of a street put through in 1817 by the spectacular developer Uriah Cotting. At first it was called Market Street, as a new way from Scollay Square to Faneuil Hall and the old town marketplace. At the far end of the Sears Crescent building, we can see a passageway to Court Street.

If we could have been looking up this alley at nightfall on December 16, 1773, we would have seen men, some with their faces charcoaled, some disguised as Indians, leaving the dwelling of newspaper publisher Benjamin Edes and heading to the harbor to the Boston Tea Party. The Edes punchbowl, from which they refreshed themselves in Edes's parlor, is now in the collection of the Massachusetts Historical Society.

The name of Market Street was later changed to Cornhill, and for many years after 1825 its distinctive attraction was provided by Boston booksellers with sidewalk book bins outside their shops in the crescent. Future President Franklin D. Roosevelt, like many another student, was a regular customer and often came to browse and read here while he was going to Harvard College.

Between Faneuil Hall off in the marketplace and the redbrick covered subway kiosk near the prow of the Sears block, there is an interesting relation. The man who designed the original Faneuil Hall (built 1740–1743), some years before its size was more than doubled by Charles Bulfinch, had his dwelling on the kiosk site, a dwelling with sufficient land for a barn in back for his horses and chaise. This was John Smibert, America's first professional portraitist. Smibert acted as architect for the wealthy merchant Peter Faneuil, who lived, as we shall see, a short distance away on Tremont Street. Smibert's portrait of Faneuil is the best we have of that philanthropic gentleman. Originally Faneuil intended to give Boston only a one-story market building, but he generously had Smibert add a second floor so that Faneuil Hall could also become, as it did, Boston's town hall.

Smibert's studio here had other well-known occupants. When John Trumbull, after a sensitive dispute over rank, temporarily left the Revolutionary army in 1777, he resumed his study of painting in this studio. Trumbull is best known today for his huge historical paintings—among them *The Battle of Bunker Hill*—in the rotunda of the Capitol in Washington, D.C. Young Trumbull regarded Smibert as "the patriarch of painting in America" and was delighted that the studio still had several copies Smibert had made of paintings by European artists. But Copley was gone from Boston and Trumbull felt he should follow him abroad. Before going, in early 1779, he helped set up a club of young men fresh from college, among them future Bay State governors Christopher Gore and William Eustis. Trumbull recalled: "The club generally met in my room, regaled themselves with a cup of tea instead of wine, and discussed subjects of literature, politics and war." Still another visitor was John Hancock, also a future governor.

Old Scollay Square has links to two of the world's greatest inventions in communication, the electric telegraph and the telephone. The inventor of the electric telegraph, Samuel F. B. Morse, son of a Charlestown clergyman, was drawn to Scollay Square as a young Yale student while he was planning a career in art. He came as a pupil of Washington Allston, when Allston, in 1809–1811, took over the former Smibert studio. As for the telephone, Scollay Square was—as we shall presently see—right by the telephone's birthplace.

Quite a few of the nation's revolutionary beginnings were in present Government Center. On the north side of Smibert's lot (roughly along the north side of the kiosk) was a narrow lane that, when widened by using some of Smibert's land, became Brattle Street. It led down past the south (right) side of the new City Hall into Dock Square. At the site of the new City Hall's southwest corner once stood the Brattle Street Church, in Brattle Square, the church of the Hancocks, Bowdoins, Harrison Gray Otis, Daniel Webster, and the patriot Dr. Joseph Warren, who was killed at Bunker Hill.

Troubles that led to the outbreak of war brought the commander of all British forces in North America, General Thomas Gage, to Brattle Square in the late 1760s. He lived in a house opposite the church. He quartered some of his redcoats in the church and in a nearby sugar warehouse. The square was like a British camp, and here occurred some of the rioting and clashes with townsmen that ended in the Boston Massacre.

John Adams made his home with Abigail and the children in a Brattle Square dwelling, prophetically called "the White House," after Samuel Adams persuaded John to leave Braintree. Dedication to impartial justice impelled John Adams, at the risk of his life, to join the legal defense of British Captain Thomas Preston and the eight other redcoats involved in the March 5, 1770, Boston Massacre.

Old Brattle Square had many great occasions. George Washington attended Sunday service in the old church, sitting in the Bowdoin pew, on his last visit to Boston.

On the short passage between the church and Dock Square was the residence of the doctor who fearlessly began smallpox inoculation in America, Dr. Zabdiel Boylston. Though it would help eliminate the scourge all over the earth, it was a technology new to his fellow citizens, and the doctor's life was endangered by mobs acting from fear and ignorance. A bomb was even tossed into the study of his most ardent supporter, the Reverend Cotton Mather. The obvious successof his experimenting finally brought triumph. The house of the pastor of the Brattle Street Church faced on the doctor's yard, and the pastor told of watching the recuperation of the doctor's patients. Dr. Boylston first inoculated his six-year-old son, his black servant, and the servant's young son. When the catastrophic epidemic of that 1721–1722 winter was over, one out of every six or seven Bostonians was dead, while of the 286 persons Dr. Boylston treated only six died. He sent a report of his success to England, and when he visited there in 1726 was honored with a fellowship in the Royal Society.

The modern design of the new City Hall was the result of a 1962 competition won by three architects teaching at Columbia University, Gerard Kallmann, Noel McKinnell, and Edward Knowles. It is truly impressive in its ten-acre setting, though a conservative architect remarked, "It looks like the box Faneuil Hall came in." Views from the offices on the top (ninth) floor facing seaward are quite rewarding. The lobby is most unusual and adapts to a variety of community events. The inverted pyramid building was designed so that the services most used by the public are most handy on the lower levels.

As mentioned, Hanover Street once continued directly across Government Center to Scollay Square. Beyond where this street ran is now the John Fitzgerald Kennedy Federal Building, with office space about evenly divided between the twin, rectangular, twenty-six-story towers and the four-story office portion. In all, the Kennedy Building, designed by Walter Gropius and Associates, has three times the space of the new City Hall and serves the entire New England region. The employees call the connecting rampway "the crossover."

In front of this crossover, between the plaza trees on the right and the sunken patio on the left, patriot orders were issued as midnight approached on the eve of April 19, 1775. Here on old Hanover Street was the dwelling of Dr. Joseph Warren. When Warren learned two days earlier, on April 16, that boats had been put over the side and nested behind the British men-of-war in Boston Harbor, he sent Paul Revere to warn Samuel Adams and John Hancock, who were attending the Provincial Congress in Concord and organizing an army. General Gage was preparing for action. He had picked his best troops, big grenadiers and fast light infantry, to go "with the utmost expedition and secrecy" to Lexington and Concord. The Sons of Liberty were watching. Warren, head of the Committee of Safety, was the top patriot still in Boston. When he was certain that the redcoats were actually embarking at the foot of the Common, he sent for two neighbors, first William Dawes to go by land and Paul Revere to go the shorter route by boat to Charlestown to spread the alarm. Revere has told of how he got a friend to raise signal lanterns in case he was captured, and then took off. Less than two months later Warren laid down his life on the battlefield.

Two sites are memorable at the head of Hanover Street, where it used to enter Scollay Square. On the southern corner was a popular gathering place of the Sons of Liberty, the Concert Hall. The Masons, so active in the Revolution, held festivities there for years. Just about all the patriots, including George Washington, enjoyed this hall. Governor Hancock sponsored a grand ball there for Admiral d'Estaing's fleet, the same comrades-in-arms for whom Madame Hancock sent servants to milk the cows on the Common.

On old Court Street, between Hanover and Sudbury at Number 109, stood a high building in which Dr. Alexander Graham Bell, then a professor at Boston University, worked to perfect his telephone. A pulpitlike stone memorial with bronze marker, near the Kennedy Building's main entrance, is on the site of Bell's 109 Court Street building, marking the birthplace of the telephone. He had a laboratory in the fifth-floor garret. For the first time ever a human voice, Bell's, traveled via wire. This was June 3, 1875.

It was not until the following March that Bell hit upon a way of sending not only sound but intelligible words. This happened in rooms Bell had rented a half-mile south of here, as we shall presently see.

During the boisterous era of Scollay Square, the square itself was often referred to as the location of the Old Howard. As the saying went, there was "always something doing from 9:00 A.M. to 11:00 P.M." at the Old Howard. Its beginnings were most sedate, the gathering place for Millerites who had calculated the date the world would end. They built their tabernacle in 1843–1844 a short way down Howard Street, which ran from opposite Hanover Street, roughly from One Center Plaza's main entrance, back to Somerset Street. The Millerites disbanded when their predetermined day passed uneventfully. The building then became a theater with the very proper Bostonian name of the Howard Athenaeum. Great plays and actors appeared. Italian opera (*Ernani*) had its first Boston performance here. By 1870 vaudeville took over and then burlesque. In its final decades there were slapstick, barroom comedy, bump and grind, and striptease. Cries of "take it off" could be heard in Howard Street by customers lined up to buy tickets—now gone, like the Millerites.

If we walk up the stone steps in the big entry of One Center Plaza, we will find a round bronze plaque atop the seat of a stone bench on the right-hand side of the little park at the top. It marks the Old Howard stage, domain of entertainment queens like glittering Ann Corio. The view from the park across Somerset Street is characteristic of Boston: The urban vista consisting of the hillside plaza between the McCormack and Saltonstall state buildings, with the medieval-style church tower of St. John the Evangelist in the background, throws into stark relief the contrast between the strident facades of the ever-changing modern boston and the abiding architectural stalwarts of old Boston.

BOSTON'S MOST HISTORIC BLOCK

Court Street

George Washington wrote in his diary that his lodgings when he came to Boston in October 1789 were at the "widow Ingersoll's . . . a very decent and good house." Ingersoll's was a four-story brick building at the corner of Court and Tremont Streets—across the street from where we first entered old Scollay Square. Here was enacted, on Washington's arrival, a political drama of far-reaching consequence. Governor John Hancock, staunch believer in state sovereignty, felt that Washington should make the first formal call. Washington, ever concerned about the precedents that he was setting, believed that the dignity of the presidency gave the federal office priority.

Hancock's attitude caused him to avoid Washington's arrival. There was delay at the approach to town, and Washington even considered not entering Boston. Town fathers urged him to enter. By the time Washington got to Ingersoll's the prepared meal was cold, like the weather that day, and only swiftly fried fish came to the rescue, with Vice President John Adams sharing the meal. Hancock soon realized that he had made a blunder. Samuel Adams, his lieutenant governor, came that Saturday night with some councillors to explain for Hancock that the governor was painfully ill with gout. The upshot of the threatened impasse came the next day when Hancock, swathed in

BOSTON'S MOST HISTORIC BLOCK

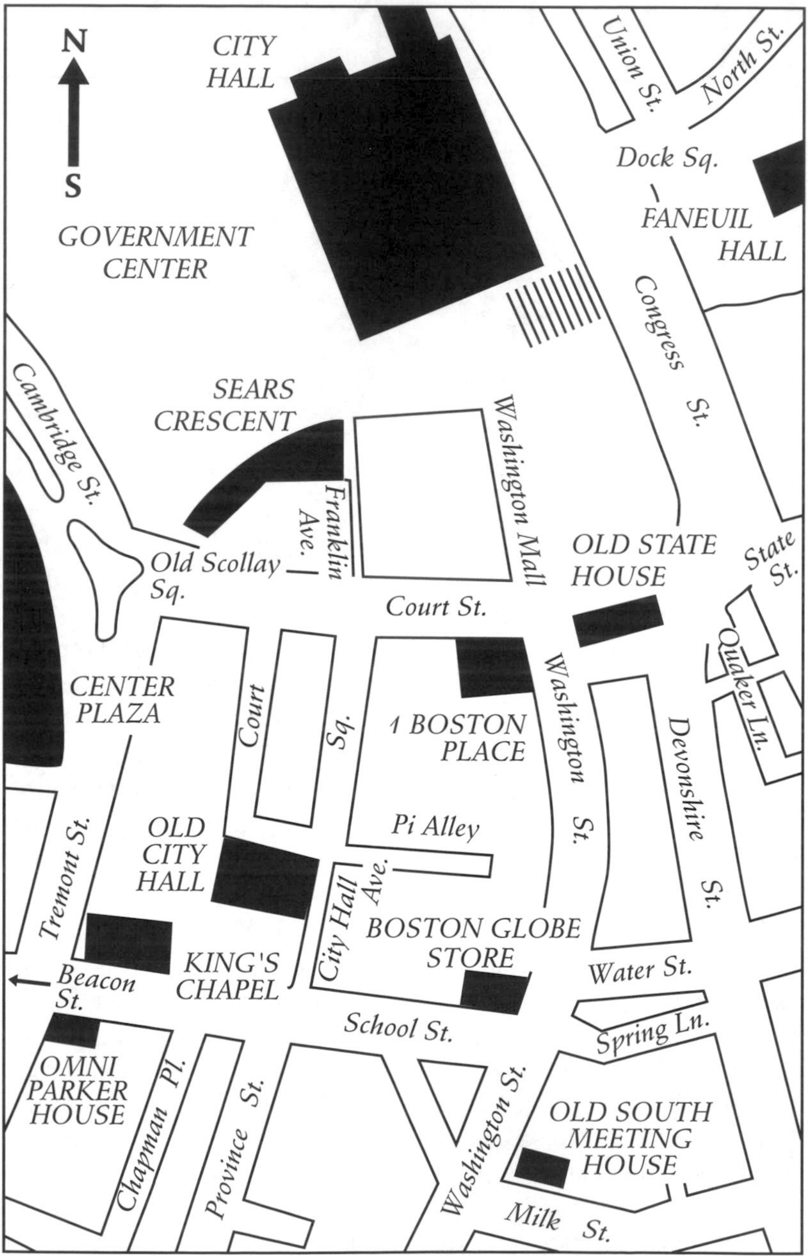

flannels and carried by servants, arrived at Washington's lodgings. Mrs. Hancock said that tears came to Washington's eyes when he saw Hancock's condition. Others argued later that Hancock's illness was merely diplomatic. Anyway Washington was gracious and, accepting Hancock's invitation, went Monday evening and "drank tea" at Hancock's mansion.

Court Street, now before us, is the north side of Boston's most historic block. Until the close of the Revolutionary War this short roadway was loyally called Queen Street, as a complement to King Street, the current State Street. Court Street was earlier called Prison Lane for the grim jailhouse where the notorious pirate Captain Kidd was held before being shipped to London, where he was hanged in 1701. That jail once stood midway down the street on the right, and the site, as we shall see, has far greater claims to fame.

It was especially interesting that Washington picked this street for his lodgings on his last visit to Boston. Back in 1776, after he had forced the redcoats out of Boston, Washington's visit had also been to this street, before setting out for Providence and New York to carry on the war. Martha and the ladies had gone ahead from Cambridge by way of Hartford. It was a little after 2:00 P.M. when Washington and his suite of three or four gentlemen stopped at the Queen Street dwelling of Colonel Henry Bromfield, Boston merchant, "to eat a snack" and then set out.

On his final visit in 1789 Washington dwelt here nearly six days, during which the town did everything it could to show admiration for "our beloved president," as the newspapers said. The place was brilliantly illuminated, bells rang, drums beat; there were artillery fire, fireworks, parades, and a brilliant assembly at Concert Hall. He went to Trinity Church as well as Brattle Street Church. He banqueted at Bowdoin's and at richly bedecked Faneuil Hall. His time was so occupied he could not sit for his portrait for Faneuil Hall until he reached Portsmouth.

This corner of Court and Tremont is fascinating for another role in the town's history. As lawyers currently flock to the buildings on streets near the courthouse in Pemberton Square, they once crowded Court Street to be near the courthouse that succeeded Captain Kidd's old prison. A luminary of the bar, Harrison Gray Otis, had his office on the widow Ingersoll's corner after he first hung up his shingle in the old Scollay Building. David Sears, Jr., one of Boston's wealthiest youths, and many others studied law with Otis. To get still nearer the courthouse Otis later moved to Court Square, right at the courthouse, and when he went as U.S. senator to Washington he gave his office to his lawyer son.

Daniel Webster had an office, too, at 46 Court Street, the old Ingersoll corner, from 1839 to 1852, when he moved from senator to secretary of state and made many runs as the Whig candidate for president. Earlier during his congressional career, from 1815 to 1827, his law office was in old Court Street opposite the head of Hanover Street. In midcareer during his first two Senate terms, 1827 to 1838, his office was at 33 Court near the west corner of Franklin Avenue. Webster always had aspiring law trainees in his offices just as he, when twenty-two, got his start up the legal ladder by training in the influential law office of future Bay State governor, aristocratic Christopher Gore.

State Street, farther downhill, was also an attraction to prominent lawyers. Old Judge John Lowell, who gave Harrison Gray Otis legal training, and John Adams both started in State Street but later moved to Court Street. Lowell, who became one of the "midnight judges" John Adams appointed in his final hours as President, wanted his office cozily "next the door to the Probate Office" on the ground floor of the courthouse. John Adams, on his return to Boston after he and patriot Josiah Quincy, Jr., courageously defended the redcoats involved in the Boston Massacre, moved into a house with a first-floor office on Court Street smartly opposite the courthouse—and Abigail came to join him with their three young sons.

Just below the Ingersoll corner at 42 Court Street, later the office of lawyer-author Richard Henry Dana, once stood a noted Boston dwelling that became the parsonage of the Brattle Street Church. This was a gift from John Hancock's Aunt Lydia, a mansion in which her father, noted Boston bookseller Colonel Daniel Henchman, raised his family. Two other noted authors studied law in Court Street but, unlike Dana, decided it was not for them: James Russell Lowell and William H. Prescott.

At 26 Court Street we come to a freestanding structure with fluted Corinthian columns from the third to the eighth floors and Corinthian pilasters, a building surrounded on three sides by Court Square. This classical edifice, currently headquarters of the Boston School Committee, was built in 1912 and served, until a few years ago, as the annex to Boston's old City Hall on School Street. It displaced the courthouse of 1833–1836.

Accounts that have come down from Judge Samuel Sewall, who knew personally some of Boston's first settlers, indicate that the courthouse and, earlier, Captain Kidd's jail were near the site of the dwelling started by the richest and foremost social figure in John Winthrop's band of Puritans, Isaac Johnson. Johnson had married Lady Arbella, daughter of the Earl of Lincoln. The only earlier builder in Boston was the hermit Reverend William Blackstone on Beacon Hill's west slope. Johnson and Blackstone were college acquaintances back in England's Emmanuel College, hotbed of Puritanism. Judge Sewall said that it was Johnson who got the word from Blackstone that there was plenty of good springwater on Beacon Hill that could help the newcomers suffering illness in Charlestown from lack of drinking water. Johnson had hardly started building here when Lady Arbella died in Salem, and a month later Johnson, only twenty-nine years of age, died, too. On his deathbed he asked to be buried at the back of his lot.

About Captain Kidd there will always be some mystery. No question, his crew engaged in piracy. But did he? Kidd, son of a Scottish clergyman, was captain of a merchant ship trading in London. He claimed that he made a deal with the Earl of Bellomont to act as privateer against pirates and that it was his crew, not he, who hoisted the black flag. The Earl came to Boston in 1698 as Bay governor and, as Kidd insisted, deceived him over the split in the loot, had him clapped in jail and shipped back for execution.

After a succession of jails and a brick courthouse, a massive granite courthouse with portico and four huge fluted columns designed by Solomon Willard was erected 1833–1836. Within its walls was held Dr. Webster's sensational trial for the Parkman murder. But far more sensational were the scenes five years later in 1854, both inside and outside the courthouse, during the trial of twenty-four-year-old Virginian Anthony Burns as a fugitive slave, the last ever to face this charge in Massachusetts.

Author Richard Henry Dana's office, at this time, was just a few steps up Court Street at then Number 32. Hearing of Burns's arrest, Dana offered to act as counsel. Boston, birthplace of the abolitionist movement, seethed with excitement during the nine days of proceedings under, as Dana said, "a tyrannical statute and a weak judge." An armed guard recruited by the U.S. marshal tensely watched the crowded courtroom.

Unitarian clergyman Theodore Parker and abolitionist orator Wendell Phillips, with others, were arrested during a Court Street riot when they attempted to smash the courthouse doors and rescue Burns. Military, militia, and police, all conspicuously armed, lined Court and State Streets to get Burns to the revenue cutter taking him back to Virginia. Crowds hissed and yelled, "Shame! Shame!" Almost all the shops along the way were closed and buildings were hung in black. It was while he was on his way home that night, just beyond old Scollay Square, that Dana was brutally attacked and stunned from behind. A bully, one of the marshal's courtroom guards, was later charged with the assault. Northern sympathizers later purchased Burns's freedom; he came to Boston to thank Dana and became a Baptist minister.

The northeast corner of Court Square, where once stood a popular Boston hostelry, Young's Hotel, is also noted as the spot where still another hotelman, Harvey D. Parker, got his start in a downstairs cafe at 4 Court Square. Dana had had his tea here before leaving for home the night he was assaulted. Parker, a man from Maine, had less than $1.00 when he arrived in Boston by packet. By the time he was twenty-seven he had saved, from his earnings as a coachman, almost $500, which he invested in his cellar cafe in 1832. He built a reputation as serving the best of food and attracted such a clientele of lawyers, newsmen, and businessmen that by the early 1850s he was ready to put some of his ideas into effect in a new hotel that he proceeded to build in School Street in 1854, the Parker House.

Farther up Court Square on the southwest corner of Pi Alley, on our left, is the Boston Public Library's interesting Kirstein Business Branch, built 1929–1930. Louis E. Kirstein, then general manager of Filene's, gave it to the city in memory of his father, Edward L. The facade reproduces the central portion of Charles Bulfinch's Tontine Crescent, Boston's first block of houses, which the architect built in 1793 on Franklin Street. This central portion was over an archway and was occupied by the private Boston Library when incorporated in 1794. A visit to the Kirstein Library, on the second floor, offers two views of the famous Tontine Crescent.

On the north side of Court Street, opposite Court Square, is a narrow passageway called Franklin Avenue. The east corner, where the New England Shelter for Homeless Veterans currently occupies a 1908 bank building in the Renaissance revival style, has many associations with pioneer newspaper publishing, the Franklins, the Boston Tea Party, and the Revolution.

Court Street and the nearby State and Washington Streets are the cradle of American journalism, understandably close to the center of authority and news, the Old State House. Failure to get State House approval brought a clamp-down on a precursor newspaper, *Publick Occurrences,* put together by Benjamin Harris, proprietor-publisher of the London Coffee House in present State Street, in 1690. The intended newspaper lasted just one spicy issue.

Boston by that time had some 7,000 residents and was the largest community in the British colonies. American printing had started on a press at Harvard College in 1638, but London newspapers seemed to supply all needs until 1704 when Boston's new postmaster, John Campbell, weary of writing news tidbits in letter form, found a Washington Street printer to publish his *News-Letter,* America's first regular newspaper, April 24, 1704. Campbell's paper did have official approval, carried official public notices, but was quite dull. He sold copies, as we shall see, around the corner in Washington Street.

Fifteen years later, in 1719, Campbell's successor as postmaster published a rival paper, the *Boston Gazette,* also dull but destined to be famous. Its printer here on the east corner was James Franklin, elder brother of Benjamin Franklin. Two years later James Franklin on this same site published his own newspaper, the lively, entertaining, crusading *New England Gazette,* with fifteen-year-old brother Benjamin as an apprentice. The story of what happened next is a New England classic—young Benjamin secretly writing for the paper, his restiveness under his older brother, his acting as publisher when independence of thought got James jailed, and finally his taking off for Philadelphia.

In pre-Revolutionary years the *Boston Gazette,* which had come under joint ownership of the patriot publishers Edes and Gill, moved to the east corner in 1768 from prior quarters, as quaintly described in days before Boston numbered street buildings, "the second house west of the Court House on Queen Street." The *Boston Gazette,* in the hectic period of rising opposition to taxes voted 3,000 miles away, became the mouthpiece of the patriot cause. Benjamin Edes was extensively active with the Sons of Liberty, consulted with them, and carried Tory-baiting articles written by Samuel Adams and others under numerous pen names. Hancock, Otis, Josiah Quincy, Jr., Joseph Warren, and the cousins Samuel and John Adams often met in the long room over the Edes and Gill shop to debate and formulate plans. As war was about to erupt, Edes smuggled his press and type by boat up the Charles River to Watertown and published for the Provincial Congress.

There are reminders of the legalistic and journalistic character of Court Street as we come to its east end. The skyscraper tower on the south corner had among its predecessors a pre–Civil War granite building with many lawyer tenants. Distinguished among them was one of the Bay State's greatest, Rufus Choate, who held many public offices and succeeded to Webster's preeminence before the bar and to Webster's senate seat in 1841.

At the north corner, 1 Court Street, the ornate, Romanesque, sixteen-floor Ames Building, 1887–1889, was built in the style of Henry H. Richardson. It was completed by his firm after his death and was Boston's first skyscraper, supported not by steel but by granite.

On its Washington Mall side, in the middle of the street, a bit north from Court Street, was in Boston's earliest years the town pump, handy to the marketplace. Notes, messages, and proclamations attached to the pump in effect fulfilled for Boston its first newspaper functions.

Old Newspaper Row

The intersection of Washington and State Streets at the west end of the Old State House, which was erected just after the devastating fire of 1711 burned the first Town House, was for generations the most important crossroads in Boston. One short road, King (present State) Street, led to Long Wharf, the town's main access to the sea, and the other, presently Washington Street but then called "the High," led to the thin isthmus that was Boston's only connection with the mainland.

That 1711 fire destroyed not only the wooden Town House but close to one hundred other buildings in the area, all those in upper State Street, all from here north to old Dock Square and just ahead of us to School Street, the route we are about to take.

So important an intersection as Washington and State has many memorable associations. Each one of the corners has its first.

Governor Winthrop tells how the northeast corner saw the establishment of Boston's mercantile life. In March 1634 John Coggan, member of a wealthy merchant family that arrived in America the previous year, set up Boston's first shop here facing the newly established marketplace. Coggan sold retail and also wholesale to shopkeepers who copied him in neighboring towns. He later became a selectman and married Governor Winthrop's widow.

On the Ames Building site, on the northwest corner, were the dwelling and garden of Harvard University's first president, Henry Dunster. He came pretty much into control of America's early printing through his college role and marriage in 1641 to the widow of the owner of the nation's first press, the so-called Day Press in Cambridge.

One of the Bay Colony's great early governors, John Leverett, had his house and garden on the southwest corner. This sturdy Puritan went back to England to fight for Cromwell and was a commander of the Ancients' Artillery. All this came in handy when a messenger from Plymouth colony, his horse white with foam, dashed to Leverett's house with word that the Indian King Philip had begun his war against the colonists. Governor Leverett held many a troubled powwow in the old Town House before Philip was defeated. King Charles II, in tribute to Leverett for his handling of King Philip's War, made him a knight, but the governor never used the title.

The southeast corner has several distinctions. Captain Robert Keayne, who founded the Ancient and Honorable Artillery and was its first commander, had his dwelling and shop here. Much has been made about the strict Puritans' admonishing and fining him one time for profiteering. Few, though, can dispute Keayne's overall magnanimity to his fellow citizens. Keayne's will left considerable funds not only for building the first Town House but for a room in it for Boston's first public library and still other bequests that led to the construction of the almshouse and granary built on Beacon Hill.

Besides Keayne's own library, which went to help form the public library, books have been heavily associated with this corner. Daniel Henchman, described by the patriot printer Isaiah Thomas as Boston's "most eminent and enterprising bookseller . . . in all British America before the year 1775," had his shop here. The first printing of the Bible in America was by Henchman. Thomas, then an apprentice in Boston, tells how Henchman privately organized its printing in the former Franklin pressroom in Court Street. A London imprint was used on the seven to eight hundred copies to disguise its source and forestall prosecution. John Hancock, a relative of Henchman, knew all about it. Hancock's uncle, from whom John inherited his great wealth, started as an apprentice in Henchman's shop.

The best-remembered and most famous apprentice here, under Henchman's successors, was future General Henry Knox, who fetched the cannon from Fort Ticonderoga to oust the redcoats and commanded George Washington's artillery. Knox was twelve years old when apprenticed. He became deeply interested in artillery from reading books ordered by British officers from London. In 1771 he opened his own shop farther down Washington Street. He married a patron of his shop, the daughter of the colony's wealthy Tory secretary, Flucker, but she, like Knox, ardently espoused the patriot cause.

Edgar Allan Poe's first book of poems, *Tamerlane and Other Poems,* currently one of America's most costly and treasured volumes, was published in the building at this corner in May 1827. The circumstances were both pathetic and prophetic of the endless disappointments ahead in his all too short life. To escape arrest for debts and a quarrel with his foster father, Poe, then eighteen years of age, took off from Richmond on a coastwise vessel. En route he met a nineteen-year-old printer who had just set himself up in business upstairs at this corner. The near penniless poetic genius gave over his poems. They were printed, to conceal their identity, as merely "By a Bostonian." None sold. Destitute, Poe enlisted in the army and was assigned down Boston Harbor at Fort Independence. Five months later Poe's outfit was shipped south from where he had fled.

The current character of this area, may be gathered by a visit to 1 Boston Place, the forty-one-story office tower facing down State Street. The tower floors of the skyscraper, built 1967–1970, were until recently the home of the busy Boston Stock Exchange, which boasted a breathtaking thirty-eighth floor overview of Boston's financial district, ever expanding with bank, mutual, savings and loan, and insurance company funds. Trading volume on the BSE grew sevenfold between 1988 and 1998, necessitating a move to roomier quarters. The fastest growing Stock Exchange in the United States now resides in the nine-story 1908 building at 100 Franklin Street.

The 1 Boston Place site embraces some highly interesting history. To the left and just off the lobby, as we enter 1 Boston Place, there is a passage to nearby Pi Alley. America's first public school, the Boston Public Latin School, was located midway down that passage when the first class assembled in the home of teacher Philemon Pormont and his wife, Susann. Future governor Leverett's father, elder of the first Meeting House, then around the corner in present State Street, wrote in the town records (handwriting still to be seen) how the parishioners agreed that Pormont, a fairly new member of the church, "shall be intreated to become schoolemaster for the teaching and nourtering of children with us." The momentous date was April 13, 1635.

By 1640 a larger Meeting House, a wooden one to replace the smaller 1632 mud-wall Meeting House, was built in front of Pormont's former dwelling and shop. After this was consumed by the 1711 fire, a three-story brick Meeting House, with bell tower and the town's first public clock, was erected here in Church Square, a site now largely covered by the 1 Boston Place skyscraper. The new Meeting House became known as Old Brick. Its bell rang alarm at the time of the Boston Massacre. When George Washington came to Boston in 1776, after ridding it of the redcoats, he and his general officers marched from the Old State House to a thanksgiving service in Old Brick.

The forty-two-story Devonshire building, on our left across Washington Street, started in 1980 and completed late in 1982 with stores, office space, apartments, and underground garage, is on the site occupied for almost a century, 1872 to 1958, by *The Boston Globe,* New England's largest daily and Sunday newspaper. Back in 1872 the heart of Boston's commercial activities was wiped out by one of the nation's worst conflagrations. A twenty-seven-year-old wounded Civil War veteran, Charles H. Taylor, suffered the loss of the 10¢ magazine enterprise he had just got going successfully and thus became available as editor—and soon publisher—of the newly founded *Boston Globe.*

IF YOU HEAR AN OWL HOOT, "TO WHOM," INSTEAD OF "TO WHO," YOU CAN MAKE UP YOUR MIND HE WAS BORN AND EDUCATED IN BOSTON.

—ANONYMOUS

The end of an era, which began with the nation's first newspapers, came when the *Globe* moved in 1958 from what was known throughout the 1800s and most of the 1900s as Newspaper Row. But by the 1950s Boston's narrow, crooked, London-style streets, plus traffic jams, had made rapid delivery of newspapers on a large scale from Newspaper Row just about impossible.

Buildings of other newspapers once part of Newspaper Row are still to be seen. Across from the *Globe* site, on the south corner of Pi Alley at 241 Washington Street, was the *Boston Post,* earlier a *Boston Herald* site. On the north corner of Water Street, at Number 262 was the Journal. The *Traveller* was on the Row opposite the Old South Meeting House. And on the south corner of Milk Street, at Number 322–328, in a building recently rehabilitated, was once Boston's high-society newspaper, *The Transcript.*

Pi Alley, directly opposite Two Devonshire Place (site for decades of *The Boston Globe*'s main entrance), goes naturally with Newspaper Row, for "pi" is a printer's term for a jumble of type. Pi Alley is still another nickname for the alley's earlier formal name, Williams Court.

The former *Globe* site has had a historic part other than in newspapering. America's first post office was located in midblock and beside it, on the *Globe* site, was the London Book Store that Henry Knox ran 1771–1775. Vandalizing of young Knox's shop during the 1775–1776 siege left Knox and his wife heavily in debt for years.

The first postmaster was the popular innkeeper Richard Fairbanks, who arrived in Boston in 1633. By permission given by the town fathers in 1638, his became the only early Boston tavern allowed to sell "wine and strong water." He sold the shop in 1652, but throughout the later 1600s a tavern, the Anchor or Blue Anchor, carried on, a jolly oasis for magistrates and members of the General Court. "The deputies treated and I treated," as Judge Sewall put it in his diary.

Just south of the tavern site, roughly at what is now the north corner of Water Street, Boston postmaster John Campbell owned the land, which he purchased in 1688–1689, presumably back to Pudding Lane (Devonshire Street) in the rear. His home and place of business were here where he sold America's first regular newspaper, *The Boston News-Letter.*

Boston's first inn, set up in 1634, was across the street on the north corner of present Pi Alley and had as host a man who came to America with Governor Winthrop, Samuel Cole. Pi Alley was then a courtyard to Cole's Ship Inn and a way to his brewhouse in back. Cole was authorized to sell just beer with his food, was fined several times for selling wine, and sold out in 1638.

The names of streets just ahead are telltale of their beginnings. Water Street originally stopped a couple of blocks down at a creek off Town Cove. Spring Lane once had a spring a few paces downhill. School Street is part of our nation's history, for it memorializes the first building specifically built for a schoolhouse.

Spring Lane was the site of the Great Spring that for more than two centuries supplied water to residents of Boston. About midway down the lane on the left is a bronze plaque marking the spot. A few steps farther down, on our right, another bronze plaque tells of Mary Chilton, who came on the *Mayflower* to New England in 1620. Then a young teenager, Mary, according to her family tradition, blithely leapt ashore from the Pilgrim longboat and was the first woman Pilgrim to land in Plymouth. She married John Winslow, brother of Gov. Edward Winslow, and they and their many children came to dwell here, where Winslow became one of Boston's thriving merchants. A daughter married Myles Standish, Jr.

Governor Winthrop's dwelling from 1643 to his death six years later was at the south corner of Spring Lane, at 294 Washington Street. He moved from his 1630 mansion on present State Street to the much smaller house he built here after his estate was robbed by a dishonest steward. British soldiers, to keep warm during the siege, used Winthrop's house for fuel. The Old South Meeting House, like the Old State House we will shortly visit, stands on what Winthrop called his "Green."

On the right as we come to School Street are some of the handful of existing early eighteenth-century brick buildings in Boston. The one at Number 277 was built as a family dwelling (1722–1728). It began its commercial life in 1795 when bookseller John West prepared one of Boston's earliest (now strikingly tiny) street directories. The shop on the corner next to it, Number 285, is among Boston's most renowned buildings, the Old Corner Bookstore, built right after the fire of 1711 and now, as we noted earlier, called The Boston Globe Store.

Old Corner Bookstore and School Street

Two names are most prominently associated with the Old Corner Bookstore and the lot on which it stands: Anne Hutchinson, a seventeenth-century martyr for religious freedom, and James T. Fields, or "Jamie," a man outstanding in the annals of nineteenth-century American book and magazine publishing. Fields's name is intimately and companionably linked with the writers of our Golden Age of Literature: Emerson, Holmes, Hawthorne, Lowell, Longfellow, and Thoreau, as well as England's Dickens and Thackeray and many others.

Anne Hutchinson, the warmhearted, public-spirited daughter of a clergyman, mother of fourteen children, in her years in Boston, 1634–1638, had many followers. Anne believed that having faith was sufficient for salvation rather than doing precisely what the orthodox Puritan clergy ordained. Her household discussions of current sermons drew many women and men, too, to the large comfortable Hutchinson dwelling. Among them were early leaders in the young colony, including the Reverend John Cotton, her pastor in England, whom she and her family followed to Boston, and the Bay Colony's twenty-four-year-old Governor Harry Vane, who eventually went back to become a top leader during Cromwell's ascendancy and later was both knighted and beheaded. Then all her neighbors, whose dwelling sites we have just passed, were attracted by her ideas: Philemon Pormont, the teacher; Samuel Cole, the innkeeper; Richard Fairbanks, the postmaster; even the devout man living across the street on the south corner of Water Street, Thomas Oliver, physician and elder of the mud-walled church on King (State) Street.

Governor Winthrop conceded that almost everyone in Boston was on her side except he and his neighbor, the Reverend John Wilson, pastor of Boston's first mud-wall Meeting House. But outside Boston Anne's thinking was pretty much held to be heretical and antinomian (against authority). Governor Winthrop feared that the Bay church was "neere to dissolution." He called her an "American Jezebel," and

Old Corner Bookstore at the foot of School Street

she was charged with "traducing the ministers."

Anne's struggle and fate are one of the most painful episodes in Boston's history. Anne, tried in Cambridge late in 1637, was ordered banished from the colony and was excommunicated by the Reverend Mr. Wilson with these dire phrases, "I cast you out. . . . I deliver you up to Satan!" In effect the banishment was a death sentence for Anne and all her children, save one. Her neighbors, and several dozen others, were required to turn in their firearms to Captain Keayne, quite a penalty for a near-frontier community so recently involved in war with the Pequot Indians.

Almost 200 years later, "Jamie" Fields, with his charming personality, came in 1830 as a fourteen-year-old apprentice to this corner, which he would make a center of American literature. In his native Portsmouth, New Hampshire, he had already read about every book in the Portsmouth Athenaeum, and he had a yen for literature and literary companions. Under a succession of booksellers he grew to be an expert in every phase of publishing and selling. By the time "Jamie" was twenty-six, with just his experience and talent as ample assets, he was made a partner by William D. Ticknor, who, back in 1832, had given up activity in his family's financial world to be a bookseller. Fields had already brought something new to the American book trade. Unlike most publishers, whom Dickens came to consider "Yankee Pirates," Fields believed that authors should get paid.

Fields's office became celebrated as a gathering place, "the exchange of wit, the Rialto of current good things, the Hub of the Hub." The two-and-one-half-story, gambrel-roof building had an entry on Washington Street and two on School Street. Fields's desk and chairs were by a window looking out School Street to the Old South Meeting House. A green baize curtain separated its serious dealing and its laughter from the main salesroom.

Emerson called Fields "the guardian and maintainer of us all." Fields led merry sorties to repasts in nearby restaurants. He went personally after material—to London, where he talked Thackeray into coming to America, or to Salem, where he arranged with the reticent Hawthorne to publish *The Scarlet Letter.* Two years later they were such good friends that in 1851 Hawthorne sent express to Fields from the Berkshires his manuscript of *The House of the Seven Gables.* When it seemed to have been lost in transit, Hawthorne dolefully told Fields: "I shall not consent to the universe existing a moment longer. I have no copy of it."

To Oliver Wendell Holmes Fields was "literary counsellor and friend." Fields published Whittier and Longfellow (copies of *Evangeline* sold like hotcakes in the winter of 1847 at 20 cents a copy), presented Robert Browning's poems to America, and added Julia Ward Howe, Thoreau, and Harriet Beecher Stowe to his list. In 1859 he took over editorship of the *Atlantic Monthly,* the country's leading periodical. At the close of the Civil War the Old Corner was simply too small for all his firm's activity and, after Ticknor's death, he moved, as we shall presently see, to Tremont Street.

Drop into The Boston Globe Store, with a display of international and domestic travel books and maps unrivaled in New England.

In midblock at numbers 15 to 17 School Street, in what was once the Hutchinson family garden, stood a 1670 dwelling that became famous in the following century as the Cromwell's Head, a two-story wooden inn with sixteen beds. Here the twenty-four-year-old colonel George Washington lodged in 1756 during a two-week visit. A signboard with a likeness of Cromwell was suspended low outside so that all, definitely including the six-foot-two Washington, had to bow to the Lord Protector on entering.

Washington in 1756 was already distinguished, as the *Boston Gazette* observed, with "a deservedly high reputation in military skill, integrity and valor, though success has not always attended his undertakings." General Braddock had suffered a devastating defeat in 1755, but it was well known that Braddock had failed to follow his aide-de-camp Washington's advice on the battlefield. Washington, now commander of his colony's militia, had encountered a British officer of lesser rank but longer service who disputed Washington's authority to command him. Concerned that "very bad consequences to the public" might result, Washington in midwinter had made the month-long, 500-mile journey to Boston on horseback to lay the issue before Governor William Shirley, commander of all British forcesin America.

Shirley's official quarters were in the Province House, just around the corner and across the street from the Old South Meeting House. Washington visited Province House several times and got a written order confirming his authority. He played cards there and made three entries, meticulous as usual, of losses totaling 5 pounds, 1 shilling, 10 pence Virginia money. He found the exchange rate with Bay Colony money so favorable that he went to a tailor for new clothing and spent about twice as much here as in all the other colonies where he lodged.

Washington's cash book shows that the colonel, like most tourists, got around town. He entered a cash gift to the crew that took him down harbor to go aboard a British frigate and another to the crew that rowed him to visit the Castle Island fortifications. He gave tips to servants and the chambermaid before departing with his two military friends and two servants, one of them a British soldier who had been valet to Braddock and had asked to serve Washington.

Boston's renown as a medical center is traceable to individuals like the man who lived in a big house with gardens and fruit trees on the corner of City Hall Avenue, immediately above Cromwell's Head. The man was Boston's foremost doctor of his day, John Warren, younger brother of the Dr. Joseph Warren killed at Bunker Hill. Dr. Warren needed a big house. He had nineteen children besides Joseph's orphans.

Dr. John Warren in 1842 laid the foundation, as his son expressed it, of the Harvard Medical School, America's first continuous medical institution. The son, one of many Warren family doctors, was Dr. John Collins Warren, who first demonstrated publicly the effectiveness of ether in surgery. The father ran a military hospital in Boston's West End during the Revolution, and the son was cofounder there of the Massachusetts General Hospital.

On the upper west corner of City Hall Avenue was the residence that orator James Otis bought soon after he shifted his law practice from Plymouth in 1748 and became a leader in the patriot cause. Later it was the parsonage of scholarly Reverend James Freeman of King's Chapel (farther up School Street facing Tremont).

Province Street, on our left off School, was formerly called Governor's Alley. It led to the garden, stables, and rear of the official residence of the royal governors whom Washington visited. Near the east corner, as highlighted on a plaque near the 24 School Street entry, Huguenots fleeing religious persecution built the small church of the French Huguenots in 1704. Peter Faneuil's uncle Andrew, a wealthy merchant, gave the church communion silver and one of his warehouses. After the Huguenots, it was Congregational for forty years until 1788, when it became Boston's first Catholic church.

A chaplain of the French navy, Abbe François Matignon, remained in Boston when the fleet departed and became Boston's first resident priest. Mass was first publicly celebrated in Boston November 2, 1788. He was joined in 1796 by future bishop Cheverus. As we shall later see, plans got under way at this chapel to buy land elsewhere and build a Catholic church, the future Church of the Holy Cross.

Old City Hall, the handsome 1862–1865 Second Empire–style granite building, resembled the new Louvre extension Napoleon III built in Paris in the 1850s. The exterior was preserved when the city government shifted in 1969 to Government Center. This hall was the domain of oft-elected Mayor James M. Curley, though he referred to his high-ceilinged mayoral office on the second floor, City Hall Avenue side, as "Agony Corner."

Preceding this building on this site was a county courthouse, a granite affair designed by Charles Bulfinch and completed in 1810. Bulfinch called it Johnson Hall after early settler Isaac Johnson. In effect the Bulfinch hall had been Boston's first separate city hall, in use from 1840 until the city government moved into this 1862–1865 building.

Outside, the statue of Josiah Quincy, who really got Boston's municipal government in place, was put up in 1879 to balance the Benjamin Franklin statue on the opposite lawn. Quincy's statue was the work of sculptor Thomas Ball. The eight-foot bronze Benjamin Franklin, Boston's first portrait statue, the work of Richard S. Greenough in 1856, is on the site of the country's first public schoolhouse, built in 1645. Franklin came as a pupil when he was eight years old. To utilize the schoolhouse yard as extra space to build the present, enlarged King's Chapel, Latin School itself was demolished and a new schoolhouse was built directly across the street in 1748.

Many distinguished Bostonians got their training at Boston Latin School, among them leaders of the Revolutionary period—Samuel Adams, John Hancock, James Bowdoin, and Josiah Quincy, Jr., the patriot. In 1812 Charles Bulfinch, also a graduate of Latin School, replaced the 1748 Latin School with a still larger schoolhouse on the same site that was later used for extending the Parker House to Chapman Place.

A big riot prior to the Boston Tea Party in 1773 erupted in School Street at the Richard Clarke mansion, on the present site of Franklin's statue. Clarke's two sons, along with their two cousins, sons of Royal Governor Thomas Hutchinson, were among the consignees of the hated tea. The Sons of Liberty had demanded that they refuse to accept the tea. First there was a riot at the Clarke warehouse on lower King (now State) Street, next came the familiar patriot whistling signal to assemble, and another crowd gathered here. When a random shot was fired from an upstairs window, the crowd attacked with volleys of rocks, breaking glass and smashing furnishings.

John Singleton Copley, who was married to Richard Clarke's daughter Susan, was represented equally by patriots and Tories. He, after a talk with Hancock, tried to get a compromise. Despite Copley's dread of seawater, he was rowed twice down the harbor to Castle Island fort, where the consignees had taken shelter. But by the time Copley reported to the gathering at the Old South Meeting House, the crisis had gone beyond compromise. Bostonians would have no part of the taxed tea.

Harvey D. Parker bought as his first School Street lot the site of the mansion of Oliver Wendell Holmes's wealthy merchant grandfather and opened his new hotel in 1856. He offered a novelty—American plan plus fine food available at any hour instead of set dining hours. Parkers expanded steadily to include nearly the entire city block. The present Omni Parker House was built in 1927, with a repeat of the corner tier of bay windows so popular in old Parkers.

Presidents, state stars, and celebrities have appeared over the years on its star-studded guest list. Many appear in portraits along the corridors. The marble fireplace on the third floor, Chapman Place corner, in suite 338, used by Charles Dickens when he was a guest in

1867–1868, may still be seen, along with the great mirror before which Dickens used to rehearse his talks, which is on the wall outside the Press Room on the mezzanine floor. A fine oil portrait of Harvey D. Parker, who personally attended Dickens's needs, also graces the exhibits there.

Understandably, there is no painting of John Wilkes Booth. The man who killed Abraham Lincoln came to Boston ten days before the assassination to visit his brother, Edwin, who was appearing at the Boston Theater. Booth occupied a room on the third floor at the head of the stairs in the Chapman Place corner section. Before checking out he spent some time practicing in a cellar shooting gallery on the opposite, east corner of Chapman Place and School Street.

High among the happy memories of the Parker House were the dinner gatherings of the highly literary Saturday Club. Richard Henry Dana has told how it developed from a "habit of Emerson" to dine with a small group of friends in the mid-1800s, particularly at the Parker House, on his Saturday jaunts to Boston. Birth of the club is usually pegged about 1855. For years membership was small, just enough for a congenial informal gathering around one of Parker's dining tables. They met on the last Saturday of each month at 3:00 P.M., then moved up the time so that out-of-towners like Emerson and Hawthorne could get home to Concord. The special room they used was the one right over the School Street entrance, above the marquee.

There were no rules; everything was spontaneous. In the early years participants might vary between a dozen and twenty, said Oliver Wendell Holmes. "You would have seen Longfellow at one end—the east end—of the long table, and Agassiz at the other. Emerson was commonly near the Longfellow end, on his left. I myself commonly sat on the right hand side of Longfellow, so as to have my back to the windows. . . ." Professor Louis Agassiz was the noted Harvard naturalist, a jovial man loaded with good humor.

Visiting celebrities were invited. Charles Dickens gave up his customary midday lunch and walk (usually 8 to 10 miles) to join the group on November 30, 1867, a cold, windy day. There were twenty-two present as "Jamie" Fields introduced Dickens to fellow members at a session that lasted well into the evening. Longfellow wrote in his diary: "A delightful dinner." From Holmes came a detailed side-light: Dickens, said Holmes, "compounded a jug anglice, or pitcher as we call it, of the gin punch for which his father was famous. No witch at her incantation could be more rapt in her task than Dickens was in his as he stooped over the drink he was mixing. . . ."

Dickens was quite particular about the gin he used. The previous Sunday, when he found it impossible to get good English gin, he sent his traveling companion and business manager, big George Dolby (a man "always," said Mark Twain, "overflowing with good nature and bursting with jollity—a gladsome gorilla") to get some. Dolby went on a tug to the Cunard liner *Cuba* on which they had arrived and, from the kindly captain, came back with two cases of gin, twenty-four bottles.

As we arrive at the top of School Street we come to a crossroads that, as we will soon see, could well be considered the Dickens land of Boston. But we will approach it by starting our walk along Tremont Street from the traffic island in old Scollay Square.

Tremont Street to King's Chapel

Tremont Street, which begins at old Scollay Square, was the southern part of the roadway that curved around the slope of Pemberton Hill, in colonial times a hillside of grandeur with mansions and terraced gardens. Governors resided here, as did top officials, merchant princes, and clergy, when the Puritan ministers filled the community role of aristocrats.

About midway on the right, between the traffic island of old Scollay Square and Beacon Street, or just opposite the northwest corner of King's Chapel Burying Ground, was the estate of merchant Peter Faneuil. The land was formerly part of Governor Bellingham's adjoining site. The Faneuil mansion, a capacious three stories with a hip roof, pilasters, and four great chimneys, was set back on the slope and approached by long steps and landscaped terraces. Behind it were stables for horses, a coach, and a chariot, and near the summit stood a summer gazebo. Elegant living and entertainment were the hallmarks of the generous and portly Faneuil, who had silver, servants, and a cellar full of the earth's choicest wines.

Late in the eighteenth century the mansion became the dwelling of still another civic benefactor, William Phillips, Jr., whose father lived in the old Bromfield mansion opposite the present Boston Athenaeum. Phillip's philanthropy helped Boston get its first general hospital. The elder Phillips left $5,000, a large sum in 1804, for a hospital. The younger Phillips quadrupled that, making the biggest private gift by far, when Dr. Jackson and Dr. Warren issued their 1810 circular appeal.

By the time Charles Dickens made his first Boston visit, in 1842, there stood, on what was originally the front lawn of the Faneuil-Phillips estate, a row of buildings that contained an enormous ballroom, at 23 Tremont Row, which was the joy of Boston's social elite. This was the dancing academy of Lorenzo Papanti, who had come from Italy as a musician on "Old Ironsides." Special arrangements for the ballroom and dressing rooms had been made on the third floors of the adjoining buildings by the owners, social lions William Appleton and Abbott Lawrence. The hall had America's first spring floor and many great pier mirrors. This was the favorite place for society's great assemblies. Papanti, teacher and proprietor, brought the waltz to America and danced the first one with Mrs. Harrison Gray Otis, Jr.

On February 1, 1842, Papanti's was the scene for Boston's honoring Charles Dickens, "Boz," just under thirty years of age. With him was his wife, Kate. Unlike his later lecturing visit, this one was intended as informal travel. The outpouring of admirers far exceeded expectations. Invitations, too many to accept, poured in. In tip-top health, he did go to many private homes for dinner and created sensations by his visit to the state senate and theaters. Crowds wherever he went around Boston cheered the author, known then only by his earliest works, *Pickwick Papers, Oliver Twist,* and *The Old Curiosity Shop.*

Twenty-two-year-old James Russell Lowell came to Dickens's hotel to invite him, on behalf of the "Young Men of Boston," to a February 1 affair. Dickens accepted. The banquet, lavish even for those nine-entree days, was specially prepared in the great kitchen of a hotel at Tremont and Beacon that gave that location its name, Albion Corner. Lowell had many of the future members of the Saturday Club on hand. Holmes wrote a special poem. Dana called Dickens "the cleverest man I ever met." Among the worshipping diners was an aspiring publisher, twenty-six-year-old "Jamie" Fields.

Quite a few houses in Boston were confiscated by the Commonwealth when their Loyalist owners, some of Boston's wealthiest, fled town with the redcoats. Peter Faneuil's mansion, then owned by plutocrat John Vassal, went the confiscatory route. So did the parsonage of King's Chapel, on our left, just north of the King's Chapel Burying Ground. The Reverend Henry Caner, the rector, dwelt here in a wooden building with roughcast—"my freehold in Boston," as he described it, "with yard, garden, orchard, etc." A Yale graduate, Mr. Caner came full of energy to revive a drive to get New England's first Episcopal church a new granite structure. The present granite King's Chapel was built in 1749–1754. When he fled, he took along the communion silver given by George III and earlier British monarchs.

The purchaser at the auction by the Commonwealth was Judge John Lowell of "Essex Junto" fame. Lowell was so admired by Samuel Adams that Adams got him to be his successor in the Continental Congress. Through Judge Lowell's action, Massachusetts abolished slavery when Lowell, a delegate, inserted into the state constitution in 1780 that all "men are born free and equal." Lowell had a Roxbury mansion "on the road leading to Dedham" and kept the Caner parsonage as a town house near his Court Street office.

Two of Boston's most distinguished institutions have had the 30 Tremont address—the Boston Athenaeum in its earliest days (1810–1822) and the Massachusetts Historical Society, founded in 1791. Massachusetts Historical, the nation's oldest historical society, spent much of its early life along Tremont Street. After being housed is an attic room in Faneuil Hall and in Bulfinch's Tontine Crescent, it was here from 1833 to 1897 in two successive stone buildings.

The Flatley Building at 18 Tremont, just north of the Caner site, was the location in 1846 of the impressive four-story granite Boston theater known, to avoid ruffling Puritan feathers, as the Boston Museum. It had its own stock company and attracted the era's stars to its stage, euphemistically called the Lecture Hall.

Directly across Tremont Street at Number 19 was the dental office of Dr. William T. G. Morton, where he did pioneer work with ether (he called it "Letheon") before the epoch-making 1846 operation at the Massachusetts General Hospital. Dr. Morton's office was on the second floor, which was just above the arcade of present Three Center Plaza.

King's Chapel Burying Ground is Boston's oldest cemetery. When about to die, Isaac Johnson requested that he be buried in back of his intended dwelling, and his prominence attracted others of the first settlers to be buried near him. As in the case of his wife, Lady Arbella, no trace other than tradition exists of his grave. Actually, grave locations in all of Boston's earliest cemeteries are far from certain because tidy gravekeepers shifted stones to mark the edges of paths. The curator and guides of King's Chapel have a plot plan and can assist in locating particular gravestones, as noted in *Ancient Gates,* a 1991 guide to King's Chapel Burying Ground.

Stone markers can be fascinating for their carvings, even when flaked, broken, or timeworn. Some are so sunken that just old coats of arms show—especially along the Tremont Street side from the tomb in the northwest corner marked "No. 1," the tomb of Oliver Wendell Holmes's great-grandfather, Jacob, a wealthy merchant whose mansion was on the nearby site of the Parker House. If we turn left as we enter, we come to the tomb of Governor John Winthrop and many Winthrop descendants. Behind it is the tomb of the Reverend John Cotton and other early clergy who lived on the slope of nearby Pemberton Hill. Near the north side, still farther down, is the grave of Captain Robert Keayne, donor of the first Town House. The white obelisk near the center of the cemetery marks the grave of William Dawes, courier for the Sons of Liberty. Just like present-day tourists, Nathaniel Hawthorne used to roam this cemetery. If, on entering, we follow the path to the right, then just after it turns left by the chapel we come to the grave of Elizabeth Pain, died 1704, the tale of whose life gives us our tragic adulteress Hester Prynne of *The Scarlet Letter.* As some gravestones indicate (the Winthrop tomb, for instance), there have been burials in recent times for descendants of these early families.

Strange as it may sound, venerable King's Chapel was an intruder on this public land. When the Bay's first royal governor, Sir Edmund Andros, arrived in Boston, he wanted to hold Church of England services. Puritan Boston was opposed. At first he used the library in the Town House, but then he demanded the keys and used the Old South Meeting House. He tried next to buy land for a chapel. Judge Sewall and other Puritan owners excused themselves from such an heretical sale. So Andros in 1688 simply took a corner in the graveyard, where he had recently buried Lady Andros, his wife, in a now unmarked grave. Soon deposed, Andros never had the opportunity to enter the chapel.

Under later governors Andros's chapel became a community center. The cornerstone for the present chapel, all its big blocks hand-cut from Quincy granite, was put in place August 11, 1749, by the church's senior warden, William Shirley, the royal governor. He was escorted from Province House to the scene and afterward, in regal manner, gave the workmen 20 pounds to drink to his health. Construction, still incomplete, went on for several years from plans the Reverend Caner had solicited from a Newport merchant and gentleman architect, Peter Harrison. Harrison sent the plans by post rider and left everything else to local workmen.

The chapel with its memorial is reminiscent of English cathedrals. Courtiers around royal governors—the Province House set—and the British military in their scarlet were customary attendants, along with many of the town's prosperous merchants. George Washington could easily recognize the building; it is pretty much as it was in 1789 when he visited the chapel to attend an oratorio of choir and organ to raise money for the portico, which was later added to the front of the chapel. Washington contributed a little more than five pounds.

Though the present chapel, now approaching its 250th anniversary, lacks the 120-foot steeple designed by Harrison in his "draught of a handsome church," it still has many attractions beyond its antiquity. The canopied pew for the royal governor contains the chair of Boston's last royal civil governor, Hutchinson. The pulpit, with sounding board, is one of the oldest in the land. The bell, recast by Paul Revere, was called by him "the sweetest bell we ever made." The organ, a copy of the chapel's 1756 organ, is successor to the first regu-

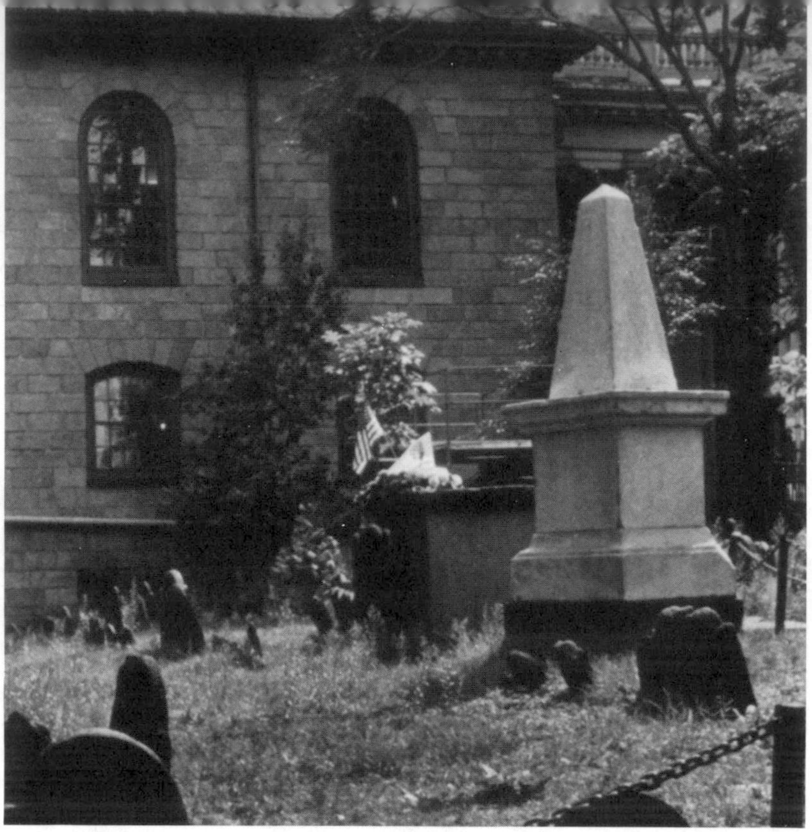

King's Chapel and Boston's oldest burying place

lar organ in America, which had initiated a new era of church music. The crypt under the chapel has two rows of high brick vaults bearing some of the foremost Boston family names from colonial times: Bulfinch, Apthorp, Gardiner, Vassall, Coolidge, Barrell, and Oliver. An additional crypt, the Strangers' Tomb, is located beneath the entry to the chapel and under the sidewalk.

Yet another distinction for the chapel is that it was, in colonial times, the first permanently established Anglican church in New England; after the Revolution it became the first Unitarian church in America. Thomas Bulfinch, father of the architect and then senior warden, invited the Reverend James Freeman to the pulpit on behalf of the vestry, and he became pastor in 1783. Mr. Freeman was the first American clergyman to call himself a Unitarian, and he revised the church's *Book of Common Prayer.* He was formally ordained in this chapel on November 18, 1787, by senior warden Bulfinch, with the congregation giving an approving "Amen!"

DOWNTOWN BOSTON

Tremont Street to Old Granary

Publisher "Jamie" Fields saw Charles Dickens during his first hours on American soil as radiantly gleeful and "all on fire with curiosity." Dickens later told the overflow gathering at the banquet for him at Papanti's, on Tremont Street, that he had been dreaming "by day and night, for years, of setting foot upon this shore. . . ." About midnight, a few hours after arriving in Boston and after Kate had gone to bed in their quarters in the Tremont House, Dickens and a young British earl he met on shipboard went out for a stroll.

A full moon was shining on the frozen snow. They went down the middle of School Street with Dickens laughing and, on arriving at the Old South Meeting House, he so enjoyed the scene that he even shouted in high spirits. He got more distinct impressions next morning on a walk to the Custom House for some baggage: "The city is a beautiful one," he wrote. "The private dwelling houses are, for the most part, large and elegant; the shops extremely good; and the public buildings handsome. . . . Boston is what I would like the whole United States to be."

The Tremont House, America's forerunner of luxury hotels, a four-story granite structure with a Greek-style portico of tall fluted pillars, built 1828–1829, stood on the south corner of Beacon and Tremont

DOWNTOWN BOSTON

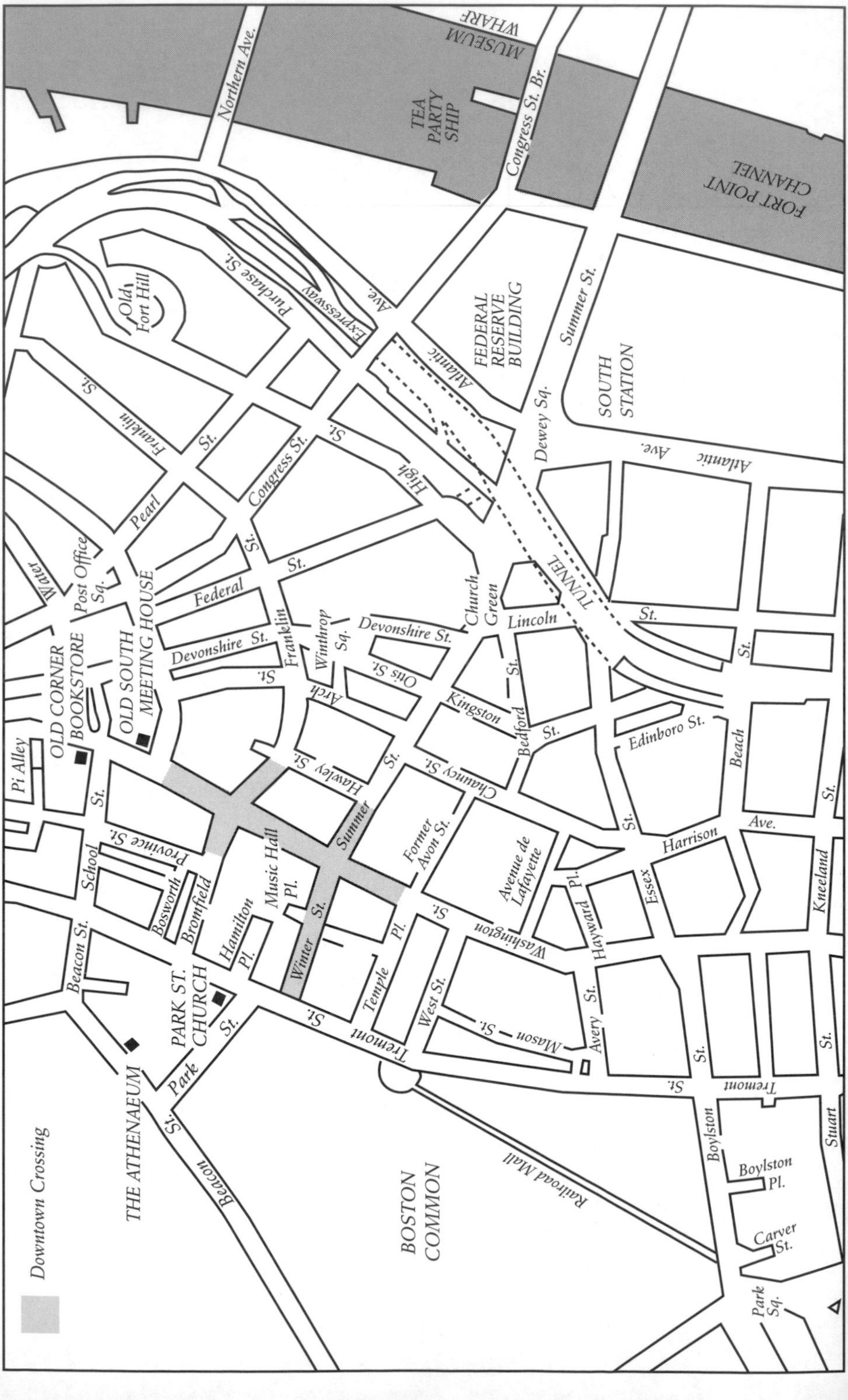

Streets and extended to the Old Granary Burying Ground. The successor, an eleven-story 1895 structure at 73 Tremont, long displayed a popular, mural-sized likeness of the old Tremont House before a 1989 renovation added two penthouse floors and a modern, two-story, lavish marble lobby.

The old hotel's bar, cuisine, and especially its bathing facilities in the cellar, fed by rainwater cisterns, were remarkable. Harrison Gray Otis, one of the hotel's owners, used to march his children from their Beacon Hill mansion "once a week for a tub bath." As for the hotel's lavish interior, Dickens, a social reformer far from being averse to luxury, pronounced it "very excellent" and added: "It has more galleries, colonnades, piazzas and passages than I can remember, or the reader would believe."

Tremont House sheltered many celebrities—stage stars, statesmen, nobles, and several presidents. President Andrew Jackson occupied the state suite on the third-floor corner overlooking the Old Granary Burying Ground. Congressman Abraham Lincoln, on a speaking tour to help elect President Zachary Taylor, "Old Rough and Ready," lodged at the Tremont House in the fall of 1848 during a week in this area. Little was recorded, though tall and thin Lincoln was said to have worn an ill-fitting bombazine suit and to have carried a twenty-five-cent straw hat, keeping notes in its sweatband. His visit, as we shall presently see, led him to file some prophetic legislation.

For Charles Dickens there was not an inactive moment during his two-week stay. He speedily engaged a secretary to help him handle the flood of requests and invitations as he squeezed in time for sittings for his portrait and bust. Dickens, a tourist at heart, missed none of Boston's historic attractions on his walks from the golden dome of the State House to the wharf of the Boston Tea Party. Longfellow, then beardless, was on hand for a farewell breakfast, and crowds waved and cheered Dickens and Kate all the way to the depot.

Tremont House and Tremont Temple, on the east side of Tremont Street, have many tales of Dickens. The much newer Parker House was Dickens's Boston residence on intermittent visits during his second and last five-month tour of America, 1867–1868, a series of readings inspired and orchestrated by "Jamie" Fields. This trip, though,

Dickens's health was failing, and the strain that he risked in order to acquire sufficient funds for his large family would contribute to his death just two years later. Dickens still tried to maintain his long, daily walks and hearty social get-togethers with literary friends. But there was no repetition of the hectic pace of his first visit.

As he arrived Dickens had contracted a cold that he called his Boston catarrh. The cold persisted through the winter, causing friends to urge him to quit all public appearances. In midwinter he did delay announcing Boston readings while, as he explained, he was "sneezing melodiously by the half hour." Dickens talked and wrote a great deal about eating and drinking, but, said Fields, "I scarcely saw him eat a hearty meal during his whole stay in the country."

Overall Dickens managed to give—and dramatically act the parts in—seventy-six of eighty planned readings in our big cities. The strain showed. He wrote his daughter that his Parker House room had "hot and cold bath in my bedroom . . . comforts not in existence when I was here before." But there was no elevator. He even got too ill for his daily walk, and part of his departure scene was the sight of big George Dolby helping Dickens down the stairs from their third floor suite. Fields remarked: "Only a man of iron could have accomplished all he did."

Arriving in front of the Tremont Temple, next to the Parker House, pause at the sidewalk curbing and look back, northward, for a magnificent view of the Old North Church—the church of Paul Revere and the lanterns. Its white spire, a replacement long ago by Charles Bulfinch, is framed between the Kennedy Federal Building on the left and the new City Hall on the right.

The Tremont Temple is also associated with Abraham Lincoln's trips to Boston. The big Free Soil rally Lincoln was to address in Court Square—between the old City Hall on School Street and the courthouse on Court Street, in front of the present Kirstein Memorial Library—was washed out by bad weather. Instead, it was held on September 22, 1848, at Tremont Temple. Lincoln's remarks and wit were "cheered to the echo," but the local papers concentrated on the two-hour speech of ex-Governor William H. Seward, who would become Lincoln's secretary of state. Seward's remarks against slavery, as well as the growing antislavery activity he encountered in New England, deeply impressed Lincoln. He told Seward: "I have been thinking about what you said in your speech. I reckon you are right. We have got to deal with this slavery question and got to give much more attention to it hereafter than we have been doing." When Lincoln got back to Washington he filed, as a starter, a bill to abolish slavery in the District of Columbia. It was defeated. But it was to be a momentous beginning.

The present Tremont Temple, built in 1895, is the fourth on this site. The first, the one in which Lincoln spoke, began life in the fall of 1827 as a theater that attracted the greatest stars of that era. In 1842–1843 it was converted into a temple by the Free Baptist Society, which held here the first integrated church meetings in America. This building and its two successors were consumed by fire. The second Tremont Temple, which had a 2000-seat capacity, the city's largest, was the setting for all of Dickens's public readings in Boston.

Longfellow called Dickens's first reading at Tremont Temple on December 2, 1867, "a triumph." When it was over Dickens had "Jamie" and Annie Fields and friends to his Parker House suite. All agreed with George Dolby's appraisal: "Never before in Boston had anything called forth such enthusiasm as that night's reading." Twenty-one-year-old Charles H. Taylor, correspondent for the *New York Tribune* and future publisher of *The Boston Globe,* sent an account to his paper of the excitement and the crush for tickets:

> *The line of carriages ran down all manner of streets . . . The moon shone out and helped the gas lamps light the gay, struggling, swarming multitude that was trying to get inside the doors, watched by the long-faced silent multitude that crowded round the doorways without tickets, with no hope of getting in at all.*
>
> *Hardly a notable man in Boston or for 50 miles about but was there. . . . There sat Longfellow, looking like the very spirit of Christmas with his ruddy cheeks and bright soft eyes looking out from the vast of snow-white hair and snow-white beard. There was Holmes looking*

crisp and fine. . . . There was Lowell, here, too, the elder Dana. . . . Yonder is Fields to whom all owe this great pleasure. . . .

The celebrated names went on and on.

First Dickens read from his *Christmas Carol.* He acted, too, the people and scenes he created, "the dolorous, surly tones of Old Scrooge . . . the chattering Crachits, poor little Tiny Tim, the dance in old Fezziwig's warehouse. . . ." The applause was thunderous.

Field slipped backstage to have a glass of champagne with Dickens, and hastened back to his seat. For his second presentation Dickens read the trial from Pickwick. Again the "rapturous applause." Dickens wrote his daughter next day that his success was "quite beyond description or exaggeration."

It was this way most of his tour. When back again for a few days in the same hall, he read from *David Copperfield* and, despite his cold, presented his *Christmas Carol* on Christmas Eve. Again there was boundless exhilaration. "Bostonians were quite astounding in their demonstration. I never saw anything like them on Christmas Eve!" Audiences clearly stimulated the innate actor in Dickens.

Tremont Temple had seen gatherings utterly different in its days as an antislavery forum. Elizabeth Peabody went to the annual meeting of the Massachusetts Anti-Slavery Society on January 24, 1861. The fifth southern state had seceded, and the flag at Fort Sumter had been fired upon. Miss Peabody had hardly found a seat when she saw a crowd in the gallery start yelling as Wendell Phillips spoke. "All hell broke loose." Phillips had invited Emerson to speak. Emerson had spoken in Concord of John Brown as "that new saint." Only the month before, a threatening crowd had broken up a meeting called "in memory of John Brown" in the nearby Music Hall, and the mob had pursued Phillips. Now, said Emerson, "the mob roared whenever I attempted to speak and after several beginnings I withdrew." Phillips, who now had some stalwart guards, and the Reverend James Freeman Clarke managed to get out their antislavery message over the outbursts and the hissing.

The jump we have seen in the height of 73 Tremont Street, though its new penthouse was set back on its south side in deference to historic Old Granary Burying Ground, underscores the possibility that the soaring towers we glimpsed in the modern downtown may be coming increasingly to this historic area and to midtown ahead of us. The 90 Tremont Street site, long home to popular Dini's restaurant, was to be filled with an eleven-story building that, by agreement on air rights, might have had an office tower extending right over Tremont Temple. And ahead, on our left at 110–120 Tremont Street, the six-story buildings were to be made twelve stories, with upper story setbacks to defer to the Boston landmark Park Street Church. Such soaring expansion, as we shall further observe, was brought to a halt by the 1989 recession.

The Old Granary Burying Ground, on our right, was opened in 1660 as the second cemetery near the town center and was named for the long wooden town granary partly on the Common, partly on the site of the Park Street Church. This cemetery is entirely on ground once part of the Common. The Egyptian-style granite gateway was an early-nineteenth-century creation of Solomon Willard, architect of Bunker Hill's granite monument. There are many noted graves from colonial times. Judge Samuel Sewall and his father-in-law, John Hull, who minted the pine-tree shillings, are both near Paul Revere's grave. There are early governors, probably including the man who served the colony the earliest and the longest, the zealous, quick-tempered John Endecott.

Endecott, governor on and off for sixteen years, has today no marked grave. His name does appear on the plaque of King's Chapel Burying Ground, but it is more probable that his ashes are in the Old Granary. Endecott died in 1665, five years after this cemetery was opened; the first one was considered full. Furthermore, town records of 1721 show that a relative established that a "tomb in the South [Granary] Burying Ground belongs to the late Governor Endecott." The relative was accordingly granted liberty to use the tomb.

Many heroes of our Revolutionary period have graves and memorials here. Benjamin Franklin raised in the center the first memorial to his parents, and, when it suffered decay, Bostonians replaced it with the present 20-foot Quincy-granite shaft, also shaped by Solomon

Willard. The path to the right of the Franklin obelisk, at the end of the next short path on the right, leads to the burial place of the family of Elizabeth Foster Vergoose, called Mother Goose for her famous nursery rhymes of 1719. Her burial spot is unmarked, but traditionally it was here. Memorials to John Hancock and James Bowdoin are on the Park Street side, south of the Franklin memorial. Revere's and Sewall's are to the west of it, and to the north is the gravestone of Robert Treat Paine, signer—like Hancock and Samuel Adams—of the Declaration of Independence. Samuel Adams, like patriot James Otis, is buried on the front, Tremont Street side. Samuel Adams rests on the right as we enter the cemetery, along with the men killed in the Boston Massacre and twelve-year-old Christopher Snider, killed in the North End anticustoms riot eleven days earlier. James Otis's stone is on the left as we enter. Just two gravestones before we reach the Otis one is the touching slate memorial to nineteen-year-old Benjamin Woodbridge (son of admiralty Judge Dudley Woodbridge), who was killed in the duel on the Common in 1728. Interestingly, the memorial is about as far away as the cemetery can provide from the grave of generous Peter Faneuil in the northwest corner. Faneuil, we recall, helped the other young duelist, his relative, escape to Europe.

One other memory goes with this Woodbridge grave. The Autocrat of the Breakfast Table recounts how he came to this cemetery on his first walk with his beloved schoolmistress. Both agreed that for two young men to get into a duel "there must have been love at the bottom of it." She dropped a rosebud she had in her hand "on the Woodbridge grave," said the Autocrat, and added sentimentally, "How women love love!"

That towering skyscraper we see as we are leaving the burying ground and look down Bromfield Street, toward the financial district, is the headquarters of one of the largest banking institutions in New England, the first national Bank of Boston (now BankBoston). Shortly we shall see the small dead-end street where the commercial acorn was planted that produced this impressive oak.

Brimstone Corner and Park Street

"Perfectly felicitous" was Henry James's impression of the 217-foot steeple of the Park Street Church, a Christopher Wren–like touch of old London. The structure itself, the design of English architect Peter Banner, was considered exuberantly by Henry James to be "the most interesting mass of brick and mortar in America." Since it was built in 1809–1810, it has certainly been among the most loved attractions near the Common.

On its site, until that time, there stood for nearly three-quarters of a century the largest building in Boston, a long wooden affair called the Granary, built to hold thousands of tons of corn and wheat to sell at low cost to the poor in times of scarcity. After the Revolution the building was used as offices for minor town officials and became renowned when its size provided a loft to make the sails of "Old Ironsides."

There is a twofold tradition about how this busy place got the name Brimstone Corner. One is that gunpowder was stored in the church during the War of 1812, in which "Old Ironsides" saved the nation's pride. The other is that the name epitomized the fervor of the Congregational preachers who filled its pulpit. It was from here in 1819 that a group of missionaries set out to Hawaii and seeded the Americanism that led to those islands becoming our fiftieth state.

In this church William Lloyd Garrison on July 4, 1829, made his first public address against slavery. He was then twenty-three years of age and urging colonization in Africa as a solution. Two years later, after he had seen firsthand in Baltimore the curse of slavery and was jailed there for his opposition, Garrison was back in Boston getting out his *Liberator* and demanding immediate emancipation.

During a children's celebration in the church on another July 4, in 1832, "America" was sung publicly for the first time. The words to "America" (set to the tune of "God Save the King") were written that year by a Bostonian, the future Reverend Samuel Francis Smith, when he was twenty-four years of age and a student at Andover Theological Seminary.

The church, when built, was at the foot of the street Charles Bulfinch put through in 1804 as a more elegant pathway to his new State House on Beacon Hill. He had become chairman of selectmen and was able to do this after ridding the old street of some public buildings that had become both inadequate and eyesores.

These buildings, from colonial to post-Revolutionary days, had been located up now-aristocratic Park Street in what was long considered a remote area of the town. Above the granary, on the site at 5 Park, was the pen for the town bull and the town pound. Our first postmaster, Richard Fairbanks, was town herder and collected twopence fees for stray calves, goats, and hogs for three years before starting to collect one-penny fees for sea letters in his tavern in 1639. Next uphill was the workhouse with its vagrants and oakum pickers. Next—on the site of the present Union Club at Number 7–8—was the bridewell (house of correction). And at the corner facing Beacon Street was the almshouse for the old, infirm, and needy. Youngsters of needy families often pathetically poked their hands through the fencing to solicit charity. By 1795 the town had shifted these institutions elsewhere and put the lots up for auction. Only the granary was moved away, to become a Dorchester hotel-tavern.

Bulfinch's design soon transformed Park Street into a Federal showplace. Prestigious residents were drawn to the uniform four-story brick houses, eight in all, that Bulfinch got under way in 1804–1805. The house at Number 1 lasted the longest as a residence; it was home for half a century to Calcutta trade merchant Thomas Wigglesworth and was family-owned into the first decade of this century. In 1953 it came into the possession of the Park Street Church, and in 1972 it was replaced by the church's six-story Ministries Building.

Senator Jonathan Mason, Harrison Gray Otis's partner in real estate, provided the new house at 2 Park for his daughter when she became the bride of medical pioneer Dr. John Collins Warren, who performed the world's first ether-assisted operation. Dr. Warren lived here the rest of his life, the best-known doctor in New England. He was physician to distinguished Bostonians from Gilbert Stuart and

John Quincy Adams to Mayor Josiah Quincy. His office was the first-floor front, with patients waiting in the hallway or on the flight of stairs. Apprentices from Harvard Medical and Massachusetts General worked in a room with a sanded floor in the rear. His library and equipment went eventually to Harvard College and Massachusetts General Hospital, where he and his father were founders, professors, and surgeons.

The Warren family has left us a fascinating picture of fashionable life the way it was on Bulfinch Row. Relatives of the large Warren family in this area included Masons, Crowninshields, Phillipses, Sullivans, and Winthrops. Traditional family gatherings were held every Thanksgiving. A doctor grandson of John Collins Warren, who inherited Number 2, said a padlocked gate in the rear led to the Old Granary Burying Ground near John Hancock's grave. He recalled:

> *Before the advent of horse-cars on Tremont Street, the enclosure afforded to the inhabitants of Park Street all the advantages of private grounds; giving protection from the noises of city life, and providing a much enjoyed breathing space in the very heart of the metropolis.*
>
> *Members of my family can still tell of picnics and other festivals held upon the quaint old table-like structures covering the graves of families with historic names. . . . The rising tide of traffic finally forced the last inhabitants into a new residential district.*

The Warrens also helped preserve the cemetery. Benjamin Franklin back in 1754 had put up a brick monument on his parents' crumbling grave. In 1827 Dr. Warren got permission from Franklin's descendants, and with the help of his neighbors and friends had Solomon Willard prepare the present obelisk.

The kingpin of the "Essex Junto," George Cabot, had 3 Park Street as his town house from 1803 to 1809. Cabot, who rose from cabin boy to captain and then became a Salem merchant and transferred to Boston, was an intimate of Alexander Hamilton. Cabot served as U.S. senator from 1791 to 1796, and during this period became president of the Boston branch of Hamilton's United States Bank. Cabot is most remembered for presiding at the ill-timed Hartford Convention of 1814, death rattle of the Federalist Party, though by then he was a moderating influence.

Ironically, Cabot sold Number 3 to wealthy lawyer and Harvard overseer Richard Sullivan, who became involved in a wild anti-Federalist tale. Sullivan's father, future Governor James Sullivan, was attorney general for seventeen years before winning the governorship in a stunning upset to the Federalists. During the campaign the father was bitterly assailed by Major Benjamin Russell's pro-Federalist Centinel. Young Sullivan encountered Russell in Scollay Square, and when Russell accepted blame for a caricature, Richard Sullivan gave Russell a caning that had Boston society aghast.

Women's Heritage Trail

5 Park Street was once the offices of the Woman's Journal, *a newspaper published by the American Woman Suffrage Association. Lucy Stone, an advocate who petitioned annually for women's suffrage, was a major force behind the* Journal. *She valued the office's proximity to the State House, once declaring "how often have women looked down from the [State House] gallery while our lawmakers voted down our rights, and heard them say, 'Half an hour is time enough to waste on it'. . . [and then] turn eagerly to consider such a question as what shall be the size of a barrel of cranberries. . . [taking] plenty of time to consider that." Lucy Stone was the first Massachusetts woman to receive a college degree (from Oberlin College in 1847). She was also the first woman to officially keep her maiden name when she married.*

It was at Number 3 that Daniel Webster made his last social call in Boston a month before he died in 1852. He had come by carriage from Marshfield to consult his doctor. The dwelling was then the home of Webster's close friend, Thomas Wren Ward, American agent for Barings of London. Ward was giving a party for the head of Barings, Thomas Barings, then on a tour of America. A melancholy glimpse of the scene has been left by a guest. Thomas Barings hastened to get a seat for the man he had known as our secretary of state. Webster, livid, shrunken, partly etherized, sought to be cheerful in the few minutes that he stayed. "All were sad and silent, and, when he rose to go, all rose with him. If a ghost had come amongst us, it could hardly have startled us more."

The old sites of 4, 5, and 6 Park, now combined at the Paulist Fathers Center and the Holy Ghost Chapel built in 1956, are linked with the Josiah Quincy family that gave Boston three mayors, with the publisher Houghton Mifflin, with bookseller Goodspeed, with famous *Atlantic Monthly* editors, and with Julia Ward Howe.

Mayor Josiah Quincy, Jr., had the joy of walking out of his dwelling at Number 4 in the fall of 1848 to take part in the gala celebration when Lake Cochituate water first gushed in Frog Pond. His father, when mayor twenty-three years earlier, had urged that the city obtain a water supply. The elder Quincy, having served sixteen years as president of Harvard, spent his still-energetic final years at Number 5, next door to his son and his grandson, Josiah Quincy III, who would be mayor for four years, 1896–1899.

By 1880 Houghton Mifflin had acquired the authors and magazines developed by "Jamie" Fields and opened Boston offices in three stories in Number 4. The Riverside Press in Cambridge, created by young Henry O. Houghton, continued to win laurels for excellent printing. The next year William Dean Howells quit as editor of the *Atlantic Monthly* to devote all his time to writing and was succeeded in Number 4 by Thomas Bailey Aldrich. Howells wrote a friend: "Aldrich is busy on the *Atlantic* and is very fond of his editorial work. He hates writing, you know, and he likes reading and talking, and he spends six hours every day at the office where I used to put in a scant afternoon a week."

Julia Ward Howe, a few years before her husband's death, became editor of the *Women's Journal* in Tremont Place, soon moved to other rooms in Number 4, and then transferred to Number 5 during her campaign, 1880–1888, for women's suffrage. Houghton Mifflin moved in 1923 into a renovated building at Number 2 that replaced the original Bulfinch building and, continuing to grow, took over the present structure at Number 3, built as a bank in 1918–1919. Goodspeed's, established in 1898 in the basement of Number 5, moved in the 1930s to its shops on Ashburton Place and then in 1935 to the Claflin Building at 18–20 Beacon Street. In 1981 the bookshop moved to 7 Beacon Street, where it continued to serve as an arbiter of good taste until it finally closed its doors in 1995.

Father Isaac Hecker, noted as probably the first American Catholic to use the term "American spirituality," was the founder of the Paulists in 1858. On his path to conversion he joined the social experiment at Brook Farm but returned to New York and became a priest in 1849 when he was thirty years of age. With other converts, Father Hecker began the missionary work of seeking converts that is now carried on at the Paulist Center Community. There is counseling here and regular masses at the chapel, a beautiful place for meditation and prayer.

The Union Club at 7–8 Park is strictly a private club. Even members long thought that both buildings were Bulfinch originals, and the tradition got around that President A. Lawrence Lowell of Harvard used to say that when he dined at the Union Club, he was in what was once the bedroom of both his grandmothers. True, Number 8, taken over by the club when it began in 1863, was once the home of textile tycoon and U.S. ambassador to England Abbott Lawrence. But the original building at Number 7, while once the home of John Amory Lowell, merchant and banker, was demolished when acquired by the club years later in 1896. This was done because the club's engineering firm advised that it was a less costly procedure than trying to adjust floors of the two buildings to the same levels.

The club started during the Civil War from division among the members of the Somerset Club, then the only exclusive gentlemen's club in town. The North was encountering ill fortune on the battlefield in 1863, and some members felt that others in the club were sympathetic to Southern cotton interests. With statesman-orator Edward Everett, former president of Harvard, as president, these members formed the Union Club, with each pledged to "unqualified loyalty to the Constitution and Union . . . an unwavering support for suppression of the rebellion." Later that year, on November 19, Union

Club President Everett was the other speaker with President Lincoln at the dedication of the Gettysburg Battlefield memorial. Members of the Union Club included many of the Saturday Club, which shifted in later years to holding its traditional get-togethers at the Union Club.

The corner lot at Park and Beacon Streets has long been regarded as Boston's most aristocratic site. Its life of elegance began here, where Boston's poorhouse had so recently stood, when Charles Bulfinch in 1804 designed and built the first Park Street residence. This Bulfinch structure, a great brick mansion with an entrance on Park Street of curving brownstone steps and white Corinthian pillars, was promptly nicknamed "Amory's Folly" because of its immense size. Beneath it, by permission of the town, were built great arched brick vaults for wine and coal. Tradition relates that Thomas Amory, the owner, was holding his housewarming party when word came of bankrupting losses at sea. The house was divided into as many as four residences, with a Greek-revival portico added on the Beacon Street side.

In August 1824, while on his national tour as the guest of America, Lafayette came to Boston for his third visit since he first came to see Admiral d'Estaing during the war. He was ecstatically received for the entire week of his stay. Mayor Quincy filled the former Amory mansion with special furnishings and a staff of servants and even restored the large original drawing room so that Lafayette would have room to hold receptions. The tall, ruddy-faced, gracious marquis, lame from a war wound in his leg, stepped out on the roof balcony to greet the applauding throng after coming from his triumphant welcome given by twenty-five hundred schoolchildren, girls in white, boys in blue jackets, singing on the Common. In the crowded days that followed there were banquets, a Harvard commencement, dinners with old comrades-in-arms, and a big military review on the Common with dinner served in a huge marquee.

Early residents in this house included renowned lawyers: Christopher Gore of Waltham, who had his town house here while he was governor; Fisher Ames, congressman and Federalist Party orator; and Samuel Dexter, U.S. senator and member of John Adams's cabinet. Over the years, as now, this building has furnished quarters for many prominent lawyers close to the functioning of our state government.

Among the most distinguished literary residents was George Ticknor, cousin of the Ticknor associated with "Jamie" Fields. He was Harvard's professor of belles lettres and noted for his hospitality to authors and celebrities. In his library, behind the three balconied windows on the second floor on the Park Street side, Ticknor assembled one of the greatest private collections in the nation. In it he wrote his history of Spanish literature. Oliver Wendell Holmes called Ticknor's library, with its manorial fireplace, the "headquarters of scholarship and hospitality." Ticknor grew highly conservative, but not about books. He lent volumes freely, gave his collection to the Boston Public Library, which he helped to form, and stood firmly for that library's satisfying "the wants of the less favored classes. . . ." To Ticknor that meant those who could not afford to have libraries of their own.

Tremont to Boston's Theater District and Old Park Square

Let us resume our walk at Hamilton Place across from the Park Street church. For a short cul-de-sac it has unusual claims to attention: Boston—actually New England—banking began here. This was where the Boston Symphony Orchestra opened its first season. On the north corner, from 1820, all during his mayoralty and until he became president of Harvard, lived Josiah Quincy, first Boston mayor of that name. And it was the south corner that became in 1865 the new location of "Jamie" Fields's thriving publishing business after it had outgrown the Old Corner Bookstore in Newspaper Row.

The soaring BankBoston building, which we glimpsed down Bromfield Street, began as the Massachusetts Bank in 1784. It occupied the center portion hall of a 140-foot-long, two-story brick Manufactory Building that had been built at the corner and along the north side of present Hamilton Place. The province built it to encourage the manufacture of linen on spinning wheels brought over by settlers from

Northern Ireland. When this manufacture died out, the wings of the building became dwellings. Then the bank bought the building and started with future Governor James Bowdoin as president.

The house Mayor Quincy occupied at the corner was a gift from his uncle, who was also a president of the Massachusetts Bank. The mayor's son has described the family home, center of Boston's political and social world, as a building "on the Common, commanding a view of the distant country and the western sky." Among old family friends who came to visit was John Adams. His last visit was in the fall of 1825 when the ex-President, just turned ninety, entered and left leaning on the arm of his son, President John Quincy Adams. Young Josiah Quincy recalled seeing "the two presidents of the United States together . . . the glow of delight which lighted up the countenance and kindled anew the eyes of the father as he looked proudly on his son and successor."

The building at the far end of Hamilton Place, most recently a theater and then a department store annex, is enclosed in some of the original walls of Boston's famous Music Hall. The location was gloriously accessible when building of the Music Hall got under way in 1852. Here, on the hall's site, was once the mansion of two of the town's leading coachmakers, the first one a Tory who fled. Their mansion grounds included not only access to Tremont Street but flower gardens large enough to accommodate a driveway across the front of the family mansion from Bromfield Street on the north to Winter Street on the south.

The Music Hall, built to furnish Puritan Boston with its first center of musical culture, was inspired and funded by the Harvard Musical Association, whose library and meeting place at 57A Chestnut Street we have already visited. The leader and association president, ex-clergyman John Sullivan Dwight, said music in Boston had been too long "in the doldrums." Boston did have the Handel & Haydn Society (since 1815) but lacked a large hall with adequate acoustics. Both were provided by the Music Hall. The 2,000 seats were even "comfortable." There was a new system of "agreeable lighting with gas," and in 1863, risking Confederate corsairs, the members brought over from Europe a great pipe organ. Soon after the war's end the Harvard

Orchestra gave its first concert on December 18, 1865. By the 1880s Boston was giving birth to other musical endeavors.

Major Henry Lee Higginson, a Boston banker and former cavalry officer wounded during the Civil War, asked composer George Henschel to form the Boston Symphony Orchestra, and it opened its first season in the Music Hall on October 22, 1881. Henschel in later years was knighted by King George V. Higginson, who acquired a lifelong love of music as a student in Vienna, gave roughly $1,000,000 to meet symphony expenses before his death in 1919. The popular Boston Pops, first called Promenade Concerts, were initiated in 1885 to help stabilize employment for the musicians.

The Music Hall also provided a pulpit and antislavery forum for the Reverend Theodore Parker, a grandson of the Captain Parker who had led the Minutemen at Lexington on April 19, 1775. In the Music Hall, from 1852 to 1859 when his health gave out, Parker, fearlessly independent, championed many social reforms. Others helped him. Wendell Phillips, after a memorial meeting here for abolition martyr John Brown was disrupted, was followed all the way to his South End residence by the threatening mob. Emerson frequently addressed Parker's congregation during Parker's absence and after his death.

On a January night in 1882, with snow so heavy that horse-car travel had to be suspended, Oscar Wilde turned the tables on some bewigged collegians who had come to mock him. The Music Hall was jammed. Wilde had been sent on an American tour by showman D'Oyly Carte to promote Gilbert and Sullivan's *Patience.* Wilde had been appearing in knee breeches like Bunthorne, a character in the operetta. Just before Wilde came onstage, sixty "Harvard students in dress coats, knee breeches and silk stockings with lilies in their buttonholes" marched two-by-two to prearranged front seats "to lampoon the world's No. 1 Aesthete." But Wilde won the audience when he emerged in conventional attire and made the jokesters the butt of the joke. After winning applause, Wilde assured the students that "there was more to the movement of aestheticism than knee breeches and sunflowers!"

The building at 7–9 Hamilton Place, its brick facade remodeled in the mid-1880s to the present imitation granite, was once the rectory of the fashionable Central Congregational Church. The church, with its pilasters and fluted stone columns, stood at 25–29 Winter Street from 1841 to 1865, when the congregation moved to a new church on Newbury Street as commerce overspread the downtown area.

"Jamie" Fields spent his last five years as a publisher on the south corner at 125 Tremont Street. Instead of the green curtain at the Old Corner, Fields had a fancy office on the second-floor front, along with a plush Authors' Room frequented by the glittering authors on his list. On the first floor was a great showroom with gas-lighted chandeliers. Here Fields got exclusive American rights to Dickens's books and arranged lecture tours for popular writers. "Boston madness!" was the way big George Dolby described the half-mile line of admirers to 125 Tremont, trying to buy tickets at $2.00 each for Dickens's first lecture. Some in the line were there from the night before with mattresses, blankets, and food. Little wonder speculators were able to ask and get $25 a ticket.

A bit farther south along Tremont Street we come to St. Paul's Cathedral, with its classical Greek portico of six massive sandstone Ionic columns and pediment. This was the creation in 1819 of two architects, Alexander Parris, soon to build the great Quincy Market next to Faneuil Hall, and Solomon Willard. As had been the case with the King's Chapel steeple, funds ran out for the bas-relief of St. Paul before the Emperor Agrippa, which Willard had planned to carve for the pediment. Costs of building had run more than double the estimates, a problem even for such wealthy Boston parishioners from Beacon Hill as Jonathan Mason, Harrison Gray Otis, David Sears, and William Appleton. Most active in seeing the cathedral to completion were Daniel Webster and Dr. John Collins Warren, long senior warden.

A visit to the cathedral is very rewarding. A hero long associated with it was Dr. Joseph Warren, killed at Bunker Hill. The British buried him on the battlefield. Friends the next year removed the body to the Old Granary, after Paul Revere positively identified the denture that he had made for Warren. Warren was interred in the cathedral crypt after it was completed, until he was removed to the Warren family plot in Forest Hills in 1855.

Next to St. Paul's on the corner of Temple Place, a Masonic Temple was built, 1830–1832, a Gothic structure with two great towers that gave the side street its name. This is where Emerson was launched as a distinguished lecturer, not by his preliminary single lecture here in 1832 after he left his North End pulpit, but by a series of ten lectures on English literature given in the winter of 1835–1836, followed the next winter by a dozen on religion and politics as well.

Two prominent teachers taught here—Bronson Alcott and Elizabeth Peabody. Bronson, regarded by Emerson as "the highest genius of his time," opened his Temple School for children in 1834. His assistant was Miss Peabody, who had most of the eighteen pupils gathered in the gas-lighted, chilly, fourth-floor room looking out "two little holes," as she called them, in the top of an arched Gothic window. The celebrated school came to an abrupt end in three years when Bronson, overruling Miss Peabody's warnings, included in his widely circulated books on his teaching techniques the then taboo knowledge: "A mother suffers when she has a child. . . . She gives up her body to God and he works upon it and brings forth the child's spirit in a little body of its own."

A Charles Bulfinch triumph, Colonnade Row, a block of nineteen brick houses along Tremont Street between West and Avery Streets, was built in 1811, with five more soon after on the south end of the row. They were all four-stories high and had iron balconies at the second-floor level supported by Doric columns that gave them their name. Their grand view of the Common to the Charles River drew residents like Amos Lawrence, William Lawrence, Jeremiah Mason, and John Lowell, the Federal pamphleteer and son of old Judge Lowell.

Lafayette, on entering the city in 1824, asked Mayor Quincy to let him know if he spotted the widow of John Hancock. As Lafayette's barouche, drawn by four white horses, was passing Colonnade Row, the Mayor pointed out where she was seated on the balcony of a friend. Lafayette, said the mayor's son, had the coachman stop, then "rose and saluted her with a profound bow." She made a curtsy and the crowd cheered. That night, after the big civic dinner of welcome, Lafayette, before going to the Quincy house in Hamilton Place, visited her at her Federal Street dwelling. The widow Hancock had been chatelaine of the Hancock mansion when, as an American volunteer officer, Lafayette came to Boston about a half-century earlier.

Tremont on the Common at 151 Tremont, a twenty-eight-story apartment building with recessed penthouses built in 1967, covers much of the acreage that was once Colonnade Row. Covering a bit more is seventeen-story Parkside completed in 1988, at 170 Tremont, just south of Tremont on the Common. Across from the south corner of Tremont on the Common is an 1888 monument to the victims of the Boston Massacre, the scene of which we shall presently visit on State Street.

At the northeast corner of Boylston Street, where we now see the 1897–1899 Grand Lodge of Massachusetts Masons, the third built on this site, Boston's second-oldest theater was raised in 1796. It was called the Haymarket for Boston's nearby South End haymarket. As feared, the big three-story wooden building soon went up in flames, but it remains a pleasant part of our nation's lore. Although "Old Ironsides" got stuck on the ways at its first attempted launching, it splashed into the water beautifully in the playlet staged that night at the Haymarket Theater.

Women's Heritage Trail

It was here at 174 Tremont Street that Fannie Farmer established Boston's first women's school for professional cooking. She revolutionized cooking in 1896 when she included scientific measurements in her newly published recipe book.

The Haymarket Theater has had many descendants in this area. From its site and on down Tremont Street—once but a short distance to the shore of the Back Bay—developed Boston's theater district.

Climbing ticket costs, ready access to videos, and a welter of electronic home entertainment options combined to depress this traditional theater district. In the late 1980s, though, the sizable growth of local and repertory groups did ignite something of a revival. The area was declared a "Midtown Cultural District" by city administrators, who hoped a revitalization of the area would effectively elbow out the denizens of the tenacious nearby red-light district, known locally as the "Combat Zone." The revitalization is well under way as the renovation of theaters and new construction proceeds apace to provide rehearsal and performance spaces for a vital theatrical population.

On our right, about halfway down the block to Stuart Street, is an example of the transformation. The old Majestic Theater, acquired by Emerson College in 1983, was designed by noted architect John Galen Howard and was truly majestic when it opened in 1903. The greatest stars have performed on its stage. As times changed, it was renamed and became part of a movie chain. Television closed it down. But the Emerson trustees, though planning to move their college to Lawrence, as we will shortly see, voted in 1988 to renovate the old Majestic as a 1,000-seat theater, which opened in the fall of 1989. Emerson has kept a contributing presence in Boston that will help local nonprofit art groups and Emerson students as the college works to expand its theater arts division.

Some dozen Boston theaters, in or close to this stretch, were the creations of one Boston architect, Clarence Blackhall, the first president of the Boston Architectural Club. A few highly regarded ones are still with us, all worth visiting for their magnificent interiors. The Colonial, just to our right on Boylston Street, Blackhall built in 1900. Ahead of us on the left side of Tremont Street is his small, delightful Wilbur playhouse, built in 1914. In 1988–1989 the Wilbur was given a magnificent renovation, with a comedy club created in the basement. A bit farther is one of the world's biggest theaters, a glittering forty-four-hundred-seat movie palace when Adolph Zukor opened it as the Metropolitan in 1925. Its stage was recently enlarged for a new opera house, and in 1983 it was renamed Wang Center for the Performing Arts, in tribute to its princely benefactor, the inventor and philanthropist Dr. An Wang. Across the street from it is the Shubert, created in 1910 by a different architect.

Historic tales go with both south corners of the intersection of Boylston Street and Tremont. On the southeast corner, where the former Renaissance Hotel Touraine of 1896–1897 (now all apartments) still stands, "62 Boylston" was the three-story house of President John Quincy Adams. While living here, he had his law office in Court Street, was chosen U.S. senator, broke with the Federalist Party, and went on, before becoming President, to be the creator of the nation's far-reaching Monroe Doctrine.

George Washington, during his 1789 visit, came early in the morning to a building on the southwest corner to see "14 girls spinning with both hands" at twenty-eight looms recently installed to produce duck, a fabric woven for sails. Those of "Old Ironsides" were made from cloth woven here. The present large structure, the Little Building at 80 Boylston Street, was also designed by Blackhall and replaced the six story Pelham Hotel of 1857, America's first apartment hotel, each floor occupied by a single family and called a French flat.

Blackhall's Colonial Theatre at 106 Boylston Street replaced the Italian villalike edifice Bostonians built in 1855–1858 as a new home and reading room for the Boston Public Library, the first major one in the United States free to all. Its collection, steadily increased by gifts of rare private libraries, was moved in 1895 to the great Renaissance building erected in Copley Square in the heart of the Back Bay, which we shall be visiting.

This part of Boylston Street was long called Piano Row for the concentration of musical businesses. Two short byways off Boylston are of special interest before we reach Park Square. First, Boylston Place. At Number 4 on the right is the Tavern Club, founded in 1883–1884 by some congenial diners-out in a second-floor studio at nearby 1 Park Square. The private club's first president, William Dean Howells, described the membership as "the best and nicest young lawyers, doctors, artists and litterateurs," high-class Bohemians with a taste for fine food and wine. With their totem, a bear, they moved here in 1887 and, along with annual plays and celebrations, have continued to entertain many of the city's distinguished visitors.

Then, the newly renamed Edgar Allan Poe Way. This alley just beyond 162 Boylston Street was once Carver Street, a long street running roughly eastward near the shore of the Back Bay. On Carver Street, within sight of the bay, Edgar Allan Poe, a sickly child, was born on January 19, 1809; his parents lived in a lodging house later designated 62 Carver Street. They were actors in a stock company at Boston's first regular theater. At 77 Carver Street, in 1845, was the home of Horace Mann, great organizer of public education. To it came his brother-in-law, Nathaniel Hawthorne, for a stay the following year. Mann and Hawthorne a few years earlier had married Elizabeth Peabody's sisters. The house of Poe's birth and the Mann and Hawthorne residences, along with most of the street, disappeared some time ago.

As we arrive at old Park Square, all filled land, we are on what was the shore of the Back Bay. The city, as part of the area's redevelopment, extensively modernized old Park Square and renamed it Park Plaza.

On our right on the southwest side of Charles Street and opening on both the Public Garden and plaza area is the Four Seasons luxury hotel-and-condominium structure completed in 1984. A short way along Charles Street on our left is the state's curving, jutty, eight-story Transportation Building, also opened in 1984, premier part of the plaza redevelopment. Just west of it is the twelve-story Heritage on the Garden, a mix of retail and office space and luxury condos completed in 1988. Besides furnishing office space for about 2,000 employees, principally of State Public Works (port, transport, and turnpike authorities), the building provides street-level shops and features a striking eight-story atrium section called City Place, where office, retail, and food outlets are intended to draw nighttime patronage to the area. The atrium passages interlink neighboring streets and the theater district.

The *Emancipation Group* statue by Thomas Ball is a replica of the one unveiled in Washington, D.C., in 1875, and was given to the city four years later. It stands in front of where Boston's first railroad depot to the south, the Boston & Providence, began operations on filled land in 1835, at the original junction of Eliot Street and Broadway, just west of the new Charles Street South extension. This was a station used by Abraham Lincoln on his visits to Boston.

Lincoln's statue faces Railroad Mall across the Common, which he used. Railroad Mall passes the grave of Gilbert Stuart, which we saw, and still provides a direct route back to Tremont Street. We can go along Tremont to School Street, and down School to the Old South Meeting House, where we will resume our walk.

Old South Meeting House to Tea Party

Americans showed how strongly they felt about the Old South Meeting House when word spread that it was in the path of the catastrophic fire of 1872, roaring through the commercial center of Boston. Bell's telephone invention was still three years away. But America had telegraph, and anxious inquiries poured in from all over the nation to learn if the Old South was still there.

The Old South that we see succeeded in 1729 a smaller cedar Meeting House, the one coveted by the first royal governor, Edmund Andros. So the Old South—Boston's second-oldest church building—was already almost a half-century old at the time of the pre-Revolutionary events that have so endeared it to America.

There are many displays and mementos of those days to be seen inside. The original sounding board is still over the pulpit where James Otis, Samuel Adams, and Joseph Warren exhorted their fellow Bostonians to demand their rights as British subjects. Behind the pulpit is the window through which Joseph Warren crawled to deliver the 1775 oration on the anniversary of the Boston Massacre. Redcoats swarmed within, jamming the steps to the pulpit and threatening Warren's life, which he would in but a few weeks give at Bunker Hill. On the east wall are the original galleries—the first is the one in which George Washington stood when he first entered Boston after forcing the redcoats to flee in their ships. The pews had been removed and used for fuel, just like John Winthrop's old house next door. Sand overspread the floor for the Meeting House to serve as a riding school for General Burgoyne's light dragoons.

What Washington surveyed was not the entire desecration and vandalizing. The Reverend Thomas Prince's great collection of books, which the Old South's minister housed in the steeple, had been looted. Missing, until found a century later in London, was Governor

Bradford's manuscript of the history of the founding of Plymouth Plantation. And the gallery in which Washington stood had been converted into an officers' bar.

Impressive reminders of two of the women honored on the Boston Women's Heritage Trail are on view. America's first Afro-American woman poet, Phillis Wheatley (c. 1753–1784), bought as a slave in childhood and raised by the Wheatley family, was an Old South member. There is a life-size likeness of Mary Tileston Hemenway (1820–1894) distinguished preservationist, who in 1876–1877 gave two checks—both on display—totaling $200,000 to help save the Old South then threatened with demolition.

Among the displays we see is some of the actual tea tossed into the harbor at the Boston Tea Party. That is linked to the most exciting event ever at the Old South. It was also the most crucial, for it led to the decree closing the port of Boston, to the arrival of regiments of redcoats to enforce that decree, to mounting tension between the authorities and the patriots, to the patriots' secreting arms to protect themselves, and to the inevitable outbreak of war when redcoats were sent to grab the arms and arrest the two men most conspicuously excluded from any royal pardon, John Hancock and Samuel Adams.

The meeting was called at 10:00 A.M. on the deadline day, December 16, 1773; if the tea was not sent back before midnight, it would be subject to duty—a tax unalterably opposed by the patriots because it had been voted by Parliament and not by their own legislature. Some 7,000 citizens from Boston and surrounding towns had come to the overflow meeting and crowded the streets outside.

Samuel Adams, a skillful showman, had planned the meeting to demonstrate to the world that the patriots had no other course than the one confronting them. Hours passed as messengers went by horseback to ask again that the royal governor grant the tea ships a pass to depart. Hutchinson was not at his official residence, diagonally across the street in Province House, but at his estate in Milton. Hutchinson was adamant. Besides, he had a conflict of interest. Two of the consignees were his sons. It was after dark when the final messenger, an owner of the tea ship *Dartmouth,* returned with Hutchinson's repeated refusal. Adams now rose and gave the signal. "This meeting," he told the throng, "can do nothing more to save the country." There was a war whoop in the gallery in answer to a band of men, some dressed as Indians, giving a loud war whoop at the Milk Street entrance of the Meeting House. The band thereupon headed down Milk Street. Most of the crowd followed from the candlelit Meeting House.

We shall take the route they took to the waterfront, taking note of some points of interest along the way.

On the opposite corner of Milk Street, firebrands from the top of the old Transcript Building, which was engulfed in flames, did set fire to the steeple of the Old South during the 1872 fire. But just at that moment rescue came with the arrival of self-propelled Kearsarge 3, a steamer with fire up, sent by rail from Portsmouth, New Hampshire. In moments a pressurized hose brought water to the Old South roof, which quenched the flames as thousands of spectators cheered the firefighters. The Transcript Building, then only twelve years old, was completely gutted, as were all the buildings along the east side of Washington Street south of the Transcript to Summer Street. Indeed, all buildings for 6 blocks down the south side of Milk Street to Pearl Street, which we will be walking, and the buildings from Washington Street east to the harbor were consumed as part of the sixty-five acres of structures that were reduced to ashes and debris.

Back in the 1600s on the site at former 19 Milk Street (now incorporated in 1 Milk Street) was the home of a widow who became the bride of Boston's first settler, the Reverend William Blackstone. After Governor Endecott tied the knot, Blackstone, with his bride riding on his steer, set out for his new domain in Rhode Island's future Blackstone Valley.

At this same site stood a two-story cottage with pitch roof that was the birthplace in 1706 of Benjamin Franklin, the fifteenth of seventeen children. On the day of his birth Ben was taken across the street to be baptized at the Old South. Pennywise Ben displayed his thrifty nature quite early in life. While helping his father get a big slaughtered pig down the bulkhead into storage, young Ben suggested that his father say grace over the entire pig. This, observed Ben, would save blessing it each time the family sat down to eat.

The twenty-two-story federal office building, post office, and courthouse at Devonshire Street was also named for John W. McCormack after his retirement as national Speaker of the House. It was built in 1931–1933 on the site of an earlier post office that was being constructed on the west half of the block at the time of the 1872 fire. The fireproof quality of the still-incomplete building gave the firemen a vantage to block the fire from sweeping westward as it roared north toward State Street. Meanwhile, over on State Street, frantic bankers were busy emptying vaults in their bank.

On the Fleet Bank Building, on the west corner at Federal and Milk Streets, a plaque reminds us that one of the nation's founders, Robert Treat Paine, lawyer, judge, and statesman, was born and resided all his life in the two-story brick mansion that stood here. Its gardens in back extended down Federal Street. Paine, also defying George III, signed just below Hancock on the Declaration of Independence.

We come now to old Post Office Square with its fairly small triangle of land around the George T. Angell memorial fountain to our left. The square, with its panoramic vistas of the ever-soaring towers of Boston's financial center, was expanded to 1.7 acres when completed in early 1990. Open space was achieved with the help of Mayor Flynn, the city, and local businessmen, who raised $82 million to demolish the 900-car city garage that once stretched between Milk and Franklin Streets, replacing it with an underground garage accommodating 1,400 cars plus the spacious, magnificent, midcity park.

A few steps beyond, at the northeast corner of Congress and Water Streets, William Lloyd Garrison, just turned twenty-six, began publishing *The Liberator* on January 1, 1831, demanding an immediate end to slavery. His small quarters were on the third floor of Merchants' Hall. The poet James Russell Lowell wrote:

The place was dark, unfurnitured and mean;
Yet there the freedom of a race began.

Most thrilling was the intrepid declaration of young, close-to-penniless newspaperman Garrison when, despite the danger, he declared in that first issue: "I am in earnest; I will not equivocate; I will not excuse; I will not retreat a single inch; and I will be heard." Vicious opposition, as we shall presently see, quickly imperiled his life.

Some background before we head along Pearl Street, which leads in 3 blocks to the scene of the Tea Party. Pearl Street in colonial times was called Hutchinson Street, after the distinguished family of our last royal civil governor. Up to 1794, when nine ropewalks stretching on the west side of the street to the waterfront burned down, among them Hutchinson property that the state had confiscated, there was only one residence on the street—that, on the northeast side, of a hated Tory customs commissioner who had fled.

Beautiful Federal residences with lovely gardens followed on the sites of the vanished ropewalks, new dwellings of some of Boston's most noted families. A great Boston merchant, James Perkins, lived at 13 Pearl Street, and a year before his death he gave it to the growing Boston Athenaeum for a new home; here it was located from 1822 to 1849. Numbering on Pearl Street at the time was old-style consecutive, as persists today on Hamilton Place. As a result, we come first on our right to the site of the mansion of James Perkins's brother, Thomas Handasyd Perkins, which was at 17 Pearl Street. This mansion Thomas Handasyd Perkins gave in 1833 to Dr. Samuel Gridley Howe's new community service for the blind, which was later renamed the Perkins School for the Blind.

The Perkins School was located just after Franklin Street, and a bit father along, about midblock, was the Athenaeum. In back of it was built the new exhibition and lecture building designed by Solomon Willard in 1826, the place where Boston was introduced to visual arts and the place where Gilbert Stuart came grouchily to the first public exhibit the following year.

At the northwest corner of Pearl and High Streets, on our left, was, from 1805 to 1815, the three-story residence of future Mayor Josiah Quincy, while he served in the state Senate and Congress. The land stretching up Fort Hill was occupied by his stable, coach house, and garden and afforded a magnificent view of the harbor and islands. A granddaughter of Thomas Handasyd Perkins tells how he loved to walk to the top of the hill, and how one spring day, taking Harrison

Gray Otis there after lunch, he spotted one of his China trade ships coming in the harbor just a year after it had sailed to the Orient.

Pearl Street, after it was transformed into a center of the boot and shoe trade, was completely burned on both sides by the 1872 fire, all the way to the sea. It has again been going through a transformation.

At the northeast corner of Milk and Pearl Streets, One Post Office Square, has now risen a forty-story office tower with garage and the 300-plus-room Hotel Meridien, a renovation of the 1922 granite-and-limestone Federal Reserve Bank. Quotes from founding fathers and state mottoes on the facade still appear on what was the Federal Reserve's first New England building after starting in 1914 in two rented basement rooms at 101 Milk Street. Stop in to view the collection of eighteenth- and nineteenth-century maps of Boston on display in the hotel lobby.

The State Street Bank Building at the Franklin Street corner, on our left, with thirty-four floors, was built in 1963–1965. This was the first skyscraper in Boston to rise higher than the nearby twenty-nine-story Custom House tower, which for a half-century had been the highest skyscraper in New England. The twenty-story New England Telephone Building (now a Bell Atlantic building) on our right, which we will visit on our next walk, was built in 1947 with a thirteen-story addition in the rear in 1966–1967.

Continuing along Pearl Street, we glance to the left as we reach High Street; forty-six-story International Place in 1986 replaced a garage that occupied what was once the summit of old Fort Hill—a view now almost blocked by the new pair of towers of 125 High Street. The Hill, of course, soared 50 feet high before being removed in 1866–1872 and used mostly to fill the outer part of old Town Cove and create Atlantic Avenue along the waterfront. In the earlier days of fine houses, Washington Square (a circle, of course) was on the hilltop. Among its noted residents in 1822 was Gilbert Stuart. High Street, incidentally, started life as Cow Lane and acquired the no-longer-descriptive name because it used to lead to the summit of Fort Hill.

Continue along Pearl Street, by the Travelers Building at 125 High Street, with its twenty-one-story and thirty-story towers and splendid lobby completed in 1990, to Purchase Street. Here the present name is descriptive. It was along here that Boston, which built and serviced ships, had its first ropewalk on the harbor side of Cow Lane. The town bought the land in 1736, put in a shore road extension, and called it Purchase Street. It was near the older, southern end of the street that Samuel Adams was born in 1722.

Griffin's Wharf was at the present end of Pearl Street and began a few feet to the left. It extended into the harbor across where we now see traffic flowing in and out of the tunnel on the John F. Fitzgerald Expressway, named for President Kennedy's grandfather, affectionately called "Honey Fitz," a congressman and Boston mayor.

A lot of planning went into staging the Tea Party. The whooping participants who came from the Old South via Pearl Street were not the only ones. Groups had prepared in at least ten places around the town in shops, houses, taverns, and clubs. They had to know how to handle tackle and have the skill and strength to move chests weighing as much as 360 pounds—in all some fifty tons of tea on three brigs—and it all had to be done fast. British warships stood only 500 yards away. The 119 known participants were in groups, each with a leader. Their spirits were heightened, if possible, as they passed the ropewalks on Pearl (Hutchinson) Street, where brawling between workmen and redcoats had led to the Boston Massacre.

British Admiral John Montagu, commander of the British warships, called from a Tory's window to a group of Tea Party patriots as they started back to town: "Well boys, you have had a fine, pleasant evening for your Indian caper, haven't you. But mind, you have got to pay the fiddler, yet." Whereupon the group's leader, Lendall Pitts, a nephew of James Bowdoin, called back: "Never mind, squire. Just come out here, if you please, and we'll settle the bill in two minutes." The admiral slammed down the window.

To get firsthand impressions of the event, walk to the right along Purchase Street to Congress Street, then left across Atlantic Avenue and the expressway to midway on the Congress Street Bridge. There is something that young Charles Dickens was too early to see when he walked to the Tea Party site with his friends Longfellow and Senator Sumner: an actual working ship, *Beaver II,* representing the original brig, along with a museum and fascinating exhibits.

While in this waterfront area take note of two interesting museums in refurbished warehouses on the far side of Fort Point Channel: the Children's Museum, which was long an attraction of Jamaica Pond, and, sharing present Museum Wharf, the Computer Museum that moved here from the high-tech area of Marlboro. They share the first floor. The Children's Museum, which shifted to the six-story-brick-and-timber former woolens warehouse in 1979, has expanded its fascinating presentation to include all but two top floors used for the computer exhibits. Museum Wharf, with ample seating among its attractions along Fort Point Channel, affords a splendid waterfront view of the 1970s and 1980s "Manhattanization" of Boston's financial district. The panorama now sweeps from one forty-six-story skyscraper to another, loftily upstaging the once all-dominating Custom House.

THIS DESTRUCTION OF THE TEA IS SO BOLD, SO DARING, SO FIRM, INTREPID AND INFLEXIBLE, AND IT MUST HAVE IMPORTANT CONSEQUENCES.

—JOHN ADAMS

The best way back is to go along Congress Street and turn left at Milk Street back to the Old South, where we will begin our next walk. On our left we see the thirty-three-story Federal Reserve, built in 1972–1976. The Federal Reserve has its own greenhouse, where plants are grown for their landscaping purposes. There are guided tours, but most of the building is out of bounds to the general public. The public is permitted to use a beautiful skylighted gallery on the first floor and a fine 400-seat auditorium in the four-story, low-rise section along Congress Street. The thirty-two-floor Keystone Building (1968–1970) at the south corner of Purchase Street and Congress, with its connecting three-sided window bays, shows a pioneer use of Travertine marble (from a quarry near Rome) on the exterior of a high rise. We also get a closer view of the huge BankBoston skyscraper, which is often given the descriptive nickname "the Pregnant Building."

Walking north, back along Congress Street, we turn left at Milk Street and return to the Old South.

Province House to Canyonland

Diagonally across Washington Street from the Old South Meeting House—just about opposite the head of Milk Street—was the finest mansion in colonial Boston, Province House, one of the two centers of political power in that era. The other, a block away, was the Old State House.

The three-story brick structure of Province House, with a great pitched and dormered roof topped with a lofty cupola, was set well back from Boston's main highway and amid spacious lawns and gardens, with great stables in the rear. It was built in 1679 by a wealthy London merchant, Peter Sergeant, a prominent magistrate and for a time a witchcraft judge. The Earl of Bellomont, quondam friend of Captain Kidd, had complained that prospering Boston had no official residence for the royal governors. So when a new governor was expected, the province took advantage of Sergeant's recent death to purchase his mansion and grounds in 1716.

The great hall and magnificent rooms of Province House were the town's official setting of gaiety and pomp during the administrations of the last eight royal governors. All the great figures of that period came up the paved path to the massive stone steps that led to the portico and the palatial entrance. The royal coat of arms that adorned the portico—as well as Shem Drowne's gilded Indian with bow and arrow atop the cupola—are still with us at the Massachusetts Historical Society.

Young Colonel George Washington used these steps more than once during his Boston visit in 1756. Losses at cards that he recorded occurred during play with fellow officers and social leaders in the lavish rooms of the mansion. And here he gave Governor Shirley a firsthand account of the death of Shirley's young son, who, fighting beside Washington, lost his life on the battlefield as part of General Braddock's defeat in the 1755 French and Indian War.

Province House was often a key setting in our nation's history. After the shocking arrest of Dr. Benjamin Church as a spy for the

British, Paul Revere recalled how surprised he had been to have witnessed Church's conviviality with British officers on the stone steps of the portico. It was in Province House that General Gage signed the fateful orders that sent the redcoats to Lexington and Concord. And it was also here that General Howe, hard pressed by Washington's fortifying of Dorchester Heights, signed orders for the hasty flight from Boston. Province House played a role in post-Revolutionary Boston's medical history. When Bostonians were trying to organize Boston's first public hospital, the Massachusetts General, the state deeded Province House and its land to the hospital to provide essential funds.

Commercial building in the area brought decline and eventual decay to Province House. In its last years, before it was destroyed by fire in 1864, it was in part an inn and tavern. Nathaniel Hawthorne, working for the Boston customs, used to drop in for a glass of port sangaree and a cigar and picked up legends from the kindly old boniface that became part of his *Twice-Told Tales.* Typical was Hawthorne's "Howe's Masquerade." As the mix of ghost story and romantic history goes, General Howe staged a masked ball "to hide the distress and danger" in beleaguered Boston in the latter part of the siege. British officers and Loyalist gentry came to the merrymaking and "the brilliantly-lighted apartments were thronged." Part of the merriment was the appearance of a group dressed in old regimentals purporting to be Washington and his officers. The never-explained part, as Hawthorne described it, was a mysterious funeral halting in front of Province House, with its slow funeral march, and then, in historical order, the ghosts of the Puritan governors and royal governors descending the stately staircase in allegorical procession. Howe himself was in it. To Hawthorne it was the funeral "of royal authority in New England."

There is irony in the fact that the fire that swept through Province House in 1864 leveled everything but some of the old brick walls. Just eight years later, when Washington Street was menaced by the great fire of 1872, not a single structure on the west side of Washington was damaged. Firemen, by using hoses, and owners, by covering buildings with wet blankets and rugs, saved them, while fire devoured everything on the east side of the street south to the present Filene's.

Midway down Washington Street between Milk and Franklin Streets, on our left, was the dwelling of one of our country's heroic young patriots, Josiah Quincy. His oratory drew crowds to the Old South. He was a complete idealist. "To inquire my duty, and to do it, is my all," he declared, and insisted that even the redcoats of the Boston Massacre were entitled to a fair trial. Despite abuse, he and John Adams defended them. Against doctor's orders, he was returning from a patriot mission in England when he died within sight of our shore. He was thirty-one.

Bromfield Street, next on our left, was named for a prominent merchant of colonial days, whose mansion occupied a historic site. It was on the south (left) side, where the old passage to the stables still goes beside the building at 30 Bromfield. Here, after merchant Bromfield's time, were successively the dwelling of a Revolutionary hero, Thomas Cushing; a stagecoach house; and then Bromfield House, an inn. On August 10, 1774, the Bay State's delegates to our first Continental Congress assembled here in the parlor of the dwelling of one of them, Thomas Cushing, Speaker of the House, an office in those days held in higher esteem than that of the royal governor. The date and place for the first congress had been set by Samuel Adams. The carriage carrying the Adamses, Cushing, and Robert Treat Paine took off from here and defiantly passed British troops on the Common.

Pre–Civil War martyr John Brown knew Bromfield Street. Abolitionist Dr. Samuel G. Howe, who developed and headed the Perkins School for the Blind, had his town office at 20 Bromfield. It was a center for antislavery fund-raising. Brown visited here and the school in South Boston. Howe recruited Free Soil emigrants to go to "Bleeding" Kansas. Brown was back here again "just before his movement on Harper's Ferry," the assault on the arsenal that led to Brown's execution in 1859.

Bromfield House is associated with the last, sad days of Hawthorne. His college mate, former President Franklin Pierce, came to Bromfield House to take the sick author for a leisurely carriage trip to New Hampshire's hills and lakes. Hawthorne—"so haggard, so white, so deeply scarred with pain"—had refused to see a doctor. His wife appealed to "Jamie" Fields to get Oliver Wendell Holmes to judge Hawthorne's condition. So Holmes set out from the Old Corner Bookstore to try. They met at Bromfield House, walked the nearby streets. Holmes reported that Hawthorne "evidently had no hope of recovering his health." A month later he died in a Plymouth, New Hampshire, hotel.

Abraham Lincoln came to Bromfield Street. On September 15, 1848, in Washington Hall, on the third floor of what was then 21 Bromfield, Lincoln made the first of his unrecorded campaign speeches in this area for future President Taylor. Most "Conscience" Whigs hereabouts, all of whom would one day support Lincoln for president, were opposed to "Old Rough and Ready" Taylor. Once again Lincoln was in strange proximity to the path of his future assassin. John Wilkes Booth, during his only professional job in Boston, in the old Museum on Tremont Street in 1863, boarded in the Bromfield House. While Lincoln's words went unrecorded, he spoke for an hour and a half in a way, the Boston Atlas said, that "for sound reasoning, cogent argument and keen satire, we have seldom heard equalled."

Before we return to Washington Street, notice a short way along Province Street, on its left-hand side, some granite steps leading to a landing and then into Bosworth Street. Overhead is an iron arch with a lantern. Province Street used to be called Governor's Alley and ran in the rear of Province House. These steps used to lead down to the gardens, stables, and coach house of Province House.

For eighteen years Dr. Oliver Wendell Holmes lived in a house at the northeast corner of Bosworth Street, after his marriage in 1840. All of his children were born here, and while living here he rose from professor of anatomy to dean of Harvard Medical School. When he was twenty-three he published two of his Autocrat articles in a magazine that failed. But Holmes remembered, and in 1857, when he resumed them in the new *Atlantic Monthly* after a gap of twenty-five years, he led off with: "I was just going to say, when I was interrupted. . . ."

Ahead of us, as we return to Washington Street, is Franklin Street, leading down into the financial district, with the soaring walls of its skyscrapers converting streets into canyons. Franklin Street, previously the prosperous center of a worldwide wool industry rivaled only by London, was in the heart of the great fire of 1872, and its buildings were totally destroyed. The street was a creation of Charles Bulfinch and he named it for one of his heroes, Benjamin Franklin. He had filled quagmire and sea inlet at the lower end, and in 1793–1795 erected buildings that began the transformation of Boston from Colonial to Federal architecture. All that remains is the curve of the street and its greater width for an elliptical park, a width that for a time gave the 1872 firefighters hope that they could halt here the fire sweeping wildly northeastward from Summer Street.

Along the curve on the south side Bulfinch built, from Hawley Street to Devonshire Street, America's first block of town houses, sixteen three-story brick houses with entrances grouped on eight sets of stone steps. He called it the Tontine Crescent, beautifully reflecting similar crescents that he had seen in England in Bath and London. All were quickly occupied by Federal-era nabobs. Bulfinch pressed on, despite a growing economic recession caused by embittered trade relations with England. He had to give up building a second crescent on the north side. Instead he started putting up four double mansions.

Had John Jay's commercial treaty with England been quickly ratified, Bulfinch would have been saved. It was not. He was declared bankrupt and lost the unfinished mansions to creditors. It was still the age of unlimited liability, so Bulfinch's bankruptcy brought financial ruin on his family as well. He was confronted with steady need, and even when he was both Boston's chairman of selectmen and superintendent of police, he was put in the Court Street jail by his creditors.

Hawley Street began as Bishop's Alley, a shortcut to the original Trinity Church on Summer Street. On our left on Hawley Street, then called Board Alley, post-Revolution Bostonians made their first sustained effort to open a theater in 1792. They erected a stage in an old livery stable, put in 500 seats, and called it, defensively, the New Exhibition Room. All the while efforts were made to repeal a 1750 law banning theaters. The sheriff appeared and arrested the director for staging a so-called moral lecture that was actually Sheridan's comedy *The School for Scandal.* Governor Hancock considered the theater an "open assault upon the laws of government." But soon, even in old Puritan Boston, the 1750 law became a dead letter.

Along our walks in the fire area are many structures, some with facades much altered or modernized, that were built right after the 1872 conflagration. Many of these usually five-story structures resemble the ones that were destroyed. Virtually all the buildings on present Franklin Street from Hawley to Devonshire went up just after 1872. An exception on our right is the beautiful five-story 1934–1935 building at Number 49, which houses at the street level the Oratory of St. Thomas More, patron saint of barristers. St. Thomas was canonized in 1935 on the 400th anniversary of his beheading by Henry VIII; within hours of that canonization William Cardinal O'Connell dedicated this oratory to him. Its busy location brings worshippers to "a sanctuary that is at once religious, artistic and reposeful." It is part of Boston's Catholic Center. Here, in the adjoining building with modernized facade, is published the diocesan paper, *The Pilot.*

Bulfinch may be credited with Arch Street. The name comes from the arch in the center of his Tontine Crescent. Through his generosity the large room over the original street was made available both to the Boston Library Society, founded two years earlier, and the Massachusetts Historical Society, founded a year before that in 1791. The library remained until 1858, when the Tontine Crescent was demolished for commercial buildings.

At the northwest corner of Arch Street is one of the best of the postfire commercial buildings. It is a five-story structure of the 1874–1875 Renaissance style with a small attic and granite facing, some rough, some smooth, at 65 Franklin Street.

As we approach Devonshire Street, we should inspect these redbrick buildings with contrasting limestone trim on the south side of the street. Notice the delicately decorative upper floors of the five-story, redbrick buildings in neo-Greco style at 85–87 Franklin, built in 1873–1875. Most impressive is the adjoining corner block gracefully curving along the sidewalk line, with all twenty-seven of its bays, right around into Devonshire Street. The first four floors were built in 1873, the fifth in 1885. Still intact are the cast-iron storefront piers and limestone lintels.

At Devonshire Street we can look right and let our imaginations picture the firebrands streaking everywhere, the roaring holocaust that faced Fire Chief John Damrell as he stood here in 1872 on the roadway into Winthrop Square. The flames were engulfing the imposing predecessor to the James M. Beebe Company—the structure we see ahead in back of poet Robert Burns's statue. This five-story, granite-faced building at 1 Winthrop Square, which Beebe rebuilt in 1873–1874 with its much detailed facade, is considered to be one of the finest of the "commercial palaces" of the postfire period. At present its modernized interior (drop in and see the photos in the lobby) has a wide variety of professional uses.

Chief Damrell's efforts to hold the fire at Franklin Street proved futile. Dynamite, against Damrell's best judgment, was then employed to level buildings north of Franklin Street to stop the flames. Chief Damrell had studied the great Chicago fire of the prior year and concluded that dynamite was ineffectual. He proved right. The fire kept sweeping north toward State Street and east to the waterfront.

Two more of Bulfinch's architectural achievements graced this part of Franklin Street. Holy Cross Church, Boston's first edifice built specifically for Catholic services, stood on the southeast corner of Devonshire Street, where we now see part of the block-long 75 Federal Street building, a twenty-two-story Art Deco skyscraper built in 1929. (This skyscraper is linked, via a sumptuous, London-like, block-long marble retail gallery, to the 101 Federal Street building completed in 1988 with a thirty-one-story tower.) Near the entry to 111 Franklin Street is a stone plaque telling of the residence of Bishop Cheverus, which was in the rear of the church. We can still see what the exterior of the church was like when we visit Hanover Street in the North End, where Bulfinch's St. Stephen's Church, virtually identical with old Holy Cross, still stands.

In 1799 Father Matignon, who had been Father Cheverus's teacher in France, and Father Cheverus found the former French Huguenot chapel in School Street too small for the growing Catholic community and bought this land in Franklin Street. This left a shortage of funds, so admiring friends, both Catholic and Protestant, headed by President John Adams, started a building fund subscription. Bulfinch made a present of his design. The parish presented Bulfinch a silver tea urn now at the Museum of Fine Arts. Father Cheverus was consecrated Boston's first Catholic bishop in 1810. From 1867–1875 the ever-growing diocese completed another structure, the Cathedral of the Holy Cross, still in the present South End.

As one of the traveled Boston gentlemen eager to rid the town of the 1750 ban on theaters, Bulfinch took time from building his Tontine Crescent to put up Boston's first theater, opened in 1794. His payment was a gold medal entitling him to free admission for life. The theater faced Federal Street, at the northwest corner of Franklin, and extended back to Devonshire Street, then, in that stretch, called Theater Alley. Bulfinch described his theater as "lofty and spacious." It was brick with Corinthian columns and pilasters and a projecting arcade for visitors alighting from carriages. Four years later it was destroyed by fire, and although patrons quickly reconstructed it, it was built much less ornately. This later theater is where the Poes were having their Boston engagement when Edgar Allan Poe was born. The site was just part of the city block on which the thirty-nine-story Fleet Bank Building at 1 Federal Street was erected in 1971–1976.

Before we walk along Federal Street, let us visit the New England Telephone Building a block beyond at 185 Franklin. Before—or after—entering the building, enjoy the expansive, indeed awesome views of high-rise, late-twentieth-century Boston from this side of newly enlarged Post Office Square. A 12-foot-high, 160-foot-long mural in the lobby depicts telephone people's activities since Professor Bell's first demonstration of his invention to the present. Just off the lobby is the actual fifth-floor attic room overlooking old Scollay Square where Bell invented the phone. His assistant, Thomas A. Watson, checked each piece of workbench and attic preserved when the building was demolished in the late 1920s. These were reassembled here in 1959 along with Bell's models and tools. It is an extraordinary exhibit—and part of it is the original attic window through which we may see the view across old Scollay Square the way Bell saw it on June 3, 1875, when human voice sounds first traveled over a wire.

Federal Street to Where the Great Fire Began

The skyscrapers towering into the skyline on many of our recent walks, through Post Office Square and Winthrop Square, leave no doubt that we are in Boston's modern canyonland.

One of the most distinctive of the skyscrapers is the tall BankBoston building at 100 Federal Street on its ample, attractive two-acre plaza. This is a Boston financial giant, born in 1784 in Hamilton Place. There are thirty-seven floors, the top one a penthouse. The facing, or "skin," is of two-inch thick slabs of polished granite. The bulge, reminiscent of the top floors of our new City Hall, is an eight-story section from the sixth to the thirteenth floors, projecting out 30 feet on all four sides of the tower.

In a national sense, few Boston sites are more historic. Our continued existence as a nation hinged on what happened here in 1788, when intensely divided delegates assembled to decide whether Massachusetts would ratify the new Constitution to replace the ill-working Articles of Confederation. Shays' Rebellion had intensified division on whether the central government would be weak or strong. The scene was the Long Lane Meeting House at the southeast corner of Franklin and Federal Streets. Congregationalists had taken over the 1744 wooden structure, successor to a refitted barn used by Scotch-Irish Presbyterians when they arrived in Boston. The 1788 delegates had found the Old State House too small and shifted here, with John Hancock presiding in the pulpit. This scene is depicted in one of the murals we could see back of the Speaker's rostrum on our visit to the State House. Samuel Adams, ever opposed to strong central government, wanted guarantees of the people's rights. He was won over when Boston mechanics, assembled by Paul Revere at the Green Dragon Tavern, voted overwhelmingly for the new Constitution. "Well," said Adams when Revere came to Winter Street to tell him, "if they must have it, they must have it." Adams, though, still wanted a

Bill of Rights—and that compromise is what the mural showed Hancock proposing to the convention.

Boston celebrated with processions through the streets, firing salutes, and giving public dinners. Long Lane's name was promptly changed to Federal Street, and the church was renamed the Federal Street Church. The Reverend Jeremy Belknap, its rector, a Revolutionary hero and historian, in 1791 persuaded some like-minded friends to form the country's oldest historical society, the Massachusetts Historical Society. In 1809 Charles Bulfinch replaced the old church. It was Bulfinch's only Gothic church, and he designed it for his friend the new pastor, the Reverend William Ellery Channing, rector from 1803 to his death in 1842, a Unitarian preacher and founder of the American Association of Unitarian Churches.

At 160 Federal is just about the best example Boston can offer of an Art Deco skyscraper. The twenty-four-floor ziggurat is the former United Shoe Machinery Corporation Building, which the company erected in 1928–1929, when it controlled about all the shoe machinery business in this country. Redone in 1986 and renamed "The Landmark," it is now linked to 150 Federal and its twenty-eight-story tower with a multistory atrium on High Street built in 1987.

The sixteen-story, pedestaled Fiduciary Trust Building at 175 Federal has thirteen floors cantilevered on a slim steel stem of caisson supports that form the first three floors. No two of the six sides of the 1975–1977 building are the same size. This remarkable engineering work was designed to overcome unique underground obstacles of a subway tunnel, plus criss-crossing electric, gas, cable, water, and sewer lines.

If we walk on the brick walkway of the pedestal building, in a few steps Purchase Street is on our left and Dewey Square directly ahead.

To our left, on land where Purchase Street was later built, was the harbor-side homestead of Samuel Adams's father, Captain Samuel Adams, brewer, merchant, and pillar of his nearby church. Here were his fine dwelling, gardens, malt house, and other structures, and in front of them, where we see Dewey Square and Atlantic Avenue, were the harbor shore and the Adams dock. From here son Samuel went to Latin School and at fourteen entered Harvard College, where he became fascinated by political rights.

Directly across Dewey Square is the granite-faced, five-story South Station with a rooftop eagle perched above the big clock. The station was built in 1898 and renovated in 1989 to combine the terminal facilities of some half-dozen railroads entering Boston from Albany and the south.

A few yards along Atlantic Avenue to the right of the South Station was the birthplace of Revolutionary War hero Henry Knox. Knox's father was a sea captain, with a wharf directly across from his house on what was then called Sea Street. The southeast corner of the forty-six-story One Financial Center, covering more than an acre, was roughly the birthplace site. This skyscraper, completed in 1983, with garage, theater, restaurants, and lounges, is one of Boston's biggest building projects. Its atrium soars six floors. Dewey Square views from the glass-enclosed atrium are quite a treat. When we step outside and glance inland, we see the age of competing high rises and lofty atriums has been well advanced around Dewey Square, with 125 Summer Street's twenty-two stories (built 1989) looking like a giant Summer Street hallmark and the bright red pyramid roof of the twenty-story 99 Summer Street (built 1987) giving the street quite a distinctive skyline.

Let us now go around the Fiduciary pedestal building and back toward Washington Street via Summer Street.

For fashionableness and beauty, Summer Street, through the Federal era to the decade before the Civil War, was certainly among the premier avenues of America. The verdant trees along the sidewalk added to the elegance of the redbrick mansions. There were three delightful churches in the neighborhood, two of them on Summer Street. Love of horticulture learned in family gardens and orchards made this the true birthplace of Boston's Horticultural Society, the Public Garden, and the Arboretum.

The elite lived along Summer Street before the aristocratic dwellings were suddenly almost swept away by expanding manufacture and commerce. The Summer Street area had not one, but four residences of U.S. senators and, for years, the residence of the national Speaker. Here lived Boston's wealthiest merchant princes.

Boston's renowned mayor, Josiah Quincy, lived on Summer Street from 1815 to 1820 while he was in the state Senate, before becoming speaker on Beacon Hill and mayor. Describing Summer Street in that period, his son Edmund called it "one of the handsomest and most commodious in Boston, with ample stable room and every convenience that was then thought essential to a gentleman's residence."

Daniel Webster lived in a new, three-story brick house at the northwest corner of Summer and High Streets, 1825–1839, during service in both the national House and Senate. Lafayette came back to Boston in 1825 to lay the cornerstone of the Bunker Hill Monument, with Webster as orator of the day. That evening the Websters, after having their drawing room joined by a doorway to that of the neighboring Thorndike residence, gave a brilliant party for Lafayette, followed by all going to Bulfinch's Federal Street Theater.

The trees and shrubs in the brick courtyard of Daniel Webster Park near the site of the senator's residence are maintained by the owners of the thirty-three-story skyscraper at 100 Summer Street, built 1972–1974.

Boston's top multimillionaire in the early decades of the 1800s, Peter Chardon Brooks, an eminently charitable man, purchased Webster's house when the senator left to become secretary of state. Brooks, who started with few funds when he was twenty-one years of age, did so well as an insurance broker that he was able to retire fifteen years later in 1803. His immediate neighbors were also distinguished and prosperous.

The short portion of Devonshire Street on our right, between Summer Street and Winthrop Square, was called Winthrop Place until 1860. On it lived and died Rufus Choate, noted trial lawyer who followed Webster in the U.S. Senate in 1841, as well as members of both the Lodge and Cabot families. Elder Senator Henry Cabot Lodge was born in 1850 in Winthrop Place, then a double cul-de-sac with Otis Street.

Church Green, the triangular junction of Summer and Bedford Streets, was named for the church that stood on the converging lot, the New South Church. This octagonal edifice of hammered granite, with four fluted Doric columns and pediment on its portico, was designed in 1814 by Charles Bulfinch and was the only Boston church directly facing the sea. It was a successor to the meeting house in which Captain Samuel Adams was deacon and stood until swept away, too, by the pressures of expanding commerce in 1868.

One of the very best of the post–1872 fire structures is the building now on the same converging corner, the five-story granite Church Green Building of 1873–1874, which succeeded to the Bulfinch church site. This is a duplicate of the one ruined by the fire, a structure that was headquarters of the shoe and leather trade that dominated this section after the Civil War.

At the east corner of Lincoln and Summer Streets has long been located fire box number 52, with an old-fashioned light above it. This is the box where, belatedly, the alarm was rung for the 1872 conflagration. Loss of life in that fire, which began at the east corner of Kingston and Summer Streets, is still uncertain. Among firefighters eleven were killed and seventeen injured, most of them severely. The fact that the fire started on Saturday night when the wholesale district, and the building it began in, were practically deserted, held down loss of life. But per acre the fire loss exceeded that of the great Chicago fire a year earlier. Very few dwellings still remained in the area. The loss of nearly eight hundred buildings, reduced to rubble in the heart of New England's wool, dry goods, leather, shoe, and publishing enterprises, threw thousands out of work.

The impressive five-story building at 83–87 Summer (1877–1878), with its cast-iron store front, replaced a similar five-story mansard. Here the fire was first spotted by theatergoers shortly after 7:00 P.M. on November 9, a moonlit, Indian summer evening. Fifteen minutes passed before the alarm was sounded by a foot patrolman making his rounds a couple of blocks away. Within minutes of discovery, the flames had shot up an elevator shaft, burst into each floor, and firebrands started falling on nearby wooden mansard roofs. Damage within the next twenty hours, until the blaze was brought under control, would approximate a billion dollars in modern terms.

The building at 83–87 Summer covers the site of several pieces of Boston's history. Among tenants renting space at Number 87 was Albert Augustus Pope, a Civil War colonel who started marketing an

English bicycle, the high-wheeler Columbia, that he had seen at the Centennial Exposition in Philadelphia. Pope went on to pioneer bicycle manufacture in America, and in his office here in 1879 he founded America's first bicycle club. Business grew so rapidly he had to move in 1881 to much larger quarters at 597 Washington Street near Hayward Place.

Otis Street, directly in the path of the appalling 1872 flames, was not cut toward present Winthrop Square until 1812. Prior to that there was a mansion set near Otis Street and considerably back from Summer Street. It was surrounded by beautiful grounds from Otis to Arch Street, for the mansion belonged to a business grandee, Thomas Russell, a banker, State Street merchant, and pioneer in high-seas trade with Russia. The Russell mansion is most remembered, however, because it became a fashionable boarding house run by Leon Chappotin, and its guests included Jerome Bonaparte, brother of the emperor, and the American portrait genius Gilbert Stuart. By 1812, when the mansion was cleared away for new residences, Otis Street became home to residents such as noted merchant Robert Gould Shaw and the great scientist-sailor Nathaniel Bowditch, author of the epochal *Navigator.*

Gilbert Stuart made his first professional visit to Boston in 1805 at the urging of U.S. Senator Jonathan Mason, who was eager to get Stuart's portraits of his family and friends. Before Stuart's family arrived some months later and he started house hunting, Stuart's quarters were in Chappotin's boarding house. Business was brisk. Sitters had to wait for the master, who was also working here on his giant painting of George Washington beside his white charger at Dorchester Heights. Stuart was warmly thanked for exhibiting this unfinished painting at a gala Fourth of July banquet in the enlarged Faneuil Hall in 1806.

When Stuart's family did arrive, they regularly attended the Trinity Church, then a block away. Stuart, pretty much a nonchurchgoer, surprised them one morning by saying he would go along. All went fine. Stuart was even able to lean over in the private pew and take his customary pinch of snuff. On the family's way out, the minister, overjoyed, shook hands most warmly. "Well," said gabby, self-centered Stuart afterward, "I do not think I shall go to church again." "Why?" inquired his daughter Anne. "Oh, I do not like the idea of a man getting up in a box and having all the conversation to himself."

Before we come to the new Summer Street Mall, notice one of the places where Boston's Public Garden, which we will presently visit, got its start. At 77 Summer Street was the dwelling of Horace Gray, son of America's—and possibly then the world's—largest shipowner. Horace Gray's garden extended in back of his dwelling along Kingston Street, and here he had a conservatory for his collection of camellias and other shrubs. These, along with plants from his Brighton estate, where he had the nation's largest grape houses, furnished the first plantings in the future Public Garden.

Opposite Horace Gray's, at the west corner of Otis Street, in a double Federal mansion he shared with the family of his brother-in-law, lived Edward Everett. Like Webster, Everett was both U.S. senator and secretary of state, also governor and president of Harvard. Everett is still best remembered as the orator who spoke for two hours at the Gettysburg Battlefield, while Abraham Lincoln delivered his immortal words so swiftly that the photographer did not have time to set up and catch the President speaking.

Summer Street Mall to West Street

Two major department stores long dominated the Summer, Winter, and Washington Streets crossroads of Boston's retail business, Jordan Marsh (now Macy's) and Filene's. "Meet you at Filene's Corner" or "Meet you at Jordan's Corner" were for generations part of Boston's shopping talk. These department stores had more in common than the city-block size of their main stores.

Both had Horatio Alger origins in the enterprising young men who came to Boston to get an economic start in life. William Filene, member of a merchant family, was eighteen years old when he came here from Germany after the Revolution of 1848, which swept Europe. He started as a cap maker and tailor. Eben Jordan, member of an old

Yankee family, arrived from Maine when he was fourteen, with a stake of $1.25 after he had paid the packet fare. He started as an errand boy. The companies Jordan and Filene founded, as we shall see, were like Boston's growth, one of rapid expansion. Also, the sites on which the stores grew have many links with Boston's history.

At Chauncy Street is now the northeast corner of Macy's seven-story replacement (1948–1949) of the old 1855 C. F. Hovey store, a lone survivor of the 1872 fire. Near the corner once stood the parsonage of Boston's First Church, the "Old Brick." Ralph Waldo Emerson was born there in 1803. His mother carried four-day-old Ralph to the "Old Brick" to be baptized by her husband, the Reverend William Emerson, namesake and son of the Revolutionary patriot parson who came running with his musket when the redcoats reached Concord's Old North Bridge. Five years after Ralph's birth the parish built a new church a short way down Chauncy Street, on the right, and, in exchange for the "Old Brick" site on Washington Street, was provided four new brick dwelling houses on the church land along Summer Street. One of these, at 27 Summer Street, became the parsonage. Young Ralph went to the South Writing School on nearby West Street, and when ten he entered Boston Latin, then in the new 1812 building Bulfinch built on the present Parker House site.

Young Ralph inherited much of his literary talent from his father, who was one of the earliest members of the Massachusetts Historical Society and a founder of the Boston Athenaeum. But his father died young, leaving his widow and six children. For a while she was allowed to keep the parsonage, but, with prices inflated by the War of 1812, she withdrew with her youngsters to relatives in Concord's Old Manse.

A well-liked, eminent Speaker of the national House, Robert C. Winthrop, for many years had his residence in one of the new buildings that replaced the old parsonage. And just across Chauncy Street, at the east corner, was the final residence of the "Essex Junto" leader George Cabot, U.S. senator, friend of George Washington and Alexander Hamilton.

The block of land on the north side of Summer Street, between Arch and Hawley Streets, offers a ready outline, an epitome, of chang-

AROUND THE WORLD

The Boston ship *Columbia* became the first American vessel to circumnavigate the world. The voyage took three years.

ing life along Summer Street from Revolutionary to present times. Back in the late 1700s it was the property and mansion of Joseph Barrell, patron of Charles Bulfinch, banker, and pioneer in Boston's China trade. Barrell in 1787 organized the epoch-making voyage of the *Columbia,* via the northwest coast, for sea otter skins that were more prized than diamonds in the marketplace at Canton. On its second voyage the *Columbia*'s skipper, Captain Robert Gray, entered the river named for his Boston vessel and established American claims to the Oregon Territory. In 1793, when Bulfinch designed Barrell a new country house, the Summer Street land with its greenery, fish pond, cove frontage, and even quagmire became available, in part, for the Tontine Crescent.

Jeffersonians as well as Federalists lived on Summer Street. Most prominent of them was Bulfinch's friend, future Governor James Sullivan. In gratitude for the help of Sullivan, then attorney general, in winning the repeal of Boston's antitheater law, Bulfinch designed Sullivan a magnificent double town house with bowfronts in which a succession of noted owners lived. Sullivan died in 1808. The following year the fabulous shipowner William "Billy" Gray quit the Federalist Party and Salem and moved into Sullivan's former mansion. Gray, who would own at least 113 ships, supported Jefferson's embargo despite its adverse effect on his fleet. He also supported Madison's war and served as lieutenant governor under patriot Elbridge Gerry. Gray pioneered in Russian as well as India and China trade. Horace Gray, whose house and gardens were diagonally across Summer Street, was one of Gray's ten children.

Fans of the delightful woodland acres of the Arnold Arboretum owe their joy initially to the next occupant of this estate, Benjamin Bussey, who started in business with $10 and ran it into a fortune. On his death in 1842, he willed his fortune to Harvard to promote knowledge of agriculture. With it went his 300 woodland acres in Jamaica Plain, where Harvard in 1870 established the Bussey Institution. Two years later James Arnold of New Bedford gave $100,000 to create the Arboretum.

Even a granddaughter of millionaire Thomas Handasyd Perkins was awed by the ostentation of still another resident of one of the big "white stone" houses at the corner of Hawley and Summer. John P. Cushing went to China when sixteen and returned from Canton in the 1830s "a rich middle aged man." She recalled how he filled his house with China's "finest and best: china, screens, silks, furniture, carvings brought by people who picked them out for themselves." To her young eyes the place seemed an "enchanted palace . . . with Chinese servants draped in blue China crepe frocks."

The 1988 "101 Arch" complex, with a lobby at 32 Summer and a twenty-one-story office tower, has preserved three floors of the brick facade, five-story, 1874 building formerly at this corner. Here the Mercantile Library of 1820, America's first, provided aspiring workers the tools of self-education. Habitues included teenage "Jamie" Fields when he was a clerk at the Old Corner Bookstore. The Massachusetts Institute of Technology recalls on a plaque that its teaching began here on February 20, 1865, with fifteen pupils in rented Mercantile Hall. Soon the class grew to twenty-three.

Bishop's Alley, presently Hawley Street, led to old Trinity Church, then on the west corner of Summer Street, now part of Filene's. In earlier days there was a tavern here where Captain Kidd dwelt while seeking in vain to come to terms with his one-time partner the Earl of Bellomont, then the Bay's royal governor. King's Chapel had flourished so well in colonial times that some parishioners by 1728 decided to build a new church because there were "no pews to be bought by newcomers." The new church was Trinity Church. Governor Shirley took part. So did Peter Faneuil. And it was in the beautiful interior of this 1734 wooden edifice that George Washington went first to church services during his last Sunday in Boston. Its successor, a granite church with an imposing high tower, built in 1828, was totally destroyed by the fire of 1872.

A late-eighteenth-century Boston showplace, the spacious Leonard Vassall mansion set endwise to the street, with great stables, grounds, and elaborate fencing, stood on the old parsonage site opposite Hawley Street. Several post-Revolutionary nabobs owned it, too. It brought a glow of royal approval to Summer Street when Prince Edward, son of George III and father of Queen Victoria, came among the wedding guests to a high-society party at the mansion.

Notice the plaque at the Washington Street entrance of Macy's 1975–1978 building. The young merchant that you see behind the counter is nineteen-year-old Eben Jordan selling a yard of cherry-colored ribbon to his first customer. This was at the start of his entrepreneurial career in 1841 in the North End of Boston. The youth from Maine had so impressed his employers that one of them helped him get his own business. Jordan, however, soon felt that he had more to learn about merchandising and went to work for Boston's largest dry goods firm, James M. Beebe Company, in its big antecedent building at 1 Winthrop Square. Two years later, in 1851, Jordan, with a fellow worker as a partner, opened Jordan Marsh Company at 129 Milk Street with $5,000 in capital. Growth was steady, and by 1861 he had a six-story stone wholesale structure on Devonshire Street in Winthrop Square and a retail store on Washington Street. He had survived the 1857 panic, when others failed, by slashing his prices in half. Luckily, a little more than a year before the great fire he withdrew from Winthrop Square and expanded his store on Washington Street. His son, who succeeded him in 1895, was both a distinguished merchant and a great patron of music. Robert Campeau, Canadian tycoon and recent owner of Jordan Marsh, had extensive plans for expansion, but the 1989 recession prevailed. The longtime flagship store was rechristened Macy's by new owners, Federated Department Stores, in 1996.

Young William Filene had to try twice before getting on the ladder to the top. On the first venture he developed stores in Boston and the North Shore, shifted to New York, had a big store on Fifth Avenue, but lost everything in the panic of 1868. He returned to New England, got stores again on the North Shore, then in 1881 concentrated on a specialty shop just west of here at 10 Winter Street. Soon he was expanding along Washington Street on the side across from Jordan's. His son, an innovator, took over in 1891.

The eight-story Beaux Arts structure of Filene's with terra cotta facade, one of the best of this type in the nation, was built in 1911–1912. The modern addition at the Franklin Street corner—with the little park put in as part of Boston's beautification—was made by Filene's in 1972–1973. Edward Filene developed, over a ten-year period, the Automatic Bargain Basement, helped create employees' credit unions, and organized the U.S. Chamber of Commerce, with the first one in Boston.

On the Washington Street side of Filene's, about midway between Franklin and Summer Streets, the Harvard Medical School took temporary quarters in rooms over an apothecary shop at 400 Washington from 1810 to 1816. Dr. John Warren, brother of the patriot and surgeon of the Continental Army, began the school's lecturing in Cambridge in 1782 but helped shift the school to Boston to get clinical advantages. His son, Dr. John Collins Warren, succeeded him in 1815 and obtained funds to get the school a new building a few blocks south on Mason Street.

Across the street at 415 Washington, until 1981, was the beautiful marquee and entrance to the Orpheum Theater, which was turned into Boston's first movie palace in 1915–1916. Essentially this was another remodeling of the historic old Music Hall of 1852 and the first large movie palace acquired outside New York City by theater magnate Marcus Loew's circuit.

The present Washington Street Mall, with its redbrick walks, plants, and canopies, was created to avoid traffic tie-ups in this shopping center, which was formerly as congested as the one on Tremont Street that inspired the first subway. Most Bostonians long associated the Summer-Winter-Washington crossroads with mounted police, honking auto-mobiles, and crowds that reach a peak at Christmas time. The new pedestrian malls are formally called the Downtown Crossing.

Entering Winter Street we come at once to a landmark site in the creation of the American textile and railroad industries. At 1 Winter, on the south corner, was the residence of Patrick Tracy Jackson. It was here in December 1821 that the Merrimack Manufacturing Company was formed. With Nathan Appleton helping to provide financing, Jackson and his brother-in-law Francis Cabot Lowell had already begun American cotton manufacture by the Charles River in Waltham. The Merrimack Company extended it to the Merrimack River, which led Jackson in 1835 to build the Boston-Lowell railroad, the first railroad to be completed leading out of Boston.

At the former subway entrance next to 10 Winter on the left, by Jackson Place, was the specialty shop where William Filene got his second successful start in business. Next, on our left, comes Winter Place and, on the opposite side, Music Hall Place, with a wall of the old Music Hall still standing at its far end.

During the 1775–1776 siege of Boston the family residence of Samuel Adams, near the far east end of Summer Street, got rough treatment from the occupying soldiers. So Adams acquired a two-story wooden house, with gardens in the rear, at the east corner of Winter Place, and it was from here that he later functioned as governor of the state he had helped to liberate.

On this same corner Elizabeth Peabody, on October 28, 1861, opened her pioneer English-speaking kindergarten at 24½ Winter Street, with thirty youngsters in what she called "a quiet, high, sunny room with seven windows to the east and south. . . . The idea of kindergarten is organized play . . . an alternnation of bodily and mental exercises," she continued. "The first day, with a full blown rose in my hand, I repeated . . . sentences about the rose, beginning 'Come and I will show you what is beautiful.'" Miss Peabody had a "great room" for a schoolroom and a "little parlor adjoining." In taking these rooms she had to modify the German educator Friedrich Froebel's kindergarten plan, because she had found "it impossible to have accommodations for growing plants or keeping animals in the neighborhood of the Common, where my children generally live." She overcame this the following September 29, 1862, when she moved her kindergarten to 15 Pinckney Street.

By walking now along Winter Place, we are taking the path that

Boston's merchant prince, Thomas Handasyd Perkins, provided to get from his new mansion, which we will presently see, to his sizable stables at the rear of his land on Winter Street. Notice the plaque to the left, commemorating the site of the home of Samuel Adams, who died here in October 1802. At 3–4 Winter Place are four- and three-story brick buildings from the early 1830s. As Locke-Ober's, a wining and dining merger with roots back to 1875, the building has for many generations been a distinctive restaurant. The Victorian interior dates to an 1886 remodeling with a large, well-equipped mahogany bar and original period decorations. Upstairs, quarters are used for private dining groups and are heavily patronized by leaders of Boston's business world.

Go through the tunnel ahead and on emerging at Temple Place, directly on the right is Perkins's Greek Revival mansion, except for its west bow and large Doric portico. It has been preserved, since 1856, by the Provident Institution for Savings, formed in 1816 as America's first mutual savings bank. Perkins built here at 36 Temple Place on leaving Pearl Street and enjoyed the companionship of his married daughters and many friends in similar residences on Temple Place. Perkins's granddaughter, Caroline Curtis, has recalled how heavy was his big front door "made of a piece of the old ship *Constitution.*" Inside she noted the "wide vestibule, with marble floor and on each side pedestals holding marble statues and steps leading up to a handsome circular hall." We can see some of this on entering. The former Perkins mansion, once heated by twenty-three fireplaces, was bought by MCLE (Massachusetts Continuing Legal Education) in 1991.

On the south side of Macy's, Temple Place once ran as Avon Street. Near the north corner of Avon was the homestead of the colony's first mintmaster, John Hull, who made the famous pine-tree shillings. Here, legend says, he put a pile of them on a scale as a dowry that equaled the weight of his eighteen-year-old daughter. Hannah's bridegroom was the future Chief Justice Samuel Sewall, diarist and repentant witchcraft justice, who later amused Bostonians by wooing wealthy widows after Hannah's death. He inherited the ample Hull estate and built himself a mansion on the land where he lived until he died in 1730.

This corner was also the site of a small wooden building in which Boston's first successful printer, Bartholomew Green, published America's first regular newspaper, the *Boston News-Letter,* April 24, 1704. Green printed it for Boston postmaster John Campbell. In 1722 Green succeeded Campbell as owner-publisher of this pioneer American journal.

By 1855 a lithographer in another shop here was looking for a boy "with a taste for drawing." A fellow volunteer fireman suggested that he had a nineteen-year-old son who fulfilled that requirement, but he had had no art training. The lithographer said he would take a chance, and thus it was that the future renowned American artist Winslow Homer began his art career.

Another block south on Washington Street brings us to West Street, on our right. A three-story 1820 row house at 15 West became, in 1840, the family residence of Elizabeth Peabody. Here she opened the first Boston bookstore run by a woman, gathering place for authors and intellectuals of the times. In 1842 her back parlor was the setting for celebrating the marriage of her sister Sophia to Nathaniel Hawthorne. Afterward the couple set out by carriage to the Old Manse in Concord, where Thoreau had put in a garden for the newlyweds. The following year in the same setting Elizabeth's sister, Mary, became the bride of the great educator Horace Mann.

While here, Elizabeth Peabody also became Boston's first woman publisher. In 1841 she took over producing *The Dial,* the magazine of the Transcendentalists. Margaret Fuller and Emerson were successively its editors and Thoreau, a writer and assistant editor. Miss Peabody published early stories of Hawthorne, and her house was used as a forum for the "Conversations" of ill-fated, brilliant feminist Margaret Fuller. As a publisher Miss Peabody kept social significance strongly in mind. Possibly the most far-reaching of her publications was Thoreau's essay "On Civil Disobedience," which inspired Mahatma Gandhi and the Reverend Martin Luther King, Jr., to practice nonviolence in their efforts to gain liberation and equality.

Earlier Boston bookselling off Scollay Square, on Cornhill and Brattle Streets, is recalled by the Brattle Book Shop at 9 West Street. This bookstore, through the proprietor Gloss family, traces continuously back to its earlier Brattle Street location where it began in 1825 as America's first antiquarian bookshop. Reminders of the old book bins in which future President F. D. Roosevelt rummaged are the book-laden push tables ("carts," Gloss calls them) wheeled on the sidewalk for fans to browse "whenever we have good weather."

Just opposite West Street, on the east side of Washington Street, Bedford Street once began and ran eastward from Washington toward Chauncy Street. On the left of the vanished part of Bedford, about midway to Chauncy, Judge William Prescott lived in "a comfortable old mansion . . . amid venerable trees." It was a mansion built by the Revolutionary-era merchant-diarist John Rowe. Here young historian William Hickling Prescott wrote his *Reign of Ferdinand and Isabella* and, laying groundwork for even greater fame, worked on his histories *The Conquest of Mexico* and *The Conquest of Peru* before moving to Beacon Street in 1845.

Old Movieland to Liberty Tree

We continue southward from West Street down Washington Street into an area of the city where extensive renewal was thwarted by the 1989 recession. By 1999, however, prosperous economic times had thrown the area into throes of renewal and reappropriation.

Farther down Washington Street, even straddling it, is an expansion of the Tufts–New England Medical Center that includes, besides hospital facilities, dental and medical schools. Contained within it is the 1796 Boston Dispensary, the first to provide outpatient care for the poor.

This part of Washington Street for decades was the prime part of a great white way of theaters and movies.

On our right, at 539 Washington, is a theater that once hosted a glamorous stage tradition going directly back to the community's first Bulfinch theater in Federal Street. The Boston Theater, successor to the Federal Street Theater, opened here in 1854. The elegance of its lobby, grand staircase, and the 3,000-seat capacity of its horseshoe interior, with three-tier balconies, ranked it immediately among the world's largest and most magnificent. A dazzling list of stars have trod its stage: Boston-born Charlotte Cushman, Edwin Booth (at the time of Lincoln's assassination), Sarah Bernhardt, "Jersey Lily" Langtry, opera singers Nellie Melba and Enrico Caruso, composer Victor Herbert, and pianist-statesman Ignace Paderewski. It was here in 1883, the year of its creation, that the Metropolitan Opera first played Boston. Several U.S. presidents have had welcomes here, as have numerous members of royalty, including Russian Duke Alexis, Hawaii's Queen Liliuokalani, who married a Bostonian, and the future King Rama of Siam.

The biggest ball of all was in 1860 for the nineteen-year-old Prince of Wales, future King Edward VII of England. What a red carpet Boston rolled out! The prince, traveling incognito as Baron Renfrew, came to Boston via the Berkshires in a sumptuous train. Equally sumptuous was the grand ball. A waxed floor was laid over the seat at a level with the stage. The theater was jammed to overflowing when the prince arrived after 10:00 P.M. He was welcomed by Boston's mayor and taken to his special royal red canopy in the balcony, as two bands played "God Save the Queen." He returned to the waxed floor to dance with seventeen envied, carefully selected, lavishly dressed partners. At 1:00 A.M., via a specially built passage from the balcony to the neighboring theater, he led all to supper served on china bearing his crest.

Future President "Teddy" Roosevelt did not fare so well when he came to the theater in 1877 for a performance of Medea. He did, in fact, fare worse than the Harvard boys who had tried to upstage Oscar Wilde. As part of his Porcellian Club initiation, freshman T. R., attired in immaculate evening dress, sat in the balcony, and applauded vigorously at the most emotional moments of the tragedy when all the rest of the audience was tensely quiet. T. R. got thrown out!

This theater was torn down, and the lavish B. F. Keith Memorial Theater was built in 1927–1928 on the foundation of the old one, as well as on the site of the former Harvard Medical School. The medical school had been just north of the Mason Street rear carriage entrance to the Boston Theater.

This was the medical school Dr. John Collins Warren had helped build back in 1816. It remained here—source of the canard that the students used corpses snatched from the nearby cemetery on the Common—until new land in the West End was given the school in 1846 by Dr. George Parkman. On this site three years later Parkman would be the victim of Boston's most sensational murder.

The Keith Memorial Theater was an opulent movie palace when it opened with George M. Cohan and Al Jolson. When built, it also partly covered the site of another theater, immediately to the south of the Boston Theater, the one in which the Prince of Wales sat down to supper after the grand ball. This was the Melodeon at 545 Washington Street, a small theater hall dating back to 1835.

Thackeray, who had been persuaded by "Jamie" Fields to give an American lecture series, spoke at the Melodeon in 1852 before an audience that included all the social and literary lights of Boston—Longfellow, Emerson, Lowell, Holmes, even ungregarious Whittier. Fields, who escorted tall, burly, broad-chested Thackeray from the Tremont House, recalled a strange scene on Washington Street: "I remember his uproarious shouting and dancing when he was told that the tickets to his first course of lectures were all sold; and when we rode together from the hotel to the lecture-hall, he insisted on thrusting both his long legs out the carriage window in deference, he said, to his magnanimous ticket-holders."

The Melodeon went through many changes in its long life, being used for concerts, lectures, oratorios, even the sermons of the Reverend Theodore Parker before he shifted to the Music Hall. In 1894 the vaudeville innovators B. F. Keith and Edward Albee, who had started a "museum" eleven years earlier in a small store immediately to the south, built at 545 Washington the showy B. F. Keith New Theater, with its glass staircase over a waterfall. They went on to parlay their low-cost "continuous vaudeville" into a chain of nearly 400 theaters nationwide. The theater's entry is now a store.

The Paramount, an Art Deco theater palace built in 1932 at Number 553 at the bend in Washington Street, is on the site of the Adams

House where Governor Calvin Coolidge was lodging when he made a typically terse statement that opened a path for him to the White House. "There is no right to strike against the public safety by anybody, anywhere, anytime," said Cal when the Boston Police went on strike in September 1919 and outlaws started openly wrecking and looting stores along Washington Street. Impressed with Cal's remarks, the GOP national convention, in rebellion against party bosses, put Coolidge on a winning presidential ticket.

Adams House got its name not from the presidential Adams clan but from an innkeeper Adams who ran a celebrated pre-Revolutionary hostelry on this site called Lamb Tavern, a two-story wooden structure. Boston's first stagecoach connection southward was from here, where passengers gathered, were guests, and rose early in predawn hours when the stagecoaches started their run to Providence in 1767. Despite hardships of travel, halting for a new pair of horses at each eighteen-mile stage, Josiah Quincy at war's end in 1783 marveled that a passenger could get to New York "after a week's hard traveling, wondering at the ease as well as the expedition of our journey."

The open space and parking space from Washington Street to Tremont Street and from the Paramount Theater to the China Trade Center at 2 Boylston Street was to become the $550 million Commonwealth Center—a thirteen-story, 400-room luxury hotel on Avery Street, two thirty-two-story office buildings, and loads of retail space. Even the Paramount Theater was to be given remodeling. But the 1989 recession had its way.

The first intelligible words to be carried by wire were the inventor's to his assistant on March 10, 1876: "Mr. Watson, come here, I want you." The place was in Bell's upstairs lab at former 3 Exeter Place. A plaque marks the site. To get there, go left at the new Avenue de Lafayette that runs alongside Lafayette Place. The telephone plaque is on the northwest corner building at 99 Harrison Avenue, facing Swissôtel.

Also here was the reception of the world's first news item transmitted by telephone. On February 12, 1877, after giving a demonstration of his phone at Salem, Bell was asked by *The Boston Globe* correspondent if he could send the news report over the wire. Bell agreed, and the newsman read it to Mr. Watson after Bell said into the phone: "Sent by telephone, the first newspaper dispatch sent by human voice over the wires."

A few steps south on Harrison Avenue bring us to Essex Street, once a shore road along Boston's South Cove. Filling this bay added miles of streets and an area nearly twice the size of the Common. It started in 1804–1807 when Harrison Avenue, then called Front Street, was extended across South Cove on a line east of and parallel to Washington Street. Then in 1833–1839 another fifty-five acres were filled in, creating Albany Street in the new South End. Most of Boston's present Chinatown, just south of Essex Street, is filled land.

The part of Harrison Avenue on which we have just walked was an extension of the original Front Street, and when extended it wiped out the house at 26 Essex Street that for forty years was the residence of the orator of abolition, Wendell Phillips. A number of noted Bostonians have lived in this neighborhood in houses that had an excellent harbor view of South Cove and South Bay. These houses replaced distilleries that flourished at this oceanside part of town until the Federal era. In still earlier times John Hull had his mint on Essex Street, just east of Kingston Street, on land that he had purchased in 1653. Near this same intersection of present Essex and Kingston, Daniel Webster, when he first came to Boston in 1804, taught in his brother's now-vanished schoolhouse before he shifted to the study of law. Among Webster's pupils was future governor and U.S. Senator Edward Everett, then ten years old and living in a house opposite where Essex Street enters Washington Street.

At 59 Essex, with its rear view across the cove, once stood Gilbert Stuart's rented dwelling, a three-story brick building near Edinboro Street, which the artist used in his last sad, impoverished years. In 1824 Secretary of State John Quincy Adams came to ask him to do a portrait of his father. Twenty years had passed since Stuart had last painted him. "Time has wrought so much change in his countenance that I wish to procure a likeness of him as he is now," said the son. Stuart went to Quincy to do it, a famous portrait of the eighty-nine-year-old patriot, John Adams. The next year Stuart suffered a stroke. His hand trembled and his left arm was slightly paralyzed. The proud, eccentric, intemperate, ever-difficult genius left eight unfinished portraits when he died insolvent in 1828. An inventory of his belongings (in its entirety only $375) placed a value of $4.75 each on these eight paintings in his front chamber. No one now knows whether these included the unfinished Martha and George Washington portraits or whether they were not itemized. The necessitous family offered these to the state for $1,000. The offer was rejected. To help the Stuart family, some members of the Boston Athenaeum raised $1,500 and bought what are now called the Athenaeum portraits, which, through a recent $5 million purchase agreement, are still available to the public alternately in Boston and in the nation's capital.

Across the street at 60 Essex, and also now vanished, was the house into which widowed Ruth Emerson, with Ralph and four other young sons, moved in 1817 and cleaned, cooked, and washed for boarders to maintain her family. "I pity all who are compelled to adopt this mode of getting a living, or rather an existence," said Ruth. Ruth, one of sixteen children, had been raised in a great mansion nearby on the west side of present Harrison Avenue, a few yards south of Essex Street where we are standing. Her father had been a wealthy merchant.

We follow Essex Street west to Washington Street. Boston's Liberty Tree—vanished like so much in this area—once stood just inside the fence of an old dwelling at the south corner of Essex Street. At the third-floor level of the present 1850 building over the Chinatown subway entrance is a freestone bas-relief marking where the tree stood until cut down by Tories and redcoats in 1775 during the siege, a spiteful destruction that caused a redcoat to fall from a limb to his death. Planted back in 1646, it was big and yielded fourteen cords of wood. For easier reading of the bas-relief, go across Washington Street to the small Liberty Tree Park at the south corner of Boylston Street. The bas-relief is duplicated in larger size on a metal plaque on the ground.

The corner 1888 Boylston Building along the back of the park replaced the freestanding 1809 three-story, brick Boylston Market Building designed by Bulfinch with cupola, stalls on the ground floor, and a grand hall on the third floor that was used for years by the

Handel & Haydn Society for concerts. Farmers bringing produce via Boston Neck could avoid market day crush at Faneuil Hall. Boylston, in 1986, became a thriving, lively China Trade Center.

The area in front of Liberty Tree, first called Hanover Square after the royal house, was changed to Liberty Hall when the Sons of Liberty met there outdoors. Secret sessions with Samuel Adams and other leaders were held in the rooms of the Chase and Speakman distillery in back of the old corner dwelling. There were exciting times at Liberty Tree in the days of the Stamp Act, when Governor Hutchinson's mansion was sacked and terrified officials fled to the castle down the harbor. A flagstaff was raised within the tree's limbs, and when the ensign went up, the Sons of Liberty assembled. Here in 1765 they forced the resignation of the intended stamp master. The hated prime minister who signed the act was hanged in effigy, paraded through town, then strung up on the scaffold out on the Neck.

Action planned at Liberty Tree in 1773 was a prelude to events leading to the Boston Tea Party. The Sons of Liberty picked a day and set high noon for the consignees to appear at Liberty Tree, resign as consignees, and send the tea back to London. None appeared. Patriot rioting in State Street and School Street followed.

Before turning back along Washington Street, a few words about this main Boston thoroughfare: Boston Neck, or "The Neck" as it was called, was the isthmus just south of us, connecting old Boston to Roxbury on the mainland. The shores of South Cove to our left and Back Bay to our right curved in so that the isthmus, about 4 or 5 blocks south of us, was little wider than a roadway, present Washington Street. A little more than half a mile south of us the roadway in early times was often dangerously overrun by high tides, and it was invariably so in storms. This was the only land entrance into Boston. It was once the narrowest width of the community, but since the filling of the bays to the left and to the right, it is now the city's widest part. Time has erased all the old landmarks: the town gate, competing fortifications built by redcoats and patriots, and the scaffold that long stood just inside the gate on the east shore, which gave the South Bay there the odious nickname of Gallows Bay.

There are some reminders that where we stand was near water. Just a block ahead of us on the left is Beach Street, which used to reach South Cove, less than a block away. And Boylston Street to our west—with a view of the high-rise Ritz-Carlton in the Back Bay—began life as Frog Lane.

Along Washington Street, as on Tremont Street, we have seen both decay and regrowth. The blight is traceable to the "old combat zone" centered at this intersection of Washington and Essex Streets. The combat zone's sharp decline, nudged by government intervention, stimulated in 1987 the creation of a Midtown Cultural District. Besides resultant plans to redo neglected theaters, the District has been developing ways to restore the magic of Boston's theatrical Broadway.

We now follow Washington Street back to the Old State House, where we begin our next walk. In London style, Washington Street in colonial times had a string of four names for its different sections, until renaming began after Washington's 1789 visit. Two of those names, Marlborough and Newbury, were preserved on two new main streets in the Back Bay. On our return walk, in good part along the central city's vibrant Downtown Crossing, we may keep in mind that this was George Washington's route when he came to Boston on a white horse in 1776 after forcing the redcoats out and again in 1789 when he came as our first President.

CENTRAL BOSTON AND THE WATERFRONT

The Old State House and State Street

When George Washington dismounted at the Old State House in 1789 at the head of State Street, the name of which had only five years earlier been changed from King Street, the building was already more than three quarters of a century old. Its redbrick walls were promptly raised after the 1711 fire that, as we have noted, burned everything in this center of colonial commerce and government from Town Dock to School Street. The new Town House of 1712–1713 is one of the oldest edifices in the land and has been called "the most important public building in American history prior to the Declaration of Independence."

Washington was quite familiar with it through his sight-seeing in Boston back in 1756 as a twenty-four-year-old Virginia colonel. The day after 10,000 redcoats and Tories left Boston's outer harbor on March 28, 1776, Washington came to the second floor of the Old State House and received an address of thanks from the General Court. In return he expressed his joy in Boston's being "now relieved from the cruel and oppressive invasions of those who . . . trample on the rights of humanity." He and his general officers thereupon walked

CENTRAL BOSTON AND THE WATERFRONT

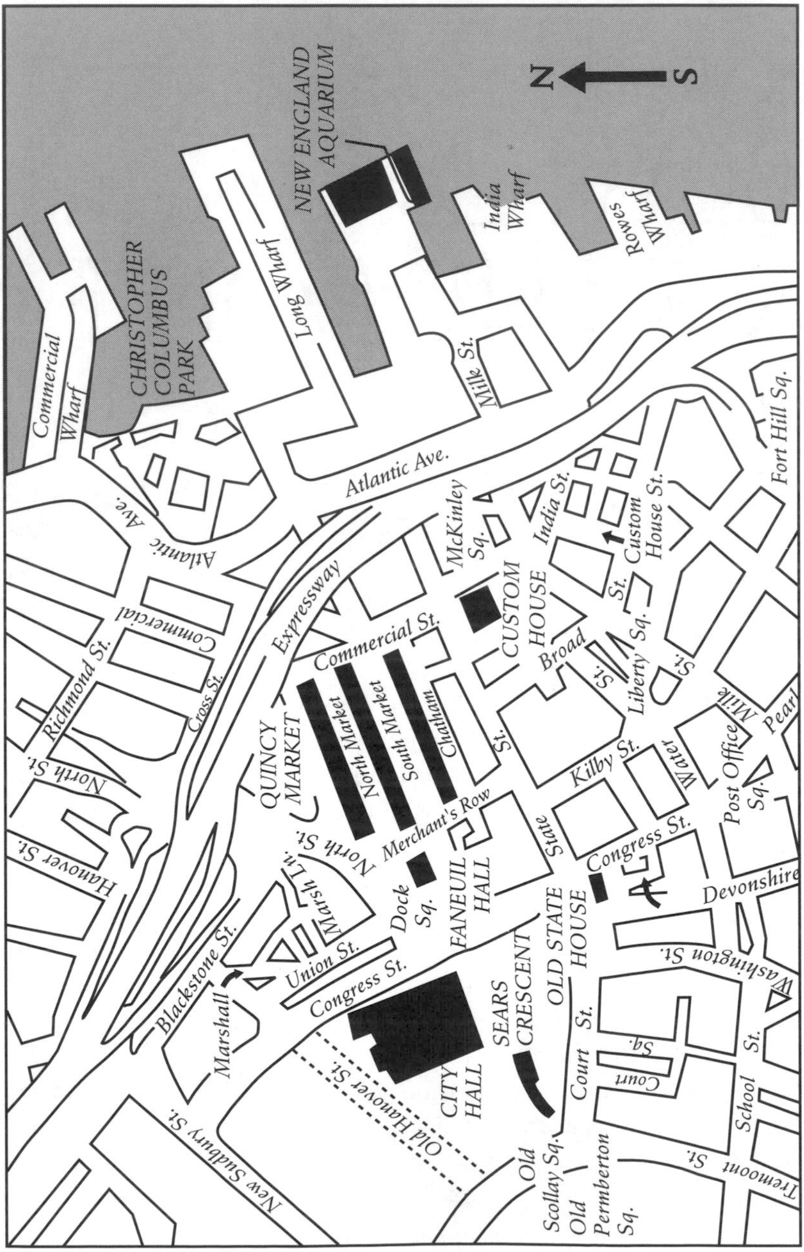

across Washington Street to a thanksgiving service in "Old Brick," the First Church of Boston.

Even before this the Old State House was a distinguished American structure. James Otis, in the upstairs front chamber of the royal governor and council, argued against the outrage of the Writs of Assistance back in 1761. "Then and there," said young lawyer John Adams, who was present and making imperishable notes, "the child independence was born."

In 1770, right after the Boston Massacre, Royal Governor Hutchinson was confronted in the same council chamber by the demand of Samuel Adams that he remove not one but both regiments of redcoats from the town. "Nothing short of their total removal will satisfy the people," Adams insisted. Eyeing Hutchinson, Adams said later, "I observed his knees to tremble; I saw his face grow pale; and I enjoyed the sight."

> FULL OF CROOKED LITTLE STREETS; BUT I TELL YOU, BOSTON HAS OPENED AND KEPT OPEN MORE TURNPIKES THAT LEAD STRAIGHT TO FREE THOUGHT AND FREE SPEECH AND FREE DEEDS THAN ANY OTHER CITY OF LIVE MEN OR DEAD MEN.
>
> —OLIVER WENDELL HOLMES, JR.

Outside the council room is a balcony looking toward the harbor. As the temper of the town rose late in 1773 on the arrival of the tea—"tea that bainful weed"—Adams would march his protesting townsmen beneath the balcony from Faneuil Hall to the larger Old South Meeting House so that Governor Hutchinson could see that they included substantial citizens. General Gage, when he succeeded Hutchinson, reported to King George III that "the people are . . . not a Boston rabble, but the farmers and the freeholders of the country. Nothing," advised Gage, "can be done but by forcible means."

From this same balcony, with ecstatic jubilation, Bostonians gathered on July 18, 1776, to hear, on its arrival from Philadelphia, the first reading of the Declaration of Independence.

There was this same ecstasy in 1789 when "our beloved president" came to Boston. Boston workers from forty-six trades—mastmakers, riggers, ropemakers, sailmakers, shipwrights, chandlers, wharfingers, seamen—each trade with its own white flag, gathered all the way along the High from the Neck to the Old State House, opened ranks, and faced inwards, as the first President passed on his white horse. Church bells rang, and as Washington approached the Old State House a thirteen-cannon federal salute was fired at each of the town's forts and batteries.

Charles Bulfinch had designed an arch across the main street with a 20-foot canopy at the peak topped with an American eagle. The arch, noted Washington, was "handsomely ornamented" and on it was gathered "a band of select singers" who sang an ode. Washington rode under the arch, entered the Old State House, went to the second floor through Senate and House chambers, and emerged through a doorway placed in the central west window to a balcony on a colonnade erected against the west facade. Armchairs had been set on a rich carpet.

After the parade passed under the arch, the President, in the company of Samuel and John Adams and a military escort, went up Court Street. Governor Hancock, in the break over precedence, had been absent. Washington told Samuel Adams, "I shall not see Governor Hancock unless at my own lodgings." And so it turned out.

Originally State Street, this relatively short street of many historic memories, was called "the Broad street leading from the Marketplace to the Sea." It was early Boston's front door to the harbor, the ocean, and the world.

The marketplace was here long before the first Town House was built in 1658. Ancient and Honorable Artillery Major Robert Keayne, whose homestead and store were on the corner at 1 State Street, left 300 pounds for a new Town House. Fully 120 other citizens chipped in, with the biggest of these gifts (20 pounds) from the town's first bookseller, Hezekiah Usher, whose house, gardens, shop, and wharf (in Dock Square) were diagonally opposite Keayne's on the north side of State Street.

The town's first library was also a gift from Keayne and was located in an east room of the new building, which was constructed above 10-foot pillars; on the open ground floor merchants could have a daily meeting place and exchange. Upstairs in this medieval wooden

During World War II the venerable golden done of the State House was painted black as a preventive measure against air raids.

building were state and town rooms, courts, and an armory for Keayne's Ancients. The pioneer town library and precious records went up in smoke in the 1711 fire. The 1712–1713 brick State House interior fell victim to fire, too, in 1747, but was quickly redone.

The Commonwealth's first governor, John Hancock, was inaugurated and served in the chamber with the balcony. We may see Hancock's once high-style inaugural attire in the same chamber, where Samuel Adams and James Bowdoin also served as governors. After completion of Bulfinch's new State House on Beacon Hill, the state functions went there in 1798. The Old State House was rented for commercial use, save from 1830 to 1841, when it was Boston's City Hall.

Incredible as it may seem, after years of alteration and commercial use there came agitation in the growing Boston of the 1870s to tear down the Old State House to make room for street traffic. Chicago offered to move the building brick by brick to the Midwest. Some citizens, about to be known as the Bostonian Society, fought to save it. They did. In 1882 the building was restored to its original appearance and placed in the care of the Bostonian Society, which assembled the painting, artifacts, and treasures now to be seen in the Old State House, a museum of Boston's and our nation's history. The glittering rebuilding of the dome, eagle with outspread wings, lion, and unicorn highlight a $6 million renovation done in 1990–1992 to preserve this national treasure.

Going in the customary south entrance of the Old State House, we recall one of its most exciting moments. Abolitionist William Lloyd Garrison, his clothing mostly torn from his body, fled on October 21, 1835, through this same doorway in an effort to escape a

Boston mob screaming, "Lynch him!" The mob, which had broken up a rally of the Boston Female Anti-Slavery Society just around the corner at 46 Washington Street, took off after Garrison, who was then publishing *The Liberator* in a room across the hall from the women's rally. Garrison, persuaded by friends, fled through a rear window and headed southward along Devonshire Street. To save him, Mayor Theodore Lyman had him arrested as a "rioter," reclothed, and taken by hack to jail. Next day Garrison was released.

There is a Visitor Center maintained by the National Park Service at 15 State Street across from the south side of the Old State House. The library of the Bostonian Society, with more paintings and mementos of Boston history, is on an upper floor.

Across Devonshire Street from the Visitor Center, on the east corner at 27 State Street, once stood Boston's First Church, beside what came to be called Quaker Lane, because at its southern end there later stood a Quaker meeting house. The first Puritan church in Boston was built in 1632, a mud-walled (mud on stones) affair with a thatched roof. The Reverend John Wilson, the first minister, had his house and garden across on the north side of the street on the lot that later belonged to the merchant-selectman-bookseller Hezekiah Usher.

So that no offenders would go unnoticed, and these soon included Quakers, the stocks, pillory, and whipping post, painfully associated with early Puritan life, were located outside the church. The first offender to sit in the stocks was carpenter Edward Palmer, who built them. His offense: overcharging. In those days a sea captain was strapped in the stocks on his return for kissing his wife on their doorstep after three years at sea. Branding, ear-clipping, and nose-slitting were other efforts of the pioneer community, on the edge of a vast continent, to prevent division in its struggle for security and salvation. The ministers preaching here, Wilson, John Eliot, and John Cotton, tried their utmost in pulpit assaults on sin and sinners.

The First Church was also used for town meetings and sessions of the General Court, which continued when the new wooden meeting house was built in 1640, predecessor to "Old Brick."

A circle of cobblestones on State Street, directly east of the Old

State House, marks the area (it actually took up all this part of the street) of the Boston Massacre in 1770. The killing was an aftermath of rioting and fighting between Bostonians and redcoats that erupted three days earlier at the ropewalks along present Pearl Street.

The forty-one-story 1968 building with modern pink-granite facing at 28 State Street occupies more than a block-sized site of historic ground. So that there could be a view from the new City Hall along what was the lower part of Washington Street, the 28 State Street building was considerately set back on its site. Along here, roughly across from the site of Paul Revere's shop, was once 46 Washington Street, from which the ruffians chased Garrison.

England's first reigning monarch ever to come to Boston, Queen Elizabeth II, and her prince, passed this way in 1976 to participate, beneath the Old State House balcony, in America's bicentennial. The Queen smiled and waved to crowds from the balcony. She also reflected on how Samuel Adams, Revere, and other patriots might react to her being here. "I think they would have been extremely surprised," she said, but she felt they would also have been "pleased to know that eventually we came together again as peoples and friends. . . ."

At the corner lot, as we have seen, John Coggan opened Boston's first shop in 1634. The two lots just eastward were those of the Reverend Mr. Wilson and later Hezekiah Usher. Devonshire, originally called Wilson's Lane, used to run northward along Mr. Wilson's land and garden to Dock Square. The only garden now on this block is one with a magnificent view of Boston—a private garden with trees, on the thirty-ninth level of the 28 State Street building.

The Royal Exchange Tavern stood at the northeast corner of State Street and now-vanished Exchange Street, which disappeared in the widening and extension of Congress Street. This tavern was a favorite gathering place of Boston's prosperous young blades, and it was here that the argument started that led to the 1728 duel and death of nineteen-year-old Benjamin Woodbridge on the Common. Most likely it was to this tavern that another young man came in 1772, Alexander Hamilton, then almost sixteen years of age, who had landed in Boston after a three-week voyage from St. Croix in the West Indies. Hamilton, on his way to college in New York—and to fame—caught the stagecoach that only a month earlier had begun the first service from the Royal Exchange Tavern to New York.

The present traffic separation in mid–Congress Street was roughly the location of the Royal Exchange Tavern. On the lower northeast corner, roughly the northwest corner of the thirty-eight-story 60 State Street skyscraper (1973–1974), was King George III's Custom House. This was the background of the opening scene on the night of the Boston Massacre.

A lone redcoat was on duty at the sentry box outside the Custom House on that cold, wintry Monday, March 5, 1770, with snow on the ground. Suddenly he got into a brawl with some passersby. Just as suddenly bells—including "Old Brick's"—started ringing as though there were a fire. A crowd quickly formed as one had during brawling over the weekend between redcoats and the waterfront workmen. Future General Henry Knox, then a nineteen-year-old apprentice bookseller at Major Keayne's corner, rushed to the sentry and warned him not to fire his musket. The crowd grew larger. Snowballs and chunks of ice were thrown as the sentry yelled for help. The post of the main guard was across from the Old State House, roughly on the site of the Visitor Center at 15 State Street. Captain James Preston and seven grenadiers responded, forcing their way through the crowd to the Custom House sentry. Knox grabbed Preston and urged no firing. "They cannot fire without my orders," Preston told Knox. At that moment a grenadier was knocked to the ground and, as he rose, his musket went off. More firing ensued. Six-foot-two mulatto Crispus Attucks, struck by two bullets, was the first to die. Three in all were killed instantly, and two more were mortally wounded. Preston got his men and the sentry back to the main guard but upbraided them for firing without orders. They said that in the melee they had heard the shout, "Fire!"

John Adams and Josiah Quincy got all but two of the grenadiers acquitted. These two were branded on the right thumb by the sheriff in the old courthouse in Court Street. Of the massacre, Daniel Webster declared: "From that moment we may date the severance of the British Empire."

A few paces down Congress Street, on our right, there stood for a decade (1808–1818) until destroyed by fire, America's first hotel, the seven-story Exchange Coffee House, designed by Asher Benjamin. Boston's commercial and financial growth in the Federal era had been attracting ever-increasing numbers of businessmen and travelers, and this hotel made something different available from the fashionable boarding houses in which Washington had lodged when he came. Many noted Boston banquets were held here; in particular, a grand feast when President Monroe's arrival in 1817 confirmed that the Era of Good Feeling definitely included even Federalist Boston. President Monroe lodged in the hotel during his visit.

The twelve-story granite Exchange Building at 53 State, built in 1889–1891, is considered one of Boston's finest examples of commercial architecture. Renamed Exchange Place in 1984 when a forty-story tower was added, it was for many years the home of the Boston Stock Exchange. It was in the rear of the Exchange Building's sturdily built 1842 predecessor that the firefighters of 1872 were finally able to bring that stunning conflagration under control. A succession of exchange buildings on this site carried on the State Street tradition of merchants busy in their counting rooms to midday, then gathering on the exchange to swap or learn the latest news, then off to a leisurely, elaborate 2:00 P.M. dinner.

Boston merchants turned to the seven seas when the Revolutionary War was followed by depression and the closing of the British empire ports to their ships. Farsighted, adventurous, resourceful men like Joseph Barrell, Thomas Russell, William Gray, Peter Chardon Brooks, David Sears, Thomas Handasyd Perkins, and William Phillips sought, serviced, or financed trade in distant lands—in the far Indies, China, and Russia—or entered businesses once reserved for the motherland, banking and insurance. State Street became the center of this flourishing activity, sporting an exciting waterfront panorama in Boston of the 1790s, encircled by the masts of 400 or more ships in a day loading or unloading cargo. State Street had seen even earlier efforts. Boston's and America's first insurance underwriter, Joseph Marion, got started in marine insurance in 1724 in old King Street. Bostonians had often in colonial days turned to the sea for prosperity. But in both fields, as well as banking, spectacular results did not come until the late years of the eighteenth century.

In the early part of the nineteenth, State Street reflected Boston's prosperity in the beauty and number of its commercial buildings. Charles Bulfinch began in State Street by remodeling two former mansions into an insurance office and a bank in 1798–1799. Then between 1803 and 1814 he graced State Street with six impressive Federal buildings with brick or granite facades for banks and insurance firms. Among them was the state's first bank, the Massachusetts Bank, now BankBoston, which moved from its initial quarters in Hamilton Place to then 64 State in 1809.

Even Jefferson's embargo and Madison's war, both opposed generally by Federalist Boston, proved to have a silver lining. The ensuing doldrums of the waterfront made idle capital available for manufacturing and later railroading. State Street came into even greater prosperity as the seaport revived in the postwar Era of Good Feeling.

Lower State Street and around the Custom House

A plaque on the northwestern corner of the Exchange Building, at 53 State Street, marks the site of the large dwelling that Governor Winthrop built on settling in Boston in 1630. This was to all the Puritan band the most interesting spot in the colony, the center of its early political life. Magistrates who ruled the colony with Winthrop as their leader met in his great hall. His house, said Winthrop, was "full of company and business." Here he entertained distinguished visitors, among them Indian chiefs who came with their retinues of braves. Plundering of his estate by his steward forced Winthrop to sell in 1643 and build a smaller house on his "green" opposite School Street.

A tavern once regarded as dispensing Boston's best bowl of punch, the Bunch of Grapes, was located, as another plaque shows, at the northeast corner of the Exchange Building near Kilby Street. This was the favorite of the patriot party. Three clusters of gilded grapes hung invitingly above the door. The lion and the unicorn, royal symbols we have just seen on the gable steps of the Old State House, are replicas. The originals, with similar royal ornaments, were hastily gathered around town, put in a heap, and burned in State Street in front of this tavern right after the Declaration of Independence was first read from the Old State House balcony. When the 1776 thanksgiving service was over at the "Old Brick," the First Parish Church across Washington Street from the Old State House, George Washington, his staff, and town leaders gathered for a banquet here.

This tavern was also the scene of other notable events. America's first Grand Lodge of Masons was formed at a gathering here in 1733 and, after the Revolution, returning soldiers who had seen the great lands of the Midwest assembled here under a cousin of General Israel Putnam in 1786 and formed the Marietta Company to open Ohio to pioneers. A few years later twenty-one-year-old Peter Chardon Brooks observed one of Boston's two or three insurance men doing business in the Bunch of Grapes and, convinced that a boom was coming in the port of Boston, decided to be a broker. He, too, adopted the business methods of Lloyd's Coffee House in London. By the time Brooks reached thirty-six years of age he was able to retire from his State Street office a millionaire.

Kilby Street in earlier days was known as Mackerel Lane and ran close to the shore of Town Cove, with wharves extending from its water side. When George Washington first entered the town after the siege he went along Kilby Street to Liberty Square, where the Sons of Liberty had burned the intended office of the king's stamp master, to old Fort Hill. He reported to President John Hancock of the Continental Congress that he had ordered the removal of all enemy fortifications. And, to make a return of the redcoats "impracticable," Washington wrote, he ordered "a large and strong work to be thrown up on Fort Hill . . . as it commands the whole harbor." A 1989 addition to Liberty Square Plaza is the bronze statue of a woman holding a child aloft, protected by a warrior, to honor the October 23, 1956, Hungarian Revolution.

Up to recent times a 7-foot-wide, irregular alley called 'Change

Avenue, directly across the street from the entrance of the Exchange Building, ran from State Street north to Corn Court and the southwest corner of Faneuil Hall. Immediately east of it on State Street was the London Bookstore, opened in 1764 with 10,000 volumes "just imported" by news publisher John Mein. The next year Mein provided Bostonians with their first circulating library, a blessing because that winter the library at Harvard College had gone up in flames. Mein, however, was a Tory and eventually fled Boston. Mein's library would have been on the right as we enter, at 60 State Street, the Sheraton Corporation's world headquarters.

Just east of the London Bookstore, at then 66 State, was the British Coffee House, a Tory favorite where patriot James Otis got into a brawl with customs officers in 1769. Otis refused damages when his attacker apologized, but the deep head wound intermittently impaired Otis's sanity and he had to withdraw from public life. The brawl scene was about where we now see a small park just east of 60 State Street.

Bostonians enjoyed their first theater play in this British Coffee House in 1750 when some English actors put on a tragedy, *The Orphan,* by the Restoration dramatist Thomas Otway. A law against theatricals was promptly enacted. The tavern's name after the war was changed to the American Coffee House, and the site was used in part by Bulfinch for Boston's first bank when that bank joined the rush of business firms to State Street.

Merchants Row, next on our left off State Street, is the only street on the north side of State Street that is in its original position. John Hancock's store was where the row reached Corn Court on the south side of Faneuil Hall. And the great warehouses and wharf of the Faneuils, uncle and nephews, were on the east side of Merchants Row roughly along Chatham Street. Facing Merchants Row at 75 State Street is a 1988 thirty-one-story skyscraper presenting a multitoned exterior and a super-modern, six-story, glass-topped lobby with rare marble and gold-toned accents that is well worth a visit.

CUNARD marked on the six-story, 1901 classical revival building on our left at 126 State recalls that the office of the Cunard Line was located here when it provided pioneer transatlantic steamship service. The success of steam in driving vessels prompted the British postal authorities to seek a fast mail route to North America. Boston was selected, and in 1840 Samuel Cunard's new company sent over its first vessel—a service not extended to New York until 1848.

Bostonians were very proud of this commercial feather in the city's cap. In February of 1844, when ice blocked the harbor, merchants met at the Exchange and swiftly raised funds to cut a channel from India Wharf to the bay so that the twelve-hundred-ton *Britannia* could depart with mail, passengers, and cargo close to schedule. Thousands of Bostonians went out on the frozen harbor to cheer the *Britannia's* passage.

About where the building at 148 State juts into the street, just east of Chatham Row, Bostonians assured deepwater mooring for their ships in 1710 by building Long Wharf as an extension into the harbor. At first called Boston Pier, it was certainly the greatest enterprise of Boston's provincial period. Long Wharf was authorized to run "from Andrew Faneuil's corner to low water, to be of the width of King [State] Street." A Yale University president traveling through New England early in the last century called Long Wharf "the most considerable structure of its kind in the United States"—1,743 feet long and 104 feet wide with seawater no less than 17 feet deep at the end. Merchants' shops, counting rooms, and warehouses were built along the north side. A portion was called T-Wharf where it joined with a bit remaining from the decayed Barricado that Bostonians had erected across the mouth of Town Cove in 1672 to keep out Spanish, French, and Dutch raiders during Britain's imperial wars.

There have been numerous exciting happenings at this centuries-old water approach to Boston. This is where redcoats disembarked and marched up King Street, where most of them boarded boats over the Battle of Bunker Hill, and where they boarded for the last time when Washington's maneuvers made holding Boston untenable.

The day before Washington left Boston in 1789 he came to Long Wharf to embark on the barge of the French admiral and inspect two seventy-four-gun warships of our French allies "about 4 miles below the town." Washington went on to say: "Going and coming I was saluted by the two frigates which lay near the wharves, and by the

The Maritime Trail and the Boston Harbor Islands

There is more to Boston's maritime heritage than cod, clipper ships, and tea. Organized in the spirit of the venerable Freedom Trail, the new Maritime Trail helps elucidate the importance of the city's waterfront in the Revolution, the China Trade and, later, as part of the Underground Railroad. Guides lead you on this free walking tour along Long Wharf and Lower State Street. Tours leave from Marriott's Custom House and Legal Sea Foods at Long Wharf. Visit www.BostonBySea.org for more information.

Don't stop at Boston's inner habor: Be sure to take a cruise among the Boston Harbor Islands. Many depart from Long and Rowes Wharves—some as an extension of the Maritime Trail. It was once quipped that these islands were meant to be the clasp of the Emerald Necklace, the system of Boston's parks as visualized by park designer Frederick Law Olmsted. These thirty-four islands have been attracting a lot of attention in the past several years, undergoing a gradual renaissance in the wake of the successful Boston Harbor Cleanup. They were recently designated as the Boston Harbor Islands National Park Area, and new visitor facilities are scheduled to open in the near future.These islands have served motley purposes through the years; though most are currently uninhabited, they have at various times been immigration stations, quarantine hospitals, World War II lookouts, camps, sewage treatment plants, and dump sites for fill from the Big Dig.

Be alert for a glimpse of the oldest and only remaining manned offshore light house, located on Little Brewster Island. It was constructed in 1716 when Boston was one of the largest seaports in the British Empire. Nearly every flight departing from nearby Logan Aiport arcs out over it.

Edgar Allen Poe was once stationed as an army private at Fort Independence on Castle Island. While there he heard the ghoulish tales that supposedly inspired him to write "The Cask of Amontillado."

Visit Fort Warren on George's Island. It took twenty-four years to build, using stones from Quincy's quarries. It was converted into a prison for a thousand Confederate soldiers during the Civil War. During its stint as a jail, a Southern woman dressed as a man slipped into the fort with hopes of helping her captive husband escape. She was apprehended, convicted as a spy, and duly hung while wearing a black robe. It is said that the "Lady in Black" still haunts the fort.

74's after I had been on board them: as also by the 40-gun ship which lay in the same range with them. I was also saluted going and coming by the fort on Castle Island."

In 1748 the Boston captain of a ship owned by the Quincy family was carrying a letter of marque and arrived at Long Wharf with 163 chests loaded with silver and gold. The skipper, confronted by a Spanish ship, played a Yankee trick. He ordered his seamen to put coats on poles on deck and lay logs to look like cannon. Whereupon the deceived captain of the threatening ship surrendered. It took four carts, guarded by armed sailors, to convey the treasure up King Street and along the High (Washington Street) to the Quincy wine cellar. The prize ship was then sold at auction at the Royal Exchange Tavern.

Bostonians principally used this wharf for their pioneer ventures to faraway, exotic lands. In 1819 a group that helped pave the way to bringing a new state into the Union left Long Wharf. The group included seven men, their wives, children, and helpers sent as missionaries from the Park Street Church to the Hawaiian Islands. In 1836 bronzed Richard Henry Dana, twenty-one, landed at Long Wharf with, as he put it, "a little more than two years spent as a common sailor before the mast," and turned his notes into a sea classic. It was at Long Wharf that young Charles Dickens first came ashore in 1842 and won the hearts of Bostonians.

Let us now go along Broad Street to see the site of the Old Custom House before we visit the present skyscraper on lower State Street.

Broad Street and India Street just east of it were built on filled land in 1805–1807 by a group of Boston businessmen headed by the distinguished developer Uriah Cotting. The new wide streets provided access to the growing waterfront. Along the streets were built rows of uniform four-story brick warehouse structures designed by Charles Bulfinch. The orderliness contrasted sharply with the older waterfront hodgepodge of zigzag alleys and helter-skelter buildings and quays. Many of these four-story Bulfinch buildings can still be seen in this area. In fact, there are at least a dozen of the sixty Bulfinch-designed commercial buildings still standing on Broad Street—more than on any other Boston street. The ones on the west and, after the bend, on the south side have been considerably altered and have additional stories. Those on the east side, especially numbers 66, 68–70, 72, and 102–104, which was originally Uriah Cotting's, have much of their 1805–1807 appearance.

The five-story, 1853 granite warehouse at 50–52 Broad Street, at the corner of Milk Street, after a $1.2 million remodeling in 1989, became the new home of the 1867 Boston Society of Architects; the warehouse includes private office space and the society's bookstore.

Despite an added fifth floor and enlarged fourth-floor windows, particular interest attaches to the 1805–1807 Bulfinch building at 64 Broad. A partner of Cotting, Francis Cabot Lowell, who had moved his business from Long Wharf to new India Wharf, used the store at 64 Broad during 1812–1814 to develop a power loom that revolutionized American textile manufacture when installed in America's first cotton-to-cloth textile factory at Waltham in 1814. Boston merchant prince Nathan Appleton, who was a financial backer of the textile venture planned by Lowell and his brother-in-law Jackson, has told how Lowell conferred with him frequently "on the Boston Exchange." The Waltham factory, a former paper mill, was already being prepared when Lowell invited Appleton to come see the vital machine that had just been perfected. They came to Number 64. "I well recalled," said Appleton, "the state of admiration with which we sat by the hour watching the beautiful movement of this new and wonderful machine, destined . . . to change the character of all textile industry." New textile plants were soon sprouting.

Thanks to recent sensitive renovation we may still enjoy as a unit Bulfinch's 64 to 70 Broad Street facades, though the buildings now utilize 64 Broad as a common entry. Vacant land adjoining 64 Broad was used for the new building's flame-finished granite lobby leading to the famous 20 Custom House Street, which we will presently see. The lofty, impressive, six-story archway facing us ahead at the far end of Broad Street is the central entry to the historically sited, fifteen-story 1987 Rowes Wharf development we will presently visit.

From Broad Street we turn left into very short Custom House Street. At Number 20, the twelve-story 1988 office building is the site of the five-story brick Custom House built here in 1810 by Uriah Cotting. It was here that impecunious thirty-four-year-old author Nathaniel Hawthorne got a customs job as a "weigher and gauger" in 1839, with the help of Elizabeth Peabody. "What possible good can it do for me to thrust my coal-begrimed visage and salt befrosted locks into good society?" wrote hardworking, innately shy Hawthorne to his future wife, Sophia Peabody, in turning down social invitations. Two years later he quit and put his $1,000 savings in Brook Farm in the hope of providing a home so that he and Sophia could be married. When that failed, they got married anyway.

Ahead, when we get to India Street, facing us from between India and Milk Streets is the handsome, Romanesque, eight-story former Chamber of Commerce, a pink-gray granite building at 177 Milk Street with a coronet of peaked dormers. It was built in 1890–1892 as the Flour and Grain Exchange. The once-lively and spacious exchange with its great chandelier occupied the space of three floors at the

Clipper Ships

"Never in these United States has the brain of man conceived, or the hand of man fashioned, so perfect a thing as the Clipper ship." —*Samuel Eliot Morison*

After a few of these walks it quickly becomes clear that you cannot go far in this area of the city without being rewarded with a water view. From its inception Boston's fortunes have been married inescapably to the sea. A romantic interlude in this long seafaring history is the age of the glamorous clipper ships, a time of unheralded speed, derring-do on the high seas, and ships with names like the *Flying Cloud, Westward Ho,* and *Meteor.* They were some of the most beautiful and inspiring vessels ever to ply these waters.

It was the 1840s. The California Gold Rush was inspiring potential prospectors all across America. People pinned their hopes on possible gold and set their hearts on speed; out of this marriage of desire, greed, and need was born the clipper ship.

Every element of her design was subsumed in the name of speed: They were long, lean ships with arched bows and "champagne glass" sterns, all topped by rakish towers of sails. This profusion of sails—on masts often as high as twenty-story buildings—was their only seeming ostentation, but it was a necessary one; ships usually sailed with each one unfurled to harness every scrap of wind, often taking the breath of those watching from shore. The term "clipper" was derived from the word "clip," as in "to go at a good clip." Some logged more than 400 miles a day on the high seas, and many set sailing records that would remain unbroken for over one hundred years. They were the stuff of myth with their feats of speed in the age of wind-powered wooden sailing vessels.

The largest and the fleetest came from the East Boston shipyard of Donald McKay. This Nova Scotian immigrant had a flair for pairing innovations in design and construction. Boston merchants would commission him to build ships to challenge those of their New York City counterparts, and the race would be on: Who would build the ship that could swiftly cross oceans and make it to San Francisco, or England, or China first?

The launching of these magnificent vessels attracted huge crowds, including notable ship afficianadoes such as Henry Wadsworth Longfellow. He often visited Donald McKay's teeming shipyard to watch the construction of ships such as the *Flying Cloud.* He was inspired to poetry at the sight of her launch into the waters of the Harbor: "She starts, -she moves, -she seems to feel/The thrill of life along her keel/And spurning with her foot the ground/With one exulting, joyous bound/She leaps into the ocean's arms!"

The romantic age of the clipper ship was short-lived, as many ardent romances are. With the end of the Civil War, the depression of 1857, and the rise of the railroad and other steam-propelled travel, clipper trade virtually disappeared. For a brief time, however, these graceful beauties held the attention and imagination of the nation in their sway.

third-floor level, but the building currently is an office building, used mainly by architects.

To the left of the former grain exchange is a row of eight four-story brick buildings, 146 to 176 Milk Street. They were once at the head of Central Wharf, which Cotting and his associates, using a Bulfinch design, had built in 1816–1817 between Long Wharf and India Wharf. These eight are all that remain of the fifty-four stores, plus a seamen's chapel in the center—"the longest continuous block of warehouses in the country"—that once stretched into the harbor. Just after the Civil War, from 1866 to 1872, Fort Hill was leveled and the gravel was mainly used to complete filling what remained of the original Town Cove. This was capped in 1868–1872 by building a new broad Atlantic Avenue across the mouth of the old cove, roughly along the line of the vanished Barricado.

Continuing along Milk Street to Atlantic Avenue and crossing, we see how Atlantic Avenue, and later the Central Artery, cut a swath right through the rows of Bulfinch warehouses. All of the row of thirty-two stores, warehouses, and counting rooms on India Wharf is now gone. On what was once the water end of India Wharf now rise the twin forty-story Harbor Towers, an apartment complex designed by I. M. Pei and built in 1971 along with the seven-story, fifteen-hundred-car garage just north of it on Atlantic Avenue.

The barques, brigs, schooners, and clippers of earlier days are gone, but there are numerous waterfront attractions.

The New England Aquarium opened in 1969 with wall exhibit tanks and a giant ocean tank 23 feet deep, 40 feet wide—the largest on earth—with seemingly endless, strange varieties of fish. More than 7,000 saltwater and freshwater varieties can be seen: sharks, piranhas, seahorses, octopuses. Dolphins and sea lions perform; the place is literally full of wonders.

Christopher Columbus Park, with its view of slips and moorings and with places to relax, makes the harbor and its pleasures more accessible to Bostonians and visitors. This space was created in part by relocating Atlantic Avenue a bit more inland. When the ocean park is completed, the best down-harbor views will be from an observation platform at the end of Long Wharf. Long Wharf is the point of embarkation for trips to the many islands of Boston Harbor, to Nantasket Beach, or across Massachusetts Bay to Provincetown.

Be sure to include the walks around this seaside park a visit to current Rowes Wharf. This lavish complex, with its stunning six-story arched entrance, towers, condominiums, grand hotel, and underground garage, epitomizes the ongoing transformation along Boston's harbor front. Once along this shore there were wharves jammed with fishing boats, freighters, and stretches of far-from-elegant warehouses. Pleasure craft have just about replaced mercantile shipping. Take time to study the large collection of seventeenth- and eighteenth-century maps of Boston on display at the Boston Harbor Hotel.

John Rowe's wharf site was the South Battery site in colonial days until the battery exploded during the great fire of 1760. This battery, also known as the Boston Sconce, along with the North Battery once on the north side of Boston's inner harbor, had artillery that commanded the sea approaches. South Battery was also an outwork of the fort that long dominated old Fort Hill, a fort best remembered as the place where irate Bostonians initially jailed Governor Sir Edmund Andros, the first coup in the bloodless Glorious Revolution of 1689, forerunner of the American Revolution of 1775.

John Rowe, Boston selectman, merchant, shipmaster, and revolutionary patriot, had his wharf only a short walk from the 1764 mansion he built, a site we noted on old Bedford Street, where historian William H. Prescott later wrote his classics. When Samuel Adams was just about to put into effect his plans for the Boston Tea Party, John Rowe became the first to suggest the action to outraged citizens overcrowding the Old South Meeting House, touching off their wild approval with, "Who knows how tea will mingle with salt water?"

To Bostonians, up to the early decades of the 1900s, the old Rowe's Wharf meant pleasure-bound families coming here to take the big ferry boats across the busy harbor to catch narrow-gauge trains to Revere Beach. Harbor shuttle services—to the airport, the North Shore, and South Shore—are now available in much smaller boats at the new Rowes Wharf's beautiful pavilion; also at hand are water taxis, charter boats for weddings and the like, and boats for dinner and evening cruises. Modern change is not confined to this side of the harbor. From Rowes Wharf's waterfront a visitor may see on the opposite side of the mouth of Fort Point Channel the Fan Pier site where, as we have noted, the new Federal Courthouse is located.

Heading back along State Street to the Custom House in McKinley Square, all of this on filled land, we pass on our left what remains of the State Street Block, a monumental granite warehouse–counting house built in 1858 by the architect Gridley J. F. Bryant. The buildings are considered among the best of a period that saw many granite structures built on the waterfront. For modern contrast, across at 200 State is a 1985 high-rise with penthouse.

Walt Whitman took a look at the granite temple that was being built as the new Custom House (while Hawthorne was working in the nearby old one) and pronounced it "one of the noblest pieces of commercial architecture in the world." Architect Ammi B. Young had placed it on 3,000 piles at the head of the dock between Long and Central wharves. It was so difficult an endeavor that it took three years, 1837–1840, just to get in the foundation. When completed in 1847 the Custom House seemed to merit fully Whitman's praise with its pedimented porticos, thirty-two monolithic Doric columns, and low Roman-style dome. Until Atlantic Avenue was built, vessels came so close that their bowsprits poked at the windows facing the harbor.

By the turn of the twentieth century, with customs requirements continuing to grow, it was decided to add the 495-foot tower. This structure was not restrained by the city's contemporary 125-foot limit on height, a limit that did not restrict building by the federal government. When raised in 1911–1915, its twenty-nine stories made the Custom House the tallest skyscraper by far in all of New England. Elevators are available. On the twenty-fifth level, above the great 22-foot-wide clock, are observation balconies on all four sides that still offer among the best skyscraper views in the heart of Boston. While visiting the tower be sure also to get off at the second-floor level to see the original rotunda and dome, a beautiful three floors in height right up to the fifth-floor level where the tower was placed. There is an original plaque going back to President Andy Jackson, who authorized the building, besides a magnificent eagle, plenty of white marble, and twelve fluted Corinthian columns. Quite a sight!

To keep public the above attractions, Mayor Flynn arranged for Boston to buy the building in 1987 after federal employees left. Many proposals were floated. Finally, in July 1990, the Boston Redevelopment Authority designated The Beal Companies to develop a hotel. The observation deck on the twenty-fifth floor will be kept available to the public.

We walk up State Street and return again to the traffic island in old Scollay Square. From there, at the foot of Beacon Hill, we will take another approach to Faneuil Hall and the waterfront.

Walkway to Old Dock Square and the Sea

Aligning ourselves with Faneuil Hall ahead, we take off again from the old Scollay Square traffic island, cross the red bricks of Government Center, and skirt the curve of the Sears Crescent.

The Sears Crescent epitomizes the Federal age, when so many of Boston's merchant families acquired great affluence. Built in 1816, it was the first of Boston's distinguished granite post-and-lintel storefronts. The Sears Block, the prow, was added in 1848.

David Sears, Jr., the heir who built the great stone mansion on Beacon Hill that is now the Somerset Club, named this crescent for his father. Sears, Jr., an only child, had inherited one of New England's largest fortunes. His father had died suddenly late in 1816 after regaling himself on a favorite Yankee repast, a Saturday night salt fish dinner. The elder Sears, who had come to Boston in 1770 to seek his fortune, had found it as a merchant in the East India and China trade. Sears, Sr., came from Plymouth, from a Pilgrim background. His marriage underscores the blending of the Pilgrim and Puritan heritages. He married a direct descendant of the foremost Bay State Puritan, Governor John Winthrop. The elder Sears was a great developer. His activities and extensive holdings in Maine, then part of Massachusetts, led to a Penobscot Bay community being named for him, Searsport. It was with local development in mind that he had just acquired the Sears Crescent land at the time he was stricken. It is a memorial to this distinctive Yankee.

As we reach the east end of the Sears Crescent, look to your left across the plaza to the area just forward of the ramp to the main entrance of Boston City Hall. This was the location of Quincy House, which faced old Brattle Square. The vanished Boston hostelry was the favorite meeting place of ward bosses whose Tammany Hall tactics dominated the city, its elections, and all municipal patronage and business for decades after Boston's nineteenth-century tidal wave of immigration. Legendary Martin Lomasney, the "Mahatma" of the West End's Ward 8, was long kingpin of these lordly meetings of what was called the Board of Strategy. President Kennedy's mother, Rose, told how both her father, "Honey Fitz," and father-in-law, P. J. Kennedy, were members of the board. Fitzgerald called Lomasney "my political godfather."

Membership did not mean that they always worked together. Fitzgerald, who became boss of the North End, and James Michael Curley, boss of the Roxbury ward where he was born, were political foes. Each, when he felt double-crossed, ran in turn with the war cry, "Down with the Bosses!" It worked magic at the polling places. The Robin Hood existence of the ward bosses, though it fell into decline, persisted until they were made obsolete by the systematized benefactions of F. D. Roosevelt's New Deal.

On the corner of old Washington Street, on our right, in the main entry of the sixteen-story 1 Washington Mall (built in 1972), a plaque tells that here was the goldsmith shop of Paul Revere. Revere was far more than a goldsmith. He had to be a jack of all trades to support his family—eight children by each of his two wives. In his climb to economic independence, Revere moved his shop fairly often. He shifted his hardware selling and silver making from about a half-mile down Washington Street near Liberty Tree to be nearer the marketplace. In a few years he moved again to nearby shops in Union and North Streets.

Revere was not the only one to find this marketplace area a path to prosperity. Some of Boston's greatest merchants started here. This section of old Washington Street was known as Cornhill, the short stretch from School Street to Dock Square just ahead of us. It was along here that a New Hampshire lad, Sam Appleton, leased "a small shop of about 20 by 18 feet" and soon was joined by his fifteen-year-old brother, Nathan. They would become multimillionaires and help finance New England's industrialization. And right here, at the corner where Washington Street used to enter Dock Square, the Lawrences began their climb when young Amos arrived from Groton in 1807 and shortly had his brother Abbott as an apprentice. Ahead for all of these entrepreneurs were mansions on Beacon Hill.

Before going down the steps at the south side of City Hall to reach Dock Square, walk out on the elevated plaza in back of the skyscraper at 28 State Street for a remarkable cityscape overview of the old Town Cove section we are about to visit. Indeed, where we stand in back of the bank was once much lower and a part of Dock Square.

Faneuil Hall, one of America's most beloved national shrines, the Quincy Market area beyond it, glimpses of the soon-to-disappear elevated Central Artery Expressway built in the 1950s, and even the four-and-one-half-acre Christopher Columbus Park beyond it—everything east from North Street on the left side of the modern, staggered, colonial saltbox style greenhouses beside Faneuil Hall to the Custom House tower on the right, and more—were built where once the tides flowed in and out of Town Cove.

Dock Square was at the head of Town Cove—just east, harborside of present City Hall. The south shore of the cove ran roughly to the right of Faneuil Hall, along Merchants Row to State Street, from State along Kilby Street to Liberty Square, then skirted Fort Hill to the South Battery, with its mounted cannon to protect the cove and harbor. The north shore ran to the North Battery, with its cannon to protect the cove, harbor, and the approach to the Charles River. The present curving, twisting North Street—a way with many former names, including Ann, Drawbridge, Fish, and Ship—still marks the north shore. Trade brought ships and sailors, and the shorefront, especially on the north side, became crowded with inns, taverns, and dens of loose living. Police took action; street names were changed.

The portion of Dock Square at the foot of the southside City Hall steps we just used was named Adams Square as Boston was getting ready to celebrate the nation's first centennial. The redone square was soon embellished with a copy of the statue that Anne Whitney, a Bay State artist, had made of Samuel Adams to join John Winthrop's statue in Statuary Hall in the Capitol in Washington. Relocated in 1928, the Samuel Adams statue could not have been given a more appropriate setting than in the foreground of Fanueil Hall where "The Father of the Revolution" furnished so much of the masterminding and inspiration that led his fellow Americans to sever their political ties with Britain. The resolute expression on Samuel Adams's face catches him at the climactic moment when he insisted that Boston be rid of not one, but both regiments of redcoats after the Boston Massacre.

Before visiting Faneuil Hall, there are a few other interesting sights at hand.

Just across North Street on our left, in the midhighway park between Union and Congress Streets, is a memorial dedicated in 1980 to Governor (but most of all Boston Mayor) James Michael Curley. There were many intriguing sides to Curley's personality. The artist, Lloyd Lillie, has portrayed two of the most prominent ones. On the bench Curley seems so approachable, so like the role he loved, "Mayor of the Poor." On his feet he appears as the orator: adroit, sparkling, so skilled that even his enemies would say, "James can charm the birds out of the trees."

At the other end of the park, in sobering contrast to the ebullient Curley statues and bustling crowds, are the stark glass towers of The New England Holocaust Memorial. The six glass columns sit on top of dark, smoldering chambers, meant to evoke Nazi death camps. Virtually every inch of each pane of glass is etched with the identification numbers of those murdered at the hands of Hitler's Third Reich, six million in all. Unveiled in October 1995, it was purposefully located at this prominent point along the well-traveled Freedom Trail and should give many passersby pause to consider the full meaning and importance of freedom.

Across from this midhighway park, on the Congress Street side opposite Marsh Lane, once stood a house at 25 Friend Street, where

View through old Dock Square to the financial district

Winslow Homer was born. The self-taught artist came of old seafaring New England stock, but his father was a hardware merchant with his store in Dock Square. Young Homer came most naturally by his love of sea and waterside life so richly presented in his paintings.

Dock Square was also home for another noted old-line family, the Daweses, who were related to Benjamin Franklin's family. Young William Dawes, Jr., was the other patriot sent out April 18, 1775, by Joseph Warren to warn that the redcoats were on their way. Dawes even managed to escape when Paul Revere was captured, held briefly, and released. The Dawes family house was at 22 North Street, opposite Faneuil Hall. Dawes, after his marriage, lived next door at 24 North, and later ran a general store in Dock Square. He was even licensed to sell rum because the selectmen, as they expressed it, found Dawes to be a man "of sober life and conversation."

> WHERE I FOUND A MUDDY LANE, I LEFT A BROAD HIGHWAY; WHERE I FOUND A BARREN WASTE, I LEFT A HOSPITAL; WHERE I FOUND A DISEASE-BREEDING ROW OF TENEMENT HOUSES, I LEFT A HEALTH CENTER; WHERE I FOUND A VACANT LOT, I LEFT A MAGNIFICENT TEMPLE OF LEARNING; WHERE I FOUND A WEED-GROWN FIELD, I LEFT A PLAYGROUND: THROUGHOUT LIFE, WHEREVER I HAVE FOUND A THISTLE, I ENDEAVORED TO REPLACE IT WITH A ROSE.
>
> —JAMES MICHAEL CURLEY

Almost from the beginnings of the town the Dock Square area has been a marketing area. Haymarket, a weekend open-air pushcart market, can still be seen just off North Street on Blackstone Street, next on the left.

The streets all around here were long the destination of farmers, and later of other suppliers, who were trucking and carting produce and meat to market. Faneuil Hall was itself part answer to the needs created by this traffic.

The water approach to the dock area lasted longer on the north side of Faneuil Hall. There was a narrow docking passage for vessels roughly along present North Market Street to Dock Square with a swing bridge, in two parts, across the dock that connected Merchants

Row, in front of Faneuil Hall, with North Street. This was long the Fish Market on the north side of Faneuil Hall.

On the south side was the Corn Market. John Hancock, who had warehouses at his wharf, one of the town's biggest, off North Street near Lewis Street, had his store by the Corn Market and Merchants Row. Hancock called it "Store No. 4 at the East End of Faneuil Hall Market," where he had "choice Newcastle coals and Irish butter, cheap for cash" as well as English and India goods. The Faneuils had their warehouses nearby on a byway called Butler's Row, pretty much in line with present Chatham Street, a very short stretch to their wharf on Town Cove.

Faneuil Hall and Quincy Market

The main entrance to Faneuil Hall is by the middle of the five doors on the Merchants Row east side. The other doors, like the ones on the west side facing City Hall, lead to the first-floor shops, now vending cake, cookies, and delicacies, instead of the earlier floor stalls whose wares, for many generations, were fresh meats from carcass to fancy cuts and produce of every variety. Faneuil Hall was, like the Old State House, undergoing a $5 million restoration in spring 1992 to preserve and make more accessible this beloved, national historical jewel.

The historic heart of Faneuil Hall is on the second floor, a citizens' forum, the most important use developed since it was presented to the town by merchant Peter Faneuil in 1742. In 1806 the building, to fit a growing town, was enlarged by Charles Bulfinch; his second-floor hall, with its galleries, is best known to Americans. In all Bulfinch doubled the width of the original structure and added a third floor, which has long been the armory of the nation's oldest military group, the Ancient and Honorable Artillery Company of 1638. A climb to the third floor will well repay a visitor with a chance to see the Ancients' meeting place, historic paintings, arms, and museum.

Besides the spacious second-floor auditorium, Faneuil Hall offers on its walls superb likenesses of national heroes and public figures. All are well identified. Most striking are the background painting above the stage, *Webster's Reply to Hayne,* and Gilbert Stuart's portrait of George Washington, picturing him taking Dorchester Heights and forcing the redcoats to flee from the menace of his artillery fire.

It is thrilling to recall the great moments and events in Faneuil Hall and the orators who made it echo with ideals and aims that have profoundly moved America. James Otis, speaking here, prophetically called it the "Cradle of Liberty." Here Samuel Adams aroused the enthusiasm of Boston's town meeting and, with Sons of Liberty as shock troops, led his fellow citizens along the path to freedom. It was within walls still standing that Bostonians protested against the Stamp Act that they saw as tyranny—and soon were able to illuminate the building to celebrate the act's repeal.

WHEN LIBERTY IS IN DANGER, FANEUIL HALL HAS THE RIGHT, IT IS HER DUTY, TO STRIKE THE KEYNOTE FOR THE UNITED STATES.

—WENDELL PHILLIPS

One of the hall's greatest moments came on November 2, 1772, when Samuel Adams proposed at a town meeting that Boston create a Committee of Correspondence and invite the other twelve colonies to do the same. By this maneuver Adams provided an effective apparatus for the citizens of all the colonies to muster united action. He never said, but it was most likely that Samuel Adams was on hand here during the Boston Tea Party that he had contrived, to be ready to act in the face of any retaliatory emergency.

Faneuil Hall, for a building in a Puritan town, had odd usage in the winter of 1775–1776 when the besieged redcoats staged theatrical shows under the guidance of playwright-general "Gentleman" Johnny Burgoyne.

After the Revolution Lafayette was given a public banquet here in 1784 on the anniversary of the victory at Yorktown. Washington, who on his 1789 Boston visit was given a public reception and banquet, called it "a large and elegant dinner" and made note that the Bostonians requested him to sit for a portrait "for the hall."

In 1812 in the present enlarged hall, "splendidly decorated" as was

THE PLAY'S THE THING

During the Revolutionary War, British soldiers ensconced themselves in Faneuil Hall. In mocking disregard for a city ordinance prohibiting plays, they used the hall as a theater. So enthralled were British officers by a performance of *The Blockade of Boston,* a farce penned by General Burgoyne, that many thought a shouted alarm that the "rebels" were marching on Charlestown Neck was a joke. It was not.

the rest of Boston, Commodore Isaac Hull of the U.S.F. (now U.S.S.) *Constitution* was given a "sumptuous" dinner to celebrate his crushing victory a few days earlier over H.M.F. (H.M.S.) *Guerriere,* forty-four guns, 700 miles east of Boston. This was the victory that produced the frigate's triumphant nickname, "Old Ironsides."

Jonathan Trumbull's immense historical paintings for the Capitol's rotunda went on tour before being installed. In December 1818 *The Signing of the Declaration of Independence* was displayed here and aging former President John Adams, then eighty-three, came to join the throng of spectators. He relived possibly the greatest scene of his life when, pointing to the canvas, he exclaimed: "There is the door through which Washington escaped when I nominated him as Commander-in-Chief of the Continental Army!"

Faneuil Hall has been cradle, too, for many other great national causes. William Lloyd Garrison's intimate ally Oliver Johnson told how a public meeting here in 1837 brought the crucial enlistment of "the orator of the anti-slavery cause." The meeting was called to protest the Illinois murder by slave-state mobsters of an antislavery newsman, the Reverend Elijah Lovejoy. Twenty-six-year-old socialite Wendell Phillips, son of Boston's first mayor, was seated in the gallery. Phillips had not come to speak but was so aroused by "the trumpet-tones of Garrison" that he made his way to the rostrum and gave his first, fiery antislavery address, taking the audience, as Johnson expressed it, "by storm."

East of Faneuil Hall on Merchants Row is the Quincy Market, with its portico of fifteen-ton, 22-foot monolithic granite Doric columns, duplicated 535 feet away on its east end, all so reminiscent of London's Covent Garden. Quincy Market with its flanking rows of warehouses and shops was long the center for the city's meat, poultry, produce, and dairy products, wholesale and retail, which had far outgrown the stalls and shops of Faneuil Hall. All the vendors moved, for still more space, toward Dorchester. By 1976 these granite-faced Greek-revival buildings of the 1820s were restored and the area transformed into one of Boston's great attractions.

It seems strange now to recall that when Josiah Quincy, then mayor, proposed this extension of the municipal market, he encountered bitter opposition. Harbor inlets, wharves, and old dock passages had to be filled out to Commercial Street. Seven new streets, including Commercial, had to be created. But the market building, with its distinctive copper dome, cupola, and rotunda designed by Alexander Parris, architect of St. Paul's Cathedral, came into existence in 1825–1826. The city built it, still owns it, and lets it under a ninety-nine-year lease.

Just as Mayor Quincy's persistence brought new life in his day to the market area, so did the renewal of the 1970s. Bostonians and visitors, young and old alike, find it a continuous indoor-outdoor festival. Trees flourish on the plazas. There are even places to sit and enjoy the antics of street performers. Its corridors, stalls, cobblestoned walkways, and more than 140 shops and restaurants are both a delightful wanderland and wonderland. There are foods and wares of all sorts, things of fun, things of fashion, gifts, flowers, jewels—and some of its old vendors still selling meat and produce. At least a dozen stalls have had the same tenant for generations. Doe, Sullivan and Company, located at old stall number 45 next to the central rotunda rest area from 1829 to 1988, was the oldest cheese wholesaler and retailer in Boston. When reopened, the six and a half acres of attractions drew some 30,000 visitors a day—more people than all the residents of Boston back in the 1820s when the market buildings were erected. Currently the daily visitors exceed 50,000.

The flanking warehouses, with their monolithic granite post-and-lintel storefronts, were built by prominent Boston businessmen according to the uniform design of Parris. Their galleries and arcades are an extension of the pleasure of the central market. At 30 North Market, opposite the rotunda, on all three levels we come to a Boston landmark going back to early in the last century, Durgin Park restaurant, enjoyably combining the old and the new.

At the east end of the Quincy Market spreads the new (1983–1984) Marketplace Center with an attractive, glass-canopied central passage to the waterfront we will visit. First, though, pause to glance back at the magnificent vista of the marketplace against its twentieth century backdrop. Also glance again at the Custom House to our right, to get a keener impression of the gracefulness of the original Greek temple base before it was topped with a tower.

Christopher Columbus Park was undertaken by the city's renewal staff in 1964. The purpose, besides renewing and revitalizing the formerly dilapidated waterfront area, was to give Bostonians a "pedestrian access to the water's edge," a direct walkway all the way through Government Center, the Faneuil Hall and Quincy Market area, "culminating at the harbor." In 1986 a garden and fount were added and named for Rose Fitzgerald Kennedy, President John F. Kennedy's mother, born nearby at 4 Garden Court, North End, which we will see shortly. In the trellis arcade center is a statue of Columbus made from Carrara marble, which Michelangelo used to carve his *Pieta, Moses,* and *David.*

The six-acre park, at which we have arrived, with its huge ship chain and black bollards near harbor's edge, its arcade and trellis, and its imaginative children's playground, is only part of this new waterfront pleasure area. Overall, it extends from docking facilities for craft near the twin Harbor Towers complex on old India Wharf northward to beyond Lewis Wharf where John Hancock's wharf once stretched seaward. All this, with harborfront attractions of wharves, coves, and marine activities, is accessible to the public.

Public access to the waterfront is slated to extend even farther. First will be the 7 miles from "Old Ironsides" in Charlestown, all along

Boston Harbor

the harborfront, to Harbor Towers, Rowes Wharf, and even to the gigantic Fan Pier development planned for the east end of Fort Point Channel. Eventually, when linked to walks along the Charles River, Boston's Harbor Walk will cover 21 waterside miles.

Old T-Wharf, demolished in 1967 when its rotted underpinnings became a hazard, will be reborn as one of the attractions of Waterfront Park. Along the old wharf, which ran beyond the present Marriott Hotel and north of and parallel to present Long Wharf, stood a three-story wooden building of lofts used for decades by the fishing industry. These very low-rent lofts were later enjoyed in the mid-1900s by about the only dwellers then living harborside along Atlantic Avenue. The wharf's reconstruction will not mean new lofts. Instead, the new T-Wharf will provide slips for private and commercial vessels, serve water transportation, and support a public viewing tower at the end of the new pier. Also, along with Long Wharf, revived T-Wharf will provide the park a convenient Visitor Service Center.

> A BOSTON MAN IS THE EAST WIND MADE FLESH.
>
> —T. G. APPLETON

Before leaving the area, drop into the 1857 Mercantile Wharf Building, 111 Atlantic Avenue, at the bend of Atlantic Avenue across from the Kennedy Garden. We can enter at the Cross Street entrance on the southwest end of the building. The atrium, open-air effect achieved in the conversion of this massive stone warehouse into apartments and a commercial ground floor is quite unusual and impressive. We make our way back through the bazaar of Quincy Market and the Faneuil Hall plazas to old Scollay Square to begin our walk to Boston's North End.

NORTH END

Washington's Route through the North End

The North End of Boston, birthplace of "Old Ironsides" and of arrangements for Paul Revere's lantern lights and midnight ride, is best approached by the departure route George Washington chose after his final visit to Boston.

Washington went in a carriage from his lodging by old Scollay Square and turned right at the Concert Hall, once at the head of old Hanover Street, where he had the night before attended a brilliant assembly and later wrote of seeing "upwards of 100 ladies. Their appearance," he went on to record, "was elegant and many of them very handsome."

The President had an escort of the Boston Corps of Horse and a cavalcade of a number of prominent citizens who later accompanied him from Charlestown to visit Harvard University, its library, and its museum before he would head north to Salem. In this farewell entourage were Vice President John Adams and future Governor James Bowdoin. As the president moved down the now-vanished part of Hanover Street, he could see on his left the dwelling of one of the Revolution's greatest heroes, Dr. Joseph Warren. It was from here that Warren in 1775 sent two neighbors, William Dawes of North

NORTH END

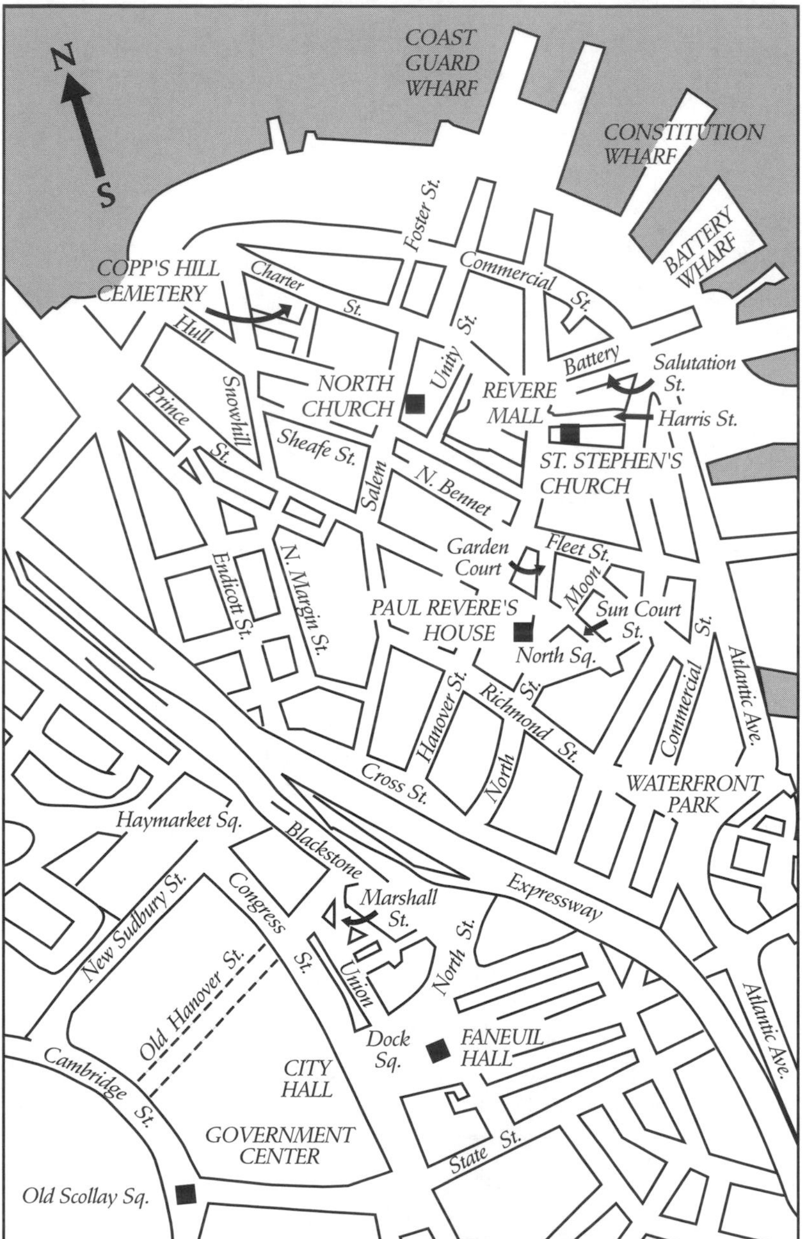
COAST GUARD WHARF
CONSTITUTION WHARF
BATTERY WHARF
N
S
Foster St.
Commercial St.
COPP'S HILL CEMETERY
Charter St.
Hull
Unity St.
Battery
Salutation St.
Snowhill
NORTH CHURCH
REVERE MALL
Harris St.
Prince St.
Sheafe St.
ST. STEPHEN'S CHURCH
Salem
N. Bennet
Garden Court
Fleet St.
Endicott St.
N. Margin St.
Moon
Sun Court St.
PAUL REVERE'S HOUSE
North Sq.
Commercial St.
Atlantic Ave.
Hanover St.
Richmond St.
North St.
Cross St.
North
WATERFRONT PARK
Haymarket Sq.
Blackstone
Expressway
Marshall St.
New Sudbury St.
Congress St.
Old Hanover St.
Union
North St.
Atlantic Ave.
Dock Sq.
FANEUIL HALL
Cambridge St.
CITY HALL
GOVERNMENT CENTER
State St.
Old Scollay Sq.

Street and Paul Revere of North Square, to warn that the redcoats were on their way.

To follow Washington's route, in part, walk to the left of the new City Hall; by descending the plaza steps or ramp and then crossing Congress Street, we come to Union Street and the remaining part of Hanover Street.

At 41–43 Union Street is the Union Oyster House, a building Washington would have surely noticed. Passing British troops used to yell for the hanging of the patriot printer on the second floor, Isaiah Thomas, publisher of the famous Revolutionary newspaper, *The Massachusetts Spy*. Only three days before the shooting war began at Lexington and Concord, Thomas smuggled press and type out of Boston by oxcart to Worcester. There he published the first official account of the opening battle.

The Georgian-style building was erected about 1714. A sergeant of the Ancients, Hopestill Capen, ran a dry goods store and had as an apprentice Benjamin Thompson, a Tory who fled America and became a famous and wealthy scientist ennobled as Count Rumford. Future French King Louis Philippe, in exile here in 1797 as the Duc de Chartres, gave French lessons in his upstairs quarters until family funds arrived for him and his two brothers. Around 1826 an oyster and clam bar was opened on the ground floor. Fishermen were then able to sail their vessels virtually to the back door. For generations the curved mahogany bar has been a magnet to oyster fans sitting on the stools or passersby watching the expert shucking through old-fashioned small windowpanes. Sawdust on the floor and whitewashed booths have long provided a setting for the serving of fish delicacies and chowders.

At the southeast corner of Union and Hanover Streets, before these roadways were widened, a blue ball suspended from an iron bracket was hung up in 1712 over the chandlery and soap-boiling shop of Josiah Franklin, father of Benjamin Franklin. The large Franklin family—Benjamin was the last son of Josiah's seventeen children—lived on the upper floor of the two-story dwelling. From here young Benjamin went to Latin School and used to walk to work by way of Dock Square and Brattle Square to his brother James's newspaper.

On President Washington's left as he reached Union Street, which used to run northwestward to Haymarket square, there stood midway down the block a two-and-a-half story building so old (it was built in 1680) that the roadway in its honor was formerly called Green Dragon Lane. The lane's name had been changed in 1708 to Union Street in honor of the formation of the British Union under Queen Anne. The building, once 84 Union Street, was the Green Dragon Tavern hailed by Daniel Webster as the "Headquarters of the Revolution." North End mechanics, workmen on the many wharves and allied shops, formed a sturdy contingent of Samuel Adams's supporters. Adams enjoyed a mug of ale and used tavern calls to win followers. When Salutation Tavern deeper in the North End became too small, gatherings were held at the Green Dragon. The Boston Caucus Club and Sons of Liberty met and helped hatch deeds like the Boston Tea Party. And more than revolution was nurtured here. In 1788, on a motion by Paul Revere, the mechanics voted in favor of adopting the federal Constitution and thereby persuaded Samuel Adams to go along with them.

Masonic groups were another heavy contributor of manpower to the Revolution. George Washington was Virginia's most prominent Mason. The Green Dragon was purchased by St. Andrew's lodge and in 1769 became the Bay Colony's first grand lodge, with Joseph Warren as grand master. Paul Revere was a Mason and, by the time he helped Samuel Adams lay the cornerstone of the State House, was grand master of the grand lodge.

The Mill Pond, which had been at the end of the block near Green Dragon Tavern, was a playground for young Ben Franklin. Living close to water, he related that he "learnt early to swim well and to manage boats." He used to fish for minnows in the Mill Pond. A born leader, he told how he got fellow youngsters to build a wharf on the pond "fit for us to stand upon." The stones they used belonged to a man planning a new house and the workmen took them back. That, said Franklin, "convinced me that nothing was useful which was not honest."

The original Green Dragon stood until 1828—well into the period when filling in the Mill Pond created fifty new acres, as much area as the Common. This was from 1810 to the late 1820s, with gravel from Beacon Hill and Copp's Hill in the North End. New streets within the pond area's roughly triangular shape were laid out from a plan of Charles Bulfinch. In June 1993 the venerable Green Dragon was restored to its rightful place on Boston's Freedom Trail, very near the original site.

Washington's route bordered the east side of the pond, Hanover to Salem Street to Prince Street and to Boston's first bridge north across the Charles River to Charlestown, replacing the ancient ferry service. We will see more of this route later.

Meantime, on the right a bit farther down Hanover Street, we come to one of Boston's oldest and shortest streets, Marshall Street, which runs diagonally back to the Union Oyster House. It developed as a shortcut from Dock Square to the Charlestown ferry. Like the North End, Marshall Street has some of the oldest sights in Boston.

Walking along Marshall Street, we find embedded in the rear of the house on the left, the one at the east corner of Marshall and Hanover Streets, something reminiscent of London, the Boston Stone. Around 1700 a painter who once had a shop on this site used the round stone as a grinder to mix pigment and linseed by rolling it in a trough; the larger stone, before it broke, was four times its present size. The date 1737, according to legend, was added by a later owner.

Across from the Boston Stone, long the starting marker for measuring distance from Boston, is a freestanding three-story redbrick building of 1760 at 10 Marshall Street, a Boston showpiece. It was originally one of four similar structures built in a block along the creek by John Hancock. John's younger brother Ebenezer had his office and house in this building when he was deputy paymaster of the Continental Army in 1778.

Admiral d'Estaing's fleet, the one hosted by Governor Hancock, brought two million of young King Louis XVI's silver crowns here to pay Washington's army, a deal arranged by Benjamin Franklin. In back of this building the tide of Town Cove once flooded and ebbed in what is now Creek Square.

In a few steps, as we continue along Hanover, we come to Blackstone Street, named for Boston's first settler. For decades this has been the locale of Haymarket, an open-air, pushcart fruit and vegetable market. This short street was originally a creek that ran between Town Cove and Mill Pond with short bridges over the creek at both Hanover and nearby North Streets. This old creek, later a canal, converted the North End into an island. In early days the North End was even called "the island of Boston."

Washington crossed the old bridge of Hanover Street that was converted in 1793 into a stone arch. We shall dodge semipermanent Big Dig construction and cross Blackstone Street. On our left, once we have crossed, at what was the northwest corner of Hanover and Blackstone, formerly stood at 168 Hanover the small dry goods shop in which nineteen-year-old Eben Jordan began his own business, a career that would lead to the creation of New England's largest department store.

Boston, as one of America's oldest communities, has had to struggle with every urban problem, including growing traffic. We have seen how Boston built the nation's first trolley subway to ease traffic along the Common. Here the city built an elevated Expressway—the Central Artery—to route north-south traffic through the city and lessen traffic on ever-congested downtown streets. The Central Artery must also handle traffic to and from east Boston via a harbor tunnel. When the Central Artery was being constructed in the 1950s, entire neighborhoods were razed for the sake of mobility, and communities such as the Waterfront and the North End were bisected and partially cut off from the rest of the city.

Now outdated, obstructive, and legendarily congested, the woefully inadequate elevated Expressway is to be put underground in what has become the single most complex highway project in the history of America. The six-lane elevated Expressway is gradually being replaced with an eight- to ten-lane underground expressway. The aging Central Artery will then be demolished, leaving twenty-seven acres of downtown open space and fostering a newly reconnected Boston. The staggeringly complex Big Dig project, which involves keeping the crumbling Central Artery open to traffic while building a massive underground tunnel directly below it, while maintaining utility service to all involved—all within feet of century-old buildings in the heart of a metropolitan city—is slated to be completed in 2004.

The Big Dig will make possible the restoration here of Hanover Street, a straightaway named for the royal house of Hanover and one of Boston's main thoroughfares. For the time being, however, Big Dig construction and the Expressway itself prevents us from continuing directly along Hanover Street. Instead, follow the red line (and signs) under the Expressway to Salem Street, turn right immediately at Cross Street for a block, and we are again on Hanover.

Royally named Hanover Street, with its waterfront about to be rejoined to the city, has seen many successive racial changes and most recently an influx of renters and condo dwellers, especially at its waterfront end.

A glance down Hanover (which goes, as we shall see, the short distance to the waterfront) once again recalls old London. At the bend ahead we can see the redbrick, Wrenlike church designed in 1804 for the Second Congregational Society in the North End, the only one remaining of five Boston churches designed by Bulfinch. Its white cupola dominates this view, still not upstaged by midcity high-rises. The church has been part of the changes wrought in this old section of Boston by tides of immigration that converted old estates into tenements and shops. The Puritans were succeeded years after the Revolution by immigrants mainly from Ireland. By 1862 this meeting house became St. Stephen's Catholic Church, the same year as fund-raising began for building of a new Holy Cross Cathedral in the South End. Late nineteenth-century immigration made the North End population heavily Jewish, and then it became chiefly Italian, as it still is. Many little alleyways, courts, and cul-de-sacs, as well as the narrow and crooked streets, underline the age of this section of Boston.

On the right, at the north corner of Hanover and Richmond, was once the parish church of Ralph Waldo Emerson. Erected in 1721 as the New Brick, later adopting the the burned Second Church's name, it was long known as the "Cockerel" for the chanticleer its builders perched on its steeple weathervane. Young Mr. Emerson came in 1829 to this church, once the meeting house of royal Governor Hutchinson. While here Mr. Emerson also served on Boston's School

Committee and, like his father, was chaplain of the state Senate. He was married while here and, little more than a year and a half later, suffered the loss of his beautiful bride to tuberculosis. By late 1832 he resigned his pastorate to pursue a literary and a broader public career.

Emerson's "powerful influence" in helping abolish slavery was lauded by Garrison's associate Oliver Johnson. Different from most other Boston clergy of that day, said Johnson, Emerson "had the courage to open his pulpit for the delivery of an anti-slavery sermon" on May 29, 1831, by the Reverend Samuel J. May. This was in the early days of Garrison's labor and the life of May, uncle of Louisa May Alcott, was often in danger. The "Cockerel" was the setting for this sermon just six months before May helped to create the pioneer New England Anti-Slavery Society.

Paul Revere's celebrated casting of church bells began with the "Cockerel," where earlier he had been baptized and where his family worshipped. Members of the North Church in North Square, after redcoats had used it for firewood, joined the "Cockerel" and brought along their bell. In 1792 it cracked. Revere, though a neophyte in bell making, offered to recast it and did. On it he molded: THE FIRST BELL CAST IN BOSTON 1792. P. REVERE.

On our left, as we approach Prince Street, at 298–300 Hanover Street, once stood the dwelling of the best known of the colonial Puritan clergy, Cotton Mather, great preacher, prolific author, beguiled by the witchcraft superstition of his era but courageously far in advance of his times in helping to introduce inoculation against smallpox. The opposition to and dread of inoculation were intense. Even five months after Dr. Zabdiel Boylston, urged by Mr. Mather, had begun inoculating his own family, Mather's dwelling came under attack in November 1721, a plague year. "Damn you, I will enoculate you with this, with a pox to you" read a note tossed with a "granado" bomb through Mather's window. The fuse shook loose and there was no explosion.

The first Italian church in New England, St. Leonard's, built in 1873, is at the northwest corner of Hanover and Prince. A restful, attractive "Peace Garden"—a brilliantly lighted scene at Yuletide—is maintained by the Franciscan Friars.

Prince Street crosses Hanover. When we turn right here it leads to one of Boston's most historic centers, North Square, where we shall presently head. Prince Street, to our left, soon crosses Salem Street and winds northwestward to the mouth of the Charles River and the bridge to Charlestown, passing in Washington's time the edge of the Mill Pond. In his diary Washington wrote that the bridge was "useful and noble ... doing great credit to the enterprising spirit of the people of this state." The 40-foot-wide bridge, with a 30-foot draw, the first attempt in America to build a bridge over a broad, deep river, was erected in 1785–1786 by a group headed by John Hancock, during the interval in Hancock's service when James Bowdoin was governor. The river at this point was deeper and several hundred feet wider than the Thames at London Bridge. The bridge was opened on Bunker Hill Day, 1786, with great ceremony, parade, music, feasting, church bells ringing, and cannon fire from Bunker Hill and Copp's Hill. For Washington's passage across the bridge Boston's *Centinel* reported that the bridge "was finely decorated with flags of all nations . . . and he was saluted by a discharge of guns from artillery posted on the celebrated heights of Charlestown."

Turn right now from Hanover Street to Prince Street and head toward North Square, a short block away. We are entering an area once just off Town Cove's north shore, an area that was the spacious setting for some of Boston's most impressive mansions during the late colonial and provincial eras of the community.

On our left on Prince Street, its front facing Garden Court Street just ahead on our left, was the three-story brick mansion with many-dormered roof built by the rich merchant and governor's councillor William Clark. Originally North Square was named Clark's Square in his honor. He owned dozens of sailing ships, was a luminary in the court circle, and lived lavishly in his twenty-six room mansion with its 10-foot-high ceilings, wainscoting, walls papered with landscapes, delicate carving, and ornamentation. During the wars with France his fortune was wrecked by the loss of forty sailing ships, and his great wharf, Clark's Wharf, roughly where present Lewis Wharf is, became the property of John Hancock's wealthy merchant uncle Thomas and was renamed Hancock's Wharf.

North Enders: A Separate Peace

Even before the Central Artery Expressway severed Hanover Street and divided the North End from Boston proper, the neighborhood had always maintained an identity distinct from the rest of the city. In colonial times it was a peculiar annual custom for North Enders and Bostonians to clash in mock battles on Guy Fawkes Day. Though staged, the affair often devolved into real fisticuffs. It was the Revolutionary War effort that finally caused North Enders and other Bostonians to set aside their differences to fight for a common cause.

Clark's mansion and gardens became the property of a wealthy, high-living descendent of Oliver Cromwell, Sir Charles Henry Frankland, who, when King George II gave him a choice of being royal governor or customs collector, picked the latter. The staircase in the mansion's main hall "was so broad and easy of ascent that Frankland used to ride his pony up and down with ease and safety." On an official visit to Marblehead Sir Charles's eye caught sight of beauteous Agnes Surraige, a maid in an inn. He took her back to Boston, as he said, to educate her. They resided, too, in his splendid country estate in Hopkinton, west of Boston. Some say inattention to duties lost him his lucrative post; others say he left for his health. He went with Agnes to Portugal. There, in the great earthquake of 1755, she saved his life when, as he said, "I was buried in ruins." From gratitude he married her and at last she became Lady Frankland.

The mansion had a later owner, Redford Webster, father of socialite John Webster, the Harvard professor who murdered Dr. Parkman.

Directly north of the Frankland mansion, also facing Garden Court Street, with gardens and fruit trees that reached back to Hanover and Fleet streets, was the mansion of Royal Governor Thomas Hutchinson, which is depicted on the bronze plaque on the current dwelling. It was another resplendently constructed brick building with Ionic pilasters, a British crown over every window, mahogany paneling in the great parlor, and costly furnishings. Hutchinson's father built the mansion in 1710.

This North End area has seen many events associated with the American Revolution. Some led up to it. In 1768 Hancock's Wharf, largest in the North End, was invaded by customs agents to seize Hancock's sloop *Liberty* for alleged smuggling of wine. Extensive and destructive rioting followed and first brought redcoats to Boston. Some of them even landed at Hancock's Wharf.

Earlier, Hutchinson's mansion was the scene of wild damage during the Stamp Act riots of 1765. Hutchinson, then lieutenant governor and chief justice, was unfairly suspected of advocating the Stamp Act. He had to flee through his gardens as the mob pillaged his mansion, smashed furnishings, drained his wine cellar, and scattered in the gutter pages of his Massachusetts history on which the scholarly governor had been working.

Unprecedented troubles with Boston's outraged colonials were by no means over.

North Square to St. Stephen's Church

Before we reach the chief attraction of North Square, Paul Revere's house, the oldest extant dwelling in Boston, there is a reminder of the period when the North End's population was predominantly Irish. Two doors down Garden Court Street, at Number 4 on the right-hand side, was the dwelling of John F. "Honey Fitz" Fitzgerald, congressman and mayor. This was the birthplace in 1890 of his daughter Rose, wife of Ambassador Joseph P. Kennedy and mother of President John F. Kennedy. Mother Rose Kennedy described the Fitzgerald quarters as "a modest flat in an eight-family dwelling." The Fitzgeralds, like the Kennedys, had come to Boston in the mid-1800s to escape the potato famine and seek a new life. For most of his life in the North End, Honey Fitz's father was a grocer on North Street and on Hanover Street. During his eight years in this house, young "Honey Fitz" became a political power in the North End and started his ascent in public life, from serving on Boston's old Common Council to winning his first term in Congress in 1894, a stepping-stone to the mayoralty.

Mother Rose told how the newcomers from Ireland loved, even reveled, in "tales of their adopted land." She, like her father, would be "dragging off" her youngsters to see historic houses and sites around them. "Jack," she recalled, "especially was fascinated by history." The North End was always a delight to both families. It was in the congressional district of both grandfather and grandson. Their love for it went back to childhood. U.S. Senator Edward M. "Ted" Kennedy told of family visits, of how he and his older brothers Jack and Bob, both of whom would be assassinated, used to play a game to see who could get across Hanover Street first "in a hop, a skip, and a jump."

Paul Revere's house at 19 North Square, with its medieval, overhanging upper floor, shingled roof, and leaded casements, is on the west side (to our right) as we enter this triangular space. The square's historic associations are about as numerous as its once-fashionable cobblestones, though one popular reminder of the past is gone, the town pump opposite Revere's house.

Revere's house was built after the great fire of 1676 that led Bostonians two years later to create a fire department with "ye engine lately come from England." Revere purchased the house in 1770, a few weeks before the Boston Massacre. He was already a Son of Liberty, a friend of Boston patriots, and winning distinction as a silversmith. His shop still remained "near the head" of Hancock's Wharf, a stone's throw from North Square, in the area where Revere was born and learned silversmithing from his father. On acquiring the house, Revere brought his first wife and five (one had already died) of his eventual sixteen children. Excepting the period when the patriot army was besieging Boston, the Reveres lived here for a decade, then rented the place to others while they doubled up with numerous relatives in the economically bleak final years of the war. They owned the house until 1800, meantime renting it out, living here, or lodging deeper in

Paul Revere's house: Boston's oldest dwelling

the North End to be near his foundry, Revere's post-Revolution business on the waterfront.

Revere had a barn, but no Revere horse went on his historic midnight ride. The Sons of Liberty kept a close eye on British movements. Only when Joseph Warren was certain that redcoats were embarking, and after he had sent Dawes, did he send off Revere. Revere had already made arrangements about the lanterns should he fail to escape town. After going back to North Square from Warren's house to get his boots and surtout, Revere hurried to his boat with two friends, who rowed him across the Charles River "a little to the eastward" of the blockading sixty-four-gun warship Somerset of George III. From Charlestown he set off at a gallop on a horse borrowed from Deacon John Larkin.

Revere had taken off from this house for many earlier exploits. From here he had gone with other North Enders to take part in the Boston Tea Party. Early next morning, dispatched by Samuel Adams, Revere took off from here on his first famous ride to carry news of the Tea Party to New York and Philadelphia. That was December 1773. The next year Revere galloped to Philadelphia, in an incredible five days, to rush the Suffolk Resolves to the First Continental Congress. The colonies would hang together! And again in icy December 1774, he sped to Portsmouth, New Hampshire, to warn that Parliament had cut off shipments of arms and ammunition. Patriots there quickly seized the powder from the king's fort—and some was soon used at Bunker Hill.

Helpful guides in the Revere house will indicate old construction and household features. There are several things besides the house that were Revere's: a bureau and five chairs; an upholstered wingback chair; four Windsor chairs from his office, one of them a rocker; and, of course, his saddlebags.

Across from the garden area beside Revere's house is one of Boston's oldest brick houses, a three-story building constructed around 1711 to 1715 and later owned by a Hitchborn cousin of Revere. Revere's mother was a Hitchborn, a member of an old Yankee family; her father owned a mansion and Hitchborn's Wharf on Fish (present North) Street. The brick house is remarkable as a pioneer example of the type of architecture (later called Georgian) that succeeded Revere's medieval-type dwelling.

By the south side of this brick house there was once an alleylike passage constructed so that Governor Hutchinson could conveniently enter the "Cockerel" by a back door. On the lower side of this passage, and facing North Square, was a house used as quarters by popular British Major John Pitcairn, commander of the British marines. Many redcoats were billeted in and around North Square. These soldiers used to muster in North Square and had shut it off on the eve of April 19, 1775, as some were to take part in the expedition to Lexington and Concord. This proved no problem to Revere, though he was already a marked man for his many courageous missions. Pitcairn would be the officer next day on Lexington Green who shouted to the minutemen, "Disperse ye rebels!" He would be mortally wounded at Bunker Hill. Rachel Revere Park and playground at the corner of North Square was named for Paul Revere's wife. The bronze plaque on the wall facing the park tells of historic people and events in this ancient area.

A church still standing on the east side of the square has special connections to literary figures. Sacred Heart Church, at the corner of Sun Court Street, with large blocks of granite framing its entrance, began as a bethel in 1833 for Methodist preacher Father Edward Taylor. Father Taylor, once a seaman himself, was so dramatic and eloquent that his fame was spread worldwide by seamen who flocked to his services.

Emerson and Father Taylor were close friends. Emerson often spoke from Mr. Taylor's pulpit. Taylor, said Emerson, was "the Shakespeare of the sailor and the poor." Charles Dickens wanted to see the North End and particularly Father Taylor, so poet Longfellow and Charles Sumner came as his guides. Dickens told how the January 1842 day was so sparkling and bracing that the trio spurned a carriage and walked from the Tremont House, via old Scollay Square to North Square, much as we have. Father Taylor always spoke extempore. Dickens, adept at shorthand, preserved for the world Father Taylor's salty phrasing and acrobatics. The three young men (Dickens was not yet thirty) were seated by a one-eyed, lame mariner in a side pew, because center church was reserved for sailors. Walt Whitman came several times to hear Father Taylor in 1859–1860 to "the quaint ship-cabin-looking church" and said, of all speakers he had heard, Taylor was the only "essentially perfect orator."

Dickens went on for further sight-seeing around the North End—as did Thackeray, walking with a Boston lawyer friend in 1852.

The church that originally carried the title "The Old North" stood on the north side of North Square, roughly at 1 North Square on the west corner, where Moon Street now enters the square. It was built in 1650 (to be Boston's Second Church) when the steady arrival of newcomers overcrowded Boston's First Church at the head of State Street. This first "Old North" was the powerful seat of the Mathers, with the pastorate, for more than three quarters of a century, passing from brother to brother and father to son. They had the prestige and authority of untitled nobility during what was the unchallenged era of the Puritan clergy. Supreme among them was the Reverend Increase Mather, father of his assistant and successor, the Reverend Cotton Mather. Increase Mather received the first D.D. degree conferred in America. His dwelling was on the site of Revere's house until the fire of 1676, which consumed the church and structures in much of the area, including warehouses and wharves on nearby Town Cove. The church was reverently rebuilt. Increase loved it so deeply that he remained its pastor during a decade and a half that he was also president of Harvard College. To make his travel easier, the college corporation purchased for him a horse.

Underscoring the respect in which he was held, Increase was chosen to go to England as the colony's agent to secure a new charter. He brought one back in 1692, along with a new royal governor, a parishioner of his church, Sir William Phips, selected by King William at Mather's suggestion. The church's fate was not so triumphant. During the siege redcoats billeted here and tore it down for cooking and fuel in 1775. Parishioners, along with their church name and records, joined the "Cockerel."

Life could be mighty stern in Puritan Boston. The dwelling of the Reverend Samuel Mather, son of Cotton, was a short way down Moon Street on the east side. It was a gift from his brother-in-law

Governor Hutchinson. Prior to Samuel, the owner was a sea captain. He was the skipper put in the stocks in 1673 for "lewd and unseemly conduct" for kissing his wife at the doorstep on returning from his long voyage.

Dickens, after service in the bethel, took a look at Revere's house through the windows (it was then unrestored and was a shop and tenement), then left by Prince Street to see the belfry made famous by Revere and the North End's centuries-old burial ground on Copp's Hill. Let us head the same way, and turn right at Hanover Street.

At the south corner of North Bennet Street, as it enters Hanover Street, was once a wooden church in which the father of Universalism in this country, the Reverend John Murray, a chaplain during our Revolution, served as its first minister from 1793 until his death in 1815. Here he preached his doctrine of universal salvation. When Mr. Murray first preached in Boston, in School Street, stones were flung through the windows. The undeterred cleric hefted one, remarking: "This argument is solid and weighty, but is neither rational nor convincing." Boston, as it learned to accept Quakers and others persecuted in earlier days, came to accept Universalists, indeed, all religions.

The little wooden church used by Mr. Murray—last of Boston's old wooden churches—was built for the last of the Mather dynasty. Samuel Mather's parishioners followed him out of the new North Church but on his death, at his wish, were reunited. The present structure at 332 Hanover, for more than a decade the North End Community Health Center, was built in 1838 and became a Baptist bethel. It still retains its church character (the cupola is up in the attic) and on the side, cut in brownstone, may be seen SAMARITAN HALL.

The turbulent post–World War I period of political unrest and red-baiting will be recalled at 383 Hanover Street, on our right, as we approach Clark Street, once the Langone Funeral Home. It was here, after their electrocution on August 23, 1927, that the immigrants Nicola Sacco and Bartolomeo Vanzetti were embalmed. A funeral cortege of thousands of sympathizers later moved along Hanover Street—past the worldwide defense committee at 256 Hanover—to Scollay Square, along the Common and other main streets.

A few steps more and on our right, between Clark and Harris Streets, we arrive at St. Stephen's Church, the beautiful Bulfinch church that we saw from further back when we first entered Hanover Street. This was a rebuilding in 1804 of what had been an early North End meeting house of 1714 called the New North. Paul Revere installed one of his bells after it was built.

Thanks to the Catholic archdiocese, Boston still has this Bulfinch church. In 1870 when Hanover Street, like virtually all early main Boston streets, had to be widened, the church was moved to save it. In 1965 Richard Cardinal Cushing assembled funds to restore the church to its original Bulfinch appearance. So when we enter we find again tall, plain glass windows, plain white walls, two big chandeliers, all accented by the red carpeting and the gilded pipes of the organ—much as it was when the Reverend Francis Parkman, father of the historian, was pastor in 1813–1849.

Old North Church and Copp's Hill

Opposite St. Stephen's Church, when we cross Hanover Street, we come to Paul Revere Mall, a neighborhood park called the Prado. It was built in 1933 and embellished magnificently two years later by Cyrus E. Dallin's equestrian statue of Revere, vibrant with purposefulness and life.

In later life Captain John Manley, a great hero of our first American navy, lived on Webster Street, which once ran through the mall from Hanover to Unity Street. Manley, who hailed from Marblehead, served in the little fleet George Washington had assembled to intercept British supplies flowing through the harbor to the besieged redcoats. Manley achieved the fleet's first success, the sensational capture of the British transport Nancy, whose virtual arsenal of cannon and shot brought abounding joy to Washington. As the redcoats were fleeing from Boston, Captain Manley captured the Elizabeth, a brig copiously filled with even more weapons for Washington's needy forces.

Ahead of us is Christ Church, familiarly known as Old North

STEEPLE CHASE

Local lore tells of a certain John Childs, who "flew" safely aboard a primitive glider from the steeple of Old North Church to the ground. This was in 1757. Dour city fathers quickly passed a law against such things.

Church, Boston's oldest church structure. Notice the three-story brick building on the left at 21 Unity Street, which, like the church, is one of Boston's oldest buildings. It was originally the dwelling of the master mason who helped to build the church, Ebenezer Clough, who built it for himself about 1715. To the right of it, at what would be 19 Unity, once stood a similar brick building that was the only one in Boston owned by Benjamin Franklin. Two of his sisters lived in it.

Paul Revere was very familiar with Christ Church, built in 1723 and quite new when Revere was a youngster. Moreover, he was one of a group of six boys who signed a contract (the church has it) to ring America's first peal of eight bells, still said to be the sweetest in our nation. They were cast in England in 1744, each duly inscribed, and they provided fifteen-year-old Paul with some new friends, music unavailable in his own church, and some pocket money. Among Revere's later friends was the sexton of Christ Church, twenty-three-year-old Robert Newman, whom Revere got to hold up the lanterns in the steeple—a deed for which Newman was promptly jailed by the British.

A visit to Christ Church is quite an experience. Many presidents and heads of state have made a pilgrimage here. The setting and memorials are reminiscent of a visit to Westminster Abbey. In a niche near the altar is the nation's first memorial to George Washington, an unusual bust. When Lafayette, then well along in years and looking back more than a quarter of a century, saw it, he exclaimed, "Yes, that is the man I knew. . . ." A wall plaque tells of this. The box pews have brass plates bearing the names of the original owners. There's one, Number 62, for General Thomas Gage, then commander-in-chief in North America. It tells how he went up the narrow steps to the steeple to witness his redcoats making their three assaults at Bunker Hill, sustaining losses that turned British victory into defeat. Major Pitcairn has a memorial. Some say that through a mistake his remains, supposedly taken to Westminster Abbey, are still here.

Guides are on hand to tell of other interesting sights and tales: the wine-glass pulpit, the early "Province House set" parishioners, sea captains, wealthy wharf owners, and Captain Daniel Malcolm (who has a plaque), a merchant on North End's Fleet Street "buried 10 feet deep in Copp's Hill safe from British bullets." Commodore Samuel Nicholson, first commander of "Old Ironsides," was a parishioner and was buried here. As in Westminster Abbey there are crypts. They are built of brick, most likely by Ebenezer Clough, for they support the hand-hewn timbers that support the main floor. There are thirty-seven of these tombs, from the one bearing Major Pitcairn's name under the altar area to Commodore Nicholson's under the church entrance. Church records say some eleven hundred were buried here. Visit the Memorial Garden on the north side of the church, which has incised stone slabs telling of historic events and personages of the parish; on the south side of the churchyard, visit the gift shop, itself a former chapel.

Women's Heritage Trail

Notice the plaques to notable North End women lining the left wall of the Paul Revere Mall. Ann Pollard, age ten, was quite possibly the first white woman to ever come ashore in Boston, landing with Governor John Winthrop at the foot of today's Prince Street. Dr. Harriot Keziah Hunt grew up on the waterfront along Hanover Street and became a self-taught doctor after she was barred from lectures at Harvard Medical School. Charlotte Cushman was an internationally known actor renowned for her ability to play both male and female roles. She established a salon in Rome to cultivate female artists.

Paul Revere statue and Old North Church steeple

Odd Offerings

During your visit to Old North church, be sure to note the four cherubs flanking the organ. They were bestowed upon the church by a pious privateer who had stolen them on the high seas. They are in good company with the sixteenth-century statue of the Virgin Mary on display. She was previously the figurehead of a Portuguese vessel.

A few more interesting locations are in the vicinity of Salem Street, on which the Old North faces.

At the second corner off Salem Street, to our left, there is narrow Sheafe Street. Sexton Robert Newman's family house was on the south corner. His mother, by the way, was a sister of the famous newspaper publisher Isaiah Thomas, who published the patriot Massachusetts Spy upstairs in the present Union Oyster House. The third man helping on Revere's lanterns was John Pulling, a vestryman. He was a seafarer and escaped British arrest only by catching the next boat out of Boston harbor.

Nearby on Sheafe Street was the birthplace in 1808 of the Reverend Samuel F. Smith, who wrote the words to "America" ("My country 'tis of thee ..."), set to the tune of "God Save the King."

Hull Street, across from the church, was originally a pasture belonging to mint master John Hull and became a gift from his daughter Hannah and her husband, Judge Samuel Sewall, to the town. We follow it up Copp's Hill.

Copp's Hill Burying Ground, Boston's second oldest (1659) is on the highest land in the North End. Its oldest stone bears the date of 1625, five years before the Puritans came to Boston. Some long thought this was a schoolboy prank, but a veteran custodian of the graveyard established it as fact. Grace Berry, he explained, died at Plymouth, and her husband removed her remains to Copp's Hill cemetery when he came here. Her gravestone, which we see presently, is among the oldest in New England.

The dynastic tomb of the Mathers, a 3-foot-high brick vault with brownstone top, is in the cemetery's oldest part, about 20 feet from the Charter Street gate and by the path running northward from the Hull Street gate where we entered. The elite used family arms. The arms of the Hutchinson family may still be seen, but the royally honored name on the gravestone was replaced by the name of a later occupant.

Along the crest of the hill a path runs westward toward Snowhill Street. As we walk it, notice the rigging of "Old Ironsides" on the right above the rooftops beyond the northwest corner of the grave yard.

Near the end of this path, on the left, is a broken granite pillar monument to Prince Hall, who fought at the Battle of Bunker Hill, the first grand master of the black Masons in Boston. His small 1807 burial stone is in back of his high memorial monument. Many blacks were buried in this cemetery, for on the north slope down to the harbor, below Charter Street, was Boston's first black community, known in the early colonial period as New Guinea.

To the left from Hall's grave and along the Snowhill Street side we will see the simple stone of sexton Robert Newman, who flashed Revere's lanterns, and near the southwest angle, the plain white stone of the man who laid the keel of "Old Ironsides," Edmund Hartt. He lived nearby, opposite the site of his shipyard and wharf, which we shall see.

On the water side of Snowhill Street, the hill rose 7 feet higher before being carted to the Mill Pond and shorefront. On it, roughly back of the Newman and Hartt graves, the redcoats built a fort and placed a battery. During the Battle of Bunker Hill its twenty-eight-pounders, under command of generals Burgoyne and Clinton, sent Charlestown up in flames.

Gravestones on Copp's Hill show scars of being used for target practice by the redcoats stationed nearby. There are at least three clear musketball marks on the gravestone of Captain Daniel Malcolm, whose memorial we saw in Christ Church. Maybe the stone's calling

Molasses Flood

Pause for a moment on Commercial Street between Copp's Hill and the North End Park playground. This unassuming stretch was the setting of a most bizarre Boston tragedy. January 15, 1919, was mild for a winter's day, unseasonably so. The temperature had increased rapidly over the past forty-eight hours, and residents of the North End were going about their business, discussing, no doubt, the weirdly balmy weather.

Workers were loading cargo into the cars of the Boston and Worcester Railroad, within earshot of the looming tanks of the United States Industrial Alcohol Company. Over two million gallons of crude molasses were being stored in a 58-by-90-foot tank. Shortly after noon workers were startled to hear sharp cracking sounds, followed by a thundering roar; it was the snapping of the tank's steel bolts as the bottom of the huge molasses tank burst open, erupting in a roiling wave of hot molasses. The tank then split entirely open, propelling molasses at a pressure of two tons per square foot. It swiftly filled the underlying loading pit, washed away the loaded railroad cars, and flooded down Commerical Street.

The thick, heavy wave crushed everyone in its path; people were pinned against walls and trapped under furniture. Houses were swept off their foundations and floors gave way, collapsing onto cellars full of horrifically asphyxiated workers. The gruesome, ever-thickening mass snapped the steel supports of the elevated train track that passed overhead and smothered people and animals in the streets as it rolled inexorably toward the ocean.

Twenty one people died, 150 people were injured, and it took weeks to clean up the wreckage. The hearings to settle the 125 lawsuits brought against the United States Industrial Alcohol Company stretched out for six years (the company argued that the collapse had been caused by a dynamite bomb rather than structural inadequacies; they lost and paid nearly $1 million in damages). Some say the dusky sweet smell still lingers.

him "a true son of liberty" drew that musket fire. The stone is in the fourth row of headstones forward of Prince Hall's. But why pick Grace Berry's 1625 stone for a target? Maybe poor shooting?

One of the most grisly hangings in Boston's colonial history once drew such a crowd to Copp's Hill that it amazed old Judge Sewall. The river between the hill and Charlestown, said Sewall, "was covered with people" in boats. A scaffold for seven pirates was raised on the Charles River flats just off the northwest corner of the graveyard. Sewall related how Captain Quelch and his cutthroats were taken from prison in Court Street and brought by boat from Town Cove. The Reverend Cotton Mather accompanied them to their execution. One pirate got a last minute reprieve. The others were strung up. "When the scaffold was let sink," said Sewall, "there was such a screech of the women" that Mrs. Sewall in the orchard by their town house heard it. And she, said Sewall, was "a full mile away!"

Dickens and his friends, after visiting Father Taylor's bethel in 1842, inspected this graveyard and Christ Church. Longfellow called the North End of his day "the little Britain of Boston." To him Christ Church was "like a parish church in London." It was not until April 6, 1860, that Longfellow wrote in his diary that he had been there again with Sumner and climbed the tower "to the chime of bells, now the home of innumerable pigeons." The visit was inspirational. A few days later his diary of April 19 reads: "I wrote a few lines on Paul

Revere's ride, this being the day of that achievement."

Dickens and his friends, on leaving, went down Snowhill Street to Prince and along Washington's route to Bunker Hill. The wounded after that battle had been brought back by the British to Copp's Hill beach. With their 50 percent casualties there was never anything again like this scene of suffering in Boston, then a place totally without hospitals. Major Pitcairn, twice wounded, bled to death in a makeshift relief station in a boatbuilder's house at 138 Prince Street, a house that long stood at the south corner of Prince Street and Lafayette Avenue and that Dickens and his friends saw.

Let us leave Copp's Hill cemetery by the Charter Street gate and turn right along Charter Street back toward Hanover. Pause to take in the views of "Old Ironsides" and the Bunker Hill Monument across the harbor.

Presently, on our left, we see Foster Street, a short downhill passage to the waterfront. Paul Revere built his new foundry at the foot of Foster Street in the early 1790s, at the east corner with Commercial Street, and here he perfected his metallurgical skills while producing products from church bells to cannon.

A fascinating Horatio Alger tales goes with the site at the west corner of Salem and Charter Streets. The royal governor whom the Reverend Increase Mather brought back from England in 1692, along with the charter (for which the street is named), had been born a poor boy in Pemaquid, Maine, then part of Massachusetts. William Phips came to Boston after being apprenticed to a ship carpenter. As a lad, says Cotton Mather, Phips dreamed that he would be rich and build himself a great mansion on beautiful Green Lane (later Salem Street) with a view of the ocean. He won himself knighthood and riches when the ship he built raised a Spanish galleon and he shared its fabulous treasure with the crown. The colony was delighted with its new governor, who promptly put an end to its witchcraft persecution. Phips indeed built his dream house at this corner.

Beyond the bend in Charter Street we come on our right to Unity Street. Two doors down on the left is Number 8, a later North End house of the "Honey Fitz" Fitzgerald family. Rose Fitzgerald Kennedy told how her father kept it as a "voting residence" after leaving

4 Garden Court. His North End roots were deep. The house in which he was born was on now-vanished Ferry Street near North Square. Motorists ride over the site every day when entering the present Callahan tunnel to East Boston.

"The Napoleon of the North End" was the way "Honey Fitz" was known by the time he took the house at 8 Unity. While he was its owner he bought a weekly, *The Republic,* for $500 and gained increased political power as well as funds to buy a fifteen-room house in Dorchester. But it was while here on Unity Street that he planned the mayoralty race that won him control of City Hall in 1905, on his promise to create "a bigger, better, busier Boston."

At the south corner where Charter meets Hanover was located a three-story brick house, with gardens and trees, in which Paul Revere lived in later life, not far from his foundry. But when a gale wrecked his shop in 1804 he acquired a new foundry in Canton, where the enterprising ex-express rider set up the nation's first copper-rolling mill. He died here in this North End house in 1818 and, with many of his church bells tolling, was buried in the family plot in Old Granary.

Three short streets on our right, as we head north on Hanover toward the waterfront, have points of interest. Hanover Avenue was formerly called Methodist Alley for a small wooden church, Boston's first Methodist church, built there in 1796.

At the bottom of Salutation Street, at the north corner where it enters North (formerly Ship) Street, was a celebrated waterfront meeting place of the Sons of Liberty, North End mechanics like Revere, who were followers of Samuel Adams and Joseph Warren in the Tea Party and the Revolution. So many meeting here were from the waterfront that they originated the term "caucus"—a briefer way of saying a meeting of the Caulkers' Club.

Battery Street led to the North Battery, built off Ship (now North) Street in 1646 to protect the river and the Town Cove. Revere, who effectively tried his hand at drawing, has left an engraving depicting the battery before the town sold it in 1789. General Gage embarked regiments and field pieces from this battery, as well as from Long Wharf, for the Battle of Bunker Hill. The site is now Battery Wharf.

As Hanover reaches Commercial Street, Constitution Wharf is on

"Old Ironsides" seen from its birthplace in Boston

our right. Edmund Hartt's shipyard (the navy then had none) was here, and here Colonel George Claghorn, then lodging nearby on Hanover Street, built "Old Ironsides." Revere's foundry supplied its bolts, spikes, and a 242-pound bell. A new Coast Guard building stands where the forty-four-gun-class frigate, with thousands of shouting huzzas, finally slipped down the heavily tallowed ways at high tide just past noon, October 21, 1797.

In another few steps across Commercial Street, we get a splendid view of the frigate itself. Just ahead of us is the U.S. Coast Guard installation. Walk out toward the end of the pier. Looking across the water, we see the nation's most famous warship, U.S.S. *Constitution* still in commission, with its three masts, black hull, and white trim. Directly in the background is the Bunker Hill Monument. The coast guardsman on duty will confirm that this is one of Boston's most photographed scenes.

On the walk back along Hanover Street we get a striking medley of yesterday and today. The gilded dome and weathervane of St. Stephen's still rise impressively above the houses of the North End—although the proliferation of skyscrapers in downtown Boston now gives a mid-Manhattan aspect to the panorama.

WEST END

Bowdoin Square to St. Joseph's

For our walk to see the attractions of Boston's West End, let us begin again from the traffic island at old Scollay Square. This was historically a pathway of hurry for those rushing to nearby Bowdoin Square to catch the semihourly omnibus to Cambridge. Charles Dickens did it on his visits. Longfellow and Dana, whose Cambridge yards and gardens were back to back, often did it.

Richard Henry Dana, heading for one of these trips in 1854, had an experience that shocked the nation. It was on the night that the fugitive slave Dana had sought to free, Anthony Burns, was sent back to his owner. Dana had worked late in his law office, and was having tea at Parker's Cafe when the bell rang for the 9:00 P.M. coach. Dana and a friend decided to walk and were going along the left side toward Bowdoin Square and passing near the west end of present Center Plaza when, as Dana wrote: "I remember observing a commotion on my left as of people pushing and instantly I received a terrible blow over my right eye. I was stunned . . . I remember standing in the street, stupefied and bleeding . . ." Dana survived this vicious attack by a hireling of the proslavers, an incident starkly illustrating the temper of the community in the years prior to the Civil War.

Another prominent man who walked the same way did not survive. Dr. George Parkman, Beacon Hill Brahmin, banker, and Boston's

WEST END

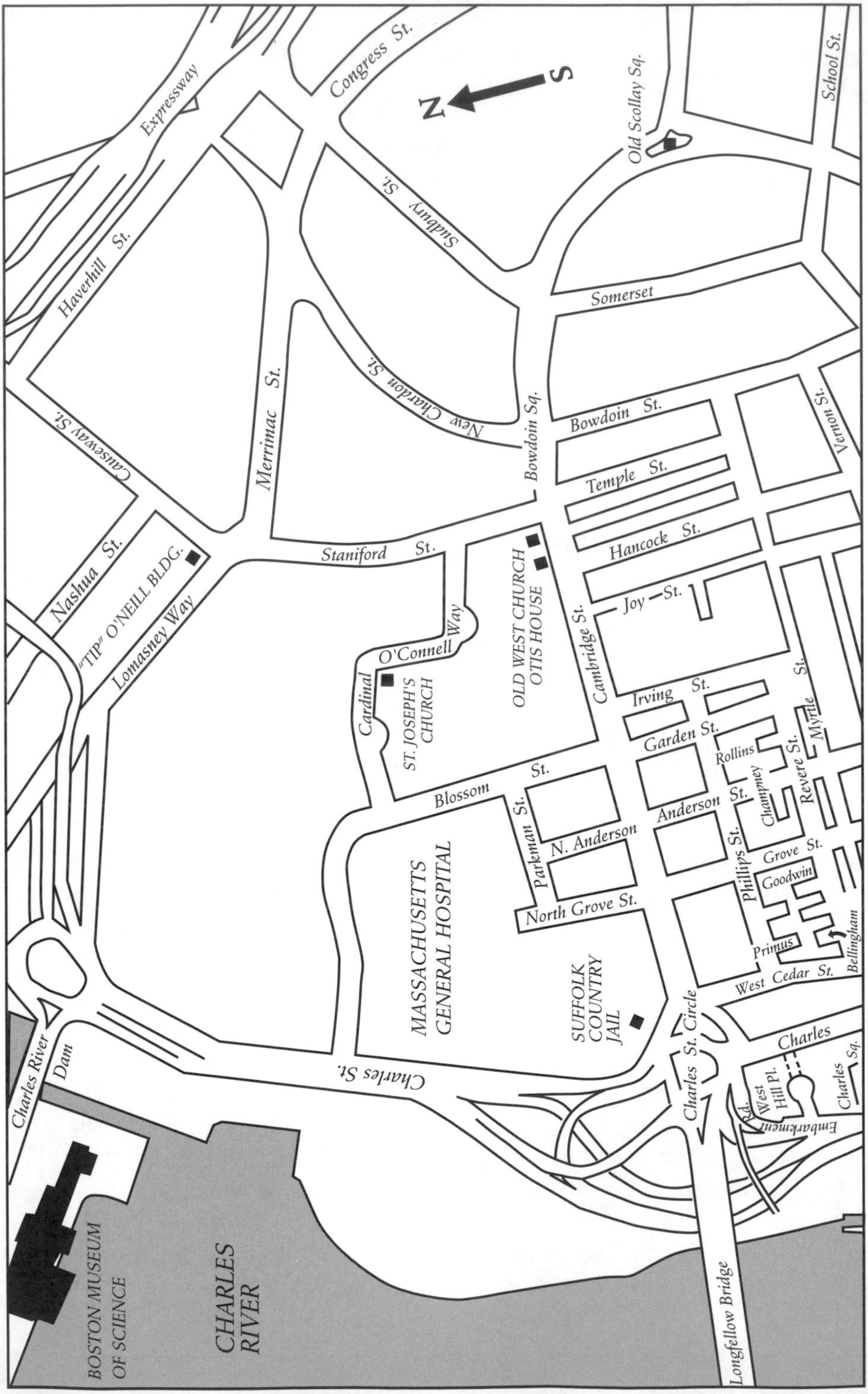
Congress St.
Expressway
N
S
Old Scollay Sq.
School St.
Sudbury St.
Haverhill St.
Somerset
Merrimac St.
New Chardon St.
Bowdoin Sq.
Bowdoin St.
Vernon St.
Causeway St.
Temple St.
Hancock St.
Staniford St.
Nashua St.
"TIP" O'NEILL BLDG.
Lomasney Way
OLD WEST CHURCH
OTIS HOUSE
Joy St.
Cambridge St.
O'Connell Way
Cardinal
ST. JOSEPH'S CHURCH
Irving St.
Myrtle St.
Garden St.
Rollins
Revere St.
Champney
Blossom St.
Parkman St.
Anderson St.
N. Anderson
Phillips St.
Grove St.
Goodwin
MASSACHUSETTS GENERAL HOSPITAL
North Grove St.
Primus
Bellingham
SUFFOLK COUNTRY JAIL
West Cedar St.
Charles St. Circle
Charles River Dam
Charles St.
Charles
Charles Sq.
West Hill Pl.
Embankment Rd.
BOSTON MUSEUM OF SCIENCE
CHARLES RIVER
Longfellow Bridge

most sensational murder victim, came through Scollay Square from his State Street bank and tried again to pick up a long overdue loan before heading back uphill to his family lunch. We shall see farther along Cambridge Street why Parkman did not appear at lunchtime.

On our left as we approach Somerset Street is the twenty-four-story Saltonstall Building, built in 1965–1966, which provides housing for some three dozen state agencies, a foot-of-Beacon Hill companion to the McCormack skyscraper at the top of the hill. Despite being members of opposite political parties, Speaker McCormack and U.S. Senator Leverett Saltonstall for years had a most friendly relationship.

Leverett Saltonstall, a direct descendent of Governor Winthrop's companion, Sir Richard Saltonstall, was the Bay State's governor for three terms during World War II and one of its most respected and admired public officials. He was noted for his modesty. He went through the dedication of this building with usual calm, then a few days later excitedly phoned his lifetime friend and secretary, Daniel J. Lynch: "Have you been down by the state building on Cambridge Street lately? I was driving by it this morning and almost lost control of the car. There was my name in letters that seemed a foot high. I never dreamed there'd be anything like that. It was quite a shocker."

One of Boston's most noted nineteenth-century hotels, the Revere House (named for Paul Revere), a hotel with no superior in the nation, used to stand on Bowdoin Square, just about the midfront of the Saltonstall Building. Royal figures of the era came as guests—among them future King Edward VII of Britain, Grand Duke Alexis of Russia, and King Kalakaua of Hawaii. U.S. presidents came, Fillmore and Pierce and Grant. Daniel Webster was a regular visitor; he even had a special chair before the great fireplace in the lobby. The banqueting room often resounded to cheers for Webster as a postprandial orator. So did crowded Bowdoin Square when Webster would speak from the hotel's columned facade, especially after political foes refused him the use of Faneuil Hall in 1850, and here he resoundingly avowed that he had not bowed to the slaveholding interests of the South.

Two plaques near the front corners of the ten-story Bell Atlantic Building, facing south on the square, tell of earlier days. One recalls the vanished bowling green.

The round plaque marks the birthplace of the great architect Charles Bulfinch. This was a stately mansion with broad lawns and gardens, the residence of his father and his grandfather, both of them noted Boston doctors, both named Thomas Bulfinch. The architect's mother was a member of the Apthorp family, one of the town's wealthiest. The Bulfinch pasture for half a century included the site of the Revere house and up Beacon Hill to hilltop Ashburton Place. This family pasture was lost in the financial crash of the architect's fortune, an economic aftermath of his creation of the Tontine Crescent. The architect's sister's marriage to neighbor Joseph Coolidge, Jr., saved the old homestead for the architect's parents, with Coolidge's father purchasing it from creditors so that the old folks could continue to live there.

After this return in 1787 from studying architecture in Europe, Bulfinch was busy beautifying this area with mansions he designed for relatives and friends. Only one of these is extant, the Otis mansion that we shall presently see. Still remembered, though, are the three-story brick mansion and gardens of Joseph Coolidge, Sr., at the west corner of present Bowdoin and Cambridge Streets; the mansion of Joseph Coolidge, Jr., at the northwest corner of the Saltonstall Building; and the great double residences of granite built for Samuel Parkman's married daughters at the west end of Bowdoin Square.

In the little triangular park opposite the Saltonstall Building—in the heart of old Bowdoin Square—a bust of Boston's beloved Cardinal Cushing was erected in mid–1981 from contributions of Humberto Cardinal Medeiros, bishops, and priests of the Boston archdiocese. At the unveiling of the bronze bust by sculptor James Rosati, Cardinal Medeiros described his predecessor as a spiritual leader who "never lacked the common touch." The archdiocese and friends in 1989 had the park redesigned by Graham Gund to provide more green space, flower beds, and benches. That same year Gund redesigned One Bowdoin Square, the impressive building that forms a backdrop to the park.

Bowdoin Square was magnificently situated in our colonial and Federal periods. The bowling green along this part of Cambridge Street led gently downhill the short distance to the Mill Pond. This water covered an area about the size of the Common and formerly separated Boston's West End from the North End.

Northwestward from Bowdoin Square, at an acute angle with Cambridge Street, ran a now-vanished main street called Green Street. It led to the ropewalks on the outer reach of the West End called Barton's Point—roughly near present Charles River dam.

Some moments of glory came to Bowdoin Square when the builder of "Old Ironsides," Colonel Claghorn, preceded by drums and fifes, led 300 men carrying on their shoulders the cable for the newly launched frigate. All the way from the ropewalks they paraded from Barton's Point, through the squares and down Hanover Street to Hartt's shipyard. Sea-loving, ship-loving Bostonians shouted and applauded.

Here at New Chardon Street, where we see now the Hurley State Services Center, was where the West End's vanished Green Street once joined Cambridge Street. Samuel Parkman's twin houses were built in the angle of the intersection. Samuel was the father of Dr. George Parkman, who walked for the last time on earth past these family buildings in what was once one of Boston's most aristocratic squares.

On approaching Staniford Street, the Hurley Services Center is set back and permits a splendid overall view of a treasure of the West End, the Old West Church, built in 1806 by the teacher-architect Asher Benjamin. For fifty-five years, 1806 to his death in 1861, this was the parish church of the Reverend Charles Lowell, son of old Judge Lowell of the "Essex Junto," father of poet James Russell Lowell. The predecessor church on the site was built in 1736. Like other Boston churches, it was used as a barracks for redcoats, who demolished the steeple in 1775 to prevent patriots from signaling their comrades in Cambridge during the siege of Boston. Cannonballs fired by those besieging continentals hit in Bowdoin Square, and even deeper into Boston, one of them lodging in the wall of the Brattle Street Church in vanished Brattle Square.

The present "Old West" has seen many changes. Before becoming a Methodist church in 1962, it was the West End branch of the public library and the polling place for the district. Early election day 1960

John F. Kennedy came with his wife to vote before taking off for the family compound on Cape Cod to await returns. Bostonians, as they had the night before at the campaign windup in Faneuil Hall, greeted the future president with frenzied applause.

For an impression of the new West End, let us turn right at Staniford Street and then left on the winding Way, named for the late Boston Cardinal William O'Connell. Shortly, on our left, we will see at Number 60 a building called Regina Cleri, a home for retired priests of the Boston archdiocese. Several still continue parish activities. Again on the left at a corner of the Way is St. Joseph's Church, built in 1823, which became Catholic in 1862.

Urban renewal leveled everything for acres in the West End, save for the Old West Church we just saw, the Otis mansion, and St. Joseph's Church. Six big high-rise apartment buildings went up, then the twin thirty-eight-story towers across from the church (towers with offices up to the mezzanines) and then more big business buildings. Prior to this clearing out, begun in the late 1950s, the West End was a jumble of old streets, rows of tenement buildings and houses, and mom and pop stores. The varieties of bread made in the small bakeries perfumed the air with the delicious odors of fresh rye and pumpernickel. Children at play turned the little, twisty streets into merry playgrounds. This has vanished. St Joseph's used to have 290 baptisms a year. Twenty years later it had only eighteen.

By the Charles River, close to St. Joseph's, the first mass in the West End was celebrated in October 1788 by the chaplain of a French man-of-war. Authorities would not allow a public celebration of the mass, but, since the French had been allies in the Revolution, they permitted its being held in the private home of Monseigneur Baury. Among the memorials and paintings in St. Joseph's is one that depicts this scene.

Pause, on returning, at the head of Cardinal O'Connell Way for a look across to 19 Staniford Street. This is the main entrance to the Hurley State Services Center. Visitors as well as employees in the building are puzzled about why there is no entrance from busy Cambridge Street into the sprawling eight-acre, six-story complex built in 1969–1972.

Old Bowdoin Square from the cupola of Old West Church

Downhill at the foot of Staniford Street, at the junction of Lomasney Way and Causeway Street, a site once part of the Mill Pond was chosen in 1981 for a giant new federal structure for the General Services Administration—an eleven-story building with a huge five-story atrium named in 1987 in honor of Speaker Thomas P. "Tip" O'Neill, Jr.

First Otis Mansion to the County Jail

On returning to Cambridge Street, glance back across Bowdoin Square, between the Kennedy Federal Building on the left and the Saltonstall Building on the right. They provide a frame for the Custom House tower rising above the new City Hall and Center Plaza, a striking picture of the change skyscrapers have made in the metropolis.

The redbrick structure on our right, just down Cambridge Street from the Old West Church, is the first Federal mansion that Bulfinch designed for Harrison Gray Otis, affable and brilliant grandson of George III's state treasurer and nephew of patriot James Otis.

At thirty years of age when he moved into this mansion in 1797, Otis was already one of Boston's most prosperous lawyers and beginning his first term as Boston's congressman. The mansion was but a stone's throw from the Bowdoin Square house in which popular "Harry" Otis was born. The high granite retaining walls for the front lawn were not there when Otis and his family were residents. The walls were placed to adjust to a 10-foot lowering of the grade of Cambridge Street.

The three-story brick mansion, headquarters for the Society for the Preservation of New England Antiquities, is well worth a visit. This great society, which has preserved dozens of residential treasures throughout New England, has restored the Otis mansion to the elegant appearance of Otis's era with original Otis family furniture, portraits, and other possessions. The society has here as well both a fascinating museum and a library.

Directly across Cambridge Street is Hancock Street, leading up to the State House. Still to be seen at Number 20—the sixth house on the left—is the dwelling from 1830–1867 of abolitionist U.S. Senator Charles Sumner. Sumner was born on Beacon Hill's North Slope only 3 blocks away, on Irving Street near Myrtle Street.

Again following the footsteps of Dr. George Parkman in November 1849, we walk along Cambridge Street and turn right to much-widened Blossom Street with its concrete center strip, a new main way into the West End. Shortly, on our left, is a street once called Vine and renamed Parkman. At this corner, when Dr. Parkman passed, there was a grocery. He dropped in and bought a head of lettuce for the midday meal and said he would pick it up on his way back.

At the end of short Parkman Street, standing on the right athwart present North Grove Street and in front of the present entrance to Massachusetts General Hospital, was once the new Massachusetts Medical College Building of the Harvard Medical School. Dr. Parkman had given the land, then on the shore of the Charles River, and had endowed the chair held by the school's dean, Dr. Oliver Wendell Holmes.

Set back on the north side of Parkman Street, partly behind the 1984 eight-story Wang Ambulatory Care Center—made possible, like the theater district's 1983 Wang Center, through gifts from high-tech inventor and entrepreneur Dr. An Wang—is the classical granite building, the original one of the Massachusetts General Hospital, designed by Bulfinch before he went to Washington to serve as President Monroe's capital architect. It was the last Boston building Bulfinch ever designed and was completed in 1821, after he left; the hospital is the nation's second-oldest (to Pennsylvania's) general hospital. In it may be seen the Bulfinch amphitheater where for the first time in the world ether was used during an operation, performed by Dr. John Collins Warren, on October 16, 1846. The best way to visit the ether dome is by the present main entrance of the hospital on North Grove Street. Ask for directions at the front desk. The amphitheater was the hospital's operating room from 1821 to 1867. When the first operation with ether (for the removal of a jaw tumor) was finished, Dr. Warren told his fascinated professional audience in the high seats,

"Gentlemen, this is no humbug." A new era in surgery had come and was quickly heralded worldwide. On display are pictures and memorabilia of that operation on a twenty-year-old youth.

Once Dr. Parkman reached North Grove Street he seemed, for a while, to have stepped off the earth. The case had sensational ingredients: great wealth, Brahmins, Harvard, and mystery. Parkman's brother-in-law, Robert Gould Shaw, offered a huge reward. Ultimately, through his own attempts at cover-up, suspicion fell on no less a personage than Boston socialite and Harvard professor Dr. John Webster, whose wife was an aunt of historian Francis Parkman. Moreover, Dr. Parkman had secured Dr. Webster his professorship. "What a tornado this caused in Cambridge," said a contemporary. Dr. Parkman's remains were finally found in a section of the foul cellar under the dissecting room and privies where the tidal Charles River flowed in and out. Top lawyers handled the case. Dr. Holmes testified. Harvard's new president, Jared Sparks, gave imperishable testimony. "Our professors," said Sparks, "do not often commit murder." Just before being hanged, Dr. Webster confessed that he had lost his temper and struck Dr. Parkman a single blow with a stick from his laboratory bench.

Look now toward the main entrance of the Massachusetts General Hospital. To the left, we can see a twenty-four-story, glass-enclosed structure that provides one of the nation's most advanced inpatient care facilities, the Ellison Building, opened in spring 1990. Together with a fifteen-story mate, they replace (and are five times larger than) the hospital's renowned Baker Building. The Eben Ellison family trust gave $10 million to help make this medical advance possible; the family had developed, in Pennsylvania, the world's largest tannery.

North Grove Street, after crossing busy Cambridge Street, becomes Grove Street and takes us partway up Beacon Hill. This was the part of the North Slope that brought the famous hill the nickname "Mount Whoredom," until Boston's distinguished Mayor Josiah Quincy and his police force, in 1823, cleaned it up. Some old street names were changed, new buildings went up, and new residents flocked in after "300 females wholly devoid of shame and modesty," as described in 1817 by a local clergyman, took flight. Ironically, this North Slope "combat zone," developed on eighteen acres of pasture that, for the most part, were owned by the ruling elder of Boston's First Church back in the 1640s and descended to his nephew, a clergyman.

There was a cliff along the north side of the hill between Revere Street and lower Phillips Street. Oliver Wendell Holmes in his Beacon Hill rambles as the "Autocrat" told his discovering the "precipitous and rudely paved cliff which looks down on the grim abode of science, and beyond to the far hills; a promenade so delicious. . . ." The grim abode was his own Harvard Medical School, where he was dean or lecturer from 1847 to 1882.

Some visitors to the hill like to inspect the quaint, short cul-de-sacs that lead off Revere Street's north side to the old cliff's edge. Up Revere Street on the left beyond Anderson Street is Rollins Place, with gaslights, trees, and the drop down the cliff blocked by a pillared facade that has the appearance of a dwelling. A short way down Anderson from Revere, on the left, is a different courtlike cliff arrangement in Champney Place. There are still three more, variously accommodating the cliff from numbers 73 to 87 Revere Street—Goodwin Place, Sentry Hill Place, and Bellingham Place.

This area was well known to modern poets Robert Lowell and John Berryman. Lowell's prose essay "91 Revere Street" tells the astounding tale of his childhood in the four-story brick dwelling at Number 91 near the corner of West Cedar. An only child, he relates how his haughty, dominating mother ruined his complaisant father's naval career. She had been reared at fashionable 18 Chestnut Street, her father's home, and considered 91 Revere—though but a short distance from Louisburg Square and purchased by her—as "barely perched on the outer rim of the hub of decency." Robert, poet-born, became a toughie. "For the Union Dead," one of his best-known poems, was written in the 1950s when he and his wife and baby daughter were living in the Back Bay at 239 Marlborough Street.

On the southwest corner of Grove and Revere, on the second floor at 49 Grove, John Berryman brought his bride Eileen in the early 1940s. He was then an instructor at Harvard and had fled his Cambridge dwelling because it was too handy for students' interrupting visits. Here, amid meager furnishings, he prized his many books, plain desk, and the companionship of fellow poets Lowell and Delmore Schwartz.

Going back down Grove Street we may, at the lower northwest corner of the intersection with Phillips Street, get the feeling of an approaching earthquake. This intersection is directly over the tunnel that carries the reverberating Boston-Cambridge rapid transit into the Beacon Hill cliffside on the way to the central Park Street Subway.

On the eastern end of Phillips Street, at numbers 14 to 18, is the Vilna Shul Synagogue built in 1919 when the West End had many Jewish residents. Its congregation dissolved in 1985. The building was given landmark status in 1990, and there have been plans to convert it into a museum and cultural center.

At 66 Phillips is the four-story brick house of abolitionist Lewis Hayden, an escaped slave, who established himself as a Cambridge Street merchant and used his house as a station on the pre–Civil War underground railroad to help other slaves escape to Canada. After the war, like John J. Smith of Pinckney Street, he was elected a black member of the state legislature.

Note a different sort of Beacon Hill dead end at Primus Avenue, on the left at the foot of Phillips Street; steps and steps, going up and down.

At West Cedar Street we turn right and go downhill to Charles Street Circle. On the far corner of Cambridge Street, behind the high walls, we can see the gray granite of the Suffolk County Jail, built by 1851 to replace the old Leverett Street Jail in the West End—just a few blocks north—where Dr. George Parkman's murderer was hanged. The present county jail was constructed on filled land over which Charles Street was extended to the Charles River dam. Most likely the most interesting occupant of the county jail was none other than the personable James Michael Curley, who was committed for ninety days in 1904. The future mayor and governor told the voters that his offense was only that he was trying to get a needy friend a job.

Curley, thirty-five years old at the time, had taken a civil service examination for a man who wanted to be a letter carrier. An attendant recognized Curley. In court Curley testified that he was merely acting "as a proxy." There is a tradition that Curley, as a VIP, did time in the sheriff's quarters, later known as "Hospitality Hall." But the superintendent of institutions saw him "sitting in his cell with four books on the table beside him. I asked what he was reading and he said, 'The Life of Jefferson.' He had already read every book in the prison library." Curley did something else while a prisoner. He ran for a seat on Boston's Board of Aldermen and a sympathetic electorate gave its judgment. He won.

Between Charles Street and the Charles River

Continuing left around the Charles Street Circle, we come to Charles Street. The weathervane, belfry, and clock tower of the 1897 Charles Street Meeting House still rising above the rooftops to our left give old-world charm to the street scene.

Immediately on the water side of Charles Street there were formerly mud flats, considered worthless, that still belonged to Charles Bulfinch after he was plunged into bankruptcy. When Charles Street was originally created by Otis and his associates in 1803–1805, besides tossing in the West Mount of Beacon Hill by dump car, he also, as he put it, used "mud from the flats." Bulfinch saw a chance to recoup some financial losses. He filled his flats over to the old wooden West Boston Bridge, predecessor of the present Longfellow Bridge, with its stone piers, just ahead of us.

Bulfinch, in fact, had been one of the group that had met at the Bunch of Grapes Tavern and built the West Boston Bridge in 1792–1793. It was Boston's second bridge to the mainland, inspired by Hancock's bridge to Charlestown, but it did not prove profitable. Optimistic Bulfinch felt sure that he would do well with the mud flats. He put his new lots up for sale in 1805 only to have his hopes dashed once again by the depression that Jefferson's embargo brought to business in Boston. "Men of large capital" like Otis, said Bulfinch, could wait for better times. As for Bulfinch, "I was obliged once more to surrender all property . . . and we were obliged to leave our neat and commodious home for a humble and inferior one."

Eventually, there were superb Federal houses along Charles Street. On crossing Charles Street, we come to a parking lot beside the four-story, redbrick, white-stone-trimmed building at 14 Embankment Road, currently the Jeffries House of the Massachusetts Charitable Eye and Ear Infirmary, founded in 1824. Here on the parking lot site at what was 164 Charles Street, "within a few doors" of his publisher friend "Jamie" Fields, lived Oliver Wendell Holmes, with the river he enjoyed right in his backyard. The "Little Professor" had left his residence near the old stone steps of the Province House garden in 1858 to be here nearer the medical school. When he first came to Charles Street it was just after he resumed his witty essays as the "Autocrat of the Breakfast Table." He lived here until 1870. By that time he felt that business and traffic had made Charles Street a noisy thoroughfare.

THERE IS ABOUT BOSTON A CERTAIN REMINISCENT AND CLASSICAL TONE, SUGGESTING AN AUTHENTICITY AND PIETY WHICH FEW OTHER AMERICAN CITIES POSSESS.

—E. B. WHITE

Above all Holmes loved the river. "My present fleet on the Charles River consists of three rowboats," said the Autocrat. Neighbor Annie Fields recalled that in those days, before embankments existed on either side, the Charles River "was wider and more beautiful. Early in the morning, sometimes before sunrise, standing at my bedroom window I have seen his tiny skiff moving quickly over the face of the quiet water. Sometimes the waves were high and rough. . . . There was little to be learned about a skiff and its management which he did not acquire."

For a view of the river, let us go up the steps or ramp, just opposite Jeffries House, to the footbridge that crosses over above Storrow Memorial Drive to the riverside park. The river from midpoint on this foot and bicycle overpass is beautiful and spacious. Those two high towers we see to the south, Hancock and Prudential, soaring over uptown Boston, are Boston's highest structures; we will visit them presently on our walk in the Back Bay. The river is quite collegiate. To the southwest is Harvard Bridge with the university farther upriver. Along the Cambridge side is the Massachusetts Institute of Technology. Nearby, going westward across the river, is Longfellow Bridge, built in 1900–1908 as successor to the old West Boston Bridge. It was in reference to the latter and with the Charles Street Meeting House in mind that Longfellow began his poem:

I stood on the bridge at midnight,
As the clocks were striking the hour,
And the moon rose o'er the city,
Behind the dark church-tower.

All along here, of course, is filled land. The parklike riverbank and embellishments, like small islands, are fairly recent. Back in 1893 the state built a 100-foot-wide promenade beyond the old seawall along the shore. In 1928–1931 a parklike embankment was added through the generosity of Mrs. James Jackson Storrow, widow of a Boston banker. Its accessibility, however, became restricted when, to solve automobile traffic problems, the present Storrow Memorial Drive was built in 1940–1951 between the houses and the river.

The river setting is still a joy. And those who can swim may join "Community Boating" at the 1940 boathouse, also given by Mrs. Storrow, and learn to sail and use the rowboats, catboats, and sloops seen sailing or moored within the curves of the islands.

Just a bit farther south is the private boathouse of the Union Boat Club, formed in 1851 when the Charles River was still tidal. This was a year before the first intercollegiate Harvard-Yale crew race. The club was formed by some gentlemen interested in rowing. They were also admirers of Daniel Webster's "Union Forever" speeches, and hence the club name. They started with a floating boathouse and then agreed to a low boathouse to spare their neighbors' river view. So the boathouse would remain small, they also built in 1909–1910 a fine new brick clubhouse—with handball and squash courts—diagonally across the Embankment Road at the foot of Chestnut Street.

Next south along the river is the Hatch Shell, named for Edward

WHAT'S A "SMOOT"?

While enjoying the charms of the Esplanade, take the time to walk out onto Harvard Bridge (where Massachusetts Avenue crosses the Charles into Cambridge) for a welcome river vista of Boston on one side, Cambridge on the other. For William Dean Howells, editor of the *Atlantic Monthly,* the view was the "stuff that dreams are made on." Between taking in the sights—and dodging runners and cyclists—look beneath your feet; you'll note the bridge is marked out in "smoots." This curious unit of measure is based on the height of a certain Oliver R. Smoot, Jr., a fraternity pledge at M.I.T. who was rolled across the bridge in the 1950s for no apparent reason.

Hatch, whose public-spirited sister, Maria Hatch, bequeathed funds for its construction in 1940 to give Boston a "public beauty spot." It was given a $5.2 million renovation in 1990–1991. This bandstand is a successor to and far fancier than the one first used by maestro Arthur Fiedler, who, with the Boston Symphony and Boston Pops musicians, inaugurated free open-air concerts by the river on July 4, 1929. The pedestrian overpass back to Beacon Street has been named Fiedler Bridge. Don't miss the huge metal Fiedler head on a nearby island.

The bridge north of Longfellow Bridge on the Charles is where in 1906–1910 a dam was completed across the river, converting it into a basin. The dam with gate is on the site of the old Craigie Bridge, Boston's third bridge to the mainland, opened in 1809. The area of the dam is now quite like a park and in 1951 became the new home of Boston's Museum of Science and the fabulous collection it began back in 1830. Its Charles Hayden Planetarium came in 1962. The latest hit is space travel in its Mugar Omnimax Theater.

The museum and planetarium make a rewarding visit. There are more than 400 exhibits, from hatching birds to a 20-foot-high dinosaur. A delightful exhibit is the layout, diorama-style, of the way the original community in New England, Plymouth, appeared. The planetarium makes our selves and our world clearer. Besides portraying trips to the stars, the museum-planetarium provides parking facilities and a skyline cafeteria.

Before returning to Charles Street by the Oliver Wendell Holmes site to continue our walk south on Charles Street, notice the Cambridge shore just west of the museum. It was here that the redcoats who embarked at the foot of the Common on the night of April 18, 1775, landed. There were many marshes on the river side at that time, and most of the redcoats were wet to their armpits before heading to Lexington.

As we return to Charles Street we note that the Charles Street Garage, ahead on our right, property of the hospitals, has two openings. The second opening into the garage became in 1856 the site of Boston's most celebrated nineteenth-century salon in the new, three-story, Federal brick home of Annie and James Fields at 148 Charles Street. Across the street, at 131 Charles, is the house where editor-author Thomas Bailey Aldrich lived as Fields's neighbor starting in 1871. We will enter the first opening at 160 Charles Street. This through-and-under opening is a right-of-way passage to the interesting circle of ten houses built at the end of World War I in West Hill Place. Before entering the archway into the circle of houses, note on the left a passage in back of the garage, which leads to a private park.

This garden, planted by the Fieldses, is all that remains of their homestead here. But the wonderful and exciting memories that go with their residence, as with the vanished Beacon Hill mansion of John Hancock, are legion. As Annie recalled: "Soon after Dr. Holmes' removal to Charles Street began a long series of early morning breakfasts ... feasts of the simplest kind. The 8 o'clock breakfast hour was chosen as being the only time the busy guests and hosts could readily call their own. There were few men, except Poe, famous in American or English literature of that era who did not appear once at least." As for the sentiments of Poe, who rarely came to Boston, he wrote Fields,

"There is no one in America whom I would rather hold by the hand than yourself."

The Fieldses bought the garden area to keep a view clear to the river. A 7-foot brick wall was recently added at the sidewalk line. Their first-floor dining room looked out on the garden, as did their library, which occupied all the second floor, a place so filled with memorabilia that Henry James called it a "waterside museum." On the third floor were bedrooms, and here Charles Dickens, breaking his rule against lodging in private homes while on tour, came as a guest. Holmes dropped by one morning in 1868 and, acceding to Dickens's urgent request, took him over to nearby Harvard Medical School to see where Dr. Parkman was murdered. Dickens found it all "horribly grim," with the furnace "smelling . . . . as if the body was still there."

There were times of merriment, too, excursions over to Longfellow's and Lowell's in Cambridge, distinguished gatherings for dinner, and a pre-Christmas repast of roast beef and plum pudding with Dickens, master of recipes, making the punch. Mark Twain has recounted "uproarious storytelling, gaiety" at gatherings in the Fieldses' house. And it was always a hospitable resort for members of the Saturday Club.

After passing one house beyond the Fieldses' redbrick garden wall, we come on Embankment Road to Charles River Square, an enclave of riverside town houses slightly older than those on West Hill Place. U.S. Senator Edward M. "Ted" Kennedy moved into a house on the left, 3 Charles River Square, soon after his first marriage, and lived here during political campaigns that carried him from county office to Congress.

Deeper in Charles River Square on the right, beside Number 18, is an opening into Revere Street that will take us back to Charles Street. Heading south on Charles Street, toward the Common and the Public Garden, we come next to Pinckney Square.

To be nearer his work Charles H. Taylor, publisher and developer of *The Boston Globe,* moved into Boston and lived for a decade, from 1880 to 1889, at 108 Charles Street, on the northwest corner, before moving to Beacon Street. One of the rungs in Taylor's rise in the newspaper world was his coverage of Dickens when Taylor was a young newsman. Taylor was able to send exclusive Dickens quotes to the *New York Tribune,* for which he was a correspondent. On Dickens avoiding the public while he was rehearsing, Taylor quoted Dickens: "My time is not my own when I am preparing to read any more than when I am writing a novel, and I can as well do one as the other without concentrating all my powers on it, until it is done."

Dr. George F. Grant, noted dentist and the first black instructor at Harvard Dental School, succeeded Mr. Taylor at 108 Charles Street in 1890, when he moved into town from Arlington Heights. Dr. Grant's first wife was the daughter of Beacon Hill's first black representative. Golf fans have a longstanding debt of gratitude to Dr. Grant, a sports enthusiast, who invented the wooden golf tee. He lived at Number 108 until his death in 1910.

Next door at 110 Charles Street was the dwelling of John A. Andrew, who was governor of Massachusetts during the Civil War, 1861 to 1865. He responded so promptly to Lincoln's first call for troops that four days later, April 19, 1861, the 6th Massachusetts Regiment was the first to shed blood in the Civil War.

As we go down Pinckney Street toward the river, note Public Alley 301 on the left. It goes between backyards and becomes River Street. En route, it presents two interesting aspects. Its park, maintained by residents, has a touch of uphill Louisburg Square. The NO PARKING signs underline an evident solution to an urgent city problem, parking. Indents in backyard fences provide parking spaces, a tactic widely repeated in Back Bay.

Turn left from Pinckney Street onto Brimmer Street. We are in a quite fashionable section. The ivy-covered house at 9 Brimmer, with trees on the lawn, has for years been the town house of the family of Admiral Richard E. Byrd, early navy pilot and flying explorer, first to fly to both the North and South poles.

The Church of the Advent at the northeast corner of Mount Vernon and Brimmer Streets, founded in 1844 in response to the High Church Episcopalian movement, moved from Bowdoin Street to this Gothic structure, built in 1879–1883. Across from the church, the red-brick house with the cream-colored doorway at 158 Mount Vernon has been the residence of Boston's ex-mayor Kevin H. White, a longtime public servant like his father.

At the corner of Mount Vernon and Brimmer, 44 Brimmer, was the family dwelling of historian Samuel Eliot Morison and of his parents and grandparents before him. He called the area "a horsey neighborhood" and wrote a delightful, nostalgic account of social life here from horsecar and herdic to Cadillac and airplane in his *One Boy's Boston.* Just across from Number 44 is private Otis Place with patrician dwellings. Justice Louis D. Brandeis lived at 6 Otis Place.

Heading now away from the river and along Mount Vernon Street, we pass on our left, at 131 Mount Vernon, the redbrick house where the elder Henry James, after his wife's funeral in February of 1882, moved from his large, longtime family house in Cambridge. Henry James, Jr., author and expatriate, who had not arrived before his mother's death, once again arrived here too late when his father died the following December in 1882.

At the corner of Charles Street stands the Charles Street Meeting House. The structure, now refitted for private use, has had so many historical associations that it was lovingly saved intact by being moved 10 feet when busy Charles Street was widened after World War I. The church was built in 1807 to the design of architect Asher Benjamin. It was built beside the tidal river for handy immersion by its congregation, the Baptist Society. Though antislavery orators were welcome in its pulpit in pre–Civil War days, a dispute over allowing a black to sit in a white pew led some members to join in forming Boston's first integrated church, Tremont Temple, in 1842. William Lloyd Garrison and Wendell Phillips, as well as Frederick Douglass and Harriet Tubman, spoke here. In 1867 the meeting house became—and remained until the 1930s—the gathering place of the African Methodist Episcopal Church and in midcentury became an active Unitarian Universalist social center.

Head south now along Charles Street, past its eateries and antiques shops, toward Beacon Street. Mrs. Mallard and her ducklings took this same route along Mount Vernon and Charles. We have seen, though, that 1951 traffic changes along Embankment Road would force her and her ducklings, if they tried it today, to fly or to use the

Arthur Fiedler pedestrian overpass. We may go as the Mallards originally did, directly to the Public Garden, and enter through the iron gates to Charles and Beacon Streets.

The charm of lawn, shrubs, and trees in this twenty-four-acre park irresistibly draws our attention, but for Mrs. Mallard it was the little island ahead in the pond that she and her ducklings sought, to await the return of Father Mallard. On the left side of the path from the iron gate to the pond we can see, in bronze, Mrs. Mallard and her trailing ducklings approaching the water. We shall have other visits to the Garden. For the present, let us return to Beacon and Charles Streets, to begin our walk in the Back Bay at the spot where its development began.

BACK BAY

What the Old Mill Dam Hath Wrought

The Back Bay community that was created in the last century—a place of long, straight, wide streets astonishingly novel to old Boston, an assemblage of superior private residences, magnificently designed churches, and cultural structures—was surprisingly not what Uriah Cotting had in mind when he got a charter in 1814 to build a dam across the bay starting at Charles and Beacon Streets.

Cotting, the remarkable developer of Federalist Boston's center and waterfront, had watched the tides flow in and out of the Back Bay and wanted to harness them as a source of mill power. To get it he would extend Beacon Street by way of a mill dam to Sewall's Point (present Kenmore Square). A short cross-dam from the mill dam to Gravelly Point (roughly present Massachusetts and Commonwealth Avenues) would be a fine location for mills to get their power as the trapped seawater flowed from the full basin on the west of the cross-dam to the receiving basin on its east. "Erect these mills and lower the price of bread," Cotting had urged his fellow citizens. He envisaged more than gristmills—all sorts of mills, more than eighty of them. However, Cotting died two years before the 50-foot-wide, mile-and-a-half-long dam to the Brookline shore was completed in 1821. Some mills were built around Gravelly Point and the cross-dam, but far from eighty. There simply was not sufficient power.

BACK BAY I

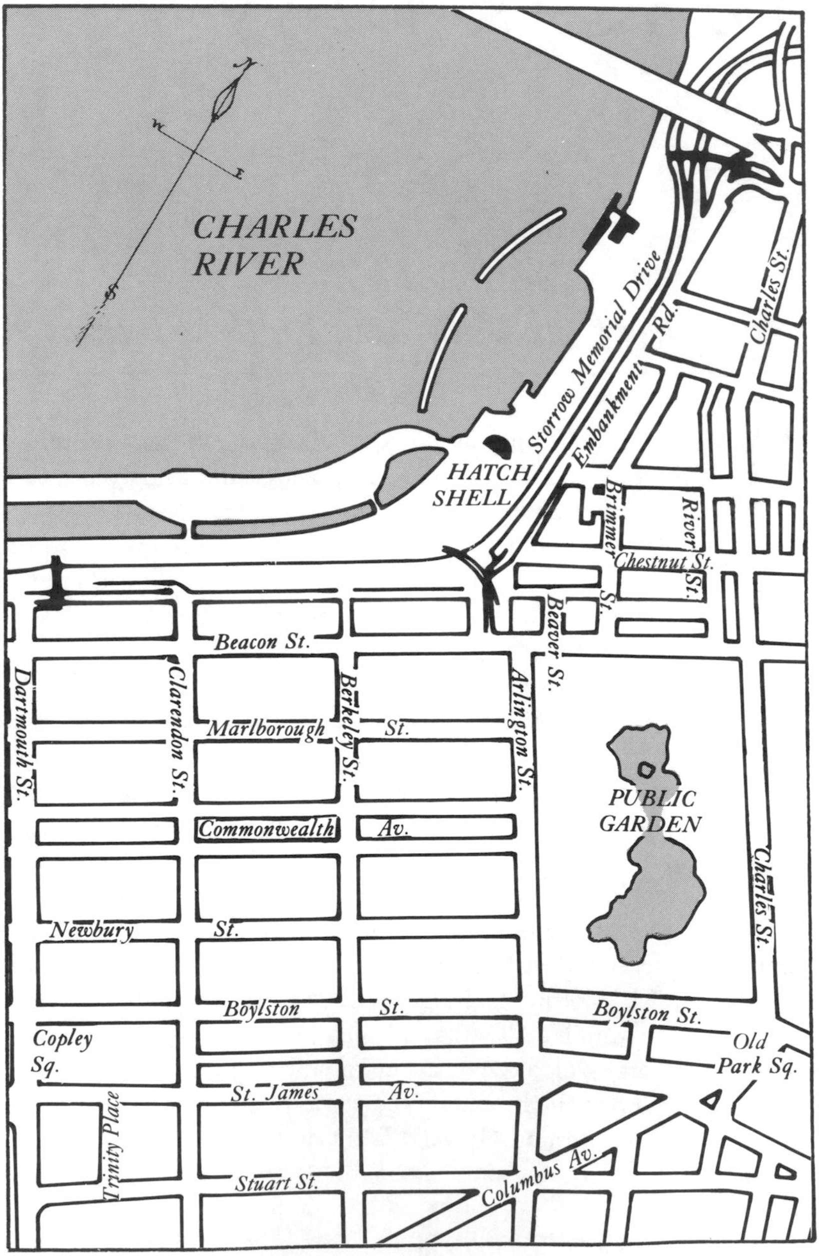
CHARLES
RIVER
HATCH
SHELL
Storrow Memorial Drive
Embankment Rd.
Charles St.
Brimmer St.
River St.
Chestnut St.
Beacon St.
Beaver St.
Dartmouth St.
Clarendon St.
Berkeley St.
Arlington St.
Marlborough St.
Commonwealth Av.
PUBLIC
GARDEN
Charles St.
Newbury St.
Boylston St.
Boylston St.
Old
Park Sq.
Copley
Sq.
St. James Av.
Trinity Place
Stuart St.
Columbus Av.

A crisscross of railroad beds, which by 1835 provided Boston's first train service to the west and south, impeded tidal flows within the Mill Dam. For these, and many other compelling reasons as we shall presently see, pressure grew to turn the Back Bay entirely into landfill, by far the biggest alteration yet in the original peninsula settled by Winthrop and his Puritan faithful.

The Mill Dam, especially as a fast route to Brookline and a superb run for sleighs in winter, got plenty of attention by Bostonians after it was opened with formal parades. Lovers loved it for strolling and sleighing. Merchant prince Thomas Handasyd Perkins's granddaughter Caroline said of it: "Where the Public Garden is now was a strip of wasteland, at high tide washed by water. The last houses on Beacon Street below Charles were the four or five white houses still there. With the water on both sides and the sunset before us, it was very pretty in the afternoon. It supplemented the Common."

The white houses (actually six), 70–75 Beacon on our right beginning at River Street, were built in 1828, the first along the Mill Dam and the oldest structures in the Back Bay. These little-altered, three-stor, Greek revival, granite faced dwellings with ridged slate roofs were designed by Asher Benjamin and built by Harrison Gary Otis and fellow Mount Vernon Proprietors as soon as they established title rights. They are still considered among the most attractive in Back Bay. The second one, Number 71, was a wedding gift in 1831 from then-Mayor Harrison Gray Otis to his son William on his marriage to the reigning society beauty, Emily Marshall. The wedding party that night at Number 71 was "enormous" with friends "serenading until the birds sang." Emily was then twenty-three. Five years later there was deep grief at Number 71 when Emily, on the birth of their third child, lost her life.

By midcentury, 1850, there were buildings along here as far as Embankment Road. Stockholders of the Cotting's developers, the Boston and Roxbury Mill Corporation, filled tidal flats and built, just west of Beaver Street, a row of eight four-story houses, numbers 92 to 99, in Italian style with rusticated brownstone main floors and upper stories of brick. Most, among them numbers 97 to 99, which were

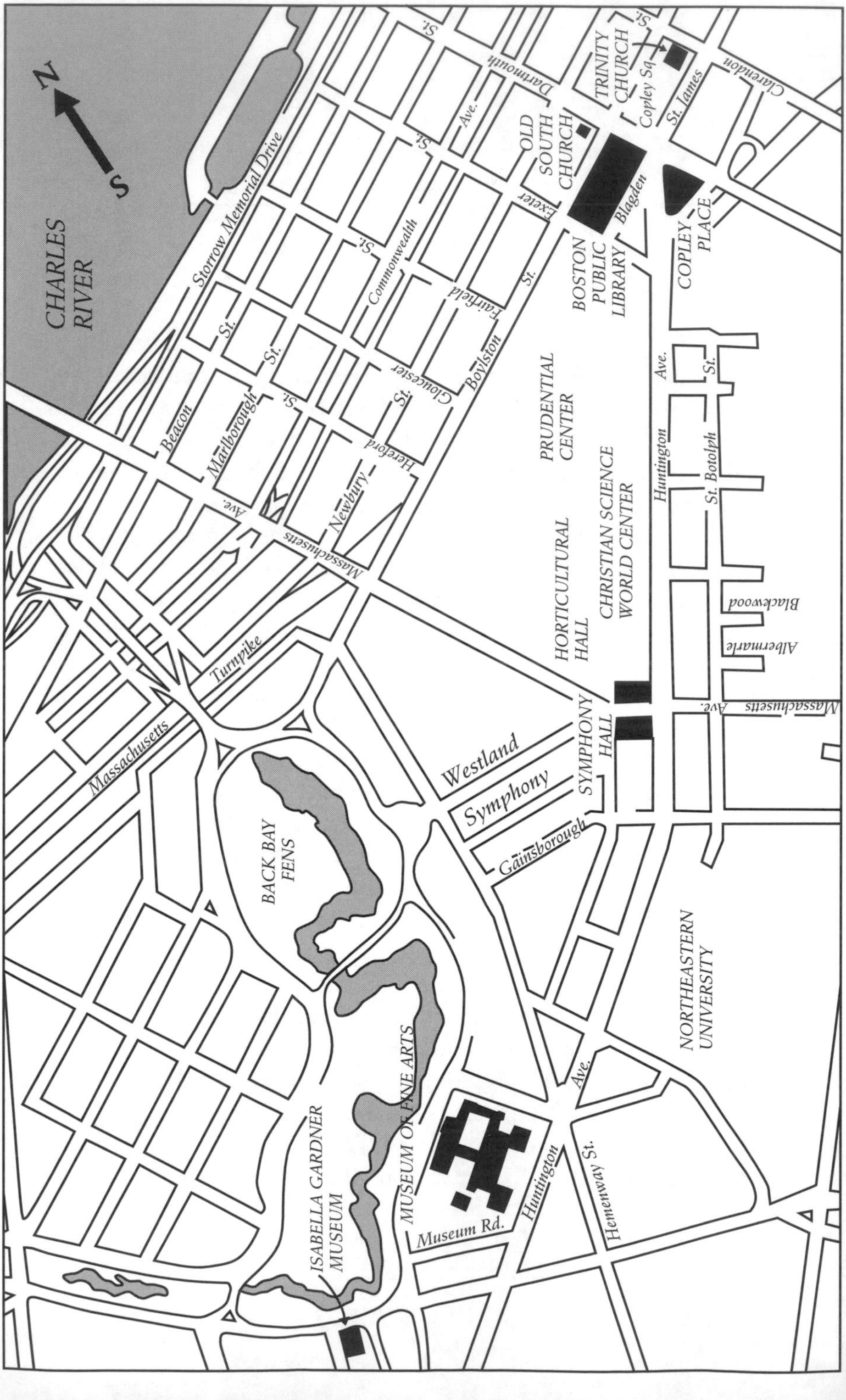
N
S
CHARLES RIVER
Storrow Memorial Drive
Beacon St.
Marlborough St.
Commonwealth Ave.
Newbury St.
Boylston St.
Dartmouth St.
Exeter St.
Fairfield St.
Gloucester St.
Hereford St.
Massachusetts Ave.
Massachusetts Turnpike
OLD SOUTH CHURCH
TRINITY CHURCH
Copley Sq.
St. James
Clarendon St.
Blagden
BOSTON PUBLIC LIBRARY
COPLEY PLACE
PRUDENTIAL CENTER
Huntington Ave.
St. Botolph St.
CHRISTIAN SCIENCE WORLD CENTER
HORTICULTURAL HALL
Blackwood
Albermarle
Massachusetts Ave.
SYMPHONY HALL
Westland
Symphony
Gainsborough
BACK BAY FENS
NORTHEASTERN UNIVERSITY
MUSEUM OF FINE ARTS
ISABELLA GARDNER MUSEUM
Museum Rd.
Huntington
Hemenway St.
Ave.

demolished to permit widening of Embankment Road, have disappeared. Only numbers 93 and 94 are still in place.

What we see along the stretch from Charles Street to Embankment Road is typical of change in the Back Bay, pronounced since the early 1930s. The nine-story structure at the corner of Charles Street is a combination of businesses and cooperative apartments. Single-family residences, with very few exceptions, have been divided into apartments, dormitories, or condominiums. Many older fine residences have been replaced.

The ten-story high rise at 81 Beacon has had an interesting political role. In 1952 during the most crucial political contest in John F. Kennedy's rise to high office, his father, former Ambassador Joseph P. Kennedy, took an apartment at Number 81, "conveniently in central Boston," as mother Rose Kennedy said, "to keep a close supervisory eye on everything." The former ambasssador, because of his isolationist reputation, knew he had to keep a low profile but was active every minute in the campaign. The race was for the U.S. Senate seat of Henry Cabot Lodge, who seemed unbeatable after he helped to get General Eisenhower to run for President that year. Mother Rose said that even Lodge attributed Jack's close victory to tea parties that the Kennedy clan organized all over the state. She heartily enjoyed the observation that her son floated into the U.S. Senate "on an ocean of tea." The Kennedy-Fitzgerald clan had a private spur to whip Lodge in 1952, for the race was sort of a return bout. Back in 1916 "Honey Fitz" had lost to the elder Henry Cabot Lodge in the state's first popular election for the U.S. Senate seat.

Crowds of visitors are a common sight outside Hampshire House at 84 Beacon Street, where they wait to go down the steps to the Bull and Finch Pub in the basement. These smiling folks are eager to see the site that inspired the setting for the NBC television series "Cheers."

This first stretch of the Mill Dam was officially known as Western Avenue until the close of the Civil War. Along here just three years later, in 1868, Charles Dickens—to amuse his friends—staged his midwinter "Great International Walking Match . . . whatsoever the weather on the Mill Dam Road" between his giant-sized agent Dolby, called by Dickens "the man of Ross," and "Jamie" Fields's pint-sized assistant, Osgood, "the Boston Bantam." Dickens was accompanied by Fields almost daily on walks. For this match, Dickens, with watch in hand, and Fields had gone over the planned course that Dickens described as "Six miles and a half, good measure, from the first tree on the Mill Dam Road, lies the little village . . . of Newton Centre. Here Massachusetts Jemmy [Fields] and The Gasper [Dickens] had established the turning point. The road comprehended every variety of inconvenience to test the mettle of the men, and nearly the whole of it was covered with snow." Moreover, the snow flew "fast and furious" and the wind was "cold and bitter" that February 29. Still Dickens and Fields, with a side bet of a hat, accompanied their champions. Tall, bulky Dolby fell behind little Osgood with the "drum stick legs." Annie Fields drove out in a carriage, found Osgood well ahead, and kept near him, as she related, "administering brandy all the way to town." All of them jumped into her carriage and "drove home with great speed to bathe and sleep before dinner." Dickens gave a lavish banquet that night at the Parker House with Longfellow, Lowell, and Holmes among the guests.

On reaching Arlington Street we are at the base of the grid of Back Bay streets stretching westward from the Public Garden, part of an infill that covered an area of the bay at least fifteen times the size of the fifty-acre Common. Yale President Timothy Dwight's appraisal of the Mill Dam (back in 1821) certainly applies equally well to the later feat of filling the Back Bay: "No enterprise of a similar nature comparable to this has been commenced on this side of the Atlantic."

Creating it, though, had become a vital necessity for the growing community. The obstruction to tidal action, the further obstruction of the railroad crisscross of lines to Providence south and Worcester west, and refuse dumping and sewage had changed the bay into an eyesore and health menace. The stench, depending on wind direction, could be unendurable. Yet the presence of the railroad beds, plus a new invention called the steam excavator, a steam shovel, suggested a solution when the mayor and aldermen, acting as a board of health, declared officially that the city had a "nuisance offensive and injurious to the large and increasing population." This was in 1849, but it was not until 1857 that legal entanglements were resolved and the trains began bringing gravel from Needham hills near the upper falls of the Charles River, 9 miles to the west.

Architect Arthur Gilman, who would build the Back Bay's first church and participate in designing the Louvre-style 1862 City Hall in School Street, was mainly creator of the spacious plan of parallel streets for the Back Bay. Commonwealth Avenue, still Boston's most resplendent boulevard promenade, is 240 feet wide between required lot-line setbacks on either side with a 100-foot-wide mall in the center.

Filling proceeded night and day, with lots auctioned as completed. Building followed—first big brownstone mansions in 1860 along Arlington Street, then westward in different styles as the project progressed. By 1882 the fill was completed. When construction was finished, the Back Bay was hailed as a living record of architectural styles in America, from the 1828 Greek-revival houses we passed on Beacon Street, at the start of Mill Dam, to late nineteenth-century chateaux we shall see when we arrive near Massachusetts Avenue.

This area of Beacon Street has been much like a college campus. The former Engineers Club, 96 Beacon, has been the Student Union for Emerson College. Emerson and Fisher junior colleges, between them, own well over two dozen Back Bay buildings for offices, classrooms, and dormitories. In spring 1992 Emerson purchased the fourteen-story building at 180 Tremont Street (near the corner of Boylston Street overlooking the Common) for media facilities, television, and radio stations.

The 1860 Gibson family five-story house we see at 137 Beacon, with its gracious furnishings from China trade wealth, has been open to the public since the 1950s as a Victorian museum.

On the water side just beyond Berkeley Street at 150–152 Beacon stood the residence of fabulous art patron Mrs. Jack Gardner from 1862 to 1902. Here she collected most of the art treasurers we shall see in the palace that she built in the Fenway. It was while she was living at Number 150–152 that John Singer Sargent painted one of the palace's treasures, a portrait of Mrs. Jack that stunned local society. Her dwelling here is now the Abbott Library of Emerson College.

As we turn left and go along the north side of Berkeley Street, two steeples ahead are instantly striking, especially when mirrored, as they most often are, in the towering glass of the John Hancock high-rise, the highest building in New England, or seen against the tall office building just to its left, Hancock's former headquarters.

The arcade entrance and damaged steeple of the First and Second Unitarian Universalist Church, the nearer church, are roughly all that survived a 1968 fire that destroyed this English Gothic edifice of puddingstone with brownstone trim, which was built in 1867 as the fifth successive meeting house of Boston's first Puritan congregation. John Winthrop's statue, first placed in Boston's old Scollay Square on the city's 250th anniversary, may now be seen most appropriately on the Marlborough Street side of the First and Second Church. Winthrop was the most important member of the church's original congregation. For a beautifully integrated, modern-style structure to go with the surviving tower and arcade, the First Church parish, which had been joined in 1970 by Boston's Second Church, turned to architect Paul Rudolph. The two ramps lead to the lobby. Off it on the left is an auditorium the church shares with Emerson College. On the right is a wonderfully imaginative, modern sanctuary of split-ribbed blocks with acoustics so unusual it is sought by many musical groups from choirs to philharmonic. Drop in. If the lobby is closed, inquire at the Parish House at 66 Marlborough just beyond Winthrop's statue.

It is certainly noticeable, as we arrive at Commonwealth Avenue, that institutions and commerce, as they did in earlier years in Boston's old South End, are increasingly taking over this formerly aristocratic area of the Back Bay. The sumptuous 1861 family mansion at the northeast corner of Berkeley and Commonwealth, set well back with balustraded yard, is called Halcyon Place, guest house for families of patients at the Massachusetts General Hospital. Walking on Commonwealth toward the Public Garden, we pass former one-family residences now divided into apartments. Emerson College has the mansion at Number 21, the Boston Center for Adult Education is at Number 5, the French Consulate General is at Number 3, and on the prestigious corner is Harbridge House. Do not fail to visit 5 Commonwealth to see firsthand the grandeur of some of Boston's former socialite residences. The Center, founded in 1933, is the nation's oldest institution for continuing education.

Originally, a son of merchant prince Abbott Lawrence built a mansion on this Number 5 site in 1861. The present structure was built in 1904 when Walter C. Baylies, successful cotton broker, wanted a bigger house for his family. The lavish Louis XIV ballroom on the west side of the mansion was added in 1912 for a daughter's debut by order of Baylies's cable from Paris to his architect and was used in 1918 for her wedding.

The residence of the French Consulate General was also built in 1861 and is pretty much like the Lawrence residence that Mr. Baylies had demolished. Originally 1 Commonwealth was built, also in 1861, by banker Samuel G. Ward, who succeeded his father as head of Barings in America, when he moved from Louisburg Square. He was a founder of the Union Club, highly convivial, and wished to be next door to members of the family of Joshua Bates, banker and Boston Public Library benefactor, who had built that same year at 12 Arlington Street. These two houses, in 1893, were combined as a single residence by art patron Mrs. J. Montgomery Sears. They are currently the quarters of Harbridge House, an international consulting firm founded a quarter century ago. Just north of them, at 8-9 Arlington, was the main office of the *Atlantic Monthly*. The prestigious magazine had James Russell Lowell, then a young professor at Harvard, as its first editor and ran in its first issue the opening chapter of Oliver Wendell Holmes's *Autocrat of the Breakfast Table*.

Across the mall, beyond Alexander Hamilton's statue, a four-story brownstone that once stood at 10 Commonwealth was the dwelling of Longfellow's brother-in-law, Thomas Gold Appleton, noted for his warm hospitality. Tom Appleton built the place in 1864 and moved here from Beacon Hill. He was a top personality in Boston's art, literary, and social worlds, a crusader for and patron of the Museum of Fine Arts, which built its first building in 1872 in nearby Copley Square. Portly, witty, bon vivant Tom was at his happiest when friends gathered at his great round dining table—artists, writers, Longfellow, Holmes, Julia Ward Howe, and other mid-nineteenth-century Boston celebrities.

Eminent among Boston's most attractive sights is the view of the

Public Garden from the Commonwealth Mall and, of course, the panorama of the city with the equestrian statue of George Washington in the forefront. With a careful eye for traffic, let us cross and enter the Public Garden.

Public Garden to the Hoffbauer Murals

Thomas Jefferson, who had a longtime acquaintance with our first president, said that George Washington was the best horseman of his age. This certainly seems undeniable as we enter the Public Garden by the Arlington Street gateway across from Commonwealth Avenue. The 38-foot-tall memorial before us, Boston's first equestrian statue, conveys Washington's skill beautifully. The artist, Bostonian Thomas Ball, worked on the model for three years before it was cast and unveiled it in 1869 on the eve of the Fourth of July. The horse Ball used as a model was Colonel T. Bigelow Lawrence's Black Prince, the mount ridden by the young Prince of Wales for the military reception on the Common during his 1860 visit.

To our left, in line with Marlborough Street, is the 30-foot *Good Samaritan* monument to commemorate "the relief of human suffering" made possible by the first use of ether in an operation at the Massachusetts General Hospital. The memorial was presented to the city in 1866 by Thomas Lee, wealthy merchant member of an old Boston family, who a year earlier also gave the granite statue of Alexander Hamilton we just passed on Commonwealth Avenue Mall. Hamilton's was the first to be erected on the mall.

Probably the best view of the little island in the Public Garden's four-acre pond is from the graceful bridge that spans it. All Mallard fans are pleased to know that, when mother and ducklings reached the rock-strewn islet, "there was Mr. Mallard waiting for them." The Mallards could spend their nights here free from foxes and turtles. In the daytime they usually "follow the swan boats and eat peanuts"—tossed, of course, by boat enthusiasts.

SWAN BOATS

In perhaps the only concession to be inspired by Wagner, after seeing a production of the opera *Lohengrin,* Robert Paget built his first swan boat in 1877 out of copper, wood, and bicycle parts. The business is still owned and operated by the Paget family. Each of these whimsical confections actually weighs several tons. The oldest of the flock was built in 1918; the newest, in 1958.

Swan boats have been a Public Garden specialty of the Paget family since Robert Paget in 1877 concealed the new bicycle propulsion technique within a swan and offered boat rides to the public. The landing from which the boats operate is near the northeast side of the bridge.

Considering the beauty that the Public Garden contributes to city life, it now seems strange that the Garden had to survive a very difficult birth. It began in 1794 when the town, shocked by recurrent fires in the ropewalks on Fort Hill, voted that if they agreed not to rebuild on Pearl Street, they could have the then-remote flats below the Common. By 1824, after more fires, the town paid the ropewalk owners for the filled land that the discouraged owners planned to sell as highly desirable house lots. But foresighted Mayor Josiah Quincy put restraints on the developers within his city council by getting the town meeting to vote that the riverbank area be "forever after kept open . . . for the use of the citizens." Even so, greed within the city council was not permanently defeated but resurfaced in later attempts to profit from the land.

Horace Gray, son of the great ship owner Billy Gray, and some horticultural friends showed the community a new use for the land. The city gave permission in 1837, and Gray and friends planted in the present Public Garden area near Charles and Beacon Streets. Gray

Swan boats at the Public Garden

gave his camellia collection from his Summer Street conservatory and built a greenhouse. An old circus building on the opposite side of Beacon Street was used for rare plants and rare birds until it, too, burned down. The first caretaker told of another attraction. "A complete bed of prize tulips, the first ever imported in the United States, valued at $1,000, but costing Mr. Gray $1,500."

River water, refuse, and other problems arose. At least four times in the 1840s and 1850s the large city council, elected by wards, again tried to sell off this land. By 1856 the state and city agreed to build Arlington Street, and by 1859 the legislature wrote a law that, other than a possible city hall, no building could ever be "erected between Arlington and Charles Streets." The next year the mayor and eight-member board of aldermen-at-large set up a competition, won by architect George F. Meacham, to draw a plan for a public garden. And so it came to life.

We pass the Ritz-Carlton Hotel on returning to Arlington Street. The new sixteen-story addition, 1979–1981, on the Commonwealth Avenue corner, with mainly condominiums above the lower floors, replaces four other 1864 brownstone mansions that stood between Tom Appleton's rendezvous of art lovers and the Arlington Street corner. The original half of the Ritz-Carlton, extending the other half of the block, also a sixteen-story structure, was opened in the spring of 1927.

Before we turn at Newbury Street, we continue along Arlington to the Boylston Street corner to see Arthur Gilman's 1859–1861 brownstone church, the Back Bay's first. Just across Arlington Street, at the southwest corner of the Public Garden, is the statue of the Reverend William Ellery Channing, who long and impressively filled the pulpit of the Federal Street Church, which, like many other congregations downtown, migrated to the new Back Bay. The statue of the great Unitarian preacher was unveiled in 1903.

Women's Heritage Trail

Look for the golden swan at 356 Boylston Street. It marks the location of the Women's Educational and Industrial Union, which was organized the same year the first swan boats were launched in the Public Garden (hence the figurehead) in response to problems caused by Boston's rapid growth and industrialization. It has helped women over the years through job training programs, placement, and advocacy for women workers.

Federal Street Church's successor is the Arlington Street Church, a Wrenlike combination of Georgian and Italian styles. The balanced rows of high Corinthian pillars in the sanctuary are very impressive, as are the Tiffany stained-glass memorial windows given from 1895 to 1930. The pulpit that Mr. Channing used in the old church, used there when Massachusetts delegates cast their crucial approval of the new federal Constitution, may be seen in the chapel. The church office is just in back of the church at 351 Boylston Street.

Near midblock, a few steps from the church office at former 141 Boylston, Harvey D. Parker chose to live in his later, prosperous years. He was on a direct route, via the Common, between his Parker House and the Museum of Fine Arts he loved, then in Copley Square. When he died in 1884 he gave the museum $100,000, up to then the largest single donation it received.

When we walk the short way back along Arlington Street, we turn and go up Newbury Street. It was once residential but is now crowded with art galleries, boutiques, fashion stores, and an endless variety of restaurants. We come quickly on the right to still another celebrated Back Bay edifice, Emmanuel Episcopal Church, built in 1861–1862 of popular puddingstone in Gothic style. Starting in the 1970s, it has been "an urban ecumenical center" with "a special ministry through the arts." It has concerts, solo to orchestral, annual Bach and Mozart celebrations, jazz celebrations, other art forms, and a puppet theater.

Three doors west of the church office, at 15 Newbury, is a Back Bay architectural treasure, the Leslie Lindsey Memorial Chapel. Gothic like the church, the chapel has lovely wood carvings, stained glass, and an altar with hand-carved white marble women saints that have also brought it the name Lady Chapel. The tale of the chapel's creation involves the profoundly sad, sudden death of a beautiful young bride and groom. The bride, Leslie Lindsey, was married in 1915 from her wealthy father's riverside Tudor castle on Bay State Road, now a social center for Boston University. The couple left for a honeymoon in Europe on board the doomed liner *Lusitania*. When her body was washed ashore in Ireland, on it was the wedding gift of rubies and diamonds that her father had given her. The family sold these to build the exquisite chapel, consecrated in 1924.

The view on reaching Berkeley Street is a delightful reminder of nineteenth-century Back Bay.

On our left, at 234 Berkeley, carefully manicured for its new tenant, Louis, the noted Back Bay clothier, is the 1861–1864 three-story, redbrick and freestone museum built by the Boston Society of Natural History to house its collections. The land was part of state gifts to education that sales of the newly filled Back Bay lots made possible. The society, as we have seen, moved to its new, much larger Museum of Science quarters on the Charles River dam. The building, under terms of the lease, is preserved with even the original museum roof over an additional third floor.

On our right-hand corner is that second steeple, a lofty 240 feet including the finial, of the Church of the Covenant, which we saw when we first turned from Beacon Street into Berkeley. "Absolutely perfect," was Dr. Holmes's description of it. This Gothic revival edifice, designed by Hobart and Richard Upjohn, was built in 1866–1867 for the Central Congregational Church, formerly on Winter Street. The glorious stained-glass windows were made by Louis C. Tiffany and installed from the 1890s to World War I; especially beautiful are the Madonna window and the sanctuary lantern of the Seven Angels. The church chapel adjoining 67 Newbury Street has shared since 1977 the current artistic life of the street as the Newbury Associated Guild of Arts (NAGA) gallery for painting, sculpture, and photography.

At 99–101 Newbury is the New England Historic Genealogical Society with its wonderfully comprehensive antiquarian collection and family research library founded in 1845. Just across the street from it is the ten-story New England Mutual Life Insurance Company Building (1940–1941), the first chartered mutual life insurance company in our nation, which we will presently visit. The company's rapid expansion into financial services in the late 1980s led to its changing its name to The New England and to construction, as we will see, of a 1988 twenty-five-story, set-back office tower—across from it at 500 Boylston Street—with a very attractive large, open courtyard.

As we reach Clarendon Street, we quickly become aware of why it is considered the country of Henry H. Richardson, the architect. The substantial Romanesque building on the corner with recessed entrance, 233 Clarendon, was designed by Richardson in 1879–1881 as the rectory for Trinity Church, which he created. A fourth story was sensitively added to the rectory after the death of bachelor Reverend Phillips Brooks, to provide for the family of his successor.

A block south of Clarendon is the landmark Trinity Church, which we will presently visit, while a block north at Commonwealth is still another Richardson creation, the 1870–1872 First Baptist Church. Particularly notice the frieze of the sacraments high up on the beautiful 176-foot square tower, the work of French sculptor Frederic Auguste Bartholdi in his mid-thirties, before he gained wide fame with his Statue of Liberty, conceived by him and presented to America by the

French nation. The giant Angels of the Judgment with gilded trumpets outreaching at each corner have for decades given a popular nickname to the Romanesque building, "The Church of the Holy Beanblowers."

We turn back south on Clarendon Street and when we come to Boylston Street, let us enter the big entrance immediately on our left, The New England building at 501 Boylston Street, to see one of Boston's foremost displays of historical murals and some very helpful dioramas. We look first at four of these dioramas just inside the Newbury Street employees' entrance. Notice in particular the two on the right side of the hallway. The first one, *The Boston Society of Natural History 1863,* gives an overall depiction of the filling of the Back Bay. The complete redbrick building is, of course, the freestanding building we have just seen on the east part of this block at Berkeley and Newbury, the one occupied by Louis the clothier. Under construction in back of it is a predecessor building to the one we are in. This was the first Massachusetts Institute of Technology building in 1863–1864 and was named after its first president, William B. Rogers. A second M.I.T. building was added on its west side in 1883. These were both replaced by New England Life in 1940–1941 and by an addition in 1961–1963. As appears in this diorama, private dwelling construction developed fastest along the river side of the Mill Dam. The spur track of dump cars west of the rising M.I.T. building runs in the line of present Dartmouth Street. West of that is the cross-dam from Gravelly Point to the Mill Dam, where some mills stand. Still farther west, where we see the trestle and Mill Dam meet, is present Kenmore Square. Tree planting on Commonwealth Avenue had about reached Clarendon Street.

Filling-in of Back Bay 1858, the next diorama on the right, looks toward Beacon Hill. Charles Street runs behind the seawall right across the diorama. On the far left we can make out the Charles Street Meeting House, the old West Boston Bridge, and Bulfinch's original Massachusetts General Hospital with the ether dome. The fill in the foreground is of the flats on the site of the present Public Garden. Dominating all, in an era of no high-rises, appears the golden dome of the State House high on Beacon Hill.

Diorama: The filling of the Back Bay

The eight large murals that we see on going back into the spacious front lobby of The New England were painted over a two-year period by the late Charles Hoffbauer. They are indeed magnificent creations. Also we may see the rotating model of "Old Ironsides."

Mid-Boylston to Mrs. Jack Gardner's

Let us pause on the top step as we emerge on the 501 Boylston Street side of The New England. The city views are fascinating. Farther out on Boylston, in back of the majestic Renaissance Boston Public Library building, rises the fifty-two-story Prudential Tower with its cluster of smaller high-rises. Straight ahead, Boston's highest high-rise of all, the sixty-two-story tower of John Hancock Insurance Company (1968–1976), upstages Hancock's own 1949

495-foot Berkeley building with its familiar weather beacon on top.

We also are at the site of an odd Boston literary tale. Mark Twain's longtime literary friend, editor William Dean Howells, called it "that hideous mistake of poor Clemens." The occasion was the 1877 dinner of *Atlantic Monthly* editors and writers for the seventieth birthday of the poet John Greenleaf Whittier, and the place was just across Boylston Street in the dining room of the Brunswick Hotel, which once stood in the southwest corner of the 500 Boylston's half-block size complex. Twain felt surefire. He described three deadbeat tramps visiting a California mining camp and passing themselves off on the innocent miners as Emerson, Longfellow, and Holmes. But Twain had not comprehended the "religious veneration in which these men were held." Everyone "was smitten with a desolating dismay." Twain himself later felt wretched. As Howells pictured the effect: "Nobody knew whether to look at the speaker or down at his plate." Howells stole a glance at Twain "standing solitary among his appalled and appalling listeners with his joke dead on his hands. I was aware of Longfellow regarding the humorist with an air of pensive puzzle, of Holmes busily writing on his menu . . . and of Emerson holding his elbows and listening with a sort of Jovian oblivion."

IN BOSTON THEY ASK, "HOW MUCH DOES HE KNOW?" IN NEW YORK, "HOW MUCH IS HE WORTH?" IN PHILADELPHIA, "WHO WERE HIS PARENTS?"

—MARK TWAIN

On the north half of the block on which The New England built 500 Boylston, it also built, in 1990 to 1991, a companion twenty-two-story tower called 222 Berkeley Street, which is occupied by the Houghton Mifflin Company. Even more striking than the gold-and-bronze ornamented, Italian marble lobby is the building's resplendent "Winter Garden," a five-story atrium with a vaulted glass skylight and public space. There is a fascinating ground-level arcade mostly on the St. James Street side that connects the two skyscrapers.

We head now past the Trinity Church parish house on the southwest corner, completed by Richardson in 1874 and used as a chapel until his Romanesque masterpiece, Trinity Church, was completed in 1877. The statue of the Reverend Phillips Brooks on the Boylston Street side of the church is the work of Augustus Saint-Gaudens; its impressiveness is accentuated by the whiteness of its pillars and canopy against the red and brown tones of Trinity's rough-surfaced stone.

Huntington Avenue used to run diagonally off Boylston Street along the way we are walking. Now Huntington Avenue starts on the far side of the Copley Square Plaza, which was created in 1969 with its fountain, trees, and benches. The plaza has recently gone through a third redoing (ridding it of a sunken park) to become a neighborhood gem. We see here the division in the plan for the Back Bay. Streets between Beacon and Boylston run parallel to the old Mill Dam. Huntington Avenue and Columbus Avenue, in the new South End, run parallel to the old Boston-Providence railroad bed.

Enter Trinity Church by the beautiful West Porch that, while part of Richardson's plan, was not added until 1897. On reaching the interior a visitor is immediately impressed by a sensation of immensity, as when entering St. Peter's in Rome or St. Paul's in London, and then by the medieval beauty of the decorations and stained-glass windows. These are the work of the distinguished artists who labored along with Richardson, John LaFarge, William Morris, and Sir Edward Burne-Jones. Even the great architect of the Boston Public Library, Charles F. McKim, worked with Richardson on Trinity Church until their views diverged. The massive tower contributes most prominently to the grandeur of the church. Among the most striking windows are the three turquoise lancet windows in the west wall over the porch we entered. They, like others here, were made of opalescent glass, which LaFarge invented. See the cloister walks and the window tracery from St. Botolph's Church in Boston, England, and visit the library and garden by the door to the parish house on the left of the altar. Volunteer guides and brochures are available here as in many of the other places we shall visit in the Back Bay.

On leaving Trinity Church from the West Porch, we go left and across St. James Avenue to the mirrorlike marvel of the John Hancock Company's home office, created by I. M. Pei and Associates. The building has more than thirteen acres of glass in its facade.

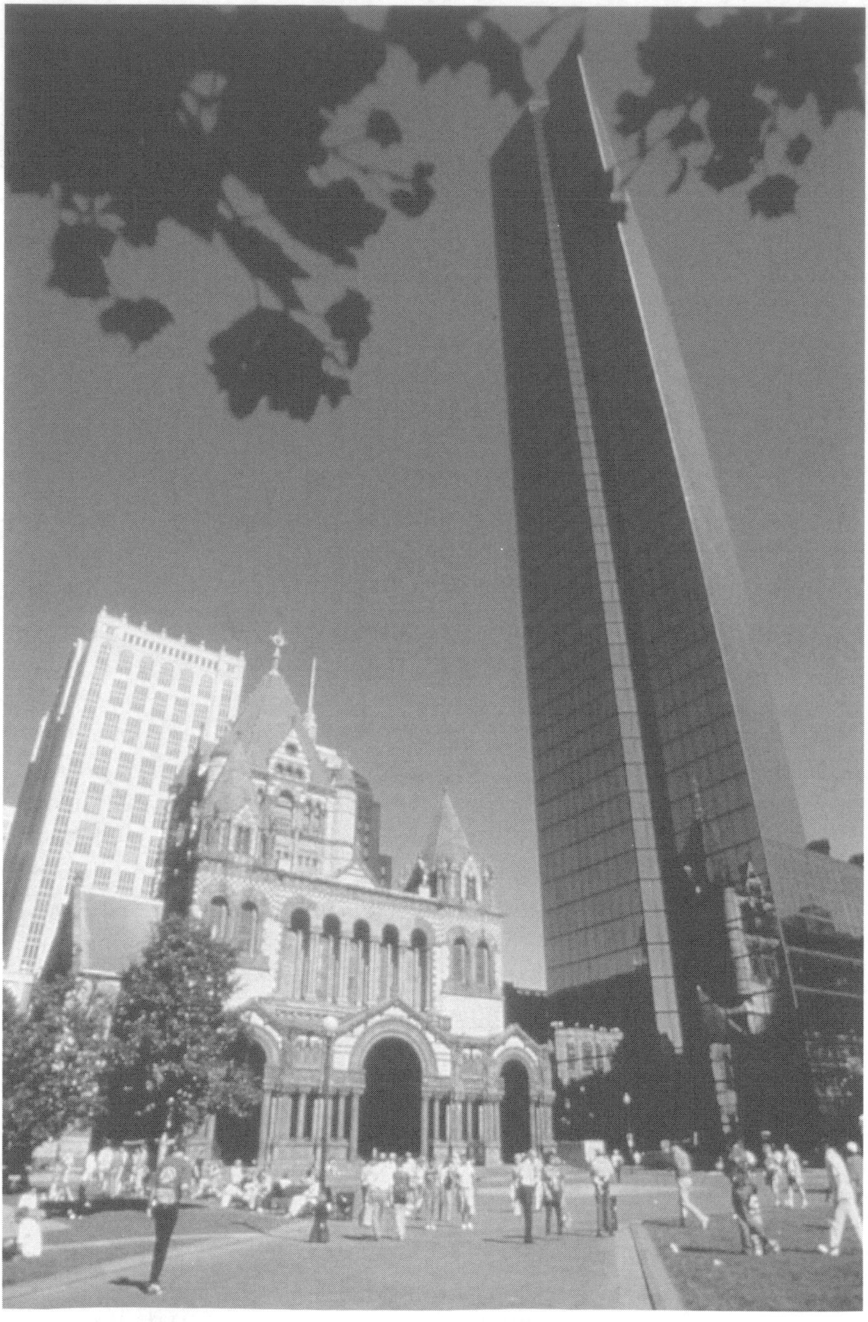

Trinity Church and the John Hancock Tower

Express elevators quickly lift visitors to the observatory on the sixtieth floor. Above it are two more utility levels. The views are literally breathtaking—the unusual bounty of islands in Boston Harbor and mountains as far as Sunapee in New Hampshire, 80 miles to the north. On clear days the view can extend 100 miles. Most impressive of all, though, is the view of Boston, day or night. Recordings, illuminated photographs, grandstand seating, telescopes, and souvenirs contribute to our enjoyment. Most helpful is *Boston 1774,* a scale model of Boston in the Revolutionary era before the filling of the coves, creeks, and the Back Bay.

The Copley Plaza Hotel, next on our left as we leave John Hancock Tower, has hosted presidents, royalty, and gala social events since opening in 1912. It stands on the site of Boston's first building for the Museum of Fine Arts, a flamboyant Victorian structure with unusual exterior terra-cotta ornamentation, built in 1871–1876. Because of space limitations, the museum moved to its current, extensive—and growing—quarters in the Fenway in 1909.

Copley Place, across Huntington Avenue from the Boston Public Library, which we will visit on our next walk, takes in a roughly ten-acre space spanning the Massachusetts Turnpike. Built in 1980 to 1984, Copley Place includes two high-rise hotels, The Westin and The Marriott, offices, restaurants, shops, two hotel atriums, two enjoyable skybridges over Stuart Street and Huntington Avenue, and a huge central atrium with a dazzling 60-foot waterfall. The Prudential Center, ahead on our right, which we will also visit later from its its front on Boylston Street, is likewise built over the turnpike. The Prudential also covers the old railroad yards and the site of the old Mechanics Building, long a Boston exposition center on Huntington Avenue.

We now walk from the Marriott lobby to the skybridge leading over Huntington Avenue to the Prudential Center. Views from the skybridge are quite impressive. As on much of our Back Bay walk we can see buildings have popped skyward like asparagus in spring—and more are coming. On our right is the triangle block beside the Public Library where a twenty-story condominium is being built. On our left, in the next block beyond the Marriott Hotel at 116 Huntington

Back Bay skyscrapers from the Christian Science Center

Avenue, is a fourteen-story office complex completed in 1991. We now go south on Huntington Avenue past the gigantic Prudential Center. Here, too, are extensive plans for high-rise and other additions.

The freestanding, twenty-eight-story, poured-concrete structure ahead at 175 Huntington Avenue is the administration building of the Christian Science Church. The expanded fifteen-acre world headquarters of Christian Science was built in 1968–1973 on the plans of I. M. Pei and Associates around the original Mother Church of Christian Science. This was the first permanent church built by the founder Mary Baker Eddy. Mary Baker Eddy called the Mother Church, the rough granite one with the square bell tower, "our prayer in stone." In it are stained-glass windows picturing great Biblical events. The four-times-larger addition is an extension (1904–1906) in composite Renaissance and Byzantine style. The cupola of its great central dome is 224 feet above the plaza. The organ is one of the largest in the Western world, and the huge open auditorium is an impressive sight.

The new administration building services 3,000 church branches throughout the world. There are two other buildings around the 670-foot reflecting pool: the 1971 Sunday School with its quarter-circle facade at the west end of the pool and the five-story 1973 Church Colonnade Building on the north side of the pool and fountain. Let us walk along the colonnade. The beautiful pool, incidentally, is part of the center's air-conditioning system, and beneath it is a garage for employees and parishioners. At the far end of the Colonnade Building, used as church offices, we turn right to the visitors center in the 1934 publishing building. Here they print the *Christian Science Monitor*, founded in 1908 by Mary Baker Eddy when she was eighty-seven years old. The *Monitor* is now read in 120 nations worldwide, as they say, "From Boston to Bombay." Visit the Mapparium in this building. It literally puts you on a bridge inside a 30-foot stained-glass globe of the earth. Helpful booklets are available.

Cultural institutions abound in the Back Bay.

Heading southeast, left along Massachusetts Avenue and as we approach Huntington Avenue, we come on the northwest corner to Horticultural Hall, headquarters of the Massachusetts Horticultural

Society founded in 1827. The 1901 building, redone in 1985 for private offices, still houses on its second floor the nation's oldest and largest horticultural library. A sure sign of spring in Boston is the society's beloved annual flower and garden show, which has been staged in ever-bigger halls since 1871. In December 1991 the Christian Science Church acquired Horticultural Hall at auction as part of its twelve-acre church center.

Symphony Hall, on the southwest corner, is another Renaissance structure created by McKim, Mead, and White for Henry Lee Higginson's Boston Symphony Orchestra in 1900, when the future of the old Music Hall in Hamilton Place seemed uncertain. Here the orchestra celebrated its one-hundredth anniversary in 1981, in a hall that has seen great artists perform and composers present their music, including Strauss, Mahler, Stravinsky, Bartok, Gershwin, and statesman-composer Paderewski. Major Higginson, preeminent music lover, sought performance that was flawless. He got Professor Wallace C. Sabine of Harvard to apply his acoustical research to the hall, the first in the world to have this advantage, with acoustics so peerless that it has been called a "Stradivarius among halls." During the annual gap in the concert season, the Symphony becomes the home of the delightful Boston Pops, which began back in 1885.

The Reverend Martin Luther King, Jr., while obtaining his doctorate at Boston University's School of Divinity from 1951 to 1954, lived in this area. For his first semester, the future civil rights martyr took a room on St. Botolph Street, a short way down from Massachusetts Avenue on the southeast side between Albemarle and Blackwood Streets. The next semester, 1952–1953, he and a student at Tufts Divinity School moved into good-sized rooms at 397 Massachusetts Avenue, just beyond the railroad bridge on our right. It was while living here that he met his future wife, Coretta Scott of Alabama, who was majoring in singing at the New England Conservatory of Music, a block southwest at 290 Huntington Avenue. In June 1953 they went back south to be married on the front lawn of the Scott home by the Reverend Martin Luther King, Sr. They then set up housekeeping in a four-room apartment in a house just in back of the Massachusetts Avenue rooms at 396 Northampton Street, a building now gone. In September of the next year the couple moved to Montgomery, Alabama, where the twenty-five-year-old Reverend King took up his pastorate.

Two of Boston's famous museums are farther along Huntington Avenue, past the New England Conservatory of Music in the 1902 building at the southeast corner of the next intersection, Gainsborough Street, and past the ever-expanding campus of Northeastern University along Huntington Avenue.

By wisely acquiring twelve acres bordering the Fenway, the Museum of Fine Arts at 465 Huntington Avenue obtained more than its spacious 1907–1909 building designed by Guy Lowell; it secured ample room for its growing collections. A west wing, begun in 1976, was opened in July 1981. The statue in front of the main entrance is Cyrus E. Dallin's *Appeal to the Great Spirit.* Guides and booklets are available to enrich our visit to see some of the world's best classical art, paintings, prints, sculpture, the Western world's foremost Oriental art, and some of the best Egyptian art outside Egypt itself, as well as John Singer Sargent's murals above the grand staircase, Paul Revere's silver, and American period furniture. The climate-controlled west wing, designed by I. M. Pei, includes an auditorium, a gallery of contemporary art, educational facilities, and an enlarged museum restaurant and museum shop.

The Isabella Stewart Gardner Museum is nearby at 280 The Fenway. On leaving the Museum of Fine Arts the way we entered, we turn right along Huntington Avenue to the next street, Museum Road, then turn right again to the Museum School on the corner of 230 The Fenway; the Gardner Museum is diagonally to our left at the bend in the Fens' Muddy River. Mrs. Gardner bought the land in 1899, nearly a decade before the Museum of Fine Arts became her neighbor. Although the Venetian palazzo-style museum carries her name and not that of her husband, actually much of its art and parts of the palace purchased in Europe were bought by both Mrs. Jack and her husband John Lowell Gardner. He first suggested the Fenway site, then newly filled land. She decided on it after his death in 1898, for they had both determined against building a museum for their private collection, Boston's greatest ever, as an addition in the rear of their former dwelling at 150–152 Beacon Street. At first she considered the Fenway site too far from the center of Boston life that she loved to bedazzle. She moved into her old-world palace late in 1901 as her home—her living quarters were on the top floor—and so it remained until her death in 1924. All the while she kept purchasing new art. She first opened the palace to her guests on January 1, 1903, receiving them at the head of her double staircase for a concert by fifty musicians of the Boston Symphony Orchestra. Logs burned that night in each room's big fireplace as guests indulged in two of her delights, doughnuts and champagne.

By her will the art treasures—works of Raphael, Titian, Van Dyck, Rubens, Botticelli, Vermeer, on and on—are displayed exactly as "at my death." The palace is simply magnificent, especially the central courtyard, which she kept filled with flowers from her Brookline greenhouses. See her private chapel, the *Europa* in the Titian Room, and in the Gothic Room her celebrated portrait by her friend John Singer Sargent, the one with strands of pearls around her waist and, if you look carefully, ruby buckles on her slippers. It becomes easier to understand how she fascinated her contemporaries.

Return by way of Museum Road, the way we came, back to Huntington Avenue and Dallin's *Appeal to the Great Spirit,* en route to the start of our next walk, Copley Square.

Copley Square and Westside Back Bay

Copley Square is a prime example of the Boston phenomenon called a "square." Planning had nothing to do with its origin. Like Topsy, it just grew—but more slowly. It was simply leftover space between the gridiron and diagonal plans of Back Bay streets, an unresolved intersection. When it was called Copley Square by the city in 1883, it consisted mainly of two unequal triangles. That was the way it continued long after Copley Square had won renown for the buildings erected on its fringes. It was not until 1969 that unbisected Copley Square Plaza emerged.

The Literary Trail

Boston is a town rife with history, historians, and walking trails. Every few years a new trail is organized in the edifying spirit of the Freedom Trail, and the pavement, cobblestones, and bricks of Boston are mapped out in new configurations. The latest addition to the historical trail scene is the Literary Trail. Though there is no painted path to follow, it traces the intertwined paths that linked the astounding number of authors, poets, social activists, and thinkers who lived in Boston, Cambridge, and Concord during the nineteenth century. The tour includes sites, gathering places, homes, and landscapes, such as the Omni Parker House and the Boston Public Library, the Longfellow House and Harvard in Cambridge, and Orchard House and Walden Pond in Concord. Learn more at www.lit-trail.org.

The Boston Public Library of 1888–1895, a Renaissance product of Charles F. McKim's artistry, was among the buildings that won fame for the square. McKim, like Richardson, studied in Paris, and the library here draws on that city's distinguished Bibliotheque Nationale. McKim lavished regard, as well as genius, on the building, and for its courtyard, one of its glories, he donated a nude bronze bacchante and child by Frederick MacMonnies. Prudery of the period excluded it from the idyllic courtyard's lawn, and it went to the Metropolitan Art Museum in New York. But Boston does have a copy in the Museum of Fine Arts.

The library, with a collection among the best in the world, had its beginnings in the nineteenth century, when library resources available to the public were very limited. Owners of private libraries did try to help. This was spurred by a French visitor to Boston, Alexandre Vattemare, who is listed among thirty famous Bostonians on the ceiling of the library's main entrance hall. On his travels Vattemare had seen books sitting idle in many libraries and wanted to circulate them by means of public libraries. He outlined his ideas to a Boston gathering in 1841, and a committee was formed. By 1847 Mayor Josiah Quincy, Jr., son of the first Mayor Quincy, offered $5,000 if the public would raise double that. Even more, he helped to get legislation on Beacon Hill the following year that made it possible for the first time to use Massachusetts tax money to finance a public library. Literary historian George Ticknor prepared a trustees' report in 1852 that inspired a $50,000 gift, a fortune then, from the library's first great benefactor, Joshua Bates, senior partner of Baring Brothers, the London bankers. Bates, born in Weymouth on the South Shore, worked as a poor young boy in Boston and remembered how his only access to books had been by reading them in a Boston bookstore. He followed his cash gift with a further one of 30,000 books. Meantime, Vattemare had sent books from France. To these were added books given by Bostonians from private libraries. In 1854 a lower room was opened in the old Adams Schoolhouse in Mason Street, near the earlier Harvard Medical School, and books could be had for use at home. By 1858 the library's first building, the Italian villalike structure on Boylston Street opposite the Common, was opened.

Gifts and acquisitions soon made that lovely building, with its huge, pillared hall named for Bates, inadequate. McKim's creation was then erected here in Copley Square on land donated by the state, with great artists using their finest talents to beautify it. Daniel Chester French sculpted the allegorical figures on the three pairs of bronze doors to the main entrance hall. On the left, before going through them, one can see a Frederick MacMonnies statue of Sir Henry Vane in dashing attire, a champion of personal liberty and the only Bay State governor to be beheaded. The luxurious staircase was hailed by Henry James for "its splendor of tawny marble." The couchant lions in yellow Sienna marble on either side of the landing were made by Louis, brother of Augustus Saint-Gaudens. Augustus made the carvings and panels on the Copley facade that complement the dignified seated figures of Art and Science sculpted in 1912 by Boston artist Bela Pratt. Pause on the landing for a view through the small windows of the open courtyard.

Murals in the buildings are considered among the world's best. Those around the staircase were by French artist Puvis de Chavannes. At the head of the staircase, around the entrance to the main reading room, is Chavanne's composition of the nine muses. In the luxurious Abbey Room, with its great fireplace, are the murals of Edwin Austin Abbey depicting Sir Galahad's *Quest of the Holy Grail.* And on the third floor are John Singer Sargent's murals on *Judaism and Christianity*, with the *Sermon on the Mount* incomplete because of Sargent's death.

The 50-foot-high main reading room, with a Roman-style, barrel-vaulted ceiling, extends the length of the Copley Square facade and was intended by McKim as the library's most impressive room. It is. And it is named Bates Hall after benefactor Joshua Bates. On the right as we enter is his bust and a portrait is at the room's south end. Another original oil of him, presented by his daughter, is in the Elliott Room (consult charts near the elevators).

Off the open courtyard on the west side is an entrance to the 1969–1972 addition to the general library—as distinct from the research library we just visited—occupying roughly the other half of the block. This was designed by Philip Johnson, in the same granite and of the same height to harmonize with the older McKim structure.

The addition is essentially functional. The enclosed courtyard was named for a remarkable benefactor of the library, John Deferrari. He was the son of an early Italian immigrant in the North End. As a youngster he sold fruit from hand baskets and pushcarts. In the 1890s he opened a fruit store at Boylston and Carver Streets and became a habitual user of the old Public Library in the same block. In 1947–1948 bachelor Deferrari set up $850,000 from his investments in stocks, bonds, and real estate to generate $3,000,000 in funds for the library's general purposes. Protecting his plain, frugal living with an assumed name, he died in 1950, when nearly eighty-seven years of age, in a Spartan $8.50-a-week room in the Beacon Chambers on Beacon Hill's Myrtle Street. To the end, Deferrari kept the family home of his father at 5 Wesley Place, one of the little cul-de-sacs off Hanover Street. In his old age he would go there alone to cook himself an abstemious meal. His bust and portrait are in the Boston Room, just off the new Boylston Street lobby of the library. The purpose of his gift was, he said, to help young people. His philosophy: "Make good use of your time. Keep working. Keep learning. Play fair as long as you live."

Treasures of the library, kept in the rare book section, represent bountiful gifts over the years. They include the original volumes assembled in the early 1700s by the Reverend Thomas Prince in the Old South Meeting House steeple, Nathaniel Bowditch's library, George Ticknor's unmatched collection of Spanish literature, Bay State and national documents, rarities from John Eliot's Indian Bible to Shakespeare's first folio, and many, many more gems.

On leaving the library by the Boylston Street lobby, we turn right toward Copley Square. On our left, across Boylston Street on the northwest corner of Dartmouth, is the New Old South Church, 1875–1877. This Northern Italian Gothic building, with a 220-foot bell tower, was built by the congregation after it gave up the Old South Meeting House and joined the migration to the Back Bay in the 1860s and 1870s. Always Congregational, its roots go back to the Puritans' First Church near the Old State House. Notice three fragments of tombstones on the wall of the arcade beside the doorway at the foot of the lofty tower. John Alden, sea captain and eldest son of Pilgrim settlers John and Priscilla Alden, was a member of this congregation. During the witchcraft hysteria Captain Alden spent fifteen weeks in the town jail until cleared and released to his family. The other two stones were found in the old church steeple. In the church are stained-glass windows in the fifteenth-century English style. The adjoining parish house has the lovely Gothic Gordon Chapel, Sunday school, library, and rooms for community activities.

We walk north along Dartmouth Street. The next building at the southwest corner of Newbury, built in 1881–1882 by architect William Ralph Emerson for the Boston Art Club, is considered among the Back Bay's best in Queen Anne style. In the intervening years since the club disbanded, this has been quarters for a bicycle club, Bryant and Stratton secretarial school, and, since 1970, a Boston schoolhouse.

The elegant 1871–1881 Hotel Vendome at the southwest corner of Commonwealth Avenue, hostelry to fabulous and wealthy guests, had lavish amenities. Its dining room in 1882 had, by means of a private generator, Boston's first incandescent lamps, four years before they were available elsewhere in the fashionable Back Bay. Presidents Ulysses S. Grant and Grover Cleveland, Vanderbilts, Carnegies, and Rockefellers, Mark Twain, stage stars and foreign celebrities from Sarah Bernhardt to Oscar Wilde have lodged within its white marble Second Empire walls. Currently business occupies the two lower floors, and those above are condominiums.

On the southeast corner of Commonwealth, at 287 Dartmouth Street, is the elegant Chilton Club organized in 1908 as a graceful retreat by its socially prominent charter members, including the poet and Bay State governor's wife Amy Lowell. We have seen, off old Newspaper Row, where *Mayflower* passenger Mary Chilton lived. Believing her to have been the first woman to come ashore, the club's founders adopted her name—even further, they adopted as the club's seal the one that was used by the Earl of Chilton, Mary Chilton's grandfather. Besides 287 Dartmouth the club acquired the adjoining brick mansion, 152 Commonwealth, and had the son of famous architect Henry H. Richardson, whose wife was a charter member, remodel the two buildings as a beautiful clubhouse.

Diagonally across Commonwealth, on the northwest corner at 306 Dartmouth, now a professional office, is an 1872 mansion purchased a decade later by Frederick L. Ames and remodeled. The architect, John Sturgis, included a grand staircase leading down to a hall considered, with its carvings, "the most palatial space in a Back Bay residence." Arriving guests entered by the porte cochere off Dartmouth, took an elevator to the second floor to leave their coats, and then, passing John LaFarge's stained-glass windows, descended the grand staircase to the reception hall.

Dartmouth Street has more noted mansions, one on each of the next two corners at the intersection with Marlborough Street.

On the southwest corner, we note the only Henry H. Richardson residence in the Back Bay other than the Trinity Church rectory. This, at 164 Marlborough, was built in 1870 for Benjamin Crowninshield and is Romanesque with quite intricate brickwork. Across the street at 163 Marlborough is an 1871–1873 mansion built for China trade millionaire Thomas C. Cushing; by architects Snell and Gregerson, it is regarded as one of the Back Bay's "handsomest." The tall, second-floor windows indicate the grandeur of the 14-foot ceilings on that floor. Nearby on Marlborough lived two college presidents, M.I.T's Rogers at 1177 and Harvard's retired Lowell at 171.

At Beacon Street we come to literary sites. On our right, at 241 Beacon, Julia Ward Howe took up residence after the death of her husband, Dr. Samuel Gridley Howe. For a dozen years she edited *Woman's Journal.* She did considerable writing and extensive speaking in the struggle for women's suffrage until her death here in 1910. Like many of its Back Bay neighbors, her home is now a lodging house.

Walking west on Beacon we pass, just beyond Dartmouth Street, the site of the Mill Dam's tollhouse. Just beyond Exeter Street, on the water side, lived the "Little Professor" Oliver Wendell Holmes and William Dean Howells. By 1870 Holmes felt Charles Street was "a noisy thoroughfare" and bought a big house at 296 Beacon "clinging to the river" he loved. He delivered a farewell address at the Medical School in 1882. The next year he wrote to Lowell, "I go to the Saturday Club quite regularly, but the company is more of ghosts than of flesh and blood to me." He died here in 1894. His house is gone, but the one next door at Number 294, which he added for his library, still remains. Three doors beyond Holmes's once stood Howells's house at Number 302. In 1884 Howells wrote to Henry James telling how he used to worry about paying for his earlier house in Belmont. "Drolly enough," he said, "I am writing a story in which the chief personage builds a house on the water side of Beacon and I shall be able to use all my experience, down to the quick. Perhaps the novel may pay for the house." Here Howells wrote the novel that won him enduring fame, *The Rise of Silas Lapham*, the tale of a man who made $1 million but could not fit into society after he shifted from the new South End to the haughtier Back Bay. That "chief personage," Silas Lapham, did indeed pay for Howells's house.

We return to Commonwealth Avenue by way of Exeter Street to see some buildings of interest.

Major Henry Lee Higginson, founder and supporter (to the tune of $1,000,000) of the Boston Symphony Orchestra, lived in the six-story

1872 building at 191 Commonwealth. Higginson, a State Street banker, served in the cavalry during the Civil War. Among his many other philanthropies were gifts to Harvard University, including Soldiers' Field in memory of close friends killed in the war.

At the northeast corner of Exeter and Newbury Streets, the distinctive, formidable-looking brownstone-and-granite building, revered Exeter Street Theater, was built in 1885 as the First Spiritualist Temple. For sixty years (1914–1974) it was a movie house. Renovated, it became a theater and cafe. In 1984 a store replaced the theater. The building's 1885 title is still carved above the marquee: First Spiritualist Temple.

Returning to Commonwealth Avenue we come to three buildings by McKim, Mead, and White. The neat, double-bay, redbrick building at 199 Commonwealth is the St. Botolph Club, founded in 1880 "to promote social intercourse among authors and artists and other gentlemen," with Francis Parkman its first president. In its first clubhouse at 87 Boylston Street, the Gardners, with their Beacon Street residence already crowded, hung some of their acquisitions. Among these was Sargent's low-neckline portrait of Mrs. Jack, which we saw at her palace. It brought so much critical comment that Mr. Gardner took it home and said it would not be exhibited again while he lived.

The magnolia trees along this part of Commonwealth Avenue, from Exeter Street to Massachusetts Avenue, reach out like a canopy of flowers over the sidewalk. They are just about the best of the all-too-brief springtime magnolia displays that greet visitors each year in the Back Bay.

The Algonquin Club, organized in 1885 for "good fellowship" by thirty prominent Bostonians, built the stately Renaissance structure at 217 Commonwealth in 1887 to the designs of Stanford White. Notice particularly over the entrance the porches superimposed on double Ionic columns. General Charles H. Taylor, publisher of *The Boston Globe*, gathered acquaintances here and served for two decades, 1898–1918, as its president. In the last two years of his life, after his wife's death, he took a house across the street from the club to be near his old friends.

The first Boston use of the detail of the double Ionic columns at ground level can be seen at 32 Hereford Street, on the northeast corner of Commonwealth. The same architects built Number 32, a four-story mainly Renaissance structure, three years before building the Algonquin Club. The iron balcony was salvaged when the Tuileries palace was burned in 1871 in rioting after Napoleon III was deposed. Since 1950 the building, originally for the son of Civil War Governor John A. Andrew, has been an M.I.T. fraternity house.

Women's Heritage Trail

"I could not hear of a liberated Boston lady going to bed with an unconventional Boston gentleman, without thinking: 'Oh, hell! They've thought it all out!' I could not imagine bed with a liberated Boston lady anyway."
—Thomas Wolfe

One of the greatest and the first of the Back Bay chateaux is the lavish, sixteenth-century-style brownstone structure that noted architect Carl Fehmer built in 1882 at 355 Commonwealth, on the northeast corner of Massachusetts Avenue. It was built for manufacturing and railroad millionaire Oliver Ames, who served as governor from 1887 to 1890. The delicately carved stone panels above the first-story windows are regarded as most noteworthy. The Ames Building accommodates the office of the college's president and executive and alumni offices.

Immediately west of Massachusetts Avenue, we observe a slight shift Commonwealth Avenue takes to the westward. This change in the axis of the mall was proposed by landscape architect Frederick Law Olmsted in his brilliant 1881 plan. This was designed to turn the Muddy River tidal flats, just a block father west, into the Back Bay Fens, the origin of American's first metropolitan park system.

Olmsted's solution to the conflict between the gridiron and diagonal schemes for the Back Bay made it possible for Commonwealth Avenue and its mall to be extended without colliding with the vital east-west railroad bed. Soon residences appeared on Commonwealth Avenue beyond Massachusetts Avenue. One of the earliest was the

1885 structure at 385 Commonwealth, which became the home of Mary Baker Eddy when she moved in 1887 from a rented house in the South End. It is still occupied by the First Reader of the Mother Church. Mrs. Eddy continued to visit here after withdrawing to New Hampshire for study and writing.

Crossing over to the south side of Commonwealth at Number 374, next to the corner apartment hotel, is the Harvard Club of Boston, built 1912 to 1913. The hotel next to it, on the corner, was built in 1925 by the family of Harvard president Charles Eliot and was named after him. Walking back eastward on Commonwealth, we come to Number 314, on the southwest corner of Hereford Street, a chateau designed by Charles Brigham and built for Albert C. Burrage in 1899. To get the location he desired, Mr. Burrage demolished a house built on the site in 1881. The mansion, with its turrets, gables, and gargoyles, has housed the Boston Evening Medical Center since 1957 and, since 1992, the Burrage House Retirement Home.

The annual Boston Marathon, with its cheering crowds, held on Patriot's Day in mid-April, enters Boston along Commonwealth Avenue and goes right up Hereford Street, then left along Boylston Street to the finish line in front of the new Boston Public Library addition. The 26-mile, 385-yard race, which starts in Hopkinton, was first run in 1897 with fifteen runners. In 1992 there were 9,500 entrants from all over the world. We now go the same way, past the Boston Architectural Center on the southwest corner of Newbury Street and the Institute of Contemporary Art at 955 Boylston in the renovated former Back Bay police station.

Before we head to the Prudential Center, note we are but a short distance from one of Boston's most venerable institutions, the Massachusetts Historical Society at 1154 Boylston, near the entrance to the Fenway. The society, formed in 1791, is America's oldest historical society. In its library are extensive documents of our American, and especially Bay State, heritage back to John Winthrop's manuscripts. These are accessible for historical researchers.

We pass next the state-owned 1962 John B. Hynes Veterans Memorial Convention Center, enlarged to the sidewalk's edge in 1984–1988 to provide Boston an ample convention center. Besides its striking new granite facade—with street-level arcade—the Hynes has quite a grand entrance hall.

Donald DeLue's monumental statue of man reaching for the heavens, *Quest Eternal*, is the sign—when not boarded off by construction—that we have arrived at The Prudential Center. The "city-within-a-city" created here on thirty-two acres by the Prudential Center seems magical to those who recall that prior to 1959 this was all a dreary stretch of railroad yards reaching from Boylston Street back to the Mechanics Building, the 1881 brick exhibition hall that were once strung along Huntington Avenue. The fifty-two-story Prudential Tower was built in 1959–1964 on bedrock 172 feet below ground level. Besides the Massachusetts Turnpike along the railroad bed to the west, beneath the plaza is a public garage for 3,500 automobiles.

Tower elevators provide quick access to the Skywalk on the fiftieth floor and to a restaurant on the fifty-second. The Skywalk gives the readiest overall view of the center with its many structures: three twenty-eight story high-rise apartment towers built 1964–1968; the twenty-five story office tower at 101 Huntington Avenue built in 1970; a second tower added to the twenty-nine-story tower of the Sheraton Boston Hotel; as well as stores and some fifteen acres of park and plaza.

The Skywalk, like the Hancock Tower, offers a magnificent panorama of Boston—its harbors and rivers, and the peninsula where we have been walking, which has grown into New England's largest metropolis. To the west we get a great view of the famous Emerald Necklace of parks, the Fenway to Franklin Field, that Olmsted contrived for the city with the golden-domed State House that "Little Professor" Holmes so pridefully and happily dubbed "the hub of the solar system."

CAMBRIDGE

Cambridge Constitutional

Many visitors consider Cambridge a mere extension of Boston proper, yet as home to two prestigious universities and with a rich cultural life stretching back to the seventeenth century, it has always been a vibrant, prosperous city in its own right. It was called Newtowne when it was founded in 1630 as the first capital of the Massachusetts Bay Colony. A few years later it was renamed after Cambridge University, the alma mater of many Colony leaders.

Cambridge grew slowly until toll bridges were constructed across the Charles River. These bridges wrought a transformation on Cambridge, which quickly became a conduit from the rest of the Commonwealth into the downtown and ports of Boston. The major routes of today—Concord Avenue, Broadway, Cambridge Street, Mount Auburn Street—were all major turnpikes of the past leading to these bridges. The city of Cambridge is currently linked to old Boston by eight bridges, though most visitors choose to take the T's Red Line to the Harvard Square stop. Upon leaving the Harvard Square "T" stop, you will surface in bustling Harvard Square, the nexus of the considerable historical, educational, and commercial forces that have shaped Cambridge from its very beginnings.

Proceed toward the calmer blocks of Brattle Street to begin your

CAMBRIDGE

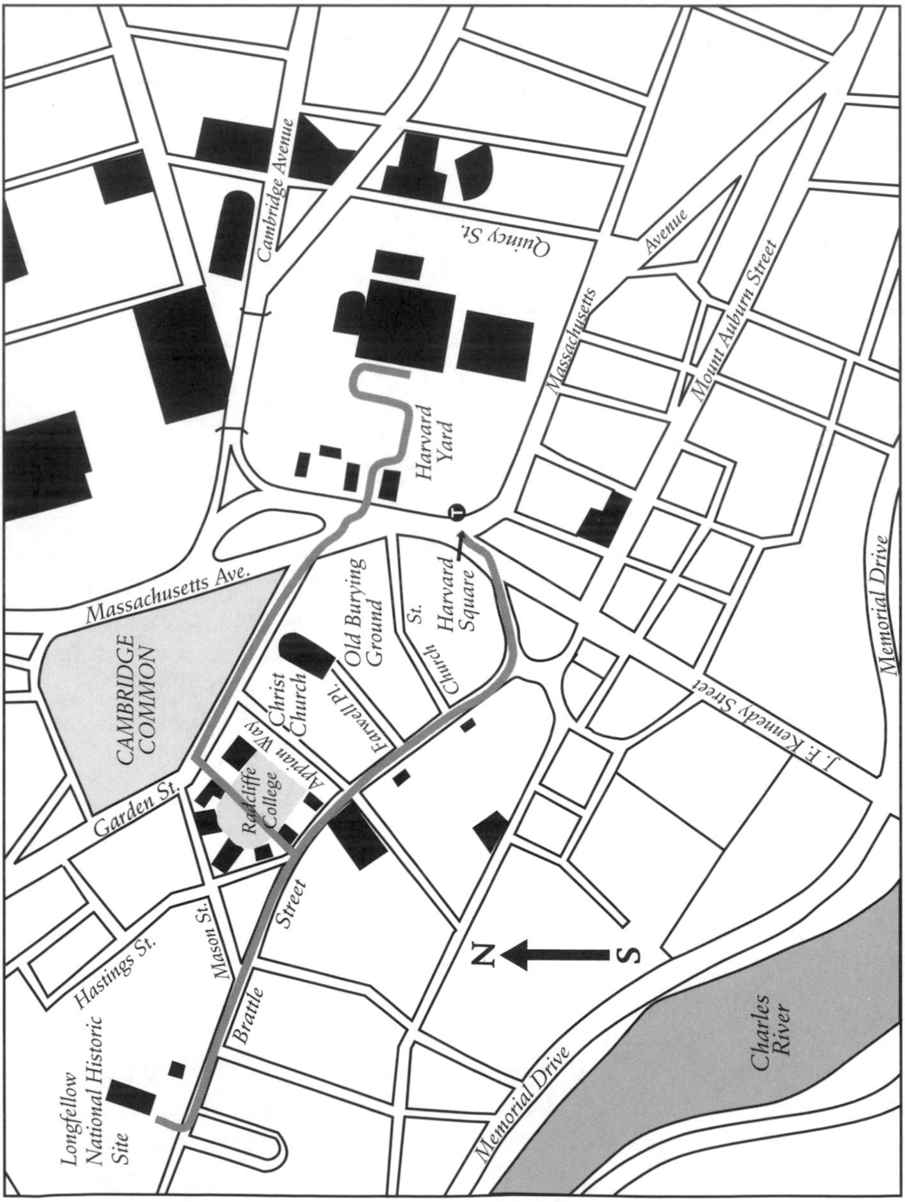
Cambridge Avenue
Quincy St.
Avenue
Massachusetts
Mount Auburn Street
Harvard Yard
Memorial Drive
Massachusetts Ave.
CAMBRIDGE COMMON
Old Burying Ground
Harvard Square
St.
Church
Christ Church
Farwell Pl.
Appian Way
Radcliffe College
Garden St.
J. F. Kennedy Street
Mason St.
Street
Hastings St.
Brattle
N
S
Charles River
Memorial Drive
Longfellow National Historic Site

exploration of Cambridge's seventeenth-century street layout, which has been altered only slightly since colonial times. Wealthy Tory merchants favored Brattle Street, as evidenced by the fine eighteenth- and nineteenth-century homes lining the street, known ever after as "Tory Row." These same Tories fled due to Revolutionary hostilities. Most of these mansions are privately owned, though the Hooper-Lee-Nichols House at 159 Brattle Street is open to the public as the Cambridge Historical Society's Headquarters.

Note 56 Brattle Street. It was once the home of Dexter Pratt, the village blacksmith who inspired his neighbor, Henry Wadsworth Longfellow, to write one of his most famous works, *The Village Blacksmith.*

Proceed to the Longfellow National Historic Site at 105 Brattle Street. This stately pre-Revolutionary mansion is replete with history. After it was abandoned by its Tory owner, George Washington took it as his residence during the siege of Boston. Later it was given to Longfellow by his new father-in-law as a wedding present when he married Frances Appleton; he lived here from 1837 until his death in 1882. It was in the well-preserved study that he wrote works such as *Evangeline* and *The Song of Hiawatha.* Note the portraits and photographs of his illustrious circle of friends, including Ralph Waldo Emerson, Nathaniel Hawthorne, Oliver Wendell Holmes, and Charles Sumner. The inkstand and quill pens given to him by Samuel Taylor Coleridge are on display, as is a chair given to him by the children of Cambridge made out of the wood of the famous "spreading chestnut tree."

Head back toward Harvard Square along Brattle Street for 2 blocks until you come to an arched entrance to Radcliffe Yard on your left. Radcliffe College was founded in 1879 so that Harvard professors could teach women, who at the time were not allowed to comingle in the classroom with Harvard men. Radcliffe and Harvard are now incorporated under the auspices of Harvard University, though Radcliffe still hosts independent programs focusing on women's issues. The airy cloister of Radcliffe Yard is the home of the Schlesinger Library on the History of Women in America and currently holds the papers of Julia Ward Howe, Harriet Beecher Stowe, Susan B.

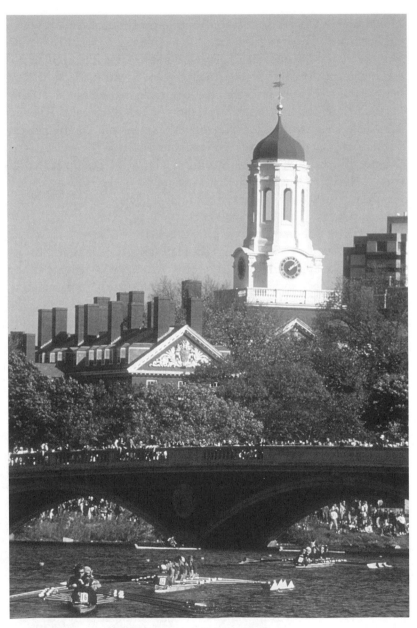

Crew teams near Dunster House, head of the Charles Regatta

Anthony, Elizabeth Cady Stanton, and Amelia Earhart.

As you exit the Yard through Gilman Gate, you'll find yourself on Garden Street, facing Cambridge Common. What was once an eighty-six-acre expanse that supported some 10,000 soldiers during the winter of 1775 is now one of the loveliest and most historic traffic medians in the city, thick with commemorative plaques and monuments. Bounded by busy Massachusetts Avenue and Garden Street, the common has been whittled down to a smallish sixteen acres, crisscrossed by studious youths and milling pigeons. According to local legend its big day came back on July 3, 1775, when George Washington took command of the Continental Army here in the shade of an elm. The elm of the legend is now gone, but not forgotten—there's a plaque.

Look for the cast hoofprints embedded in the traffic island to the south of the common. They commemorate the midnight ride Williams Dawes made on April 18–19, 1775, to warn citizens of approaching redcoats.

Turn back to Garden Street for a view of the spare, shingled lines of the oldest church in Cambridge. Christ Church was built in 1761 for the convenience of Cambridge's largely Tory Anglican community, who had wearied of the long trek to Boston's King Chapel. When these same Tories fled in 1774, the church became a matter of convenience for colonial troops, who commandeered it as a barracks. Though they melted the organ pipes for bullets, the church was restored in time for George and Martha Washington to worship there in 1775.

Adjacent to Christ Church is The Old Burying Ground (also known as God's Acre), which contains the worn gravestones of many Cambridge notables.

For many, Cambridge is synonymous with Harvard, and rightly so. Harvard became the first college in the country when it was founded in 1636 to provide training for ministers. It is now one of the most renowned educational institutions in the world, and covers nearly 400 acres in the Cambridge-Boston environs.

Cross busy J.F.K. Street, and enter the well-ordered enclave of academic buildings and housing that comprise Harvard Yard. Harvard's

M.I.T.

Stretching along more than a mile of riverfront, the Massachusetts Institute of Technology looms large as Cambridge's other intellectual power house. The campus is mainly of interest to visitors because of its modern architecture and sculpture, with buildings by Eero Saarinen and I. M. Pei. Student-led tours of the campus leave from the Information Office located at 77 Massachusetts Avenue.

most historic buildings form this courtyard at a quiet remove from the hurtling cars of Massachusetts Avenue. Harvard has all freshmen housed in the Yard, in buildings that once housed young Emerson, Thoreau, and countless others American luminaries.

Over the years Harvard has commissioned talented architects to build additions to this storied Yard, and there are architectural gems at every turn. On your right as you enter is the oldest, Massachusetts Hall.

In the center of the Yard is University Hall, designed by Charles Bulfinch, distinguished by its use of granite as opposed to the ubiquitous red Harvard brick of the other buildings. The building also serves as a point of demarcation between the pre-Revolutionary buildings of the "Old Yard" and eighteenth- and nineteenth-century buildings of the "New Yard."

Before you proceed, however, notice the John Harvard statue by Daniel Chester French, located directly in front of University Hall. It has long been customary for Harvard graduates to have their pictures taken with what is commonly known as the "Statue of Three Lies." As there was no record of John Harvard's appearance, Daniel Chester French used a Harvard student as his model—so it's not really John Harvard with whom people are posing. The inscription names John Harvard as the founder of the University, when he was simply a

Harvard Yard, spring

benefactor. To add insult to historic injury, the inscription lists the wrong date for the founding of the school. (It was founded in 1636, not 1638).

Not to be missed is the massive, impressively colonnaded Widener Library, located along the south side of the "New Yard." It is the largest university library in the world and often has a copy of the Gutenberg Bible or a First Folio of Shakespeare on display. The library was named for Henry Elkins Widener, a Harvard student who died with the sinking of the *Titanic* because he couldn't swim to nearby lifeboats. His family donated funds to help in the building's comple-

◄○►

Harvard graduates used to line up according to the social status of the parents, rather than in alphabetical order.

tion with the stipulation that all Harvard students be required to demonstrate that they could swim 50 yards, or learn how. Step inside the lobby to view the three historical dioramas of the development of Harvard Square in 1667, 1775, and 1936, as well as the John Singer Sargent murals adorning the walls.

When you have completed your tour of the library, head back through the gates to the bustle of Harvard Square.

For a more subdued exploration of the past, make your way down Mount Auburn Street (by foot, or by bus from the Harvard Square T stop) to Mount Auburn Cemetery.

MOUNT AUBURN CEMETERY

The first thing you should notice about Mount Auburn Cemetery is how radically different it is from the crowded colonial burial grounds of Boston proper. Mount Auburn is what is known as a rural garden cemetery, and its spacious, Arcadian arrangement stands in stark contrast to the close-knit rows of tombstones we have been viewing thus far. When consecrated in 1831 it was the first cemetery of its kind in America; its designers intentionally incorporated the gentle winding roads, ponds, hills, and picturesque plantings to be found in ideal pastoral settings, in a calculated effort to soothe and accommodate the mourners.

This welcome greensward within striking distance of populous city neighborhoods quickly became a popular destination for weekend outings. Recreating in a cemetery was not as jarring a prospect then as it may seem to us now; death was far more a part of everyday life for nineteenth-century families. It is still an outstanding place for bird-watching in spring.

The cemetery, which is still active, has been the final resting place of choice for many celebrated figures from Boston's past: Christian Science founder Mary Baker Eddy, architects Charles Bulfinch and R. Buckminster Fuller, Fannie Farmer, Isabella Stewart Gardner, reformers Julia Ward Howe and Dorothea Dix, poet Henry Wadsworth Longfellow, Harrison Gray Otis, author Bernard Malamud, historian Francis Parkman, painter Winslow Homer, and Harriet Jacobs, author of the autobiographical *Incidents in the Life of a Slave Girl.* Observe the various evolving monument styles and inscribed sentiments for an illuminating tutorial in the social and artistic history of America.

Maps for self-guided tours are available at the front gate at 580 Mount Auburn Street.

PUBLIC TRANSPORTATION TO NEARBY HISTORIC SIGHTS

Best routes to nearby historic places by public transportation can change. It is prudent to check.

Consult www.mbta.com before your visit, or stop at these handy information sources downtown: the Boston Visitor Information Booth opposite West Street on the Common; the National Park Service Visitor Center at 15 State Street; and the information booth in the Park Street subway station of the "T" (MBTA) near Brimstone Center. The third one, down in the subway, is open the longest hours and in all seasons. Even though it is inside the subway station, requiring payment of a fare, the route to most of the nearby historic places begins in the subway. To go from there to:

"Old Ironsides" (U.S.S. *Constitution* Museum): Go to Haymarket Station or Sullivan on the Orange Line; then upstairs and take Bus 92 or 93.

Bunker Hill: Go to Haymarket Station on the Orange Line; then upstairs and take Bus 92 or 93.

Dorchester Heights: Go to Broadway Station on the Red Line; then take bus 9.

John F. Kennedy Library and Museum: Go to J.F.K./U. Mass Station on the Red Line; then a few blocks by bus.

Massachusetts State Archives: Use same "T" service as to John F.

Kennedy Library and Museum.

Cambridge Common (Craigie House, Washington's headquarters): Go to Harvard Square stop on the Red Line; then walk.

Concord (Old North Bridge, Minuteman National Historic Park): Go to the Concord Commuter Rail stop; then take a 2 mile walk.

Lexington Green (Buckman Tavern, Munroe Tavern, Hancock-Clarke House, Museum of Our National Heritage): Take Red Line to Alewife; then Bus 62 or 76.

Plymouth (Plymouth Rock, *Mayflower II*, Pilgrim Hall Museum, Plimouth Planatation): Go to South Station on Red Line; then upstairs to Plymouth and Brockton bus.

Quincy (Adams National Historic Site): Take Red Line to Quincy Center (be sure you take the subway train marked "Braintree"); then bus.

Salem (Peabody Museum, Essex Institute, House of Seven Gables, Pioneer Village): Go to Haymarket Station on the Orange Line; then upstairs and take Bus 450 or 455.

While you are in the Park Street subway, notice, on the north wall just inside the turnstiles, a big mosaic mural that depicts the first streetcar entering the subway. A woman rider in the mural is holding up *The Boston Globe* of that September 1, 1897. Be careful not to walk on the tracks. The grinding noise of the streetcar wheels as they twist around the subway's tight bends is a community legacy for Boston's having built the first trolley subway in America. The noise can also be a helpful warning.

INDEX

Abbey, Edwin Austin, 299
Abbot Library, 277
Abiel Smith School, 62
abolition movement, 6, 39, 122–25, 153, 213–14, 226; New England Anti-Slavery Society formed, 63–64; slavery abolished in Massachusetts, 115; *see also Liberator, The*
Academy of Arts and Sciences, 69
Acorn Street, 43; Number 20, 51
Adams, Abigail, 87, 94
Adams, Charles Francis, 88
Adams, Charles Francis, Jr., 38
Adams, Henry, 32, 38
Adams, John, 79, 87, 91, 94, 98, 135, 158, 179, 185, 213, defends Boston Massacre redcoats, 79, 94, 153, 190; and Washington's Boston visits, 79, 185, 219
Adams, John Quincy, 38, 135, 141
Adams, Samuel, x, xi, 5, 33–34, 69, 87, 115, birthplace of, 149; and Boston Tea Party, 144; and Committee of Correspondence, 69, 212; and U.S. Constitution, 159, 222; and First Continental Congress, 153; education of, 111, 160; grave of, 126; and laying of State House cornerstone, 43; statue of, Faneuil Hall, 208; and Washington's 1789 visit, 91, 185; will of, 79; Winter Place residence of, 5
Adams, Captain Samuel, 160, 163
Adams House, 177
Adams Schoolhouse, 298
Adams Square, 208
Advent, Church of, 65, 267
African Baptist Church Society, 62
African Meeting House, 62
African Methodist Episcopal Church, 268
Aga Khan, 19
Agassiz, Louis, 112
Albany Street, 178
Albee, Edward, 176
Albion Corner, 115
Albion Hotel, 115
Alcott, Bronson, 53, 59, 138
Alcott, Mrs. Bronson, 59, 60
Alcott, Louisa May, 12, 53, 56, 59, 60, 68, 226
Alcott, May, 56, 68
Alden, Captain John, 300
Aldrich, Lilian, 56
Aldrich, Thomas Bailey, 40, 53, 55, 56, 131
Algonquin Club, 304
Allston, Washington, 86
"America" (song), 127, 240
American Anti-Slavery Society, 63
American Coffee House, 194
American Revolution, *see* Revolutionary War
American Woman Suffrage Association, 130
Ames, Fisher, 133
Ames, Frederick L., 301
Ames, Oliver, 304
Ames Building, 98, 99, 304
Amherst, Lord Jeffrey, 11
Amory, Thomas, 133; house of, 133
Ancient and Honorable Artillery Company, 16, 100, 186, 211
Anderson Street, 259
Andrew, Governor John A., 11, 48, 49, 267, 304
Andros, Sir Edmund, 117, 143, 203
Andros, Lady, 117
Angell, George T., 146
Ann Street. See North Street
Anthology Society, 71
Anthony, Susan B., 309
Appalachian Mountain Club, 37
Appeal to the Great Spirit (Dallin), 295
Appleton, Fanny, 27
Appleton, Frances, 309
Appleton, Mary, 21
Appleton, Nathan, 21, 27, 29, 71, 171, 198–99, 207
Appleton, Samuel, 21, 29, 207
Appleton, Thomas Gold, 279
Appleton, William, 21, 116, 138
Arbella, Lady, 95, 116
Arch Street, 156, 166
Archives and Museum, State House, 32
Aristides the Just, statue of, Louisburg Square, 52
Arlington Street, 277, 282; Numbers

8–9, 279; Number 12, 279
Arlington Street Church, 283
Arnold, James, 168
Arnold Arboretum, 168, 161
Art Deco style, 157, 160
Ashburton Place, 67, 132; Number 1, 67; Number 3, 67; Number 13, 67
Atlantic Avenue, 48, 161, 202, 217
Atlantic Monthly, 40, 52, 73, 108, 131, 154, 279
Attucks, Crispus, 190
Autocrat of the Breakfast Table; *see* Holmes, Oliver Wendell

Back Bay (cove), 17, 141, 181; filling of, 269, 276–79, 271, 286, 291
Back Bay community, 291; *see also individual street names*
Back Bay Fens, 304
Ball, Thomas, 110, 142, 281
Ballou, Maturin M., 60
Bancroft, George, 58
BankBoston, 126, 134, 150, 159
Banner, Peter, 127
Baptist Society, 268
Barings, Thomas, 130
Barnum, P. T., 54
Barrell, Joseph, 167, 191
Bartholdi, Frederic Auguste, 286
Barton's Point, 253
Bates, Joshua, 279, 298, 299
Battery Street, 245
"Battle Hymn of the Republic," 48
Battery Wharf, 245
Baury, Monseigneur, 254
Bay State Charter, 32
Bay State Road, 284
Baylies, Walter C., 279
Beach Street, 181
Beacon Chambers, 299
Beacon Hill, xii, 17–74, 100, 252; Christmas celebration on, 44, 52; cliff on, 259; condominium conversions on, 46; development of, 24; used as fill for Mill Pond, 222–23; gardens on, 19, 45; "Hidden House" of, 57; North Slope of, 51, 61, 62, 64, 257, 258; private passageways on, 57, 59; removal of top of, 35; *see also individual street names*
Beacon Hill Friends House, 49
Beacon Hill Reservoir, 35, 65
Beacon Street, 5, 6, 15, 17–34, 68–74, 271–80, 302; and Bowdoin Street, 68; and Charles Street, 271; and Joy Street, 29; Number 1, 73; Number 7, 70, 73; Number 9 (Hinckley mansion, Somerset Club), 73, Number 10½, 71, 72; Number 14, 70; Number 16, 70; Numbers 18–20, 70, Number 25, 31; Number 30, 3; Number 31, 31; Number 32, 31, Number 33, 30, Number 34, 30; Number 39, 27, 71; Number 40, 71; Number 42, 25, 73; Number 43, 25; Number 44, 24; Number 45, 23, 24, 25, 41; Number 46, 22; Number 48, 22, Number 50, 21; Number 53, 21; Number 54, 20, 21; Number 55, 20; Number 61, 19; Number 63, 19; Number 64, 19; Numbers 70–75, 273; Number 71, 273; Number 81, 275, Number 84, 275; Numbers 92–99, 273; Number 96, 277; Number 137, 277; Numbers 150–152, 277, 296; Number 241, 302; Number 294, 302; Number 296, 302; Number 302, 302; and Park Street, 6, 133; and Somerset Street, 72, 75; and Tremont Street, 119; and Walnut Street, 28
Beacon Street Mall, the Common, 7, 22, 31
Beaver II (Tea Party ship), 149
Beaver Street, 273
Bedford Street, 174, 203; and Summer Street, 171
Beecher, Reverend Lyman, 65
Belknap, Reverend Jeremy, 160
Bell, Alexander Graham, 89, 158, 178
Bell Atlantic, 148, 251
Bellevue Hotel, 67
Bellingham, Penelope, 78
Bellingham, Governor Richard, 78, 113
Bellingham Place, 259
Bellomont, Earl of, 95, 151, 168
Benjamin, Asher, 43, 191, 253, 268, 273
Berkeley Street, 277; and Commonwealth Avenue, 278; Number 222, 288; Number 234, 284
Bernhardt, Sarah, 175, 301

Berry, Grace, 240; gravestone of, 240
Berryman, John, 259
"Big Dig," 224
Bishop's Alley; *see* Hawley Street
Black communities, 56, 241
Black Heritage Trail, 62
Blackhall, Clarence, 140, 141
Blackstone, Reverend William, xiii, 4, 22, 24, 50, 95, 145
Blackstone Street, 210, 224
Blaxton; *see* Blackstone, Reverend William
Blossom Street, 257
Board Alley; *see* Hawley Street
Bonaparte, Jerome, 164
Booth, Edwin, 45, 112, 175
Booth, John Wilkes, 45, 112, 154
Boston & Lowell railroad station, 77
Boston & Maine Station, 14
Boston & Providence Station, 14, 142
Boston and Roxbury Mill Corporation, 273
Boston Architectural Center, 1, 305
Boston Architectural Club, 140
Boston Art Club, 300
Boston Athenaeum, 57, 66, 71, 72, 84, 115, 147, 179
Boston Atlas, 154
Boston Bar Association, 70
Boston Caucus Club, 222; *see also* Caulkers' Club
Boston Center for Adult Education, 278
Boston City Hall; *see* City Hall
Boston Common; *see* Common, the
Boston Corps of Horse, 219
Boston Evening Medical Center, 305
Boston Female Anti-Slavery Society, 188
Boston Gazette, 98, 108
Boston Globe, 4, 58, 60, 103, 123, 178, 266
Boston Globe Store, 58, 104, 108
Boston Harbor Hotel, 208
Boston Herald, 102
Boston Horticultural Society, 161
Boston Journal, 102
Boston Library Society, 97, 156
Boston-Lowell railroad, 171
Boston Marathon, 305
Boston Massacre, 79, 87, 94, 102, 126, 143, 153, 190
Boston Massacre monument, the Common, 139
Boston Museum, 115
Boston Neck, 180, 186
Boston News-Letter, 97, 103, 173
Boston Pier; *see* Long Wharf
Boston Place, Number 1, 101
Boston Pops, 136, 264, 294
Boston Post, 13, 102
Boston Public Latin School, 31, 71, 80, 101, 110, 111
Boston Public Library, 97, 134, 141, 279, 291, 297–300; Kirstein Library, 97
Boston Radical Club, 48
Boston School Committee, 95, 225
Boston Society of Architects, 198
Boston Society of Natural History, 285
Boston Stock Exchange, 101, 191
Boston Stone, 223
Boston Symphony Orchestra, 134, 264, 294, 302
Boston Tea Party, 14, 69, 85, 111, 144, 149, 180, 212, 232
Boston Tea Party ship (*Beaver II*), 149
Boston Theater, 46, 112, 175, 176
Boston Transcript, 57, 103
Boston Traveller, 102
Boston University, 46, 70, 89, 284, 294
Boston Women's Heritage Trail, 32
Bostonian Society, 57, 187
Bostonians, The (James), 67
Bosworth Street, 154
Bowditch, Nathaniel, 164, 300
Bowdoin, Elizabeth, 64
Bowdoin, James, 28, 64, 69, 111, 135, 187, 219, 227; grave of, 126; house of, 12, 69
Bowdoin Square, 56, 251, 252
Bowdoin Street, 64–65, 67; and Beacon Street, 69; and Cambridge Street, 254; Number 122, 66
Bowdoin Street Meeting House, 64
Boylston, Dr. Zabdiel, 87, 226
Boylston Building, 179
Boylston Market Building, 180
Boylston Place, Number 4, 141
Boylston Street, 141, 180, 291, 299; and Arlington Street, 283; and Clarendon Street, 286; and Dart-

mouth Street, 300; Number 62, 141; Number 80, 141; Number 87, 303; Number 141, 283; Number 162, 141; Number 351, 283; Number 500, 288, Number 955, 305; Number 1154, 305; and Tremont Street, 139; and Washington Street, 180
Braddock, General, 108, 151
Bradford, Governor William, 144
Bradlee brothers, 14
Branch Street, Number 66, 19
Brandeis, Louis D., 268
Brattle Book Shop, 173
Brattle Square, 86, 253
Brattle Street, 86
Brattle Street Church, 87, 94, 253; parsonage of, 94
Brewer, Gardner, 3
Brewster, Elder, 70
Bridgman, Laura, 39
Brigham, Charles, 305
Brimmer Street, 267; and Mount Vernon Street, 267–68; Number 9, 267; Number 44, 268
Brimstone Corner (Park and Tremont Streets), 4, 127
British Coffee House, 194
British consul general, residence of, 49
Broad Street, 198; Number 64, 199; Number 66, 198; Numbers 68–70, 198; Number 70, 199; Number 72, 198; Numbers 102–104, 198
Broadway, 307
Bromfield, Edward, 69
Bromfield, Colonel Henry, 93
Bromfield House, 153
Bromfield-Phillips mansion, 69, 114
Bromfield Street, 126, 135, 153–54; Number 20, 153; Number 21, 154; Number 30, 153
Brooks, Peter Chardon, 162, 193
Brooks, Reverend Phillips, 289; statue of, Trinity Church, 289
Brown, John, 49, 124, 136, 153
Brunswick Hotel, 288
Bryant, Gridley, J. F., 204
Bulfinch, Charles, 5, 27, 40, 48, 84, 85, 122, 167, 186, 198, 252; Amory house, 133; bankruptcy of, 80, 155, 252; plan for Beacon Hill, 24, 51; 39 Beacon Street, 27; 45 Beacon Street (third Otis house), 23; Boston Public Latin School, 111; Boylston Market Building, 180; Broad Street warehouses, 198, 64 Broad Street, 199; Bulfinch Row, 5, 129; Cambridge Street (first) Otis house, 254; 6–8 Chestnut Street, 49; 13–17 Chestnut Street, 48; 29A Chestnut Street, 45; Colonnade Row, 138; column, Beacon Hill, 35; enlarges Faneuil Hall, 85, 211; Federal Street Church, 160; Federal Street Theater, 162; creates Franklin Street, 155; Holy Cross Church, 110, 157; Johnson Hall, 110; Massachusetts General Hospital building, 257; layout of Mill Pond fill, 222; Mount Vernon Street row houses, 37; 55 Mount Vernon Street, 38; 59–67 Mount Vernon Street, 40; 85 Mount Vernon Street (second Otis house), 41, 57; 87–89 Mount Vernon Street, 41; New South Church, 163; lays out Park Street, 6, 128; Perkins house, 36; St. Stephen's Church, 157, 225, 236, 247; State House, xvii, xviii, 5, 24, 33, 186, 306; State Street buildings, 180; Sullivan town house, 167; Tontine Crescent, 84, 97, 115, 155, 156
Bulfinch, Thomas, 118, 252
Bulfinch Row, 5, 129
Bull & Finch Pub, 275
Bunch of Grapes, 192, 261
Bunker Hill, Battle of, 14, 143, 241, 245, 247; Monument, 26, 125, 162, 244; transportation to, 317
Burgoyne, General John, 12, 69, 143, 212, 241
Burne-Jones, Sir Edward, 289
Burns, Anthony, 96, 249; trial of, 96
Burns, Robert, statue, 157
Burrage, Albert C., 305
Burrage House Retirement Home, 305
Bussey, Benjamin, 168
Butler's Row, 211
Byrd, Richard E., 267
Byron, Lord, 39

Cabot, Edward C., 71
Cabot, George, 129, 166

Cambridge Common, 311
Cambridge Street, 249, 251, 254, 256, 257
Cambridge University, 307
Campbell, John, 97, 103, 173
Campeau, Robert, 169
Caner, Reverend Henry, 115, 117
Capen, Hopestill, 221
Cardinal William O'Connell Way, 254
Carson, Rachel, 73
Caruso, Enrico, 175
Carver Street, 141, 300; Number 62, 142; Number 77, 142
Cascieri, Arcangelo, 1
Castle Island, 109, 197
Cathedral of the Holy Cross, 157, 225
Catholic Center, 156
Caulkers' Club, 245; *see also* Boston Caucus Club
Causeway Street, 54, 77, 256
cemeteries, 14, 116; *see also* Central Burying Ground; Copp's Hill Burying Ground; King's Chapel Burying Ground; Old Granary Burying Ground
Center Plaza, 77, 79, 249, 256; Number One, 89; Number Two, 83; Number Three, 80, 116
Centinel; see Columbia Centinel
Central Artery, 202, 207, 224
Central Burying Ground, the Common, 13, 14
Central Congregational Church, 137, 285; rectory of, 137
Central Wharf, 29, 202
C. F. Hovey, store, 166
Chamber of Commerce, 199
Champney Place, 259
'Change Avenue, 194
Channing, Reverend William Ellery, 41, 160, 283
Chapman Place, 111
Chappotin, Leon, 164
Charles I, 4, 32
Charles II, 78, 100
Charles Hayden Planetarium, 264
Charles River, 15, 21, 257, 258, 262–64; bridges, 223, 262, 263; dam, 253, 260, 263
Charles River Square, 266; Number 3, 266; Number 18, 266
Charles Street, 36, 50, 51, 56, 261–62, 264, 265; and Beacon Street, 19, 22, 268, 271; Number 108, 266; Number 131, 265; Number 148, 265; Number 161, 265; Number 164, 262
Charles Street Circle, 261
Charles Street Garage, 265
Charles Street Jail, 260
Charles Street Meeting House, 263, 268
Charter Street, 244, 245; and Hanover Street, 245; and Salem Street, 244
Chase & Speakman distillery, 180
Chatham Street, 105, 211
Chauncy Street, 166
Chavannes, Puvis de, 299
"Cheers," 275
Chestnut Street, 36, 43–49, 50–51, 263; Number 1, 48, 49; Number 4, 49, Numbers 6–8, 49; Number 10, 49; Number 13, 48, 49; Number 15, 48; Number 16, 48; Number 17, 48, 49; Number 29A, 45; Number 31, 45; Number 37, 45; Number 43, 45; Number 50, 44; Number 51, 51; Number 52, 44; Number 57A, 44, 135
Cheverus, Bishop, 110, 157
Children's Museum, 150
Chilton Club, 301
Chinatown, 178
China Trade Center, 180
Choate, Rufus, 98, 162
Christ Church (Old North Church), 82, 122, 236–38, 243
Christian Science Church, 293
Christian Science Monitor, 293
Christopher Columbus Park, 202, 207, 215
Christopher Columbus statue, Louisburg Square, 51
Church, Dr. Benjamin, 151
Church Green, 162; Church Green Building, 163
Churchill, Winston, 26, 73
Church of St. John the Evangelist, 65, 90
Church of the Advent, 65, 267
Church of the Covenant, 285
Church of the French Hugenots, 110, 157

Church of the Holy Bean-blowers (First Baptist Church), 286
Church of the Holy Cross, 110
Church Square, 102
City Hall, new (Government Center), 82, 86, 110, 122, 159, 189, 206, 221, 256
City Hall, old (School Street), 77, 95, 110, 277
City Hall Avenue, 109
City Place, 142
Civil War, 11, 132
Claflin, William, 70
Claflin Building, 70
Claghorn, Colonel George, 247, 253
Clarendon Street: and Boylston Street, 286; Number 233, 285
Clark, William, 227
Clark Street, 236
Clark's Square; *see* North Square
Clark's Wharf, 227
Clarke, Reverend James Freeman, 48, 58, 67, 124
Clarke, Richard, 111
Clarke, Susan, 111
Clinton, General Sir Henry, 12, 30, 241
Clough, Ebenezer, 238
Club of Odd Volumes, 41
"Cockerel" church, 226, 233
Codman, John, Sr., 57
Coggan, John, 99, 189
Cohan, George M., 176
Cole, Samuel, 103, 105
Coleridge, Samuel Taylor, 309
Cole's Ship Inn, 103
Colonial Theater, 140, 141
Colonnade Row, 139
Columbia (ship), 167
Columbia Centinel, 36, 37, 227
Columbus Avenue, 289
"combat zone", 89, 140, 181
Commercial Street, 214, 242, 244
Committee of Correspondence, 69, 212
Committtee of Safety, 88
Common, the, 1–16, 19, 22, 125, 135; Beacon Street Mall, 7, 22, 31; Boston Massacre monument, 139; Brewer fountain, 3; cattle on, 8, 30; Central Burying Ground, 12, 13; duel on, 11; established, 1, 3; executions on, 10–11, 16, Flagstaff Hill, 9, 12, 16; Founders' Monument, 22; Frog Pond, 9, 25; Great Elm, 9–10; Information Booth, 1; Lafayette Mall, 4; Long Path, 7, 8; MacArthur Mall, 15; military exercises on, 11–12; Parkman Bandstand, 12; Parkman Plaza, 1; public punishment on, 10; Railroad Mall, 12, 13, 14, 142; Robert Gould Shaw Memorial, 6; Soldiers' Monument, 10; Tremont Street mall, 3
Commonwealth Avenue, 43, 271, 277, 280, 285, 286, 301, 303–5; and Berkeley Street, 278; Number 1, 279, Number 3, 278; Number 5, 278; Number 10, 279; Number 21, 278; Number 191, 303; Number 199, 303; Number 217, 303; Number 314, 305; Number 355, 304; Number 374, 305; Number 385, 305
Commonwealth Center, 177
Computer Museum, 150
Conant, James B., 43
Concert Hall, 88, 93, 219
Concord Avenue, 307
Congregational House, 70
Congress Street, 149, 190, 208, 221; Number 344, 150; and Purchase Street, 150; and Water Street, 146–47
Constitution, U.S., adopted, 159, 222
Constitution, U.S.S; *see* "Old Ironsides"
Constitution Wharf, 245
Coolidge, Calvin, 177
Coolidge, Joseph, Jr., 252
Coolidge, Joseph, Sr., 252
Copley, Elizabeth, 31, 78
Copley, John Singleton, 25, 78, 86,111; house of, 48
Copley, Mrs. John Singleton; *see* Clarke, Susan
Copley Place, 291
Copley Plaza Hotel, 291
Copley Square, 298
Copley Square Plaza, 289, 298
Copp's Hill, 227, 241
Copp's Hill Burying Ground, 240, 241
Corn Court, 194
Corn Market, 211
Cornhill, 207

Cornhill Street; *see* Market Street
Cotting, Uriah, 29, 85, 198, 199, 271
Cotton, Reverend John, 78, 105, 116, 188
Cotton Hill; *see* Pemberton Hill
Courthouse, Federal, 146, 204
Court Square, 94, 95, 96, 122; Number 4, 97
Court Street, Number 1, 98; Number 26, 95; Number 32, 96; Number 42, 94; Number 46, 94; Number 109, 89; and Tremont Street, 82, 93
Covenant, Church of the, 285
Cow Lane, 148; *see also* High Street
Craigie Bridge, 264
Craigie House, Cambridge, 27; transportation to, 318
Cram, Ralph Adams, 44
Creek Square, 223
Cromwell's Head, 108
Cross Street, 225
Crowninshield, Benjamin, 301
Crowninshield, Benjamin W., 73
Cunard, Samuel, 195
Cunard Line, 194
Curley, James Michael, 26, 34, 66, 83, 110, 208, 260; memorial, 208
Curtis, Caroline (T. H. Perkin's granddaughter), 168, 172, 273
Cushing, John P., 168
Cushing, Richard Cardinal, 236, 252; bust of, in Bowdoin Square, 252
Cushing, Thomas, 153
Cushing, Thomas C., 302
Cushman, Charlotte, 175, 238
Custom House: in 1770s, 190; of 1810, 199; of 1847, 204; tower, 148, 204
Custom House Street, Number 20, 199

Dallin, Cyrus E., 32, 236, 295
Damrell, John, 157
Dana, Richard Henry, Jr., 45, 51, 96, 112, 115, 198, 249
Dana, Richard Henry, Sr., 45, 124
Daniel Webster Park, 162
Dartmouth Street, 301; and Boylston Street, 300; and Marlborough Street, 302; and Newbury Street, 300; Number 306, 301
Dawes, William, 88, 116, 210, 219, 232, 313
Day Press, 99
Declaration of Independence, 183, 193
Defarrari, John, 299
DeLue, Donald, 306
Derby, Captain Richard Crowninshield, 46
Derne Street, 35, 64
Devonshire Building, 102
Devonshire Street, 103, 146, 162, 188; and Franklin Street, 146, 156–57; and State Street, 188
Dewey Square, 160, 161
Dexter, Samuel, 133
Dial, The, 173
DiBaccari, Adio, 1
Dickens, Charles, 17, 107, 112–13, 137, 149, 234; visits in North End, 235; and Parkman murder case, 50, 260; quoted on Boston, 5, 19, 119; quoted on Channing, 41; quoted on rehearsing, 267; on Thanksgiving, 1867, 55, 112; reading at Tremont Temple, 121; first visit (1842), 5, 41, 114, 119, 121, 198, 233, 234; visit of 1867–1868, 55, 112, 121–22, 266, 275; and walking contest, 276
Dickens, Kate, 114, 121
Dini's restaurant, 125
Dock Square, 80, 86, 99, 189, 207
Doe, Sullivan & Company, 214
Dolby, George, 113, 123, 137, 275
Dorchester Heights, transportation to, 317
Doric Hall, State House, 34
Douglass, Frederick, 6, 268
Downtown Crossing, 171, 181
D'Oyly Carte, Richard, 136
Drawbridge Street. *See* North Street
Drowne, Shem, 151
duel on the Common, 1728, 11
Dunster, Henry, 99
Durgin Park, 215
Dvorak, Antonin, 44
Dwight, John Sullivan, 135
Dwight, Timothy, 276
Dyer, Mary, 6, 10; statue of, 32

Earhart, Amelia, 311
Eddy, Mary Baker, 293, 305

Edes, Benjamin, 85, 98
Edgar Allan Poe Way, 141
Edinboro Street, 178
Edward, Prince, 52, 169
Eliot, Charles W., 31, 305
Eliot, John, 70, 188, 300
Eliot Street, 142
Elizabeth II, 189
Ellison, Eben, 258
emancipation; *see* abolition movement
Emancipation Group Statue, Park Square, 142
Embankment Road, 263, 266, 273; Number 14, 262
Emerson, Ellen, 72
Emerson, Ralph Waldo, 33, 43, 49, 53, 59, 72, 107, 124, 138, 176, 233, 279; and abolition, 124, 226; and the Alcotts, 53, 59–60; birthplace of, 166; childhood of, 72, 166, 179; edits *The Dial,* 173; and Whitman's *Leaves of Grass,* 7; lecture at Masonic Temple, 138; and Saturday Club, 112
Emerson, William, 166
Emerson, Reverend William, 72, 166
Emerson, Mrs. William (Ruth), 72, 166, 179
Emerson, William Ralph, 301
Emerson College, 140, 277
Emmanuel Episcopal Church, 284
Endecott, Governor John, 10, 22, 80, 125
Engineers Club, 277
Episcopal Diocese of Massachusetts, 65
"Essex Junto," 37, 51, 74, 115, 129
Essex Street, 178; and Kingston Street, 178; Number 26, 178; Number 59, 178; Number 60, 179; and Washington Street, 179
d'Estaing, Admiral, 30, 88, 133, 223
Eustis, William, 86
Evangeline (Longfellow), 108
Everett, Edward, 132, 165, 178
Exchange Place, 191, 193
Exchange Coffee House, 191
Exchange Street, 189
executions, public, 9–10, 16, 243
Exeter Place, Number 3, 177
Exeter Street, 302
Exeter Street Theater, 303
Expressway; *see* Fitzgerald, John F., Expressway

Fairbanks, Richard, 103, 105, 128
Fan Pier, 204, 216
Faneuil, Andrew, 195
Faneuil, Peter, 11, 85, 115, 126, 211; mansion of, 113–14
Fanueil Hall, 11, 82, 85, 93, 115, 164, 207–14; Samuel Adams statue at, 208; enlarged, 85, 211; markets of, 207; Washington portrait at, 93, 164, 212
Farmer, Fannie, 139
Federal Reserve Building, 148, 150
Federal Street, 147, 159–60; and Franklin Street, 159; and Milk Street (Fleet Bank), 146, 158; Number 1 (Fleet Bank), 158; Number 75, 157; Number 100 (First National Bank), 159; Number 101, 157; Number 150, 160; Number 160, 160; Number 175, 160
Federal Street Church, 160, 283
Federal Street Theater, 158, 162, 175
Federalist Party, 37, 130
Fehmer, Carl, 304
Fens, the, 304
Fenway, The, 295, 306; Number 230, 295; Number 280, 295
Fidiciary Trust Building, 161
Fiedler, Arthur, 264
Fiedler Bridge, 264, 269
Fields, Annie, 55, 123; quoted, 262, 265, 276
Fields, James T. "Jamie," 20, 55, 59, 61, 73, 107, 112, 119, 154, 168, 262; Charles Street residence of, 265; and Dickens's 1842 visit, 121; and Dickens's 1867–1868 visit, 55–56, 112, 121, 275; publishing career of, 59, 61, 73, 107–8, 131, 134, 137; and Thackeray lectures, 176
Filene, Edward, 170
Filene, William, 165, 171
Filene's, 97, 166, 170
fire of 1676, 230, 234
fire of 1711, 99, 102, 183, 187
fire of 1872, 148, 155, 163, 166, 169; extent of damage from, 145, 166;

on Franklin Street, 155; and Old South Meeting House, 145; on Pearl Street, 148; on Washington Street, 152
First and Second Unitarian Church, 278; parish house of, 279
First Baptist Church, 286
First Church: of 1632, 188, 300; of 1640, 188, 234; "Old Brick," 166, 188, 193; parsonage of, 166
First Spiritualist Temple, 303
Fish Market, 211
Fish Street; *see* North Street
Fisher Junior College, 277
Fitzgerald, John F. "Honey Fitz," 68, 149, 206, 230, 245, 275,
Fitzgerald, John F., Expressway, 149, 225
Flagstaff Hill, the Common, 8, 9, 10
Flatley Building, 115
Fleet Bank, 146
Flour and Grain Exchange, 199
Flynn, Mayor Richard, 83, 146, 205
Ford Hall Forum, 67
Fort Hill, 71, 148, 193, 203, 281
Fort Point Channel, 150, 204
Foster Street, 244
Founders' Monument, the Common, 22, 45
Four Seasons Hotel, 142
Fox Hill, 15
Frankland, Sir Charles Henry, 228
Franklin, Benjamin, 69, 98, 110, 129, 155, 222, 223, 237; birthplace of, 145; and memorial to his parents, 125, 129, 145; statue of, old City Hall, 110
Franklin, James, 98, 221
Franklin, Josiah (father), 145, 221
Franklin Avenue, 97
Franklin Field, 306
Franklin Street, 85, 155; and Arch Street, 156; and Devonshire Street, 156–57; and Federal Street, 159; and Pearl Street, 148; Numbers 85–87, 156; Number 111, 157; Number 185, 158
Free Baptist Society, 128
Freedom Trail, 1
Freeman, Reverend James, 109, 118
French, Daniel Chester, 34, 312
French Consulate General, 279
French Hugenots, Church of the, 110, 157
Friend Street, Number 25, 210
Froebel, Friedrich, 60, 171
Frog Lane; *see* Boylston Street
Frog Pond, the Common, 7, 23, 131
Front Street; *see* Harrison Avenue
Frost, Robert, 43
Fuller, Margaret, 67, 173

Gage, General Thomas, 11, 29, 86, 152, 185, 238, 245
Gallows Bay, 180
Gandhi, Mahatma, 178
Garden Street, 311
Garden Court Street, 227; Number 4, 215, 229
Gardner, Isabella Stewart (Mrs. Jack), 73, 277, 295, 303
Gardner, Isabella Stewart, Museum, 295
Gardner, John Lowell, 73, 295, 303
Garrison, William Lloyd, 37, 65, 127, 146, 214, 226, 268; attacked by mob, 37 188; and New England Anti-Slavery Society, 63, 65
General Services Administration, 256
George III, 13, 30, 83, 115, 169, 185
Gerry, Elbridge, 167
Gibson family residence, 277
Gilman, Arthur, 277, 283
Gilman Gate, 311
Glapion, Louis, 61
God's Acre, 311
Good Samaritan monument, Public Garden, 280
Goodspeed's, 70
Goodwin Place, 259
Gordon Chapel, New Old South Church, 300
Gore, Christopher, 86, 94, 133
Government Center, 75, 82, 83, 86
Governor's Alley; *see* Province Street
Granary, the, 125, 127, 128
Grant, Dr. George F., 267
Grant, Ulysses S., 15, 251
Gravelly Point, 271
Gray, Horace, 165, 281
Gray, Captain Robert, 167
Gray, William "Billy," 167, 191, 281
Great Elm, the Common, 9–10, 16, 78

Great Spring, 103
Green, Bartholomew, 173
Green Dragon Lane; *see* Union Street
Green Dragon Tavern, 159, 223
Green Lane; *see* Salem Street
Green Street, 253
Greene, Gardiner, 31, 78
Greene, Mrs. Gardiner; *see* Copley, Elizabeth
Greenough, Richard S., 110
Griffin's Wharf, 149
Gropius, Walter, and Associates, 88
Grove Street, 55, 258, 259
Gund, Graham, 252

Halcyon Place, 278
Hall, Primus, 62
Hall, Prince, 62, 241
Hamilton, Alexander, 129, 189; statue of, Commonwealth Avenue Mall, 279
Hamilton Place, 135, 147, 192; Numbers 7–9, 136
Hampshire House, 275
Hancock, Ebenezer, 223
Hancock, John, 32, 69, 86, 88, 98, 100, 111, 146, 193, 223; and erection of Charlestown bridge, 227; and U.S. Constitution, 32, 159; inaugurated governor, 186; mansion of, xiii, 3, 5, 12, 13, 29, 32, ; memorial to, 126; and New Exhibition Room, 155; and repeal of Stamp Act, 13; store of, 194, 211; and Washington's 1789 visit, 93, 185; will of, 79
Hancock, Mrs. John, 88, 93, 138
Hancock, Thomas, 29, 227
Hancock Avenue, 32
Hancock Building (1949), 278, 291
Hancock Street, 35; Number 20, 257
Hancock Tower, 262, 278, 287, 289
Hancock's Wharf, 229
Handel & Haydn Society, 135, 180
Hanks, John, 15
Hanover Avenue, 245
Hanover Square; *see* Liberty Hall
Hanover Street, 23, 82, 87, 88, 157, 223, 225, 226–27, 236, 244, 300; and Charter Street, 245; and Marshall Street, 223; Number 168, 224; Number 256, 235; Numbers 298–300, 226; Number 332, 235; Number 383, 235; and North Bennet Street (wooden church), 235; and Prince Street, 223; and Richmond Street, 225; and Union Street, 221
Harbor Towers, 202, 215
Harborwalk, 216
Harbridge House, 279
Harding, Chester, 70
Harris, Benjamin, 97
Harris Street, 236
Harrison, Peter, 117
Harrison Avenue, 178
Hartt, Edmund, 241, 247
Harvard Bridge, 263
Harvard Club of Boston, 305
Harvard College, 26, 85, 97, 129, 160, 168, 194, 234; *see also* Harvard University
Harvard Dental School, 267
Harvard, John, 312
Harvard Medical School, 109, 129, 154, 170, 176, 238, 257, 302
Harvard Musical Association, 44, 136
Harvard Orchestra, 136
Harvard Square, 307
Harvard University, 43, 99, 219, 302; *see also* Harvard College
Harvard Yard, 311–12
Hatch Shell, 263
Hawley Street, 155, 166; and Summer Street, 166
Hawthorne, Nathaniel, 17, 72, 112, 116, 142, 154, 199; wedding to Sophia Peabody, 58, 173; writings of, 107, 152, 173
Hayden, Lewis, 260
Haymarket, 210, 224
Haymarket Square (open-air market), 14, 222
Haymarket Theater, 139
Hayward Place, 164
Hecker, Father Isaac, 132
Hemenway, Mary Tileston, 144
Henchman, Colonel Daniel, 94, 100
Henry Esmond (Thackeray), 20
Henschel, George, 136
Herbert, Victor, 175
Hereford Street, 304; and Newbury Street, 305; Number 32, 304
Heritage on the Garden, 142

Herter, Albert, murals, State House, 20, 34
Herter, Christian A., 19
Hibbins, Mrs. Ann, 78
"Hidden House" of Beacon Hill, 57
Higginson, Major Henry Lee, 136, 294, 302
Higginson, Stephen, 37
Higginson, Stephen, Jr., 37
High, the; *see* Washington Street
High Street, 148, 160; and Pearl Street, 148; and Summer Street, 162; Number 125, 148
Hillard, George, 58, 67
Hinckley, David, 73
Hoffbauer, Charles, 287
Holmes, Jacob, 116
Holmes, Oliver Wendell, 12, 49, 50, 111, 126, 154, 176, 258, 259, 279, 288; Autocrat articles of, 154, 259, 262, 279; Beacon Street residence of, 302; Charles Street residence of, 262; and Dickens's Boston visits, 114, 123, 266, 276; proposes marriage, 7; and Parkman murder case, 50, 258, 266; quoted on Beacon Street, 23; quoted on Fields, 108; quoted on Saturday Club, 112; quoted on State House, 306; quoted on Ticknor's library, 134
Holmes, Oliver Wendell, Walk; *see* Long Path
Holy Bean Blowers, Church of the (First Baptist Church), 286
Holy Cross, Cathedral of the, 157, 225
Holy Cross, Church of the, 110, 157
Holy Ghost Chapel, Paulist Center, 131
Homer, Winslow, 173, 210
Hooker, Joseph, statue of, 34
Hooper-Lee-Nichols House, 311
Horticultural Hall, 294
hotel, America's first, 191
Hotel Meridien, 148
Hotel Touraine, 140
Hotel Vendome, 300
Houghton, Henry O., 131
Houghton Mifflin Company, 40, 73, 131, 288
House of the Seven Gables, The (Hawthorne), 108
Howard Athenaeum, 89
Howard, John Galen, 140
Howard Street, 89
Howe, Julia Ward, 39, 48, 49, 54, 60, 108, 131, 279, 302
Howe, Maud, 61
Howe, Dr. Samuel Gridley, 39–40, 49, 147, 153, 302
Howe, General William, 152
Howells, William Dean, 52–53, 131, 141, 288, 302
Hull, Hannah; see Sewall, Hannah
Hull, Isaac, 213
Hull, John, 125, 172, 178, 240
Hull Street, 240
Hunt, Dr. Harriot Keziah, 238
Huntington Avenue, 289, 291, 293–95, 306; Number 101, 306; Number 116, 291
Hurley State Services Center, 254
Hutchinson, Anne, 6, 105; statue of, 32
Hutchinson, Governor Thomas, 79, 111, 117, 144, 185, 233; and Boston Tea Party, 144; mansion of, 229; meeting house of, 225; and Stamp Act riots, 229
Hutchinson Street; *see* Pearl Street

Independent Chronicle, 48
India Street, 199
India Wharf, 29, 198, 202
Information Booth, the Common, 1
Ingersoll's, 94
Institute of Contemporary Art, 305
International Place, 148
Isabella Stewart Gardner Museum, 295

Jackson, Andrew, 9, 121, 204
Jackson, Dr. James, 75, 114
Jackson, Patrick Tracy, 77, 171, 199
Jackson Place, 171
James, Henry (elder), 49, 67, 268
James, Henry (younger), 53, 67, 127, 266, 268, 298, 302
James M. Beebe Company, 157, 169
Jefferson, Thomas, 72, 280; embargo of 1807, 24, 192
Jeffries House, 262

J.F.K. Street, 311
John B. Hynes Veterans Memorial Convention Center, 305
John Hancock Tower, 289
John Harvard Statue, 312
John Paul II, Pope, 16
Johnson, Isaac, 95, 110, 116
Johnson, Oliver, 63, 213, 226
Johnson, Philip, 299
Johnson Hall, 110
Jolson, Al, 176
Jordan, Eben, 23, 44, 165, 169
Jordan Marsh Company, 44, 165, 169
journalism, 97–98, 102–3
Joy, Benjamin, 41, 45
Joy, Dr. John, 28, 29, 36, 40, 41
Joy, Mrs. John, 29
Joy Street, 7, 28, 30; and Beacon Street, 30, 36; and Mount Vernon Street, 38; Numbers 1–5, 37; Number 46, 61

Kallmann, McKinnell and Knowles, 87
Keayne, Captain Robert, 100, 107, 116, 186
Keith, B. F., 176
Keith, B. F., Memorial Theater, 175
Keith, B. F., New Theater, 176
Kenmore Square, 271, 286
Kennedy, Senator Edward M. "Ted," 44, 230, 266
Kennedy, John F., 32, 66, 215, 230, 254, 275
Kennedy, John F., Federal Building, 80, 88, 122, 256
Kennedy, John F., Library and Museum, 32; transportation to, 317
Kennedy, Joseph P., 229, 275
Kennedy, P. J., 206
Kennedy, Robert, 230
Kennedy, Rose Fitzgerald, 206, 215, 230, 244, 275; Kennedy Garden, 217
Keystone Building, 150
Kidd, Captain, 93, 95, 151, 168
Kilby Street, 192, 193
King, Reverend Martin Luther, Jr., 173, 294
King Street; *see* State Street
King's Chapel, 71, 77, 110, 115, 116–18, 168; parish house of, 19; parsonage of, 71, 109, 115; rectory of, 19
King's Chapel Burying Ground, 113, 115, 116, 125
Kingston Street, 165; and Essex Street, 178; and Summer Street, 163
Kipling, Rudyard, 26
Kirstein, Edward L., Memorial Library, 97
Kissinger, Henry, 49
Kitchen Street, *see* Branch Street
Knowles, Edward, 87
Knox, Henry, 48, 72, 100, 103, 161, 190

Lady Chapel, Emmanuel Church, 284
LaFarge, John, 289, 301
LaFayette Hotel, 177
Lafayette, Marquis de, 4, 10, 34, 133, 139, 162, 237
Lafayette Mall, the Common, 4
Lafayette Place, 177
Lamb Tavern, 177
Langone Funeral Home, 235
Langtry, "Jersey Lily," 175
Larkin, John, 232
Late George Apley, The (Marquand), 57
Lawrence, Abbott, 114, 132, 207, 279
Lawrence, Amos, 138, 207
Lawrence, Colonel T. Bigelow, 280
Lawrence, William, 138
Leaves of Grass (Whitman), 7
Lee, Thomas, 280
Leslie Lindsey Memorial Chapel, 284
Leverett, John, 101
Leverett Street Jail, 260
Lewis Wharf, 215
Lexington Green, transportation to, 318
Liberator, The, 65, 127, 146, 188
Liberty (sloop), 229
Liberty Hall, 180
Liberty Square, 193
Liberty Tree, 13, 180, 206
Liberty Tree Park, 180
Lillie, Lloyd, 208

Lincoln, Abraham, 45, 63, 112, 133, 154; log cabin displayed, 15; visits Boston, 15, 122, 123, 154
Lincoln, Frederick Walker, 51
Lincoln, Robert, 14
Lincoln Street, 163
Lind, Jenny, 54
Lindsey, Leslie, 284
Little Building, 141
Locke-Ober's, 172
Lodge, Henry Cabot (elder), 31, 40, 162; memorial to, 32
Lodge, Henry Cabot (younger), 275
Lodge, John Ellerton, 31
Loew, Marcus, 170
Lomasney, Martin, 206
Lomasney Way, 256
London Book Store (1771–1775), 103
London Bookstore (1764), 194
London Coffee House, 97
Long Lane; *see* Federal Street
Long Lane Meeting House, 159
Long Path, the Common, 8, 9
Long Wharf, 99, 197, 202, 217, 245
Longfellow, Anne, 27
Longfellow, Henry Wadsworth, 27, 49, 72, 108, 176, 249, 263, 288, 309; and Dickens's 1842 visit, 123, 233; and Dickens's 1867–1868 visit, 55, 112, 121–22, 275; wedding of, 27
Longfellow Bridge, 261
Longfellow National Historic Site, 309
Louis XVI, 223
Louis Philippe, 221
Louisburg Square, 22, 43, 50, 51, 79; Number 3, 52; Number 4, 53; Number 8, 54; Number 10, 54; Number 16, 52; Number 19, 51, 52; Number 20, 54
Lovejoy, Reverend Elijah, 213
Lowell, Amy, 301
Lowell, A. Lawrence, 132, 302
Lowell, Reverend Charles, 51, 253
Lowell, Francis Cabot, 74, 171, 198
Lowell, Guy, 295
Lowell, James Russell, 8, 49, 51, 94, 114, 146, 253, 276, 279
Lowell, Judge John, 51, 74, 94, 115, 253
Lowell, John (son of judge), 138
Lowell, John Amory, 132
Lowell, Robert, 259
Lulu (Louisa May Alcott's niece), 54, 57, 68
Lyman, Theodore, 37, 188
Lynch, Daniel J., 251

MacArthur Mall, the Common, 15
McCloskey, Robert, 17; *see also Make Way for Ducklings!*
McCormack, John W., 66, 146, 251
McCormack, John W., Building (state offices), 67, 89, 251
McCormack, John W., Federal Building, 146
McIlvain, Isabel, 32
Mackerel Lane; *see* Kilby Street
McKim, Charles F., 289, 297
McKim, Mead and White, 294, 303
McKinley Square, 204
McKinnell, Noel, 87
MacLean, Arthur, 39
MacMonnies, Frederick, 297
Madison's war; *see* War of 1812
Majestic Theater, 140
Make Way for Ducklings!, 17, 55, 268, 280
Malcom, Daniel, 238
Manley, Captain John, 236
Mann, Horace, 66, 67, 142, 173; statue of, 34
Manufactory Building, 134
Mapparium, 293
Marion, Joseph, 191
Marketplace Center, 215
Market Street, 85
Marlborough Street, 181; and Dartmouth Street, 301; Number 66, 278; Number 163, 301; Number 164, 301; Number 239, 259
Marquand, John P., 26, 57
Marriott Hotel, 216, 291
Marsh, Julia, 44
Marshall, Emily, 273
Marshall Street, 223
Mason, Jeremiah, 138
Mason, Jonathan, 24, 36, 128, 137, 164; Mount Vernon Street residence of, 36, 38
Mason Street, 170, 176, 298
Masonic Temple (Tremont and

Temple Streets), 138
Masons, 34, 88, 193, 222; Grand Lodge of (Tremont and Boylston Streets), 139, 193
Massachusetts Anti-Slavery Society, 124
Massachusetts Avenue, 277, 293, 304; Number 397, 294
Massachusetts Bank, 135, 192; *see also* First National Bank of Boston
Massachusetts Bay Colony, 307
Massachusetts Hall, 312
Massachusetts Continuing Legal Education (MCLE), 172
Massachusetts General Hospital, 75, 109, 116, 129, 152, 258, 278; Bulfinch building, 257; created, 75, 109, 114; ether first used at, 116, 257, 280
Massachusetts Historical Society, 84, 115, 151, 156, 160, 305
Massachusetts Institute of Technology (MIT), 168, 264, 286, 304
Massachusetts Medical College Building, Harvard Medical School, 257
Massachusetts Spy, 221, 240
Massachusetts Turnpike, 291, 306
Mather, Reverend Cotton, 10, 87, 226, 234, 243, 244
Mather, Reverend Increase, 234, 244
Mather, Reverend Samuel, 234
Mather tomb, Copp's Hill, 241
Matignon, Abbe Francois, 110, 157
Maude, Daniel, 80
May, Reverend Samuel J., 226
Meacham, George F., 282
Mechanics Building, 291, 306
Medeiros, Humberto Cardinal, 252
Meeting House: first (mudwall), 101, 105; of 1640, 101; "Old Brick," Church Square, 102
Meeting House School, 62
Mein, John, 194
Melba, Nellie, 175
Melodeon, 176
Mercantile Library, 168
Merchants Row, 194, 207, 211, 214
Meridien, Hotel, 148
Merrimack Manufacturing Company, 171
Methodist Alley; *see* Hanover Avenue
Middleton, George, 61
Midtown Cultural District, 140, 181
Mifflin, George Harrison, 73
Milk Street, 102, 145, 146, 199, 202; and Federal Street (Fleet Bank), 146, 158; and Franklin Street, 148; Number 19, 145; Number 101, 148; Number 129, 169; Number 146, 202; Number 177, 199; and Pearl Street, 148
Mill Dam, 29, 273, 275, 286, 289, 302
Mill Pond, 224, 227, 252, 256
Millerites, 89
Milmore, Martin, 10
Molineux, William, 68
Monroe, James, 9, 25, 34, 191
Montagu, John, 149
Monthly Anthology, 71
Moon Street, 234
Morison, Samuel Eliot, 268
Morris, William, 289
Morse, Samuel F. B., 86
Morton, Dr. William T. G., 116
Mother Church of Christian Science, 293
Mother Goose, 126
Mott, Lucretia, 49, 63
Mount Auburn Street, 314
Mount Vernon (hill), 51, 55
Mount Vernon Place, Number 8, 36
Mount Vernon Proprietors, 24, 36, 40, 45, 46, 51, 61, 273
Mount Vernon Street, 24, 25, 35–43, 46, 48, 50, 51, 53, 55, 59; and Brimmer Street, 267–68; and Joy Street, 36; Number 32, 39; Number 34, 39; Number 47, 39; Number 49, 37; Numbers 50–60 (stables), 41; Number 51, 38; Number 53, 38; Number 55, 38; Number 57, 38; Number 59, 40; Numbers 59–67 (Mason house), 40; Number 65, 40; Numbers 70–72, 46; Number 77, 41; Number 80, 39; Number 83, 41; Number 85 (Otis house), 41; Number 87, 41; Number 88, 43; Number 89, 41; Number 131, 268; Number 158, 267
Mount Whoredom, 55, 258
Muddy River, 295, 304
Mugar Omni Theater, 264
Murray, Reverend John, 235

Museum of African-American
History, 62
Museum of Fine Arts, 48, 72, 279, 283, 291, 295, 297
Museum of Science, 264, 284
Museum Road, 295
Museum School, 295
Museum Wharf, 150
Music Hall, 44, 124, 135, 170, 294
Music Hall Place, 171
Myrtle Street, 55, 64, 257

National Park Service Visitor Center, 188, 317
Newbury Associated Guild of Arts (NAGA) gallery, 285
Neck, The; *see* Boston Neck
Neill, William C., 63
New Chardon Street, 253
New England, The, 287–88
New England Anti-Slavery Society, 63, 226
New England Aquarium, 202
New England Conservatory of Music, 294
New England Gazette, 98
New England Historic Genealogical Society, 285
New England Shelter for Homeless Veterans, 97
New England Mutual Life Insurance Company Building, 285
New England Holocaust Memorial, 208
New England Shelter for Homeless Veterans, 97
New England School of Law, 39
New England School of Pharmacy, 46
New England Telephone Building, 148, 158, 251
New Exhibition Room, 155
New Guinea (black community), 241
New North (meeting house, 1714), 236
New Old South Church, 300
New South Church, 162
New York Tribune, 123, 267
Newbury Street, 181, 284–85; and Dartmouth Street, 300; Number 15, 284; Number 80 (New England Mutual Life Insurance Company Building), 285; Number 101, 285
Newman, Robert, 237, 240
News-Letter; see Boston News-Letter
Newspaper Row, 102, 134
Newtowne, 307
New Yard, 312
Nichols, Rose Standish, 38
Nichols House Museum, 38
Nicholson, Samuel, 238
North American Review, 31
North Battery, 207, 245
North Bennet Street and Hanover Street wooden church, 236
North Church, 226; *see also* Old North
North End, 82, 157, 219–47; *see also individual street names*
North End Community Health Center, 235
North Grove Street, 257
North Market Street, 210; Number 30, 215
North Slope of Beacon Hill, 55, 61, 62, 64, 257
North Square, 221, 226, 227, 229–36; 1711–1715 brick house in, 232; Number 1, 234; Number 19 (Paul Revere's house), 230–32, 234
North Station, 54, 77
North Street, 208, 210, 211; Number 22, 210; Number 24, 210; and Salutation Street, 245
Northampton Street, Number 396, 294
Northeastern University, 295
Northumberland, Lord Percy, 16, 29

Oberlin College, 130
O'Connell, William Cardinal, 156, 254
Old Brick (First Church), 102, 166, 185, 193; parsonage of, 166
Old Brick (Meeting House, Church Square), 102
Old Burying Ground, 311
Old Corner Bookstore, 57, 58, 104, 105, 134, 154, 168; *see also* Boston Globe Store
Old Granary Burying Ground, 121, 125, 129, 245

Old Howard, 89
"Old Ironsides" (U.S.S. *Constitution*), 34, 114, 127, 139, 141, 215, 238, 247, 253, 287; transportation to, 317
Old North (original North Church), 234
Old North Church (Christ Church), 82, 122, 236–38, 243
Old South Meeting House, 102, 104, 107, 109, 119, 143–45, 153, 300
Old State House, 11, 82, 84, 99, 102, 104, 151, 159, 186, 193
Old Yard, 312
Old West Church, 51, 66, 254
Oliver, Thomas, 105
Olmsted, Frederick Law, 304, 306
One Financial Center, 161
O'Neill, Thomas P. "Tip," Jr., 84, 256
O'Reilly, John Boyle, 7
Oriental Tea Company, 84
Orpheum Theater, 170
Osgood (Fields's assistant), 276
Otis, Harrison Gray, 23–26, 51, 86, 94, 121, 128, 137, 148; and Back Bay development, 51, 261, 273; and Beacon Hill development, 24, 51, 273; Beacon Street house of, 24, 25, 26; Cambridge Street house of, 256; 85 Mount Vernon Street house of, 41, 57
Otis, Mrs. Harrison Gray, Jr., 114
Otis, James, 23, 98, 109, 126, 143, 185, 194, 212, 256
Otis, Sally, 25
Otis, William, 273
Otis Place, 268; Number 6, 268
Otis Street, 164; and Summer Street, 164
Otway, Thomas, 194

Paderewski, Ignace, 175
Page, Lieutenant Thomas H., 12
Paget, Robert, 281
Pain, Elizabeth, 116
Paine, Robert Treat, 49, 126, 146, 153
Palmer, Edward, 188
Papanti, Lorenzo, 114
Paramount Theater, 177
Park Plaza, 142
Park Square, 12, 142; Number 1, 141
Park Street, 3, 4, 127–34; and Beacon Street, 5, 133; Number 1, 128; Number 2, 128; Number 3, 129; Number 4, 131; Number 5, 131; Number 6, 131; Number 7, 132; Number 8, 132; and Tremont Street (Brimstone Corner), 3, 127
Park Street Church, 3, 74, 125, 127, 198
Park Street Church Ministries Building, 128
Park Street subway station, 260, 317, 318
Parker, Captain, 136
Parker, Daniel, 72
Parker, Harvey D., 96, 111, 283
Parker, Reverend Theodore, 96, 136, 176
Parker House, 96, 111, 112, 121, 276, 283
Parkman, Francis, 44, 258, 303
Parkman, Reverend Francis, 236
Parkman, Dr. George, 50, 95, 176, 228, 249, 251, 257, 258, 266
Parkman George Francis, 1, 30, 50
Parkman, Samuel, 252, 253
Parkman Bandstand, the Common, 12
Parkman Plaza, the Common, 1
Parkman Street, 257
Parris, Alexander, 25, 137, 214
Paulist Fathers Center, 131, 132
Paul Revere Mall, 238
Peabody, Elizabeth, 58, 60, 124, 138, 173, 199; bookstore of, 59, 173; kindergartens of, 60, 67, 171
Peabody, Mary, 67, 142, 173
Peabody, Sophia, 17, 58, 70, 142, 173
Pearl Street, 147–49, 189; and High Street, 147; and Milk Street, 148; Number 13, 71, 147; Number 17, 147
Pei, I. M., and Associates, 202, 289, 293, 295
Pelham Hotel, 141
Pemberton Hill, 31, 75, 78, 113
Pemberton Square, 75–82, 93
Pemberton Square Courthouse: of 1866, 77, 79; of 1936–1939, 79
Pepperell, Sir William, 11

Percy, Lord; *see* Northumberland, Lord Percy
Perkins, James, 71, 147
Perkins, Thomas, 36, 45
Perkins, Thomas Handasyd, 36, 72, 147; granddaughter of (Caroline Curtis), 168, 172, 273; mansion of, 172
Perkins School for the Blind, 147
Philip, King, 100
Phillips, John, 27, 28
Phillips, Wendell, 27, 64, 96, 114, 124, 136, 178, 213, 268
Phillips, William, 69, 70, 114, 191
Phillips, William, Jr., 114
Phillips Street, 259; and Grove Street, 260; Numbers 14–18, 260; Number 66, 260
Phips, Sir William, 234, 244
Pi (Pie) Alley, 96, 101, 102
Piano Row, 141
Pierce, Franklin, 153, 251
Pilot, The, 156
Pinckney Square, 266
Pinckney Street, 22, 50, 51, 55–61, 267; Numbers 5–7, 61, 64; Numbers 12–22, 59; Number 13, 60; Number 14, 61; Number 15, 60, 171; Number 18, 59; Number 20, 59; Number 24, 40; Number 43, 56; Number 54, 58; Number 57, 57; Numbers 58–66, 57; Number 62, 58; Number 74, 57; Number 74½, 57; Number 81, 56; Number 84, 56; Number 86, 56
Pitcairn, Major John, 233, 238, 244
Pitts, Lendall, 149
Plymouth, transportation to, 318
Poe, Edgar Allan, 9, 100, 158, 265
police strike of 1919, 177
Pollard, Ann, 238
Pope, Albert Augustus, 163
Pormont, Philemon, 80, 101, 105
Pormont, Susann, 101
Post-Boy, 13
post office, America's first, 103
Post Office Square, 148, 159; Number One, 148
Portia School of Law, 39
Prado (Paul Revere Mall), 236
Pratt, Bela, 298
Pratt, Dexter, 309
Prescott, Colonel William, 20
Prescott, Judge William, 174
Prescott, William Hickling, 20, 44, 94, 174
Preston, James, 190
Preston, Captain Thomas, 87
Primus Avenue, 260
Prince, Reverend Thomas, 143, 300
Prince Street, 226; and Hanover Street, 227; Number 138, 244
Prison Lane; *see* Court Street
Provident Institution for Savings, 172
Province House, 108, 117, 151, 154
Province Street, 109, 154
Prudential Center, 291, 306
Prudential Tower, 262, 287, 306
Public Alley, 267
Public Garden, 17, 55, 142, 161, 165, 266, 278, 280, 281, 283
public transportation; *see* subway system
Publick Occurrences, 97
Pudding Lane; *see* Devonshire Street
Pulling, John, 240
punishment, public, 12, 188
Purchase Street, 149, 160
Putnam, Israel, 193

Quaker Lane, 188
Queen Anne style, 300
Queen Street; *see* Court Street
Quelch, Captain, 243
Quest Eternal (DeLue), 306
Quincy, transportation to, 318
Quincy, Edmund, 162
Quincy, Josiah, Jr. (patriot), 98, 110, 153, 177; defends Boston Massacre redcoats, 94, 153, 190
Quincy, Mayor Josiah, 5, 8, 129, 131, 135, 147, 162, 214; cleans up Beacon Hill, 258; and Lafayette's visit, 133; and Public Garden, 281; statue of, Old City Hall, 110
Quincy, Mayor Josiah, Jr., 110, 131, 298
Quincy, Josiah, III, 131
Quincy House, 206
Quincy Market, 137, 214

Rachel Revere Park, 238
Radcliffe College, 309

Radcliffe Yard, 309
Railroad Mall, the Common, 13, 14, 142
Red Line, 307
Regina Cleri, 254
religious oppression/tolerance, 10, 234
Revere, Paul, 13, 32, 34, 117, 137, 152, 232, 237, 244, 295; casts bell for the "Cockerel," 226; casts bell for King's Chapel, 117; casts bell for New North, 236; and U.S.S. *Constitution,* 247; foundry of, 244; grave of, 125, 245; house of, 230; as Masonic leader, 34, 222; ride of, 88, 210, 221, 232; shops of, 206; and repeal of Stamp Act, 13; will of, 79
Revere House, 251
Revere Street, 259, 266; Numbers 73–91, 259; and West Cedar Street, 62, 259
Revolutionary War, 3, 11, 15, 153, 195; Battle of Bunker Hill, 238, 241, 245; siege of Boston, 29, 253
Richardson, Henry H., 35, 98, 285, 289, 297, 301
Richmond Street, 225
Ripley, Reverend George, 67
Rise of Silas Lapham, The (Howells), 302
Ritz-Carlton Hotel, 181, 282
River Street, 267, 273
Riverside Press, 131
Rogers, William B., 286
Rollins Place, 259
Roosevelt, Franklin D., 16, 66, 73, 85, 174, 206
Roosevelt, Theodore, 40, 175
Rosati, James, 252
Round Marsh, 16
Rowe, John, 174, 203
Rowes Wharf, 203, 204, 216
Royal Exchange Tavern, 189
Rudolph, Paul, 278
Rumford, Count; *see* Thompson, Benjamin
Russell, Benjamin, 36, 130
Russell, Thomas, 164, 191

Sabine, Wallace C., 294
Sacco, Nicola, 235
Sacred Cod, State House, 33
Sacred Heart Church, 233
St. Botolph Club, 303
St. Botolph Street, 294
Saint-Gaudens, Augustus, 6, 289, 298
Saint-Gaudens, Louis, 298
St. James Avenue, 289
St. James Street, 288
St. John the Evangelist, Church of, 65, 89
St. John the Evangelist, Society of, 65
St. Joseph's Church, 254
St. Leonard's Church, 226
St. Margaret's Convent, 52
St. Monica's Home, 52
St. Paul's Cathedral, 16, 137
St. Stephen's Church, 157, 225, 236, 247
St. Thomas More, Oratory of, 156
Salem, transportation to, 318
Salem Street, 225, 240, 244; and Charter Street, 244
Saltonstall, Leverett, 251
Salstonall Building, 89, 251, 252, 256
Saltonstall, Sir Richard, 251
Salutation Street and North Street, 245
Salutation Tavern, 222
Sandy Hill; *see* Pemberton Hill
Sargent, John Singer, 277, 295, 299
Saturday Club, 54, 112, 133, 266, 302
Scarlet Letter, The (Hawthorne), 107, 116
Schlesinger Library, 309
School Street, 28, 96, 99, 103, 104, 105–13; Numbers 17–19, 108; Number 24, 110; riot in, 111
Schwartz, Delmore, 260
Scollay, William, 82, 84
Scollay Buildings, 83, 94
Scollay Square, xvii–xviii, 71, 75, 80, 82–89, 91, 113
Scott, Coretta, 294
Sea Street; *see* Atlantic Avenue
Sears, David, 69, 73, 137, 191, 205
Sears, David, Jr., 25, 26, 73, 94, 137, 205
Sears, Mrs. J. Montgomery, 279

Sears Block, Scollay Square, 84, 205
Sears Crescent, 85, 205
Second Church (original Old North Church), 234
Second Congregational Society, 225
Sentry Hill Place, 259
Sergeant, Peter, 151
Sewall, Hannah, 172, 240, 243
Sewall, Judge Samuel, 95, 103, 117, 125, 172, 240, 243
Sewall's Point, 271
Seward, William H., 15, 122
Shaw, Robert Gould (elder), 29, 164
Shaw, Colonel Robert Gould, 6, 29, 258
Shaw, Robert Gould, Memorial, 62
Sheafe Street, 240
Sheraton Boston Hotel, 306
Ship Street; *see* North Street
Shirley, Governor William, 11, 108, 117, 151, 168
Shubert Theater, 140
Shurtleff, Arthur, 44
Sierra Club, 37
Signing of the Declaration of Independence, The (Trumbull), 213
6th Massachusetts Regiment, 267
slavery; *see* abolition movement
Smibert, John, 85, 86; studio of, 85, 86
Smith, Abiel, 62
Smith, Lieutenant Colonel Francis, 15
Smith, John J., 56, 64, 260
Smith, Reverend Samuel Francis, 127, 240
Smith Court, 56, 62–64; Number 3, 63; Number 5, 64; Number 7, 64; Number 7½, 64; Number 8, 62; Number 10, 64
Snell and Gregerson, 302
Snider, Christopher, 126
Snowhill Street, 241
Society for the Preservation of New England Antiquities, 256
Society of St. John the Evangelist, 65
Soldiers' Field, 303
Soldiers' Monument, the Common, 9, 10
Somerset Club, 26, 73, 132, 205
Somerset Court, 67
Somerset Street, 72, 75, 89, 251; and Ashburton Place, 67; and Beacon Street, 73
Song of Hiawatha, The (Longfellow) 309
Sons of Liberty, 13, 68, 88, 98, 180, 212, 222, 232, 245; and Boston Tea Party, 111, 180; and Stamp Act, 13, 180
South Bay, 178
South Cove, 178
South End, 13, 56, 139, 158, 178
South Station, 161
Sparks, Jared, 67, 258
Spring Lane, 28, 103
Spruce Court, 50
Spruce Street, 22, 45, 50
stagecoaches, 177, 190
Stamp Act, 180, 212; repealed, 13; riots, 229
Staniford Street, 253; Number 19 (Hurley State Services Center), 254, 255
Stanton, Elizabeth Cady, 311
State House (Beacon Hill), xviii, 3, 23, 28, 187, 306; Archives and Museum, 31; cornerstone of, 5, 33; Doric Hall, 34; extension of, 31, 35; grounds of, 3, 64; Lodge memorial, 31–32; murals in, 19, 32; Sacred Cod, 33; statue of Mary Dyer, 11, 32; statue of Anne Hutchinson, 32; *see also* Old State House
State Street, 94, 97, 105, 111, 146, 183–195, 205; and Devonshire Street, 188; Number 1, 186; Number 15 (Visitor Center), 188, 190, 317; Number 27, 188; Number 28, 189, 207; Number 53, 191, 192; Number 60, 194; Number 64, 192; Number 66, 194; Number 75, 194; Number 126, 194; and Washington Street, 99–102, 189
State Street Bank Building, 148
State Street Block, 204
Stewart, Isabella "Belle;" *see* Gardner, Isabella Stewart
Stone, Lucy, 130
Storrow, Mrs. James Jackson, 263
Storrow Memorial Drive, 263
Story of a Bad Boy, The (Aldrich), 56

Stowe, Harriet Beecher, 65, 108
Stuart, Anne, 165
Stuart, Gilbert, 13, 70, 72, 128, 142, 147, 164–65, 178; portraits of Washington, 72, 164, 179, 212
Sturgis, John, 301
subway system, 4, 224, 317–18
Sudbury Street, 80
Suffolk University, 27, 64
Sullivan, Governor James, 130, 167; mansion of, 167
Sullivan, Richard, 130
Summer Street, 155, 161–65, 166, 167; between Arch and Hawley Streets, 168; and Bedford Street, 162; and Hawley Street, 168; and High Street, 162; and Kingston Street, 163; and Lincoln Street, 163; Number 27, 166, Numbers 83–87, 163; Number 87, 163; Number 99, 161; Number 100, 162; Number 125, 161; and Otis Street, 164
Summer Street Mall, 165; *see also* Downtown Crossing
Sumner, Charles, 20, 58, 149, 233, 243, 257
Sun Court Street, 233
Surraige, Agnes, 228
Swan, Hepzibah, 41, 45, 48
Swan, James, 41, 48
swan boats, Public Garden, 280, 281, 283
Symphony Hall, 294

T-Wharf, 195, 217
Tamerlane and Other Poems (Poe), 100
Tavern Club, 53, 141
Taylor, Charles H., 102, 123, 266, 303
Taylor, Father Edward, 233, 234, 243
Taylor, Zachary, 14, 121, 154
Tea Party; *see* Boston Tea Party
Temple, Lady; *see* Bowdoin, Elizabeth
Temple, Sir John, 64
Temple Place, 138, 172
Temple School, 138
Temple Street, Numbers 44–46, 64
Thackeray, William Makepeace, 6, 20, 107, 176, 234
Theater Alley; *see* Devonshire Street
theater district, 139, 174–76
Theological School and Methodist Chapel of Boston University, 46
Thomas, Isaiah, 100, 221, 240
Thompson, Benjamin, 221
Thoreau, Henry David, 108, 173
Ticknor, George, 72, 134, 300
Ticknor, William D., 61, 107
Ticknor & Fields, 61
Tiffany, Louis C., 285
Tontine Crescent, 84, 97, 115, 155, 156
Tory Row, 309
Touraine, Hotel, 140
Town Cove, 103, 148, 195, 202, 207, 223, 227, 234; filled, 148, 202
Town House, 99, 100, 183, 186; *see also* Old State House
Transcript Building, 145
Transportation Building, 142
transportation, public; *see* subway system
Travelers Building, 148
Tremont House, 119
Tremont on the Common, 139
Tremont Place, 74
Tremont Row, 83; Number 23, 114; *see also* Tremont Street
Tremont Street, 3, 13, 14, 16, 83, 84, 113–18, 119–26, 137–41; and Beacon Street, 115, 119; and Boylston Street, 139; and Court Street, 91, 93; Number 18, 115; Number 19, 116; Number 30, 115; Number 73, 121, 124; Number 90, 125; Numbers 110–120, 125; Number 125, 137; Number 151, 139; and Park Street (Brimstone Corner), 127
Tremont Street mall, the Common, 3
Tremont Temple, 54, 121, 122, 123, 124, 268
Tremont Theater, 54
Trinity Church, 93, 288–89; on Summer Street, 168; parish house of, 288; rectory of, 40, 285
Trumbull, John, 85–86, 213
Trumbull, Governor Jonathan, 26
Tubman, Harriet, 268
Tuckerman family, 31

Tudor, Frederic, 29
Tudor, William, 71
Tufts–New England Medical Center, 174
Twain, Mark, 53, 113, 266, 288
Twenty-first Amendment, 67–68
Two Devonshire Place, 103
Two Years Before the Mast (Dana), 45

Union Boat Club, 263
Union Club, 55, 128, 132, 279
Union Oyster House, 221, 240
Union Street, 206, 208, 221–22; and Hanover Street, 221; Numbers 41–43, 221; Number 84, 222
Unitarian Universalist Association, 31
United Shoe Machinery Corporation Building, 160
Unity Street: Number 8, 244; Number 19, 237; Number 21, 237
University Hall, 312
Upjohn, Hobart and Richard, 285
Usher, Hezekiah, 186, 188

Vanderbilt, William K., 54
Vane, Sir Harry, 78, 105; statue of, Boston Public Library, 298
Vane, Seaborne, 78
Vanzetti, Bartolomeo, 235
Vassall, John, 115
Vassall, Leonard, mansion, 169
Vattemare, Alexandre, 297, 298
Vendome, Hotel, 300
Vergoose, Elizabeth Foster, 126
Village Blacksmith, The (Longfellow), 309
Vilna Shul Synagogue, 260
Vine Street; *see* Parkman Street
Virginians, The (Thackeray), 20
Visitor Center, 15 State Street, 188, 190, 317

Wales, Prince of (Edward VII), 52, 175, 280
Walnut Street, 27, 40, 50; and Beacon Street, 22; Number 8, 50
Wang Ambulatory Care Center, 257
Wang, Dr. An, 140, 257
Wang Center for the Performing Arts, 140, 257
War of 1812 (Madison's war), 9, 25, 29, 127, 192
Ward, Samuel, 54
Ward, Samuel Gray, 54, 279
Ward, Thomas Wren, 130
Warren, Dr. John, 109, 170
Warren, Dr. John Collins, 77, 109, 114, 128, 137, 170, 176, 257
Warren, Dr. Joseph, xv, 88, 98, 109, 137, 143, 222; sends Dawes and Revere on warning ride, 88, 210, 222, 232
Washington, George, 27, 88, 168, 213, 222; visit of 1756, 108, 151, 183; during siege of Boston, 12, 27, 30, 193, 236; visit of 1776, 11, 30, 93, 102, 143, 181, 183, 193; visit of 1789 (last), 4, 69, 87, 91, 92, 117, 141, 181, 183, 195, 213, 221, 227; library of, 72; memorial to, Christ Church, 237; route through the North End, 219–27; Stuart portraits of, 72, 164, 179, 212; statue of, Public Garden, 280
Washington, Martha, 93; Stuart portrait of, 72, 179
Washington Hall, 154
Washington Mall, 98, 170; Number 1, 206
Washington Square, 148
Washington Street, 28, 84, 145, 151–53, 154, 169–70, 173, 174–77, 180–81, 207; and Boylston Street, 179; and Essex Street, 179; Number 46, 189; Number 241, 102; Number 262, 102; Number 277, 104; Numbers 281–283 (Old Corner Bookstore), 104, 105; Number 294, 104; Number 400, 170; Number 415, 170; Number 539, 174; Number 545, 176; Number 553, 176; Number 597, 164; and State Street, 99, 189
Water Street, 103, 105; and Congress Street, 146
waterfront, 149–50, 195–98, 199, 202, 215–17
Watson, Thomas A., 158, 177
Webster, Daniel, 26, 38, 66, 77, 86, 178, 251; and Bunker Hill Monument, 162; last illness of, 130; law

offices of, 94; quoted, 190, 222; and building of St. Paul's Cathedral, 137; statue of, 34
Webster, Dr. John, 95, 228, 258
Webster, Redford, 228
Webster Street, 236
Wendell, Oliver, 28
Wesley Place, Number 5, 299
West, John, 104
West Boston Bridge, 263
West Cedar Street, 43, 260; Number 9, 43, 45; Number 43, 57; and Revere Street, 62
West End, 109, 249–69; *see also individual street names*
West Hill Place, 265, 266
Westin Hotel, 291
West Street, 12, 14, 173, 174; Number 15, 173
Western Avenue, 275
Wheatley, Phillis, 144
Whig Party, 14, 20
White, Kevin H., 268
White, Stanford, 303
Whitman, Walt, 6–7, 204, 234
Whitney, Anne, 43, 208
Whittier, John Greenleaf, 49, 53, 108, 176, 288
Widener, Henry Elkins, 313
Widener Library, 313
Wigglesworth, Thomas, 128
Wilbur Theater, 140
Wilde, Oscar, 136, 175, 301
Willard, Solomon, 26, 65, 95, 125, 129, 137, 147
Williams Court; *see* Pi (Pie) Alley
Willow Street, 50
Wilson, Reverend John, 10, 105, 188
Wilson's Lane; *see* Devonshire Street
Winter Place, 171; Numbers 3–4, 172
Winter Street, 137, 159, 170–71; Number 1, 171; Number 10, 171; Number 24½ 60, 171; Numbers 25–29, 137
Winthrop, Governor John, 10, 22, 32, 80, 143, 205, 278; acquires the Common, 4; and Anne Hutchinson, 105; School Street house of, 192; State Street residence of, 192; statue of, First and Second Church, 278; tomb of, 116; Washington Street residence of, 104; writings of, 10, 99, 305
Winthrop, Robert C., 166
Winthrop, Thomas L., 28
Winthrop Place, 162
Winthrop Square, Number 1, 157, 169
Women's City Club, 27
Women's Educational and Industrial Union, 283
Women's Journal, 130, 302
Women's Heritage Trail, 6, 144
Woodbridge, Benjamin, 11, 126, 189
Woodbridge, Judge Dudley, 126

Yale, Elihu, 80
Young, Ammi B., 204
Young's Hotel, 96

Zukor, Adolph, 140